ypsky

CONTEMPORARY LABOR ISSUES

WADSWORTH CONTINUING EDUCATION SERIES

Leonard Freedman, General Editor

CONTEMPORARY LABOR ISSUES

Edited by
WALTER FOGEL and
ARCHIE KLEINGARTNER
University of California, Los Angeles

Wadsworth Publishing Company, Inc., Belmont, California

L. C. Cat. Card No.: 66–24536
Printed in the United States of America

Preface

There are a number of readings books on labor which are presently available. Why, therefore, add another one?

The major reason is that we believe the books now available are not as useful as they might be for purposes of teaching, either in college or adult programs. The content of most of these books is arranged according to the structure of the academic interests of the authors—labor economics, sociology of work, human relations, etc. Chapter titles frequently correspond to the divisions of professorial fields. In other words, most readings collections on labor are oriented toward the instructor and not the student. As a consequence they are conventional, overly-intellectual, and non-provocative for laymen.

This book represents an attempt to provide a more exciting approach to the study of labor. Our experience in teaching courses in labor and industrial relations has convinced us that a high degree of student interest in these courses can be awakened by exposing the students to important current *issues* in the field of labor—issues which have contemporary meaning to people who are interested in what is going on in the world in which they live. Too often, a seminal intrigue with labor problems is stifled by an excessively intellectual or uninspiring presentation of traditional academic subjects. We believe that an issues approach will stimulate interest in labor problems which will be accompanied and followed by effective learning of appropriate subject matters.

We do not imply that what professors know about labor need not be taught. Indeed it must, through textbooks and lectures, but this can be done most effectively when the students are motivated, when they have *feelings* about a variety of labor problems. This book is meant to awaken such motivation, by its use as a supplement to a textbook in college courses or as the basis for discussion in adult programs where the participants already have some understanding of labor and industrial relations.

Another departure from conventional reading collections is brought to this volume by a broad definition of "labor." We do not see that term as many of our precursors apparently do—synonymous with organized labor, or with the trade union sector of the society. Certainly unions are a very important part of the labor picture, clearly the most visible part because of their organizational machinery and their interaction with other institutions in the society. Yet, union membership includes only about one-quarter of the labor force (though, admittedly, union policies have an immediate impact on a much larger fraction). More importantly, many of today's labor issues exist independently of unions. The problems of unemployment, minority welfare, leisure, and automation are not more related to union activity than they are to the conduct of other institutions—employers, schools, civic groups, and political parties, for example. These labor issues need to be presented in their own right—not just in their relation to the organized sector of the labor force. Three chapters in this book provide this kind of presentation. They are in "Part One: The Broad Context." "Part Two: Labor's Involvement," includes six chapters which are oriented largely, though not completely, around organized labor. Several chapters in each part are divided into sections so that the reader may easily grasp the major issues that are covered.

We believe that this book can be used profitably in any course where attention is given to labor as a sector of the economy or society, whether it is offered in departments of economics, political science, sociology, or business administration. It also is appropriate for adult-learning and labor-education programs. We hope that it is as exciting to use as it was to prepare.

The editors owe special appreciation to Franklin Tom and Edward Passman for research assistance, to their wives for a spirit of toleration, and to Rose Price for secretarial help.

Walter Fogel
Archie Kleingartner

Contents

3. Work and Leisure   137

WORK

LEISURE

PART TWO: LABOR'S INVOLVEMENT

4. Is There Still a Labor Movement?   185

5. Must Union Membership Decline?   222

Part One
The Broad
Context

1
Unemployment

Unemployment was the major labor problem of the first half of the 1960's; whether the problem will persist in the new era of the efficiently managed economy remains to be seen. During 1965, the nation's unemployment rate declined steadily and appeared to be heading below a level of 4 percent of the labor force. But there is no assurance that we can hold unemployment down to that level. Reduction in military spending and increases in technological innovation could quickly increase the numbers who are without work. Even a 4-percent rate means that three million people are unable to find jobs. Doubtless, unemployment will continue to be an important issue, if not the major one, for some time to come.

A mere citation of the number of men and women who are without work does not disclose the full seriousness of the problem, for unemployment is a major contributor to other unsolved problems of our time. It increases the difficulty of adjustments to labor-displacing automation and other forms of technological change. It slows the progress of minority groups struggling to raise their socioeconomic status nearer to that of the majority. And it brings deprivation and, eventually, poverty to millions of Americans.

Unemployment in the 1960's is not nearly so great as that of the 1930's, when 20 to 25 percent of the labor force was without work. But this fact gives no comfort to those who are idle now. If anything, it makes their situation worse. The fact that most people have steady jobs often has a grave psychological effect on the small fraction who do not.

3

In addition to the fear that almost inevitably accompanies joblessness, there is another effect—one of anger—stimulated frequently by charges that the unemployed really don't want to work. Neil Chamberlain answers that charge in the first article in this chapter; though the statistics he cites refer to the beginning of the 1960's, the nature of the unemployment described is still relevant. Chamberlain points out that there are many kinds of unemployment, all of which fall unevenly among the citizenry. This unevenness suggests specific remedial policy programs, some of which are now in operation.

Though today's unemployed are fewer than they once were, unemployment is still a serious problem because our aspirations have also changed over the years. The American people expect more from their economy than they used to. Even 5 to 6 percent idleness in our labor force is too much. The question of how to reduce this percentage has raised an issue that has dominated the public discussion of unemployment in the last several years. Is our unemployment a result of a shortage of jobs or a shortage of skills among those seeking jobs? The Heller and Killingsworth selections present the alternative arguments. The debate on this question is not merely an academic exercise, insensitive to the plight of its presumed subjects; for the answer itself will suggest the ways to go about putting people back to work.

If the answer is too few jobs, a tax cut or some other demand-creating measure is called for. If the answer is inadequate skills among the unemployed, a tax cut would create jobs with no one to fill them, and the result would be higher wages and prices. In the latter case, training and retraining to increase the skills of those out of work would be more effective than a tax cut.

By now, most experts agree. Both lack of jobs and inadequate skills are involved in today's unemployment, and both job-creating and retraining policies are needed. In the last several years, Congress has enacted programs for training or retraining *some* of the unemployed. In 1964, federal taxes were reduced.

A final evaluation of these policies cannot yet be made. But by the middle of 1965, unemployment was down to 4.5 percent of the labor force (the lowest rate since 1957), and inflation-producing, labor-supply "bottlenecks" had not yet appeared—results that must have been satisfying to the tax-cut proponents. The selection from the *Manpower Report of the President* and the report by Gerald Somers offer preliminary evaluations of our current measures to battle forced idleness.

Regardless of the cause or the numbers involved, being out of work often brings crushing consequences to those who must endure it. The six case histories from *Newsweek* remind us of this discomforting fact.

One reason unemployment is so difficult a problem is that annual increments to the labor force now total about one and one-half million persons, and the number is rising. Another reason is that automation or, more accurately, technological change each year reduces the number of persons required to produce a given amount of goods and services.

The issue of the relationship of automation to unemployment arose at least ten years ago, when the nation's press first startled the public with a recitation of the amazing feats performed by electronic data-processing machines (computers). The importance of the issue continues to increase among a population that asks "How can anyone be sure that science will not bring inventions which will soon make most of us obsolete?"

But is the automation occurring *now* any different in its impact on workers than the improvements in production methods that have constantly taken place in the industrial history of the United States? Charles Killingsworth thinks so and tells why in the first selection in the section on the challenge of automation. Killingsworth thinks automation is more of a job threat than is generally realized, because it is being accepted so rapidly by all kinds of businesses and because no new consumer products, whose production would absorb displaced workers, are readily visible. The Ad Hoc Committee on the Triple Revolution would, no doubt, consider these views—based on assessments of current events—to be insensitive to the threat to employment that they see posed by automation. Peering into the future, with perhaps more insight than ordinary mortals, the members of this group are confident that cybernetics will soon make it possible to produce all the material goods we need with just a fraction of the present labor force.

If automation is really something new, then productivity (output per man-hour) should be increasing much faster now than formerly. The figures for the last few years do show greater than average gains in productivity, but even these gains have been matched at various times in the past. Thus, we will have to wait for future developments to see whether annual productivity gains will rise to new high levels.

A few voices are now beginning to be heard against the wails of the automation prophets. Charles Silberman's article reassures us that there will be a need for labor for a long time to come—even unskilled labor. Machines are replacing men; but, at the same time, our seemingly insatiable wants provide other tasks for which labor is needed, he says. In the final selection, Walter Heller takes a similar view, and reminds us of the ultimate gains to be had from improvements in technology. Heller and Killingsworth express differing views on the effects of automation to complement their respective positions on the nature of unemployment, presented in the first section of the chapter.

dimensions and solutions

Neil W. Chamberlain
THE MANY FACES
OF UNEMPLOYMENT

Unemployment is an ugly word. It is not now, as it was only a few decades ago, so directly associated with hunger, disease, and privation; but it still brings with it insecurity, dependence, feelings of personal inadequacy and frustration. The brave and the bluff seek to keep these ghosts under cover, but unemployment insists on bringing them out into the open.

Approximately 4½ million Americans saw the New Year in with unemployment as an unwanted guest whose presence was very much felt. Only about 10 percent of this number had actually invited unemployment. (These were the persons who have given up one job in order to move to or shop around for another.) For them, joblessness probably would not persist long enough to be burdensome. Another 20 percent consisted of those who had not previously or recently been working and who were now looking for a job. For many of these, too, the situation, while unpleasant, was not serious.

Unemployment, then, was probably not a searing experience to about 30 percent of the jobless at the beginning of 1961. But this still left more than 3 million who were exposed to its sharp, psychological thrusts.

About 1 million of this number, or almost one out of every four

Reprinted by permission from *Challenge, The Magazine of Economic Affairs,* 475 Fifth Avenue, New York, N.Y. 10017, March 1961.
Mr. Chamberlain is Professor of Economics at Yale University.

unemployed, had been out of work for 15 weeks or longer. Most of them had not yet experienced hardship, but this is no test of the seriousness of their situation. In our society today it is no longer the physical but the psychological impact of unemployment which is most destructive.

At the end of 1960 some 500,000 workers had been without a job for 6 months or more. They were distinguished, invidiously if impersonally, from their neighbors and associates by being economically unwanted.

TURNOVER AMONG UNEMPLOYED

. . . Most joblessness lasts only a short time. There is a turnover among the unemployed just as there is turnover of the employed.

In 1957, for example, every month saw about 1.5 million people leave the category of the unemployed, and an equal number move into this status. Of those leaving, about 1 million found new jobs or returned to their former jobs, and the other half-million withdrew from the labor force altogether. (Many of the latter were older people or housewives who gave up trying to find employment, and students who returned to school. Some of them might return to the job hunt later. But included also were heads of families on short or indefinite layoff from companies where business was bad.) In 1958 more than 14 million persons were unemployed at some time during the year. In the first 10 to 11 months of 1959 about 12 percent of all family heads in the labor force had experienced some spell of joblessness.

This turnover among the unemployed means that the hardships of unemployment are spread among many people and not concentrated on the same group throughout the year. From another point of view, however, it indicates how much more widespread the impact of unemployment is than a figure of 4½ million at any one time would suggest.

"HIDDEN" UNEMPLOYMENT

Moreover, part of the turnover of the unemployed is due to individuals leaving the labor force because they feel they have no prospect of getting a job. To that extent the net figures of unemployment understate it. This is sometimes referred to as "hidden" unemployment, because it does not get into the statistics. In addition, hidden underemployment exists when individuals looking for work are driven to accept a job below their capabilities. In periods of manpower surpluses, skills and talents often go wasted on jobs that do not demand them. This is a psychological hardship to the individual as well as an economic loss to society.

The job situation in the United States, then, as 1961 began, was roughly as though fate had tapped every 15th person in the labor force, marking him as one to be taken from his job and segregated into a giant compound. Of those in this compound, one out of four had asked to be included, but three out of four went unwillingly. Every day the gates to the compound are opened; some are let out while others take their places. But one out of every four has been kept there for more than 3 months, and one out of eight has been there for half a year or longer.

This picture stresses the psychological aspect of unemployment which is perhaps most important—the individual's feeling that he is controlled by external circumstances, and that short of making the usual discouraging round of employment offices, there is little he can do but wait. Those who maintain that assistance to the unemployed tends to rob them of self-reliance might consider whether unemployment itself does not do so far more effectively.

Other employment effects associated with declines in economic activity have less of a psychological and more of a straightforward economic impact. These are the reduced length of the working week and the amount of part-time employment. . . .

NOT A NEW PHENOMENON

Unemployment is not a new phenomenon. The United States has always had recurring periods when jobs were hard to find. Is there any reason to be especially concerned now? Has the nature of the unemployment problem changed so that it requires reexamination? The answer to both these questions is probably "Yes."

In the postwar era the recoveries from the recessions have been less than complete: the pool of unemployed has grown proportionately larger and more persistent. . . .

There have been several explanations for this discouraging performance of the economy. Some have sought the reason in excessively tight monetary policy, which has restrained recovery and held it within too-limited bounds. Since productivity is increasing, the same amount of industrial output can be secured with less manpower at the end of a recession than at its beginning. As there are also additions to the labor force, unemployment can be held to previous levels only if production increases. If monetary policies or other governmental programs restrain industrial expansion, recovery may not be pushed to the record levels needed to keep unemployment within the same bounds.

Another explanation is that the changing composition of the labor force contributes to a higher degree of employment instability. If the proportion of people in the labor force who are most susceptible to layoffs increases, and those who have a higher degree of unemployment stability become of less importance in the total, then unemployment levels may be harder to keep under control than formerly—even though there may be no change in governmental policies, monetary actions or business or union activities.

The changing structure of the economy, as reflected in a changing composition of the labor force, may have produced the postwar employment pattern. For example, the reduction in the numbers of farmworkers and their shift into other forms of employment undoubtedly had its impact on unemployment levels, since farm employment is much more stable than nonfarm. Similarly, the addition of proportionately more women to the labor force might be expected to have the same effect of increasing unemployment levels, since women typically are employed in more marginal jobs than are men. It seems unlikely, however, that changes of this nature can, by themselves, account for the higher unemployment plateau.

In any event, we are faced with a problem. It is a question of legitimate concern as to why the United States has lagged behind many foreign economies in the postwar period, not only in its rate of growth but also in its control of unemployment.

Let us take a closer look at the unemployed. Who are they? Why are they jobless?

First, there are several different kinds of unemployment. Of these, perhaps the most important are frictional, seasonal, cyclical, and structural. The frictionally unemployed are those who are temporarily out of a job—sometimes because they have been laid off for a spell, sometimes because they have changed jobs, sometimes because they have been fired, and so on. There are always frictionally unemployed people, and their presence should cause no anxiety. They are the mark of people's freedom to quit jobs, to move around, to try to better themselves, just as they are the mark of a free economy in which some firms are declining and laying off, while others expand and add more workers.

INTRACTABLE PROBLEM

Seasonal unemployment is a more intractable problem. Some industries are seasonal in their very nature—canning and harvesting, for example. Others, such as construction and mining, are dependent on weather. They are indispensable activities and cannot be eliminated. Despite efforts at dovetailing—combining a swimming pool with an ice-skating rink, for example—to cover a full year, some seasonality of employment is unavoidable. All that we can say—after all efforts have been made to reduce this source of unemployment—is that compensation programs should seek to mitigate the harshest financial burdens so that annual incomes are adequate for minimum needs.

Cyclical unemployment occurred as waves of rising joblessness rolled over the economy four times in the postwar period. It can be partially met through unemployment compensation and supplementary unemployment benefit programs, if its duration is short enough. But it often calls for special governmental programs designed to bolster economic activity. The 1946 Employment Act, which made the Government responsible for encouraging and maintaining economic activity at levels consonant with full employment, is largely addressed to cyclical unemployment.

Structural unemployment is the most difficult of all to combat. It is caused by the rise and fall of industries, occupations, and regions, and by radically changing technologies and markets. It is hard to offset because it is concentrated in a particular town, region, or industry. So many of the unemployed are lumped together that they create a "chronic" condition, which prosperity in the Nation at large will never correct. For these groups of workers, as groups, there is nothing but a bleak future.

SELECTIVE PATTERN

The two types of unemployment which most demand attention are cyclical and structural. If the people in these categories were drawn at random from the population at large, we could proceed directly to try to do something about these kinds of unemployment. But the characteristics of the unemployed show that the pattern is not random, but selective. Unemployment tends to be concentrated among the young, the old, the nonwhites, workers in the goods-producing industries, blue-collar workers, and the unskilled and less educated. To some extent women are more affected than men, but on an overall basis their plight is not so striking as that of the other groups listed.

Let us first consider the young. To many people it is surprising that unemployment tends to be most heavily concentrated in the 14 to 24 age group. Among youngsters in the 16 to 19 category the rate of unemployment is three times that of the labor force at large. And in the course of a year boys 18 to 24 have proportionately the heaviest incidence of unemployment of 15 weeks or more—about twice that for men in the 45 to 64 category.

The reason is that most of these young people are getting adjusted to the world of work. Typically, in their first year or two of employment, they will switch jobs up to half a dozen times before they satisfy themselves that they have done about as well as they can expect to do. With experience, then marriage, family, and home ownership, this period of shopping around for a good job comes to an end.

While improved counseling services might well help to curb some unnecessary movement, probably most of this frenetic job activity is part of the experience of growing up. It seems unlikely that the heavy concentration of unemployment in this group is anything about which much can be, or perhaps should be done.

At the other end of the age spectrum the situation is different. The rates of unemployment among workers 45 and over are very comparable with those for workers in the prime age group of 25 to 44. The statistics collected do not show that the former group is disproportionately represented among the unemployed. Numbers of older workers, however, withdraw from the labor force altogether because they have no luck in finding a job after having lost one; perhaps they go on social security or private pension before they would have liked to. This hidden unemployment of an unknown number of persons makes it probable that a problem exists. Moreover, the duration of spells of unemployment is longer for the older than the prime age group.

CLEAR-CUT PROBLEM

The problem of the nonwhite worker is clear cut. For colored members of the labor force, unemployment rates are twice as high as for whites, and spells of unemployment last almost twice as long. In part, this is attributable to the relegation of colored workers to unskilled jobs, where unemployment tends to strike more frequently; their relatively more limited education, born of limited opportunity, also exposes them to adverse employment experience. In any event, the effect of discrimination is evident in the statistics.

Among industries, workers in mining and construction have the greatest incidence of unemployment (12.7 and 15.9 percent respectively in December 1960), with those in manufacturing following (almost 7.5 percent in the same month). In contrast, 4.5 percent of the workers in industries providing services were unemployed last December, and of those in finance and public administration only 3.1 and 3.2 percent, respectively. Clearly, goods producers are more likely to lose their jobs than are service producers.

Joblessness is related to occupation in that blue-collar workers are more unemployment prone than white-collar workers. On a skill level, the unskilled have a much heavier incidence of unemployment than the semiskilled (15.6 percent of the former were out of work in December 1960, as against 9.9 percent of the latter). And semiskilled operatives have a higher unemployment rate than craftsmen (9.9 percent as against 7.4 percent). But clerical and sales employees experienced only about 3.7 and 2.7 percent unemployment respectively, while for professional and technical employees that rate was 1.7 percent.

The fact that the jobless fall into these major groups indicates that unemployment is not as general a problem as once was believed. It is also probably true that the concentration of unemployment on special groups has gone further today than in the past, though statistics to prove this are imperfect or lacking.

In any event, it has become the fashion among the experts to say that unemployment is now a matter of class rather than mass. However, if unemployment rises much above the 7-percent level, it begins to suck in numbers of those outside the susceptible groups.

The corollary usually drawn from the apparent change in the composition of those out of work is that the kind of broadside attack on unemployment which used to be recommended is no longer very helpful. Governmental fiscal and monetary efforts to stimulate economic activity, it is said, make sense only when dealing with the unemployed who are drawn at random from all parts of society. In that kind of situation, the promotion of business activity will encourage more hiring, and people with all kinds of skills will be called back to work.

But the situation is different when the unemployed are largely people who are less wanted than other workers—those discriminated against, those with limited education, and those in declining occupations and industries. Then, say the experts, special policies are needed for each special group. . . .

The fair employment practices approach to discriminatory hiring based on race has been urged as one means of lessening the disproportionate impact of unemployment on Negroes and other nonwhites. This proposal is often met by stubborn insistence that "you can't legislate people's sentiments," but this is an irrelevant response. It is not sentiment but behavior which such legislation would seek to affect.

SPECIAL TREATMENT

The approach that the ranks of the unemployed are made up of groups which require special treatment has considerable merit. At the same time, any suggestion that our postwar levels of unemployment can be handled solely by such efforts is mischievous. Insuring that more youngsters complete their high school education makes them more employable, but it does not automatically provide them with jobs. Removing some of the discrimination against Negroes will put them on a more equal footing with whites in the competition for work, but it will not guarantee either blacks or whites that they will find it.

After all such special-group efforts have been made, a booming economy is needed to keep everyone—except the frictionally unemployed—at work. The Employment Act of 1946 is still necessary, and should be utilized.

That act has suffered an ironic fate. It was founded on the haunting memories of from 12 million to 20 million unemployed during the great depression of the 1930's and on the determination that such mass unemployment should not be permitted to happen again. But the act had scarcely passed before it became a dead letter. In the postwar years the old ghost of mass unemployment gave way to the spectre of inflation. For more than a decade the Federal Government was more concerned with rising prices than with rising unemployment.

CONDITIONED IDEAS

What we now need to recognize is that in regard to the reemployment of specially disadvantaged groups there is no basic incompatibility between approaches to full employment and control of inflation. If we need to put people back to work to provide them with income and security, we also need their labor to turn out the goods and services to match the money which people spend, thereby helping to keep prices stable.

Our ideas about unemployment have been conditioned by our thinking of it in mass rather than class terms, and our ideas about inflation have been similarly distorted. As long as one believed in random or "mass" unemployment he could argue that at least it was something of a curb on inflation. Workers couldn't push wages up so easily when other workers were looking for jobs, and employers wouldn't push up prices if their costs weren't rising.

But the jobless are not a "random" group and their unemployment, instead of curbing inflation, may actually make it worse. At times when demand is pressing on supply, at current prices, their numbers contribute nothing to output. On the other hand, because of their special characteristics they cannot readily be substituted for other workers, and hence fail to act as a brake on wages and prices.

It is not a matter of choosing between two approaches to unemployment—the group problem and the broadside approaches. In fact, both are needed, and one is ineffective without the other.

Programs directed at the problems of particular groups could include: Counseling young workers; attacking racial discrimination in hiring; inducing youngsters to complete their high school education and go on to college, if they have the intellectual capacity for it; encouraging employers to recognize that older workers bring assets as well as liabilities with them; and retraining workers for jobs in growing industries or needed occupations. But to believe that all these useful and necessary programs will be enough in themselves to put people to work is wishful thinking. Such measures will not do away with recessions, and when recessions appear the old broadside measures of fiscal and monetary policy, and perhaps some fresh overall approaches as well, will be needed.

It is equally fallacious to assume that the broadside treatment can be effective without the special measures. We can spend and spend, and we still will not put people back to work if they are unemployed for special reasons. At least we will have to spend more than otherwise would be necessary to make their marginal employment worthwhile to some employer, and in the process we will revive the old concern of whether we are not spending ourselves into inflation.

But if we first attack the special disabilities of the unemployed groups, and then—or concomitantly, since the unemployed cannot wait indefinitely—sustain, by federally inspired efforts under the Employment Act, the general buoyancy of our economy whenever it flags, we shall be moving effectively on both the unemployment and inflation fronts. The more well-trained people are used to best advantage, the less likely is it that the supply of goods will fail to keep up with wants.

TOO MUCH CODDLING?

Some few people will perhaps argue that this double-barreled program represents too much coddling of people who should learn to look out for themselves. Let me be blunt. The fear, still encountered in some quarters, that "too much" attention to the unemployed, "excessive" efforts to give them assistance, coupled with payments to them when they are out of work, will have a damaging influence on the self-reliance of our people, is an outmoded superstition.

The fact is that the kinds of self-reliance which are needed change. None of us would be particularly successful at surviving in the conditions of the distant past. What is more, it would be a shameful farce to make every youngster learn how to make fire by friction or to track a wild animal through the woods instead of acquiring a knowledge of physics and economics. The latter studies are certainly more intimately related to his survival in today's world than is the woodsman's lore.

Similarly, though the capability of carving a job out for oneself in the economic jungle of a young economy was once essential to survival, our improved arts of organization and economics have now put us a stage or two beyond that primitive state. Governmental programs to reduce special disabilities associated with particular groups in our society, followed up by broad programs to mobilize the improved talents of the members of these groups in productive channels, can scarcely be thought of as debilitating to their character unless we have lost all sense of perspective. Their characters can as readily be tempered on a job as in repeatedly or protractedly seeking one.

Charles C. Killingsworth
UNEMPLOYMENT
WITH LABOR SHORTAGES

. . . The President's Council of Economic Advisers has repeatedly declared that automation and "structural unemployment" are not responsible for the gradual creep of unemployment above the 4-percent level of 1957. For example, the 1963 report of the Council includes the following passage (p. 25):

"The problems of structural unemployment—of imperfect adaptation of jobs and workers—are persistent and serious, and they are thrown into bold relief by the prolonged lack of sufficient job opportunities over the past 5 years. *But these problems of adaptation have not constituted a greater cause of unemployment in recent years than in earlier periods.* The source of the high unemployment rates in recent years, even in periods of cyclical expansion, lies not in labor market imbalance, but in the markets for goods and services." [Emphasis not in original.]

This analysis of the unemployment problem—that it is caused primarily by a lagging growth rate—is the basis for the administration's emphasis on a large tax cut as the top-priority item in the program to "get the economy moving again." Chairman Walter Heller of the CEA has repeatedly said that there is a "good prospect" that the tax cut would reduce unemployment to the 4-percent level.

From testimony before the Senate Subcommittee on Employment and Manpower, 1963.

Mr. Killingsworth is University Professor of Labor and Industrial Relations, Michigan State University.

I think that it can be demonstrated that the Council is the victim of a half-truth. The lagging growth rate is only a part of the problem, and it may not be the most important part. I think that it is extremely unlikely that the proposed tax cut, desirable though it is as a part of a program, will prove to be sufficient to reduce unemployment to the 4-percent level. Perhaps it is true that in politics you can't get everything all at once. But I feel compelled to say that my analysis leads me to the conclusion that the administration's economic program is seriously incomplete. It gives woefully inadequate attention to what I regard as a key aspect of the unemployment problem of the 1960's; namely, labor market imbalance.

The Council's position on labor market imbalance, quoted above, rests on meticulous and extensive statistical studies. I am sure that the members of the Council, who are scholars of the highest competence and integrity, are willing to go where the facts lead them. The trouble is that their staff studies have not analyzed the figures which, in my judgment, clearly show a growing problem of labor market imbalance.

Let me preface my own analysis of those figures with a brief restatement of my argument to this point. The fundamental effect of automation on the labor market is to "twist" the pattern of demand—that is, it pushes down the demand for workers with little training while pushing up the demand for workers with large amounts of training. The shift from goods to services is a second major factor which twists the labor market in the same way. There are some low-skilled, blue-collar jobs in service-producing industries; but the most rapidly growing parts of the service sector are health care and education, both of which require a heavy preponderance of highly trained people. . . .

Table 1 shows the relationship between rates of unemployment and levels of education of males 18 and over in 2 years—1950 and 1962.

The overall unemployment rate was substantially the same in

TABLE 1. *Education and unemployment, April 1950 and March 1962*
(males, 18 and over)

| | UNEMPLOYMENT RATES | | PERCENTAGE CHANGE, |
YEARS OF SCHOOL COMPLETED	1950	1962	1950 to 1962
0 to 7	8.4	9.2	+9.5
8	6.6	7.5	+13.6
9 to 11	6.9	7.8	+13.0
12	4.6	4.8	+4.3
13 to 15	4.1	4.0	−2.4
16 or more	2.2	1.4	−36.4
All groups	6.2	6.0	−3.2

both years—6.2 in 1950, and 6.0 in 1962. But there was a redistribution of unemployment between these 2 years. The unemployment rates at the top of the educational attainment ladder went down, while the rates at the middle and lower rungs of the ladder went up substantially. The most significant figure in this table, I think, is the one showing the very large decrease in the unemployment rate of college graduates. . . .

It is important to note that all of the improvement in the unemployment situation in 1962, as compared with 1950, was concentrated in the elite group of our labor force—the approximately 20 percent with college training. In all of the other categories, which have about 80 percent of the labor force, unemployment rates were substantially higher in 1962 than in 1950. These figures, I contend, substantiate the thesis that the patterns of demand for labor have been twisted faster than the patterns of supply have changed, and that as a result we had a substantially greater degree of labor market imbalance in 1962 than in 1950.

But these figures do not fully reveal the power of the labor market twist. The "labor force" enumeration includes (with minor exceptions) only those who say that they have jobs or that they have actively sought work in the week preceding the survey. Those who have been out of work so long that they have given up hope and are no longer "actively seeking" work—but who would take a job if one were available —are simply not counted either as unemployed or as a member of the labor force. The percentage of a given category of the total population that is "in the labor force" (under the foregoing definition) is expressed as the "labor force participation rate." It seems probable that worsening employment prospects for a particular group over a long period would force down the labor force participation rate—i.e., would squeeze a number of people out of the labor market altogether, in the sense that they would give up the continuing, active search for jobs. Conversely, it seems probable that improving employment prospects would tend to pull more people into the labor market and thus to raise the labor force participation rate. These two trends are indeed observable since 1950. The squeezing out of people at the lower end of the educational ladder and the pulling in of people at the upper end is another manifestation of the labor market twist. . . .

The important point that I want to make with these figures is that in all likelihood the official unemployment statistics substantially understate the size of the labor surplus of men with limited education. If we found jobs for most of those now officially reported as unemployed, the news of improving opportunities would undoubtedly bring back into the labor force many men who are not now counted as members of it. Unfortunately, we cannot count on the same flexibility of supply at the top of the educational scale. Even the most extreme pressures of demand cannot pull the participation rate much above 98 or 99 percent, which (as just stated) is the current rate in some college-trained age groups.

Our overall unemployment rate has now been above 5 percent for more than 5 years, and we cannot be sure what effects a substantial increase in spending by consumers, businesses and Government (i.e., an increase in aggregate demand) would have on the patterns of employment, unemployment, and labor force participation just discussed. Many respected economists believe, as one of them once put it, that the hard core of unemployment is made of ice, not rock, and that it would melt away if overall demand rose high enough. As already noted, the Council of Economic Advisers has virtually guaranteed that the administration's tax cut program—which in its current version would put about $11 billion in the hands of consumers and businesses—would reduce unemployment to an "interim target" rate of 4 percent by 1966. This line of reasoning assumes (either implicitly or sometimes explicitly) that no serious bottlenecks of labor supply would appear before the achievement of the overall unemployment rate of 4 percent. I seriously question the validity of this critically important assumption under the labor market conditions of today and the foreseeable future. . . .

Bear in mind that the unemployment rates for the lower educational attainment groups (those with 80 percent of the men) are now higher than in 1950, and that the unemployment rate for college graduates is now substantially lower than in 1950. Also bear in mind that the labor force participation rate figures strongly suggest a large and growing "reserve army"—which is not counted among the unemployed—at the lower educational levels, and that there is no evidence of any such reserve of college-trained men. Finally, bear in mind the differences between the lower end of the educational scale and the upper end in responsiveness to overall decreases in the unemployment rate.

When you put all of these considerations together, I believe that you are ineluctably led to the conclusion that long before we could get down to an overall unemployment rate as low as 4 percent, we would have a severe shortage of workers at the top of the educational ladder. This shortage would be a bottleneck to further expansion of employment. I cannot pinpoint the level at which the bottleneck would begin to seriously impede expansion; but . . . it seems reasonable to believe that we could not get very far below a 5-percent overall unemployment level without hitting that bottleneck.

The most fundamental conclusion that emerges from my analysis is that automation and the changing pattern of consumer wants have greatly increased the importance of investment in human beings as a factor in economic growth. More investment in plant and equipment, without very large increases in our investment in human beings, seems certain to enlarge the surplus of underdeveloped manpower and to create a shortage of the highly developed manpower needed to design, install, and man modern production facilities.

The Manpower Development and Training Act is aptly named, soundly conceived, and well administered. This program was not originally intended to provide general literacy training as such; separate legislation was proposed for that purpose but was not adopted. Experience under the Manpower Development and Training Act has shown how essential literacy training is as a prerequisite for specific occupational training. (In 1962, 40 percent of the unemployed males had 8 or fewer years of schooling, but only 13 percent of the Manpower Development and Training Act male trainees had that little education.) If the House agrees with action already taken by the Senate to provide literacy training under the Manpower Development and Training Act, the original scope of the program will be broadened in a highly desirable way. But I doubt that even the most enthusiastic supporters of the Manpower Development and Training Act program (and I count myself among them) would argue that its present or projected size is really commensurate with the size of the job to be done. We ought to be thinking in terms of helping two or three times as many people as this program is now expected to reach. . . .

To my mind, the greatest shortcoming of the administration's program for reducing unemployment is the failure to recognize the crucial need to break the trained manpower bottleneck. I recognize that the administration has recommended what many people regard as very ambitious measures for Federal aid to higher education. But . . . even the largest appropriations within the realm of remote possibility would leave virtually untouched the most difficult aspect of the financing of higher education. That is the investment that the student, or his parents, must make in his subsistence costs during 4 or more years of training. For most students today, the minimum cost is $5,000.

To put a complex matter briefly, we must find a fundamentally new approach to the financing of at least this important part of the cost of higher education. We must make it as easy for an individual to finance his own investment in higher education as it is for him to finance the purchase of a home. I have proposed that we make provisions for loans to college students up to a maximum of $12,000, with a repayment period as long as 40 years, at a subsidized interest rate of 2 percent. Repayment should be on the basis of a flat percentage of income—a kind of social security system in reverse. Others may think of better solutions; the means are less important than the end which is to make higher education readily available to all who can benefit from it.

I would give a considerably higher priority to the stimulation of investment in human beings than I would to such measures as the proposed tax cut. But I would still rate the tax cut as important. Denying that the tax cut is the "ultimate weapon" against unemployment is not denying that it can make some contribution to the reduction of unemployment. After all, even to get below a 5-percent unemployment rate would be a considerable achievement today. But a really effective attack on the complex problem of unemployment requires a whole arsenal of powerful weapons.

And we don't have all the time in the world. Human history has been described as a race between education and catastrophe. In the past dozen years, education has been falling behind in that race.

Walter Heller

TAX REDUCTION AND
STRUCTURAL UNEMPLOYMENT

. . . In the period of vigorous business activity in 1947 and 1948, unemployment averaged 3.8 percent of the labor force. After the recession of 1949 and the recovery of 1950, the rate was relatively stable from early 1951 to late 1953, averaging 3.1 percent. Since that time, the rate has drifted upward. In the period of stable unemployment from mid-1955 to late 1957, unemployment averaged 4.3 percent, an increase of more than one-third above the 1951–53 period. In the first half of 1960, unemployment averaged 5.3 percent, nearly one-fourth above the 1955–57 level. Following the recession and recovery of 1960–61, the rate fluctuated within a narrow range averaging 5.6 percent in 1962 and 1963 to date, a little higher than early 1960. Looking at the 1947–57 period, the average unemployment rate was below 4 percent in each of the following years: 1947, 1948, 1951, 1952, and 1953, and below 4½ percent in 1955, 1956, and 1957.

When one looks behind these figures to get a grasp of the economic conditions that produced them, the most notable difference

From testimony before the Senate Subcommittee on Employment and Manpower, 1963.

Mr. Heller was chairman of the President's Council of Economic Advisers when he presented this statement.

between the pre-1957 and post-1957 periods is found in the strength of market demand. In the first postwar decade, markets were strong. Backlogs of consumer demand had to be worked off. The demands of the Korean conflict had to be met. Outmoded plants and equipment had to be replaced or modernized, and capacity had to be enlarged. Deficiencies in housing, office facilities, and public works had to be made up. . . .

But 1957 marked a watershed. In the ensuing period, demand has slackened at a time when our labor force growth has been accelerating in response to the postwar jump in the birth rate. Business fixed investment dropped off from 10 to 11 percent of the GNP to only 9 percent—indeed, the level of such investment in 1962 barely struggled back to its level in 1956, while GNP was rising by nearly one-fifth (both in constant prices).

Thus, the clearest and most striking change since 1957 is the weakening of demand. So the clearest and most urgent need today is to remove the overburden of taxation which is retarding the growth in demand to full employment levels. Income tax rates enacted to finance war and fight inflation—though reduced in 1954—are still so high that they would yield a large surplus of revenues over expenditures if we were at full employment today. They are, in short, repressing demand and incentives in an economy operating well short of its capacity.

To avoid misunderstanding, it is important to stress that any employment program would be unbalanced and incomplete without determined measures (a) to upgrade and adapt the skills and education of the labor force to the more exacting demands of our advancing technology and (b) to facilitate the flow of workers from job to job, industry to industry, and place to place. Nevertheless, our principal reliance for a return to the 4-percent-or-better levels of unemployment we took for granted in the early postwar period must be on measures to boost demand for the products of American industry and agriculture. . . .

The Persistent Problems of Structural Unemployment

The tax cut would thus increase demand to levels consistent with a 4 percent rate of unemployment. It would ease our most pressing unemployment problems. But no one can assume that our worries about unemployment would then be over. Some of its most distressing and inequitable aspects would remain.

To be sure, tax reduction will create new jobs in every community across the Nation and expand employment in every industry. The overwhelming majority of American families will benefit directly from the income tax cuts that will accrue to 50 million taxpaying individuals and 600,000 taxpaying corporations. Their direct rise in after-tax income will soon be translated, through the marketplace, into stronger markets for all kinds of goods and services and a quickening of the business pulse in all communities. With average working hours already at a high level, this added demand and activity will in large part be translated, in turn, into additional jobs, and income for the unemployed. Thus, the nontax-paying minority will, in a very real sense, be the greatest beneficiaries of the tax program.

Experience clearly shows (1) that the unemployment rate will decline for every major category of workers and (2) that the sharpest declines will occur where the incidence of unemployment is the highest: among teenagers, the Negroes, the less skilled, the blue-collar groups generally.

But even so, the unemployment rates of many groups will still be intolerably high. Back in 1957, for instance, when the average unemployment rate was just over 4 percent for the whole economy, the rates were much higher for many disadvantaged groups and regions—e.g., 10.8 percent for teenagers, 8 percent for nonwhites, 9.4 percent for unskilled manual workers, and 11.5 percent for workers in Wilkes-Barre-Hazleton, Pa.

These high specific unemployment rates, which persist even when the general rate falls to an acceptable level, are the essence of the problem of structural unemployment. Even a fully successful tax cut cannot solve problems like these by itself. They require a more direct attack.

To reduce the abnormally high and stubborn unemployment rate for Negroes requires a major improvement in their education and training and an attack on racial discrimination. To reduce the persistent high rate for the unskilled and the uneducated groups demands measures to help them acquire skills and knowledge. To reduce excessive unemployment associated with declining industries and technological advance requires retraining and relocation. To reduce high unemployment in distressed areas of Pennsylvania, Michigan, Minnesota, and elsewhere calls for special measures to rebuild the economic base of those communities and assist their workers.

Both the administration and the Congress have recognized that these measures must be taken concurrently with measures to expand aggregate demand. Coal miners in Harlan County are structurally unemployed now, and so are Negro and Puerto Rican youths in New York City. Yet, programs to reduce structural unemployment will run into severe limits in the absence of an adequate growth of demand, i.e., in the absence of rapid expansion of total job opportunities. Such expansion is needed to assure that retrained and upgraded workers, for example, will find jobs at the end of the training period and will not do so at the expense of job opportunities for other unemployed workers. As structural programs create new and upgraded skills, they will in some cases fit the participants for jobs that had previously gone begging. But for the most part, the needed jobs must be created by expansion of total demand.

Quite apart from the human significance of structural unemployment, it also has great economic importance. For only as we reduce structural and frictional unemployment can we achieve the higher levels of total output which would be associated with unemployment rates below our 4-percent interim target. The council emphasized this point in its 1963 annual report (p. 42), as follows:

"Success in a combined policy of strengthening demand and adapting manpower supplies to evolving needs would enable us to achieve an interim objective of 4-percent unemployment and permit us to push beyond it in a setting of reasonable price stability. Bottlenecks in skilled labor, middle-level manpower, and professional personnel [now] tend to become acute as unemployment approaches 4 percent. The result is to retard growth and generate wage-price pressures at particular points in the economy. As we widen or break these bottlenecks by intensified and flexible educational, training, and retraining efforts, our employment sights will steadily rise."

Every worker needlessly unemployed represents a human cost which offends the sensibilities of a civilized society. But each worker needlessly unemployed also represents a waste of potential goods and services, which even an affluent society can ill afford. More intensive measures to attack structural unemployment are necessary to reduce the unemployment rate not merely to 4 percent, but beyond.

Has Structural Unemployment Increased?

The preceding section addressed itself to structural unemployment as a human and social problem and considered its role in the process of lowering the unemployment rate to and below 4 percent. But it is also appropriate to ask: Has structural unemployment increased to such an extent since 1957—the last time unemployment was near 4 percent—that it will impede the expansionary effects of demand-creating measures in general and the tax cut in particular?

An affirmative answer would, we believe, represent a misreading of the facts. As we have already pointed out, there are serious structural problems, and prompt action is needed both to root out the inequities and hardships they inflict and to help us reach our employment goals. But this conclusion need not—and does not—rest on a belief that there has been a disproportionate surge in structural unemployment since 1957.

A reading of the evidence on this score must focus principally on what happens, over time, to the unemployment rates of particular groups —teenagers, untrained and unskilled workers, Negroes, and other disadvantaged groups and regions—in relation to the total unemployment rate. It would clearly be misleading simply to compare unemployment rates for such groups in a year like 1957, when the total rate was about 4 percent, with the corresponding rates in 1962–63, when the total rate has averaged 5.6 percent. Rather, it is the relationship between the total rate and the group rates—and its historical development—that reveals whether the structural problem is getting worse or not. And this relationship has been remarkably stable. . . .

Shifting Educational Requirements and Possible Skilled Manpower Bottlenecks

In recent weeks—partly before this committee, partly elsewhere —particular attention has been given to one aspect of the problem of structural maladjustments. This is the question of whether a recent shift in the pace and character of technological change has accelerated the long-term rise in job educational and skill requirements in a way that imposes a new bottleneck on expansion. The issue merits special discussion because of the obstacle to the employment-expanding effects of the tax program that this skilled manpower bottleneck is alleged to present. . . .

It is feared that, as demand increases, there will not be enough highly educated workers to fill the key technical and professional positions that must be manned if production is to expand to levels consistent with 4-percent unemployment; that, in consequence, expansion of output will be frustrated: and that, because of this, high percentages of the remainder of the labor force—including poorly educated workers —will be left unemployed. . . .

The nub [of the issue] is the failure of the bottleneck hypothesis to make any allowance for the proven capacity of a free labor market— especially one endowed with a high average level of education and enterprise and expanding programs to improve labor skills and mobility —to reconcile discrepancies between particular labor supplies and particular labor demands.

If relative shortages of particular skills develop, the price system and the market will moderate them, as they always have done in the past. Employers will be prompted to step up their inservice training programs and, as more jobs become available, poorly skilled and poorly educated workers will be more strongly motivated to avail themselves of training, retraining, and adult education opportunities. Government manpower programs begun in the 1961–63 period will also be operating to help ease the adjustment of specific shortages.

As for the personnel with the very highest skills, many—for the very reason that they are scarce—have been "stockpiled" by their employers and are not working to capacity when business is slack. As business picks up, they will be used more fully—and they will be used more efficiently. As engineers become scarce, and more expensive, their talents will be concentrated on engineering assignments, leaving drafting (for example) for draftsmen, who can be trained more quickly.

Naturally, most college graduates will have jobs no matter how high the unemployment rate in the whole economy, even if they have to work below the level for which they are qualified. If they are already in the supervisory or technical jobs for which they are best qualified, their employers will not have to increase by 10 percent the number of such jobs in order to increase total employment by 10 percent. And to the extent that they are not already in such jobs, they are a hidden reservoir of superior talent.

The highly educated manpower bottleneck argument arrives at its alarming conclusion by projecting to new situations a perfectly static set of educational requirements. The argument makes no allowance for flexibility in the system. Flexibility, of course, is not unlimited. If we were talking about accomplishing a massive increase in output within a few months, manpower bottlenecks might indeed become critical. But we find it unrealistic to believe that they represent a major constraint upon an extra $30 billion of output in what will soon be a $600 billion economy —especially when (a) there are virtually no current signs of tension in either labor markets or product markets and (b) the demand expansion that will accomplish the closure will be spread over 2 or more years in which continuing new supplies of highly trained manpower will be entering the labor market. . . .

Conclusions

This statement has been . . . necessarily complex. But the issues involved are of the highest urgency and significance for the economic future of our Nation, and they are far from simple. In so characterizing them we know we share the view of this subcommittee, which has been so tirelessly pursuing all aspects of this subject.

We have tried to draw our conclusions from the evidence as we have gone along, and therefore need only pull them together here. These are our principal conclusions:

1. Enactment of the major tax reduction program which is now before the Senate is a necessary condition for solution of the problems

that concern this subcommittee. It will directly add $30 billion to total output and create 2 to 3 million extra jobs. Without the continuing lift in total demands for goods and services that the tax program is designed to accomplish, little progress can be expected in reducing and eliminating problems of excessive unemployment for the Nation as a whole. Had this lift in demand been effective in the years 1958 through 1963, it would have overcome economic slack; achieved a considerably higher level of output of needed goods and services; maintained unemployment rates comparable with those realized in the years before 1957; and—in the process—reduced or eliminated our budget deficits.

2. Although tax reduction will alleviate, it will not by itself cure, longstanding problems of structural unemployment, of incomplete adaptation of the structure of our labor force to the structure of demand, of regional imbalances, and of consequent hardship, inequity, and inefficiency. The need to attack these problems stems, first, from our concern to alleviate unnecessary human distress. Second, it stems from the desire to convert unproductive and unwanted idleness into productive employment, so that we can increase our output of needed goods and services even beyond the potential output associated with our interim target of a 4-percent rate of unemployment. And third, if the rate of technological displacement of workers is in the process of accelerating, it will need to be matched by a similar increase in the mobility and adaptability of our labor force.

This administration has placed high priority upon measures to accelerate our productivity gains—through the stimulation of investment by tax measures, the improvement of technology in lagging sectors of the civilian economy, and in other ways—with the urgent purpose of improving the competitive position of American producers in world markets and of stepping up our long-term growth rate. It has promoted policies designed to realize the benefits of maximum productive efficiency—policies which may require shifts in our resource use and consequent displacements of labor.

It would be irresponsible not to complement these policies with others designed to facilitate the transfer of resources and to ease necessary burdens of adjustment—as, indeed, was due in the "adjustment" provisions of the Trade Expansion Act.

Without attempting to be comprehensive, we can indicate some of the important channels of attack on structural problems:

> Improved labor market information services.
> Improved guidance and placement services.
> Improved programs of apprenticeship.
> Strengthened programs to reduce discriminatory hiring and employment practices by race, sex, or national origin.

Expanded and more effective programs of vocational education, general adult education, and retraining.

Basic improvements in the quality of our educational system at all levels.

Measures to enlarge educational opportunities for children of low-income families and minority groups.

Programs to assist the geographical movement of workers.

Expanded policies to strengthen the economic base and to speed the economic growth of distressed communities and regions.

The tax cut and other measures to expand total demand are no substitute for policies like these; while these policies, in turn, are no substitute for a tax cut. Yet a more vigorous expansion of demand will release forces that will powerfully aid in the solution of structural problems. The existence of a stronger demand for labor will by itself strengthen the incentives for workers to undertake training or retraining and for employers to help provide it; will attract workers to move to the places where jobs are plentiful and stimulate employers to assist such movement; will ease the financial burdens on local communities in undertaking improvements in their educational systems; will reduce discriminatory practices both by employers and by unions; and will increase the effectiveness of the free market price system in encouraging appropriate adjustments of both labor supply and labor demand, the need for which is now partly obscured by slack markets.

3. Important as is the attack on structural problems, we need not fear that structural obstacles will block a healthy expansion of jobs and output resulting from the tax cut. The feasibility of our 4-percent interim target assumes not some newly perfected system of labor market adjustment but the labor market as it exists today with its present adjustment mechanism. Possible and desirable improvements in our labor market adjustment processes can smooth and accelerate achievement of the interim target. And they can permit us to penetrate beyond it to even lower unemployment rates. But it is on demand stimulus that we must rely to get to the provisional 4-percent objective. . . .

Manpower Report
of the President
IMPACT OF THE TAX CUT

The tax cut was designed to stimulate output and employment through an expansion of personal and business expenditures, and its impact on income and expenditures has been substantial; the tax cut directly added about $9 billion to consumer expenditures in 1964 as a whole. The stimulus to business investment has also been significant.

The tax cut also had a similarly impressive impact on employment. The relationship between changes in gross national product and employment is not stable, especially in the short run, but some rough idea of the magnitude of the impact on employment of the tax-cut-generated increase in GNP can be obtained.

The increase of $39 billion in GNP between 1963 and 1964 can be traced through to its employment impact in a general way, as follows:

> About $11 billion was the direct result of price increases of 1.9 percent and did not reflect real increment in the quantity of goods and services produced in the economy.

> Thus, close to $28 billion represents real increase in gross national product over the year (in 1964 dollars).

> However, about half ($14 billion) of this rise in real gross national product was necessary to maintain the level of employment in the face of increases in productivity (about 3 percent in the private economy) over the year. This amount of growth in GNP produced no net growth in employment; rather it offset the effects of automation and other factors affecting productivity.

> This left about $14 billion in additional real GNP for generating employment to meet the job needs of a growing labor force and reducing unemployment.

As pointed out earlier, about two-thirds of the $14 billion—about $9 billion—was a direct result of the tax cut on consumer expenditures. Without the tax cut, it is likely that unemployment would have increased over the year rather than declining by half a percentage point.

From *Manpower Report of the President, 1965,* Washington, D.C., U.S. Government Printing Office, pp. 11–12.

The employment expansion of 1964 impressively demonstrated the effectiveness of properly designed fiscal actions in creating employment opportunities. The nature of the employment growth also provided some measure of the extent to which we can look to acceleration of economic activity to solve specific manpower problems.

Many of the sectors of the economy and groups in the labor force that had faced the severest employment problems in the late 1950's and early 1960's benefited substantially from the employment growth in 1964. As compared with the annual average change from 1957 to 1962, in 1964:

Jobs expanded sharply in the private nonfarm sector of the economy, up by 1.2 million versus 270,000 in the earlier period.

Employment in goods-producing industries rose by 420,000 as opposed to a decline of 100,000.

Blue-collar employment increased by 550,000 versus an annual average decline of 120,000.

Full-time employment was up by 1.3 million versus an annual increase of 250,000.

Nonwhite employment rose by 250,000 versus an average annual increase of only 75,000 in the earlier period.

But in spite of these job gains, the major improvement in unemployment in 1964 occurred among adult males, who had the lowest unemployment rate of any group in the labor force. Although there was a substantial increase in teenage employment in 1964, it was just enough to employ the rapidly expanding labor force, and their unemployment rate remained close to 15 percent.

Despite the substantial employment expansion in goods-producing industries, most of the increase over the year occurred—as has been the case for many years—in the service industries; the goods-producing industries barely held their own as a proportion of total employment, even under the stimulus of the tax cut. Similarly, although the growth in manual occupations has been a dramatic feature of the recent employment expansion, it is among white-collar and service occupations that the largest and most rapid increases in employment have been taking place.

In summary, the outstanding employment increases of 1964 do not appear to have reversed the basic longer-run shifts in the occupational and industry distribution of employment which have particular relevance to the unemployment problems of manual workers. The past year has underlined the fact that opportunities for employment for these workers are certainly enhanced during periods of rapid employment growth. But it has also indicated that generalized improvement of employment opportunities is not an adequate solution to the extremely high unemployment rates that are a measure of the employment disabilities of Negroes, younger workers and the undereducated and unskilled of any age.

Gerald G. Somers
RETRAINING THE UNEMPLOYED

OBJECTIVES OF RETRAINING

The conclusions reached by a number of critics of retraining are disheartening. They are disheartening not because retraining lacks potential for longrun good, but because the programs to date appear to have had such limited shortrun impact on the hard core of unemployment. The disillusionment is greater because the initial expectations were so high. In the various Congressional hearings on unemployment policies, retraining proposals met with an almost "unanimous chorus of praise." After all, training is education, and who can be opposed to education? Training is the vehicle for occupational mobility, and in a dynamic economy of structural change who can be opposed to mobility?

But the expectations and current experience must both be seen in perspective. Retraining has three major objectives: (1) Shortrun increase in employment; (2) longrun economic growth; (3) improvement in the welfare and general well-being of the trainees and society. Regardless of any shortrun deficiencies, there can be little doubt that retraining the unemployed, like the educational process as a whole, is a worthwhile enterprise from the standpoints of the longrun economic growth of the American economy and the general well-being of its citizens. Indeed, some authorities are now saying that the investment in human resources, through education and training, has accounted for a greater part of our economic growth than the investment in capital equipment. Even if immediate employment does not result, the acquisition of new skills and

From a statement delivered to the Senate Subcommittee on Employment and Manpower, 1963.
Mr. Somers is Professor of Economics, University of Wisconsin.

knowledge by the unemployed is likely to make some future contribution to their own advancement and that of the economy.

Retraining allowances will usually take the place of unemployment compensation or relief payments for unemployed workers. Even if there were small additions to the costs for society, in what better way can the unemployed spend their moments of enforced idleness than in the acquisition of new skills? Our research provides ample evidence that retraining can give a new sense of pride, confidence, and social status to unemployed workers; and these represent substantial social gains regardless of immediate labor market consequences.

Therefore, one may well favor a greatly expanded program for retraining of the unemployed even if it could be demonstrated that no immediate jobs were created thereby. But most of those who have supported recent retraining measures have been more concerned with the current problems of unemployment than with longrun growth and well-being. And herein lies the disillusionment. The shortrun concern can be seen in the Manpower Development and Training Act provisions which restrict retraining to those who have a "reasonable expectation of employ"; in the incorporation of retraining provisions in the Area Redevelopment Act's attack on depressed areas; in the inclusion of retraining to meet the dislocation which may result from the Trade Expansion Act; in the retraining provisions espoused in the youth conservation bill; and in the many State and local efforts to reduce relief rolls through retraining.

IMMEDIATE EMPLOYMENT EFFECTS OF RETRAINING

It is clear from national statistics as well as our own surveys that Government-subsidized retraining has achieved only minor reductions in unemployment to date. This is primarily because of the limited period of experience with retraining, the small scale of the enterprise, and the state of the economy. In small part, the poor showing stems from deficiencies noted in a number of criticisms of the current programs; and our own research, although still in process, supports many of these findings. Some deficiencies are minor. They are recognized by the training authorities and can be corrected with the passage of time. Our responses from trainees, employers, unions, and Government officials indicate that some of the current Area Redevelopment Act and Manpower Development and Training Act courses are too short for the occupational objectives they seek to achieve; equipment is often inadequate in quantity and quality, and frequently it is available to unemployed trainees for only a few hours in the evening; instructors may be out of touch with the latest techniques; training allowances are often inadequate; retrained workers are not provided the tools which they are expected to bring to the job; local advisory committees have not always functioned effectively; and the complicated relations between the Office of Manpower, Automation and Training, the Bureau of Employment Security, and Health, Education, and Welfare—both in Washington and at the local level—have sometimes served to delay the inception of programs and impair their effective functioning.

However, these are growing pains; many of these problems are now being solved and they can be expected to diminish further as greater experience is gained. The relatively meager accomplishments of the retraining programs to date are basically attributable to the fact that they have just begun, but the real concern for their future success stems from more fundamental causes.

The crucial issues are (1) whether the retraining programs are currently enrolling the hard core of the unemployed, and (2) whether sufficient job vacancies now exist to justify a substantial lowering of selection standards.

The answer to the first question clearly depends on one's definition of hard-core unemployment. The national data indicate that the Area Redevelopment Act and Manpower Development and Training Act trainees include more long-term unemployed but fewer older and less-educated workers than are found among the unemployed as a whole in the areas from which they are drawn. This has led some to recommend that selection standards be lowered so as to include more hard-to-place workers. From the standpoints of longrun economic growth and general well-being this would be justified: but such a lowering of standards would probably lead to a lower placement ratio in the present status of the economy.

Even under the present selection standards the placement ratio of Area Redevelopment Act trainees is 65 percent and of Manpower Development and Training Act trainees, 70 percent, according to national data sources. . . .

ATTITUDE OF NONTRAINEES

The differential employment experience of trainees and nontrainees can be illuminated by reference to the preliminary data on attitudes of nontrainees, drawn from West Virginia surveys. . . . Those who applied for retraining but were found unacceptable felt overwhelmingly that they could have done the work in the training occupation to which they aspired. Only 4 percent indicated that they were not qualified. Almost all of these so-called rejects took the general aptitude tests administered by the Employment Service, and three-fourths felt that the tests were fair in spite of their disqualification. . . .

The bitterness of many of the "rejects" was directed not at the tests but at the Employment Service. Only one-fifth felt that the local office personnel took appropriate steps in informing the applicant of the reasons for his failure and in counseling him concerning his future course in the labor market. Seventeen percent first learned of their nonacceptance from the survey interviewer, even though considerable time had elapsed since their applications had been processed in most cases. The discouragement and bitterness evinced by the "rejects" lead to the conclusion that a major opportunity for fruitful counseling can be found among these unemployed workers.

A surprisingly large proportion of workers do not enroll in a training course after having been accepted on the basis of their test results and interviews; 36 percent of these did not report for training because they found employment prior to the beginning of the course. Because of limitations in training facilities or prospective employment opportunities, 27 percent could not be accommodated in the training course.

For dropouts, too, the temptation of an immediate job is a major factor in their decision to withdraw from the retraining program. Dropouts were especially numerous under the West Virginia area vocational program because trainees do not receive a weekly allowance during training under this program.

AGE AS A SELECTIVE FACTOR

Nonaccepted applicants for retraining are considerably older than those who are referred to the courses by the Employment Service. . . . In one area of West Virginia almost half of the "rejects" were over 45 years of age in contrast with only 14.6 percent of accepted applicants. The higher age of the "rejects" contributes to their failure to pass the aptitude tests and also serves as an independent factor causing their rejection by Employment Service counselors. Thus the youth of trainees in Government programs, relative to the average of the unemployed, can be explained only in part by the lack of motivation of older workers. Even those who are sufficiently well motivated to apply for admission to a retraining course are less likely than younger workers to have their applications accepted. . . .

TRAINEE VIEWS ON RETRAINING

West Virginia workers who experienced retraining were well pleased with the training they had received, but their satisfaction diminished somewhat with the passage of time following the completion of the course. Of 86 workers who were still engaged in training at the time of the initial interview surveys, 77 percent "liked the course very much" and 86 percent felt that they had chosen "the right course." Among 627 workers who had completed the retraining course or had withdrawn from the course at the time of the initial survey, 64 percent "liked the course very much" and 70 percent felt that they selected the appropriate course.

On the other hand, respondents' views on the difficulty of the course material appeared to benefit from a sense of detachment. Whereas 21 percent of the "in-training" sample found the course "pretty hard," only 12 percent of the "dropouts" and "completions" expressed this view. The remainder in both groups found the course "pretty easy" or "about right."

Relatively few persons withdrew from retraining because of difficulties with the course material. From the standpoint of the trainees, it appears that the aptitude testing is accurately gauged to the course material; but there is reason to believe that a reduction in standards for selecting trainees in the typical Area Redevelopment Act courses would not greatly increase the dropout rate attributable to difficulties with the course material.

EMPLOYER EXPERIENCE WITH RETRAINEES

The proof of retraining must be sought in posttraining employment experience and the values found in the programs by potential employers. Unfortunately our data on employer views are even more meager than those for trainees. However a sample survey of 44 West Virginia employers provides some insights into employer reactions to the Area Redevelopment Act and State programs. On the basis of their experience with the trainees they had hired, 47 percent of the employers indicated that the qualifications of the trainees were good and 32 percent stated that they were adequate. The remainder noted inadequacies in qualifications or were unable to express an opinion. Although most of the employers expressed satisfaction with the quality of instruction and placement procedures, their major reservation was on the length of the training course. Thirty-five percent stated that the course was too short, and only slightly more than half felt that it was about right in length.

The major suggestions for improvements in the retraining program made by employers were (1) an increase in the length of the training course, (2) more effective standards for screening and selecting trainees, and (3) greater efforts to place trainees in the specific jobs for which they were trained. . . .

Newsweek Magazine
SIX CASE HISTORIES

. . . The brunt of the [unemployment] burden falls on those least able to bear it—the young and the old, the Negro, the man with outmoded skills or no skills at all, the man living in a depressed area, and the unskilled woman, either widowed, divorced, or deserted, who must toil to support herself and her children. Theirs is what Labor Secretary Wirtz last week called "the human tragedy of life without opportunity." Worse still is the gnawing fear of permanent uselessness—the fear of millions that they will still be on the no-help-wanted list when the nation's economy moves on to new record heights. From the major categories of America's unemployed, here are six case histories:

Alfred Michel, 54, of West Mifflin, Pa., is a gap-toothed, broken-nosed steelworker who hasn't worked in three years and who will probably never work again. Like a third of the long-term unemployed, he is too old. ("When jobs are tight," says Wirtz, "the day a man over 45 loses his job is the day he becomes 'old.'") Despite his 37 years in the mills, Michel was furloughed when United States Steel closed its outmoded and inefficient open-hearth plant at Clairton, near Pittsburgh, and he was placed in U.S. Steel's huge "labor pool" to await reassignment. He is still waiting.

Nor is he alone in his predicament. There are currently 100,000 steelworkers drawing supplemental unemployment benefits (up to 65 per cent of base pay); there are many more, like Michel, who have long since exhausted such benefits. His sole subsistence is a relief check for $78.10 every two weeks, out of which he must pay $54 a month on the house into which he has sunk his life's savings. At the moment, he is a year behind in his payments.

Were there only Michel and his wife, he wouldn't complain. But though he has raised five children on his laborer's pay, he still has two daughters to go, one 14 years old and the other 16.

"I don't mind so much," Michel says, his voice choked with emotion, "but it's the girls. They're growing up. They want to go to dances and parties and things. They need pretty dresses and things so they don't feel ashamed, so they don't feel different from other people. But I can't give it to them. I can't give them nothing."

Does he feel bitter? "No," he says, yet he adds quietly, like a child: "But they did away with my plant. They ought to get me a new plant."

Anthony Rocha, 17, of Atlanta, Ga., is a small, slight youngster who exudes a nail-chewing nervousness; he is a high-school dropout; he has never had a real job. Of average intelligence, but two years behind his class because of illness and accidents, Rocha quit Atlanta's Fulton High School two weeks before Christmas while in the ninth grade, against his parents' wishes.

Dressed in a white shirt and tan, tight-legged trousers, lounging on a couch in his modest home, he tried to explain why. "Some people find an interest in school, but I just didn't. [So] me and a friend of mine decided we would just quit and get us a job. I didn't realize it would be so hard to find one. I've tried to get jobs at service stations, a bakery, and all the grocery stores out here, but there just aren't any jobs for a person like me."

There were other reasons, of course, for his leaving school. Anthony's step-father, who never finished high school himself, is a warehouse stockman who earns only $62.50 a week, with which he must support a family of five.

"All I wanted to know when I quit school," adds Rocha, "was that I could support myself and stop mooching on my mother and father. I realize now I definitely made a mistake."

But the wisdom came too late, as it frequently does. That's the main reason there are more than 500,000 unemployed teen-agers in the U.S. today, more than 10 per cent of the unemployed. These figures are even more chilling in view of Labor Department predictions that of the 26 million youngsters who will enter the work force during the 1960s, 7.5 million will be high-school dropouts, ill-equipped for space-age work. "What can a kid do about unemployment," asks Wirtz, "pick up his phone and call his congressman?"

Buster Taylor is 57, he has a minimal education ("I can print pretty fair"), and he has little to offer an employer but a strong and willing back. But his worst handicap is the fact that he is a Negro in Chicago, a city where Negroes account for 13 per cent of the work force but make up a full 40 per cent of the unemployed.

According to the National Association for the Advancement of Colored People, the same is roughly true in Detroit, Philadelphia, and St.

Louis, and to a lesser degree in Los Angeles and New York. While these estimates are impossible to check, the Labor Department last week placed the nationwide unemployment rate among Negroes at 13.3 per cent, more than twice the national average. "For the white, it's a mild recession," asserts Herbert Hill, forceful labor secretary of the NAACP. "For the Negro, it's a full-blown depression." Hill's answer: a double-barreled attack on discrimination in company hiring policies and in trade-union hiring-hall policies and apprentice-training programs. But for a fellow like David Blackshear, a 34-year-old New York textile examiner jobless since September, Hill's attack is meaningless. "I don't think it's prejudice," says Blackshear. "The garment industry is just stagnant."

Nor is Hill's solution enough for Buster Taylor. Taylor and his wife, Laura, came out of rural Mississippi in the early '40s. Lucky at first, Taylor found a steady job in a meat-packing plant, then served his time in the service, and returned to civilian life as the operator of a fork-lift truck for the same firm. Like some 30,000 other packinghouse workers, he was automated out of his job. Although he quickly found employment in a nearby produce market, driving a truck and hauling 100-pound sacks of potatoes, his workweek eventually dwindled from five to four days, then three, then—two months ago—nothing. And because he worked on a day-to-day basis on his last job, Taylor is ineligible for unemployment compensation.

How have he and his wife survived? On Mrs. Taylor's $24-a-week unemployment compensation, a "windfall" from her brief period of employment as a sorter last year with a Chicago feather wholesaler, plus an occasional visit to the market where Taylor used to work. "They give me some of the potatoes or lettuce they can't use," Taylor explains, "and that keeps us from starving. But you can't get meat like that. And it doesn't put any oil in the burner."

Antonio Moreno of Visalia, Calif., has worked at his trade since he was 15 years old. Now he is 61, the father of eleven children, and he has only one remaining ambition in life: "I want a full-time job and to be paid a just wage for my labor." But because he is a migrant farm worker, Antonio Moreno hasn't a chance of achieving that ambition. Indeed, he is lucky to work at all.

Things have changed little for the migrant farm worker since John Steinbeck chronicled their frightful estate in "The Grapes of Wrath." He may benefit from workmen's compensation, limited disability insurance, and improved housing. But to most migrant farm workers, these mean little. The reason is simply that there never has been sufficient work to provide a decent year-round living. And with automation edging its way into the fruitful lands of the southern San Joaquin Valley, the work for the Antonio Morenos becomes less and less.

In lush Tulare County, for example, there were 25,000 seasonal jobs for 25,000 farm workers four years ago; last year there were only 17,000 jobs. The other 8,000 had been replaced by gigantic, ponderous mechanical cotton pickers, 15 feet tall, 8 feet wide, and 10 feet long, each capable of picking more cotton a day than 30 to 50 men, depending on the terrain. With similar automatic equipment cutting a wide swath through the South and Southwest, one in every five migrant farm workers is, in effect, permanently unemployed.

Moreno, slight and stooped, his face the color of tanned leather, recalls that he was once assured at least four to five months' work in the cotton fields. "Now, maybe, I get one month," he adds. "And then I can only pick where the machines can't go, in the mud, in the weeds, where the crop is poor."

Still, Moreno is one of the lucky ones. He has a four-room house that he built with makeshift skills and makeshift materials on a lot that he bought for $200. And with pooled earnings of about $2,000 a year, he has managed to keep his whole family together.

To keep his family together over the next two years, however, will take a minor miracle. Moreno had to borrow $346 from the Visalia finance company to meet emergency medical payments and other pressing money needs. Since he already owed $477, he was forced to mortgage his house, its furnishings, and his lot for a total of $1,032, including $207 in carrying charges. Net result: he must pay $43 a month for the next 24 months, a fantastic amount for a migrant farm worker.

Mrs. Florence Almeida, 40, of New Bedford, Mass., is petite, blond, and pretty. If she would smile, she would be very pretty, but she finds little to smile about these days. She is a widow with three children and she hasn't got a job.

By some standards, Mrs. Almeida is well provided for; she receives $111 a month in aid to dependent children and $75 a month as the widow of a veteran. But with $48 monthly to pay on her 1959 Plymouth and the expense of a growing family, she has to work to live, and since Christmas, the living has been anything but easy.

A $1.75-an-hour presser in a garment factory, she was furloughed "temporarily" just before the holiday; called back early this month, she was furloughed permanently after a week's work.

At times, Mrs. Almeida seems resigned to it. "I'm not a worrier by nature and I accept things," she states matter-of-factly. "I think about leaving New Bedford, but the living here is so nice and I'm settled." In the next breath, however, she adds: "But if I didn't have security at home, I don't know where I'd look for it. I don't know where I'd find work."

Thomas Pastellak of Scranton, Pa., is a handsome, black-haired, 26-year-old with the cut of an Ivy Leaguer. He quit school after the ninth grade to help support his mother (his father had vanished); nonetheless, he is an articulate, well-read person. One of the first to sign up for an electronics course under the Manpower Development and Training Act (MDTA), he graduated near the head of his class. That was Dec. 4, and he still hasn't found a job.

Pastellak lives in a depressed area.

Theoretically, MDTA courses are designed to train men for existing job opportunities within the communities in which the classes are conducted. Unfortunately, in their effort to rush an electronics program into being, Scranton school officials misgauged the market. Of the first eleven electronics graduates, only two have found employment utilizing their new-found skills. Dr. Richard F. McNichols, superintendent of Scranton schools, now admits that in Scranton, a depressed area for a decade, "the job potential just isn't there." And wherever else Pastellak has gone in search of a job—in other Pennsylvania cities, in New Jersey, and in New York—the jobs available in electronics have been either committed to local residents or demand a knowledge and training far beyond any MDTA program.

To Pastellak the problem is deeply personal and intimate. He wants to marry. "I met a girl here in Scranton three years ago," he says, "when I was a seaman on the Great Lakes. I realized then that it was no life for a married man. I gave her a ring in 1961 and came home to stay. I haven't had a steady job since. We were supposed to have been married last year, but how can you get married without a job?"

the challenge of automation

Charles C. Killingsworth

AUTOMATION IS DIFFERENT

. . . A great many people today argue that automation is essentially no different from earlier technological developments like the assembly line. In my opinion, this argument is a source of error. The magnitude of the error is revealed, I believe, by a consideration, first, of the changed economic environment of today, and second, of some intrinsic characteristics of automation which make it different from such developments as the assembly line.

The economic environment in the United States today is far different from what it was when the steam engine, electric power, the assembly line and other major technological changes of the past appeared. Today, we live in a rather fully developed mass-consumption society. Let me illustrate the point by reference to . . . automobile registrations. The year when Henry Ford introduced his revolutionary idea of a moving assembly line was 1913. In that year, the automobile industry was in its early adolescence—a period of explosive growth and great potential for further growth. . . . The country had only about a million automobiles registered in that year, which was 1 car for every 100 people in the country. The assembly line greatly increased productivity in Ford's factory; direct labor requirements were cut by 90 percent on the assembly line. But sales increased enormously. . . . The number of cars registered increased tenfold in the 10 years following 1913, and most of them were Fords. By 1923, there was 1 car for every 10 people. So the

From testimony before the Senate Subcommittee on Employment and Manpower, 1963.

rapidly growing market for cars enabled Ford to employ more workers despite his laborsaving inventions. It should be added that the growth of the market was stimulated by Ford's big price cuts.

Compare that 1913 situation with the situation in the 1950's, when the transfer machine—"Detroit automation"—made its appearance. This new device in some major installations typically achieved direct labor savings of about 90 percent—about the same as the assembly line. But in the 1950's we had an automobile industry which had completed the rapid growth phase of its development. There were already 40 million cars registered in the United States, which was 1 car for every 4 persons. The market was not completely saturated, but the growth potential was much more limited than it was in 1913. In the decade of the fifties (the most prosperous period this country had seen up to that time), the total number of automobile registrations continued to climb. But the growth in 10 years was 50 percent, compared with the increase of 1,000 percent in the 10 years following 1913. We moved from one car for each four persons in 1950 to one for three in 1960.

I think that this comparison illustrates a point of fundamental importance. When a major laborsaving invention is introduced in an industry which is in its rapid growth stage—its adolescence—the invention may help to spur further rapid growth, especially through price cuts, and total employment in the industry may increase substantially. This is the historical pattern which prompts many people to argue that "machines make jobs." But the fact is that when an industry has reached maturity—for example, when there is already one car for each three people—it just is not possible to achieve further dramatic increases in sales, even with the largest price cuts within the realm of reason. The improved productivity made possible by laborsaving machines simply enables the industry to keep up with the normal growth of the market while employing fewer production workers. This is what happened in a number of our major industries in the 1950's.

Look across the whole range of consumer goods and you will see that our mass consumption society has done a highly effective job of supplying the wants of the great majority of consumers. About 99.5 percent of the homes that are wired for electricity have electric refrigerators; 93 percent have television sets; 83 percent have electric washing machines; and we have even more radios than homes. The only sharply rising sales curve in the consumer durables field today is that of the electric can opener industry. The electric toothbrush and electric hairbrush industries are starting to grow rapidly, too. But the growth of employment in these new "industries" will not offset the declines in the older, larger consumer goods industries.

The doctrine that "machines make jobs," to the extent that it rests on research rather than faith, is drawn primarily from studies of the periods 1899–1937 and 1946–1953. These were mainly years when the growth potential of most markets for goods was still very great. I think that it is a major source of error to assume that the markets of our great mass-production industries will grow at the same prodigious rate in the 2d half of the 20th century that they achieved in the 1st half. Without that kind of growth rate, the doctrine that "machines make jobs" will surely be as obsolete as the model T.

I do not mean to suggest that all consumer markets in the United States are approaching saturation and that consumers will soon be buying only replacements for what they already have. One of the few things that we can predict with reasonable certainty in economics is that as consumers' incomes rise, their spending will rise too. But our history reveals some longrun changes in the patterns of consumer spending. These changes have an important effect on patterns of employment. [There is the] recent decline of employment in the goods-producing industries and the long-term rise in employment in the service-producing industries—banking, trade, health care, education, and Government. This slow shift in emphasis from the production of goods to the production of services appears to be characteristic of the mature stage of a mass-consumption society. The United States is the only country in the world in which the jobs in services outnumber the jobs in goods industries.

Will the growth of jobs in the services offset the loss of jobs in goods industries? This kind of offset is possible, but by no means inevitable. We cannot safely accept the convenient assumption of economic theory that all labor is homogeneous, and the conclusion that only inertia or ignorance can impede the free flow of laborers from one industry to another as the patterns of consumer spending change. The displaced assembly line worker may be readily adaptable to work in a filling station; he may be much less acceptable as a clerk in a department store; and, without years of training, he cannot qualify as a teacher or a nurse. Adapting the labor force to changes in the supply of jobs is a matter of crucial importance in our society today.

The economic environment today is so different from that of 40 or 50 years ago that simply more of the same kinds of technological change that we experienced in the first half of the century would have a different impact now. But automation differs in some respects from most of the earlier technological changes.

One major difference is the much broader applicability of automation. The steam engine had a number of uses, but mainly in factories and in transportation. The cotton gin, the spinning jenny, the linotype, and others had a substantial impact, but each in only one industry. The examples that I have already given of automation applications illustrate the versatility of the techniques. Computer technology in particular seems likely to invade almost every area of industrial activity.

A related difference is that automation appears to be spreading more rapidly than most major technological changes of the past. It is difficult if not impossible to measure the diffusion of technology in quantitative terms, of course. But I find these facts suggestive: About a century was required for the general adoption of the steam engine in those activities where it could be employed; the comparable time span for electric power was about 50 years. The first automatic accounting systems were installed in banks some 7 or 8 years ago. Today, about half of the banks are in the process of converting to this system. When the first large-scale computers were introduced early in the 1950's, there were estimates that only about 10 or 15 of them would ever be needed in the entire United States. Today, nearly 4,000 fully transistorized computers are in use, and the number on order is about double that, so that in 2 or 3 years we will have about three times as many in use as we have today. . . .

Ad Hoc Committee
THE TRIPLE REVOLUTION

This statement is written in the recognition that mankind is at a historic conjuncture which demands a fundamental reexamination of existing values and institutions. At this time three separate and mutually reinforcing revolutions are taking place:

The Cybernation Revolution: A new era of production has begun. Its principles of organization are as different from those of the industrial era as those of the industrial era were different from the agricultural. The cybernation revolution has been brought about by the combination of the computer and the automated self-regulating machine. This results in a system of almost unlimited productive capacity which requires progressively less human labor. Cybernation is already reorganizing the economic and social system to meet its own needs.

Excerpted from a memorandum prepared by the Ad Hoc Committee on the Triple Revolution, Santa Barbara, California, March 1964. The memorandum, sent to President Johnson and Congressional leaders, was signed by W. H. Ferry, Michael Harrington, Robert Heilbroner, Ralph Helstein, Linus Pauling, Bayard Rustin, Ben B. Seligman, Robert Theobald, and about 25 others.

The Weaponry Revolution: New forms of weaponry have been developed which cannot win wars but which can obliterate civilization. We are recognizing only now that the great weapons have eliminated war as a method for resolving international conflicts. The ever-present threat of total destruction is tempered by the knowledge of the final futility of war. The need of a "warless world" is generally recognized, though achieving it will be a long and frustrating process.

The Human Rights Revolution: A universal demand for full human rights is now clearly evident. It continues to be demonstrated in the civil rights movement within the United States. But this is only the local manifestation of a world-wide movement toward the establishment of social and political régimes in which every individual will feel valued and none will feel rejected on account of his race.

We are particularly concerned in this statement with the first of these revolutionary phenomena. This is not because we underestimate the significance of the other two. On the contrary, we affirm that it is the simultaneous occurrence and interaction of all three developments which make evident the necessity for radical alterations in attitude and policy. The adoption of just policies for coping with cybernation and for extending rights to all Americans is indispensable for the creation of an atmosphere in the United States in which the supreme issue, peace, can be reasonably debated and resolved. . . .

THE NATURE OF THE CYBERNATION REVOLUTION

Cybernation is manifesting the characteristics of a revolution in production. These include the development of radically different techniques and the subsequent appearance of novel principles of the organization of production; a basic reordering of man's relationship to his environment; and a dramatic increase in total available and potential energy.

The major difference between the agricultural, industrial and cybernation revolutions is the speed at which they developed. The agricultural revolution began several thousand years ago in the Middle East. Centuries passed in the shift from a subsistence base of hunting and food gathering to settled agriculture.

In contrast, it has been less than two hundred years since the emergence of the Industrial Revolution, and direct and accurate knowledge of the new productive techniques has reached most of mankind. This swift dissemination of information is generally held to be the main factor leading to widespread industrialization.

While the major aspects of the cybernation revolution are for the moment restricted to the United States, its effects are observable almost at once throughout the industrial world and large parts of the non-industrial world. Observation is rapidly followed by analysis and criticism. The problems posed by the cybernation revolution are part of a new era in the history of all mankind but they are first being faced by the people of the United States. The way Americans cope with cybernation will influence the course of this phenomenon everywhere. This country is the stage on which the Machines-and-Man drama will first be played for the world to witness.

The fundamental problem posed by the cybernation revolution in the United States is that it invalidates the general mechanism so far employed to undergird people's rights as consumers. Up to this time economic resources have been distributed on the basis of contributions to production, with machines and men competing for employment on somewhat equal terms. In the developing cybernated system, potentially unlimited output can be achieved by systems of machines which will require little cooperation from human beings. As machines take over production from men, they absorb an increasing proportion of resources, while the men who are displaced become dependent on minimal and unrelated government measures—unemployment insurance, social security, welfare payments. These measures are less and less able to disguise a historic paradox: that a growing proportion of the population is subsisting on minimal incomes, often below the poverty line, at a time when sufficient productive potential is available to supply the needs of everyone in the United States.

The existence of this paradox is denied or ignored by conventional economic analysis. The general economic approach argues that potential demand, which if filled would raise the number of jobs and provide incomes to those holding them, is underestimated. Most contemporary economic analysis states that all of the available labor force and industrial capacity is required to meet the needs of consumers and industry and to provide adequate public services: schools, parks, roads, homes, decent cities, and clean water and air. It is further argued that demand could be increased, by a variety of standard techniques, to any desired extent by providing money and machines to improve the conditions of the billions of impoverished people elsewhere in the world, who need food and shelter, clothes and machinery and everything else the industrial nations take for granted.

There is no question that cybernation does increase the potential for the provision of funds to neglected public sectors. Nor is there any question that cybernation would make possible the abolition of poverty at home and abroad. But the industrial system does not possess any adequate mechanisms to permit these potentials to become realities. The industrial system was designed to produce an ever-increasing quantity of goods as efficiently as possible, and it was assumed that the distribution of the power to purchase these goods would occur almost automatically. The continuance of the income-through-jobs link as the only major mechanism for distributing effective demand—for granting the right to consume—now acts as the main brake on the almost unlimited capacity of a cybernated productive system.

Recent administrations have proposed measures aimed at achieving a better distribution of resources, and at reducing unemployment and underemployment. A few of these proposals have been enacted. More often they have failed to secure Congressional support. In every case, many members of Congress have criticized the proposed measures as departing from traditional principles for the allocation of resources and the encouragement of production. Abetted by budget-balancing economists and interest groups, they have argued for the maintenance of an economic machine based on ideas of scarcity to deal with the facts of abundance produced by cybernation. This time-consuming criticism has slowed the workings of Congress and has thrown out of focus for that body the inter-related effects of the triple revolution.

An adequate distribution of the potential abundance of goods and services will be achieved only when it is understood that the major economic problem is not how to increase production but how to distribute the abundance that is the great potential of cybernation. There is an urgent need for a fundamental change in the mechanisms employed to insure consumer rights.

FACTS AND FIGURES

No responsible observer would attempt to describe the exact pace or the full sweep of a phenomenon that is developing with the speed of cybernation. Some aspects of this revolution, however, are already clear:

The rate of productivity increase has risen with the onset of cybernation.

An industrial economic system postulated on scarcity has been unable to distribute the abundant goods and services produced by a cybernated system or potential in it.

Surplus capacity and unemployment have thus coexisted at excessive levels over the last six years.

The underlying cause of excessive unemployment is the fact that the capability of machines is rising more rapidly than the capacity of many human beings to keep pace.

A permanent impoverished and jobless class is established in the midst of potential abundance.

Evidence for these statements follows:

1. The increased efficiency of machine systems is shown in the more rapid increase in productivity per man-hour since 1960, a year that marks the first visible upsurge of the cybernation revolution. In 1961, 1962, and 1963, productivity per man-hour rose at an average pace above three and a half per cent—a rate well above both the historical average and the post-war rate.

Companies are finding cybernation more and more attractive. Even at the present early stage of cybernation, costs have already been lowered to a point where the price of a durable machine may be as little as one-third of the current annual wage-cost of the worker it replaces. A more rapid rise in the rate of productivity increase per man-hour can be expected from now on.

2. In recent years it has proved impossible to increase demand fast enough to bring about the full use of either men or plant capacities. The task of developing sufficient additional demand promises to become more difficult each year. A thirty-billion-dollar annual increase in gross national product is now required to prevent unemployment rates from rising. An additional forty-to-sixty-billion-dollar increase would be required to bring unemployment rates down to an acceptable level.

3. The official rate of unemployment has remained at or above five and a half per cent during the Sixties. The unemployment rate for teenagers has been rising steadily and now stands at around fifteen per cent. The unemployment rate for Negro teenagers stands at about thirty per cent. The unemployment rate for teenagers in minority ghettoes sometimes exceeds fifty per cent. Unemployment rates for Negroes are regularly more than twice those for whites, whatever their occupation, educational level, age or sex. The unemployment position for other racial minorities is similarly unfavorable. Unemployment rates in depressed areas often exceed fifty per cent.

These official figures seriously underestimate the true extent of unemployment. The statistics take no notice of underemployment or featherbedding. Besides the five and a half per cent of the labor force who are officially designated as unemployed, nearly four per cent of the labor force sought full-time work in 1962 but could find only part-time jobs. In addition, methods of calculating unemployment rates—a person is counted as unemployed only if he has actively sought a job recently—ignore the fact that many men and women who would like to find jobs have not looked for them because they know there are no employment opportunities. Underestimates for this reason are pervasive among groups whose unemployment rates are high—the young, the old, and racial minorities. Many people in the depressed agricultural, mining and industrial areas, who by official definition hold jobs but who are actually grossly underemployed, would move if there were prospects of finding work elsewhere. It is reasonable to estimate that over eight million people are not working who would like to have jobs today as compared with the four million shown in the official statistics.

Even more serious is the fact that the number of people who have voluntarily removed themselves from the labor force is not constant but increases continuously. These people have decided to stop looking for employment and seem to have accepted the fact that they will never hold jobs again. This decision is largely irreversible, in economic and also in social and psychological terms. The older worker calls himself "retired"; he cannot accept work without affecting his social-security status. The worker in his prime years is forced onto relief: in most states the requirements for becoming a relief recipient bring about such fundamental alterations in an individual's situation that a reversal of the process is always difficult and often totally infeasible. Teenagers, especially "drop-outs" and Negroes, are coming to realize that there is no place for them in the labor force, but at the same time they are given no realistic alternative. These people and their dependents make up a large part of the "poverty" sector of the American population.

Statistical evidence of these trends appears in the decline in the proportion of people claiming to be in the labor force—the so-called labor-force-participation rate. The recent apparent stabilization of the unemployment rate at around five and a half per cent is therefore misleading: it is a reflection of the discouragement and defeat of people who cannot find employment and have withdrawn from the market rather than a measure of the economy's success in creating jobs for those who want to work.

4. An efficiently functioning industrial system is assumed to provide the great majority of new jobs through the expansion of the private-enterprise sector. But well over half of the new jobs created during the period 1957–1962 were in the public sector—predominantly in teaching. Job creation in the private sector has now almost entirely ceased except in services; of the four million three hundred thousand jobs created in this period, only about two hundred thousand were provided by private industry through its own efforts. Many authorities anticipate that the application of cybernation to certain service industries, which is only beginning, will be particularly effective. If this is the case, no significant job creation will take place in the private sector in coming years.

5. Cybernation raises the level of the skills of the machine. Secretary of Labor Willard Wirtz has recently stated that the machines being produced today have, on the average, skills equivalent to a high-school diploma. If a human being is to compete with such machines,

therefore, he must at least possess a high school diploma. The Department of Labor estimates, however, that on the basis of present trends as many as thirty per cent of all students will be high school drop-outs in this decade.

6. A permanently depressed class is developing in the United States. Some thirty-eight million Americans, almost one-fifth of the nation, still live in poverty. The percentage of total income received by the poorest twenty per cent of the population was 4.9% in 1944 and 4.7% in 1963.

Secretary Wirtz recently summarized these trends: "The confluence of surging population and driving technology is splitting the American labor force into tens of millions of 'have's' and millions of 'have-nots.' In our economy of sixty-nine million jobs, those with wanted skills enjoy opportunity and earning power. But the others face a new and stark problem—exclusion on a permanent basis, both as producers and consumers, from economic life. This division of people threatens to create a human slag heap. We cannot tolerate the development of a separate nation of the poor, the unskilled, the jobless, living within another nation of the well-off, the trained and the employed."

NEED FOR A NEW CONSENSUS

The stubbornness and novelty of the situation that is conveyed by these statistics is now generally accepted. Ironically, it continues to be assumed that it is possible to devise measures which will reduce unemployment to a minimum and thus preserve the overall viability of the present productive system. Some authorities have gone so far as to suggest that the pace of technological change should be slowed down "so as to allow the industrial productive system time to adapt."

We believe, on the contrary, that the industrial productive system is no longer viable. We assert that the only way to turn technological change to the benefit of the individual and the service of the general welfare is to accept the process and to utilize it rationally and humanely. The new science of political economy will be built on the encouragement and planned expansion of cybernation. The issues raised by cybernation are particularly amenable to intelligent policy-making: cybernation itself provides the resources and tools that are needed to ensure minimum hardship during the transition process.

But major changes must be made in our attitudes and institutions in the foreseeable future. Today Americans are being swept along by three simultaneous revolutions while assuming they have them under control. In the absence of real understanding of any of these phenomena, especially of technology, we may be allowing an efficient and dehumanized community to emerge by default. Gaining control of our future requires the conscious formation of the society we wish to have. Cybernation at last forces us to answer historic questions: What is man's role when he is not dependent upon his own activities for the material basis of his life? What should be the basis for distributing individual access to national resources? Are there other proper claims on goods and services besides a job?

Because of cybernation, society no longer needs to impose repetitive and meaningless (because unnecessary) toil upon the individual. Society can now set the citizen free to make his own choice of occupation and vocation from a wide range of activities not now fostered by our value system and our accepted modes of "work." But in the absence of such a consensus about cybernation, the nation cannot begin to take advantage of all that it promises for human betterment.

PROPOSAL FOR ACTION

As a first step to a new consensus it is essential to recognize that the traditional link between jobs and incomes is being broken. The economy of abundance can sustain all citizens in comfort and economic security whether or not they engage in what is commonly reckoned as work. Wealth produced by machines rather than by men is still wealth. We urge, therefore, that society, through its appropriate legal and governmental institutions, undertake an unqualified commitment to provide every individual and every family with an adequate income as a matter of right. This undertaking we consider to be essential to the emerging economic, social and political order in this country. We regard it as the only policy by which the quarter of the nation now dispossessed and soon-to-be dispossessed by lack of employment can be brought within the abundant society. The unqualified right to an income would take the place of the patchwork of welfare measures—from unemployment insurance to relief—designed to ensure that no citizen or resident of the United States actually starves.

We do not pretend to visualize all of the consequences of this change in our values. It is clear, however, that the distribution of abundance in a cybernated society must be based on criteria strikingly different from those of an economic system based on scarcity. In retrospect, the establishment of the right to an income will prove to have been only the first step in the reconstruction of the value system of our society brought on by the triple revolution.

The present system encourages activities which can lead to private profit and neglects those activities which can enhance the wealth and the quality of life of our society. Consequently national policy has hitherto been aimed far more at the welfare of the productive process than at the welfare of people. The era of cybernation can reverse this emphasis. With public policy and research concentrated on people rather than processes we believe that many creative activities and interests commonly thought of as non-economic will absorb the time and the commitment of many of those no longer needed to produce goods and services. Society as a whole must encourage new modes of constructive, rewarding and ennobling activity. Principal among these are activities, such as teaching and learning, that relate people to people rather than people to things. Education has never been primarily conducted for profit in our society; it represents the first and most obvious activity inviting the expansion of the public sector to meet the needs of this period of transition.

We are not able to predict the long-run patterns of human activity and commitment in a nation when fewer and fewer people are involved in production of goods and services, nor are we able to forecast the over-all patterns of income distribution that will replace those of the past full employment system. However, these are not speculative and fanciful matters to be contemplated at leisure for a society that may come into existence in three or four generations. The outlines of the future press sharply into the present. The problems of joblessness, inadequate incomes, and frustrated lives confront us now; the American Negro, in his rebellion, asserts the demands—and the rights—of all the disadvantaged. The Negro's is the most insistent voice today, but behind him stand the millions of impoverished who are beginning to understand that cybernation, properly understood and used, is the road out of want and toward a decent life. . . .

Charles E. Silberman
THE REAL NEWS
ABOUT AUTOMATION

One of the most sensational pieces of news about the performance of the U.S. economy in this era of radical change and dire prediction

Reprinted from the January 1965 issue of *Fortune Magazine* by special permission; © 1965 Time, Inc.

Mr. Silberman is on the Board of Editors of *Fortune*. He is also the author of a recent study of the Negro in America, *Crisis in Black and White.*

is contained in a statistic that has been ignored by all but a handful of Labor Department economists. The statistic is this: employment of manufacturing production workers has increased by one million in the last three and a half years (from the first quarter of 1961 to the third quarter of 1964). This increase dramatically reversed the trend of the preceding five years, when 1,700,000 production-worker jobs were eliminated and "the work of the hands" appeared to be going out of style. Such work is very much in style now.

This turnaround in blue-collar employment raises fundamental questions about the speed with which machines are replacing men. It was the large decline in blue-collar employment in manufacturing during the late 1950's and early 1960's, more than the persistence of high over-all unemployment rates, that persuaded so many people that automation was rapidly taking hold, condemning the unskilled and the poorly educated to a vast human slag heap. "The moment of truth on automation is coming—a lot sooner than most people realize," the Research Institute of America warned its businessmen-subscribers a year ago. "Cybernation," said the sociologist-physicist Donald N. Michael, who coined the term (to refer to the marriage of computers with automatic machinery), "means an end to full employment." The Ad Hoc Committee on the Triple Revolution, a diverse but influential group of private citizens, goes even further: in its view "cybernation" means an end to *all* employment, or almost all. Unless "radically new strategies" are employed, the committee warned President Johnson last March, "the nation will be thrown into unprecedented economic and social disorder." It argued that "cybernation" makes a mockery of any attempt to provide jobs for either white or Negro workers. Technological change— the most crucial of the three revolutions the committee is concerned about (the other two are in civil rights and military weapons)—is creating an economy in which "potentially unlimited output can be achieved by systems of machines" requiring "little cooperation from human beings."

Nothing of the sort is happening. Six months of field research and economic and statistical analysis by *Fortune* makes it clear that automation has made substantially less headway in the U.S. economy than the literature on the subject suggests. (*Fortune* is indebted to industrial economist Alan Greenspan of Townsend-Greenspan & Co. for his assistance with the economic and statistical analysis.) Fifteen years after the concepts of "feedback" and "closed-loop control" became widespread, and ten years after computers started coming into common use, *no fully automated process exists for any major product in any industry in the U.S.* Nor is any in prospect in the immediate future. Furthermore, the extent and growth of several partially automated processes have been wildly exaggerated by most students of the economy. There is, in fact, no technological barrier to full employment.

This is not to deny that technology is changing; clearly it is. Nor is it to deny that such change displaces substantial numbers of workers. Technological innovation is always doing that, and is always painful to the individuals directly affected—the blacksmiths, harness makers, and coachmen whose jobs were destroyed by the automobile, and the insurance-company clerks now being displaced by computers. But the question raised by Michael, the Research Institute, and the self-appointed Committee on the Triple Revolution is not whether innovation causes displacement of labor. It is, rather, whether technological displacement is occurring at a substantially faster rate than in the past—at a rate so fast, in fact, as to threaten a crisis of mass unemployment similar to that of the 1930's.

THE VIEW FROM BROOKLYN

The answer, to be elaborated in this article, is no. Unemployment *is* too high, and has been for some years, but automation, in any meaningful sense of the term, is only a minor cause. The auto workers in South Bend who lost their jobs when Studebaker shut down, the packing-house workers thrown out of work in Chicago and Kansas City when the meatpackers decentralized their slaughtering operations, the coal miners in. Appalachia made idle by the loss of coal's biggest markets, the shipyard workers in Brooklyn and Portsmouth whose jobs will end when the Navy closes its yards—all are in trouble and many are in need of help. But they are no more the victims of automation than were the New England textile workers of the 1920's, made idle when the cotton mills first started moving south, or the southern cotton pickers of the 1930's and 1940's, thrown on relief when the mechanical cotton picker came into use.

To the men in question, of course, this fine distinction may seem brutal and irrelevant: what matters to them is not the particular reason they are idle but the poverty—of the spirit even more than of the body—that idleness causes. But to those concerned with relieving and preventing unemployment, the causes *must* be central. There can be no greater disservice to the unemployed—indeed, no greater act of contempt—than to substitute easy slogans for ruthless honesty in analyzing the causes of their joblessness, and thus fail to ease their plight.

. . . There are two kinds of pitfalls in trying to understand an age like ours. One is to take comfort in some such platitude as "the more it changes, the more it stays the same," thereby underestimating or ignoring altogether what might be termed "the cosmic changes" going on. The other is to become so enamored of the cosmic—to focus so completely on all the possibilities of contemporary science and technology—that one loses sight of the realities of the present. Too many of the people writing about automation and "cybernation" have fallen into the latter trap: they have grossly exaggerated the economic impact of automation. At the same time, curiously enough, some of them may have underestimated or simply ignored its psychological and cultural impact. For technology—*any* technology—has a logic of its own that affects people more or less independently of the purpose for which the technology may be used. The assembly line, for example, dictates a particular organization of work and a particular set of relations among workers, and between workers and managers, whether the line is turning out automobiles, breakfast cereals, or insurance-company records. . . .

THE IMPORTANCE OF IMITATION

A good deal of the confusion over what's happening stems from a failure to distinguish between what is scientifically possible and what is economically feasible. For technological change is *not* purely a matter of invention, of scientific or technical capability—a fact most defense contractors have had to learn the hard way. On the contrary, as Albert Wohlstetter of the Council on Foreign Relations puts it, technological change "has to do with such grubby matters as costs, and uses, and competing purposes: in short, with politics, sociology, economics, and military strategy." Indeed, the great economist Joseph Schumpeter used to argue that invention per se played a relatively minor role in technological change. What was crucial, he insisted, was "innovation"— the process of finding economic applications for the inventions—and "imitation," his term for the process by which innovation is diffused throughout the economy. The time lag between these three steps may have been truncated by the growth of industrial research and development and by the growing recognition that knowledge is the most important form of capital. But a time lag does remain, and it can be substantial, as the disappointingly small civilian fallout from military and space research and development activities attests.

We have misunderstood what is happening, moreover, because discussions of the future of science and technology have turned into "a competition in ominousness," as Wohlstetter describes it. In their eagerness to demonstrate that the apocalypse is at hand, the new technocratic Jeremiahs seem to feel that any example will do; they show a remarkable lack of interest in getting the details straight, and so have constructed elaborate theories on surprisingly shaky foundations.

To explain how automation is revolutionizing the structure of production and of employment, for example, Professor Charles C. Killingsworth of Michigan State University told Senator Clark's Employment and Manpower Subcommittee about Texaco's computerized petroleum refining unit in Port Arthur, Texas, which, Killingsworth said, processes "several million gallons of raw material daily." He picked a poor example; the installation actually demonstrates how small the bite of automation is, and how large and numerous are the obstacles to its rapid spread. The unit in question produces about 80,000 gallons a day, 0.6 percent of the refinery's total throughput. (Killingsworth apparently confused cubic feet of raw-material input with gallons of output.) The computer installation has been successful, to be sure. But the payoff has not come in reduced employment—the number of workers remained at three per shift—but in the greater efficiency with which the unit converts gases into polymers. (Killingsworth told the Clark committee that it was his "guess" that the computer had "replaced a half dozen men in the control room.") More to the point, this particular process was picked for computerization because it was "relatively simple when compared with other refinery processes" and because it was one of the few processes for which good historical data (essential if control is to be shifted from people to computers) was available.

Since the first installation Texaco has put a second computer in control of some of the operations in a large catalytic cracker; the number of workers on this process has remained unchanged.

Killingsworth's mistakes about the capacity of the original computerized refinery unit and his exaggeration of its significance typify most of the literature on automation. Donald Michael's influential essay, "Cybernation: The Silent Conquest," published in 1962 by the Fund for the Republic, contains several other such exaggerations. . . . Two examples:

Michael goes to some lengths to show how "cybernation permits much greater rationalization of managerial activities," e.g., "The computers can produce information about what is happening now . . . built-in feedback monitors the developing situation and deals with routine changes, errors and needs with little or no intervention by human beings. This frees management for attention to more basic duties." Michael instances "an automatic lathe . . . which gauges each part as it is produced and automatically resets the cutting tools to compensate for tool wear." The lathe "can be operated for 5 to 8 hours without attention, except for an occasional check to make sure that parts are being delivered to the loading mechanism." This description of the lathe came from 1955 testimony before a congressional committee by Walter Reuther, who in turn was quoting from *American Machinist* magazine. Michael's reference to the lathe is almost a complete *non sequitur*. For one thing, whatever its impact on the machinists in the shop, it did not affect managerial activities at all. For another, no computer was involved. The machine was simply an improved version of a standard automatic lathe that machine-tool manufacturers had been making for several decades.

To show how cybernation permits rationalization of management —in this instance by "combining built-in feedback with a display capability"—Michael also cites the Grayson-Robinson apparel chain's use of a computer to handle "the complete merchandise and inventory-control function." Actually, the chain had neither "feedback" nor "display capability." It did use a computer to give management a weekly report of sales and inventory, but Grayson-Robinson merchandise men did all the buying and reordering. Perhaps the chain would have been better off if the computer *had* handled "the complete merchandise function," for it started a bankruptcy proceeding in August, 1962, and was declared bankrupt last November.

THE ANONYMOUS GHOSTS

Not to be outdone by Michael's invention of the word "cybernation," the writer, Alice Mary Hilton, has coined the term "cyberculture" to describe the new "age of abundance and leisure" that computer-run factories will soon be forcing everyone to enjoy. Writing about the "cybercultural revolution" in the fall issue of the *Michigan Quarterly Review*, Miss Hilton offered a few original examples of her own:

> In Texas and New Jersey, in the oil refineries—the silent, lifeless ghost towns of this century—crude oil is processed into different grades of gasoline and various byproducts—the proportions determined automatically and flexibly as consumers' demands vary. Crude oil is piped in—gasoline and byproducts emerge, hour after hour, day after day, without pause for sleep or rest or play, without coffee breaks or vacations, sick leaves or strikes. *There are no workers, no supervisors, no executives; just a few highly trained engineers standing by in the central control room*, watching their brainchild fend for itself. (Emphasis added.)

Unfortunately, Miss Hilton is closely guarding the identity of these refinery "ghost towns." In Port Arthur, Texas, however, the Texaco refinery alone employs 5,000 people, the Gulf refinery 4,000.

Computers are producing fuel for human consumption as well as for machines, according to Miss Hilton. "In a Chicago suburb, in a bakery as large as a football field," she wrote, "bread and rolls and cakes and cookies are produced for millions of households throughout the country by a team of machines, called a system . . . *All the blue-collar and white-collar workers—of all levels—have been replaced by a silent machine system that labors twenty-four hours every day* . . . The bakery runs itself; the system even maintains itself," her awe-struck report continued. *"The few human beings still inside the 'black box' are only nursing the infant cybernation to maturity."* (Emphasis added.) Miss Hilton presumably was describing the Chicago bakery of Sara Lee, a subsidiary of Consolidated Foods. An elaborate computer system does indeed control the blending of the ingredients and part of the baking process, to ensure uniformity of product, but people are still required to perform a wide range of activities—e.g., braiding Danish pastry dough and spreading chocolate icing. And, "the few human beings still inside the 'black box' " come to about 450 per shift—300 of them in direct labor.

Walter Reuther, from whom Michael took his example of the automatic lathe, has provided other instances of the devastating impact of automation. Appearing before Senator Joseph Clark's Subcommittee on Employment and Manpower in May of 1963, Reuther compared the production methods used when he went to work for Ford in 1927 with those now in use. Once it took three weeks to machine the engine block for a Model T; in Ford's "automated" engine plant in Cleveland, which Reuther had visited after its opening in the early 1950's, the machining took only 14.6 minutes, because "the technology in that plant is built around computers." He added, "The thing we need to understand in order to grasp this revolutionary impact of such technology is that this automated engine line . . . is already obsolete."

Indeed it is—but not for the reason Reuther suggested. The engine line he described was taken out more than four years ago, because it was just too inflexible. When Ford redesigned its engines in 1959–60 it had to rebuild almost the entire Cleveland factory. The computers Reuther talked about were not replaced, however—because the factory never had any computers in the first place.

CAUGHT ON THE HORN OF PROPHECY

The view that computers are causing mass unemployment has gained currency largely because of a historical coincidence: the computer happened to come into widespread use in a period of sluggish economic growth and high unemployment. Thus it was natural that some who were not looking too closely at the evidence would attribute the unemployment to computers and automation, and would assume that a lot more automation must mean a lot more unemployment.

One of the first to push the panic button was W. H. Ferry, vice president of the Fund for the Republic. In a widely publicized essay entitled "Caught on the Horn of Plenty," published in January, 1962, and still being distributed, Ferry stated flatly that "The United States is advancing rapidly into a national economy in which there will not be enough jobs of the conventional kind to go around." He then proposed a test: "The next three years ought to suffice to determine whether a liberated margin [his term for the "technologically displaced"] is in fact in the making. If by 1964 the unemployment rate is close to 10 percent, despite the use of all conventional medications, we may be ready to agree that once again, as in the Thirties, the nation is in a radical dilemma, a dilemma of abundance."

The three years have passed. The unemployment rate has not risen to 10 percent, as Ferry believed it would; it has, instead, declined from its high of 7.1 percent in May, 1961, to 5 percent in November, 1964. There is little reason for comfort, and none for complacency, in these figures; 5 percent represents nearly four million people without jobs. And the number of unemployed could increase this year if the growth in output slows down.

But there is even less reason for chiliastic pessimism. To compare our situation with that of the 1930's, when 13 million people—25 percent of the labor force—were unemployed, is to indulge in reckless distortion. The persistence of high over-all unemployment and the changes in the occupational structure of the labor force have been due less to automation or technological changes than to a combination of quite different (and in some instances, quite temporary and reversible) economic forces. These will be analyzed in detail next month. The remainder of this article will examine what in fact is happening to productivity, and consider why automation has proceeded so much more slowly and has had so much less impact on employment than so many had expected.

THE SOURCES OF PRODUCTIVITY GROWTH

If technology were in fact threatening mass unemployment, the threat should be reflected in an acceleration of the rate at which productivity—i.e., output per man-hour—is increasing. What *has* been happening to productivity? Do the statistics of output per man-hour show any evidence of revolutionary changes in the structure of production? In general, the rate of productivity increase tends to accelerate over time, for productivity feeds upon itself. For the last 115 years, however—about as long a period as we can measure—the acceleration has been gradual, averaging about 0.2 percent per decade. Gross private (nongovernmental) output per man-hour grew at an average rate of only 1.3 percent a year between 1850 and 1889. The average jumped to 2 percent during the next thirty years (1889 to 1919), and then to 2.5 percent between the two world wars. Between 1947 and 1960 productivity gains averaged 3.1 percent a year; since 1960 the annual increase has averaged 3.6 percent.

The productivity gains these last four years, it should be pointed out, are running ahead of *Fortune's* 1959 forecast of a 3.1 percent average annual increase for the 1960's as a whole—a forecast that most academic and business students of productivity dismissed at the time as extravagantly optimistic. But note several things about these large productivity gains: Even larger gains have been registered over comparable or longer periods a number of times in the past—for example, from 1920 to 1924 and 1947 to 1953. More important, such figures reflect a lot more than technological change. Firms increase productivity, for example, by making their employees or their machines work harder; by hiring employees with more education or training, or by giving employees on-the-job training; by changing the way in which work is organized (e.g., using a typing pool instead of individual secretaries); or by changing the product "mix" (making more high-priced products).

It is inherent in the way productivity is measured, moreover, that above-average gains are recorded during periods of rising output and below-average gains during periods of stable or falling output. Productivity had been held down from 1955 to 1960, partly because output itself had been very sluggish, partly because the huge capital expenditures of 1955–57 and the enormous buildup in R. and D. activities had both, so to speak, diverted manpower from current to future production. When the current boom finally got under way, therefore, business had a reservoir of new products and new production processes to draw upon. More important, almost every industry had some excess capacity, which meant that until the past six months or so firms could fill incoming orders using only their newest and most efficient facilities. They could also concentrate their capital expenditures on equipment designed to increase the efficiency of existing facilities rather than spending to increase capacity. In addition, high unemployment rates made it possible for employers to be very choosy about whom they hired. Taking everything together, there are good reasons for viewing the productivity gains of the past few years as not entirely sustainable for the rest of the decade.

If the Triple Revolutionists were right—if we were in fact developing "a system of almost unlimited productive capacity"—it would follow that business firms could realize substantial increases in production without having to spend very much on new plant and equipment. But the current business expansion has triggered the greatest capital-goods boom in history—twice the size and duration of the capital-goods boom of the mid-Fifties.

Moreover, if a "new era of production" had really begun, it would have to show up in manufacturing, the most critical sector of the economy. Yet productivity has been growing a bit more *slowly* in manufacturing than in the economy as a whole. In the entire postwar period manufacturing productivity has increased by 2.8 percent a year, vs. 3.2 percent for the private economy. There has been an acceleration in the last four years, to be sure, but the manufacturing productivity gains are still below those for the whole economy—i.e., 3.5 vs. 3.6 percent a year. Furthermore, these recent gains in manufacturing are smaller than the gains realized in the decade following World War I, when technology was being revolutionized by the assembly line and the endless-chain drive. Between 1919 and 1929, output per man-hour in manufacturing increased by 5.6 percent a year. The acceleration in over-all productivity growth since the 1920's has come about because mechanization and rationalization have been applied elsewhere in the economy—e.g., in finance, insurance, retail and wholesale trade.

THE BREWMASTER'S NOSE

If there is not now any "cybernetic revolution" in manufacturing, perhaps there will be one soon. How likely is any such event? The answer seems to be—not very. Consider some obstacles that have been encountered in trying to automate continuous-process industries like oil refining, chemicals, and paper.

These industries looked like sitting ducks to manufacturers and designers of computer systems. They are characterized by enormous capital investment in processes in which relatively small increases in efficiency can yield large improvements in profit. By the mid-1950's they had actually gone pretty far toward automation. All that had to be done to achieve complete automation—or so it seemed at the time—was to substitute computers for the human beings monitoring the instruments and controlling the variables of the production process.

The next step was never taken; there are now about 300 process-control computers in use in the U.S., but the essential control of the production process remains in human hands and minds. Refineries and chemical plants, with their miles of pipes and tubes, and paper mills, with their gigantic machines dwarfing the handful of attendants, may *look* as though they were controlled by machines, but they're not. What is literally meant by "automation" or "cybernation," i.e., a process in which a computer or some other machine controls all aspects of the process from injection of the raw material to the emergence of the final product, determining the proper mix and flow materials, sensing deviations from the desired operating conditions and correcting these deviations as they occur, or before they occur—we are a long way from all this. In the electric-power industry, for example, which has more than a third of all installations, computers are used mostly as data loggers, recording what happens in the process for the engineers to analyze and study. So far no more than a half dozen or so plants are using computers to control the elaborate sequence of events involved in starting and shutting down a generating station, and only a few plants are using computers to determine the optimum distribution of power throughout the system. In pulp and paper mills, computers serve primarily as data loggers.

Most of these industries have realized large gains in productivity in recent years. But the gains have come less from computers than from better material handling, and from installation of larger and more efficient machinery of the conventional sort: for example, bigger electrical turbines and generators, bigger cat crackers in oil refineries, larger-diameter oil and gas pipelines, bigger and faster paper machines. The computers themselves have displaced very few people, if any at all, partly because computers are being used to perform functions that had not existed before; partly because the number of employees involved in controlling the process had already been reduced to the bare minimum needed to take care of emergencies. Computer manufacturers today try to justify their systems by pointing, not to savings in manpower, but to reduction in raw-material costs and increased efficiency in operation.

Full automation is far in the future because, as Peter F. Drucker has observed, "There's no substitute for the brewmaster's nose." The productivity of a paper mill, for example, hinges in large part on such things as a machine operator's ability to establish the proper "freeness," and this he does by watching the water "go along the wire." (The operator watches a mixture of water and fiber going past him; if he feels that the water is traveling too far before draining out, or not far enough, basic operating adjustments have to be made.) There is no *scientific* reason why such operations cannot be automated; in principle, the brewmaster's nose can be too, and in time it probably will. But the costs of doing so are inordinately large, and the time inordinately long: no industry understands its production process well enough to automate without huge investments of time and capital.

Consider, for example, the basic oxygen process for making steel. The system designers discovered very rapidly that they didn't have data precise enough to enable them to set up a mathematical model describing what actually goes on in an oxygen converter—the first step in designing a computer-controlled system. The data were too crude because the instruments being used were too crude. And the instruments were crude because steelmen didn't know what quantitative information they needed —not because they were uninterested, but because before computers came along they had no use for more refined data. Hence the computer manufacturer must study the process long enough to determine what information is needed, then find instruments sensitive enough to yield that information in quantitative form, then hook up these instruments to a computer to monitor the process long enough to determine what happens, and to identify the critical variables. Only then can it try to develop a mathematical model of what goes on in the process.

And setting up the model can be the most intractable job of all. It turns out, for example, that the mathematics of controlling an oxygen furnace, an oil refinery, or a paper mill are in some ways more complicated than the mathematics of controlling a missile or a satellite. The only mathematical technique now available for handling as many variables as are found in most industrial processes is "linear programing." Unfortunately, as Bunker-Ramo's T. M. Stout puts it, "practically no relationships in nature are linear." Thus, designers of computer process-control systems have had to develop their own mathematical techniques as they went along.

Each new computer installation, of course, makes the next one easier; in time, computers will be able to control more and more production variables. The point is that the change will be gradual and that it will not lead to people-less plants. The most fully automated refineries, paper mills, and generating stations now imaginable will still require a work force something like the present one. Even if computers could handle all the operating variables in a paper mill, for example, the number of operators probably would not be reduced below the present seven per machine. As one production man explains it, "at least fourteen hands are needed immediately to rethread the paper when it breaks"— and the paper breaks an average of twice a day.

THE ELEPHANTS AND THE MAHOUTS

The obstacles are multiplied several times over when firms try to automate the production of more complicated products that have to be assembled from a large number of parts. Automation, like mechanization in general, proceeds in two ways—either by taking over functions that men perform, e.g., substituting the automobile or the plane for man's feet, substituting the lever, the wheelbarrow, or the power-driven machine for man's arm and shoulder muscles; or by eliminating some of the functions that have to be performed, e.g., eliminating the setting of type through the use of punched tape, eliminating the thousands of operations that are needed to assemble an electronic circuit through the use of printed circuits. Changes that involve the elimination of functions may have great impact when they come—but they come very infrequently.

Most technological change, therefore, involves the mechanization of existing functions—what the brilliant Canadian student of technology, Marshall McLuhan, calls "extensions of man." Three broad kinds of function can be distinguished: muscle power or sheer physical strength; sensory-manipulative operations such as picking things up and moving them elsewhere, or guiding a shovel to the right spot with the right amount of force (as distinguished from the exertion of that force); and problem solving, using the brain to analyze a problem, select and process the necessary information, and reach a solution. What distinguishes the computer from most previous technological innovations—what makes it so awesome—is that it can tackle the second and third of these functions, not just the first. This enormous potential of the computer is the kernel of truth—a very large kernel—that the Triple Revolutionists have got hold of, and that gives their arguments so much surface plausibility.

But when we try to apply this newest extension of man to the process of physical production, we start running into difficulty. Many kinds of gross physical activity have already been mechanized out of existence, or soon will be, by simple and relatively inexpensive means, such as conveyer belts, lift trucks, and overhead cranes. The odor of perspiration has largely disappeared from the factory and the construction site. Most of the people left in the production process are involved in sensory-manipulative operations like assembling automobiles or directing a steam shovel. And these tasks—relatively unskilled and uncomplicated as they may appear—are the hardest operations of all to automate.

In addressing a meeting some five years ago on the theme "The Corporation: Will It Be Managed by Machines?" Professor Herbert Simon of Carnegie Tech, one of those working on the furthest frontiers of computer utilization, reflected on a tableau that had been enacted outside his office window the week before, when the foundations for a new building were laid. "After some preliminary skirmishing by men equipped with surveying instruments and sledges for driving pegs," Professor Simon observed, "most of the work has been done by various species of mechanical elephant and their mahouts. Two kinds of elephants dug out the earth (one with its forelegs, the other with its trunk) and loaded it in trucks (pack elephants, I suppose). Then, after an interlude during which another group of men carefully fitted some boards into place as forms, a new kind of elephant appeared, its belly full of concrete, which it disgorged back into the forms. It was assisted by two men with wheelbarrows—plain old-fashioned man-handled wheelbarrows—and two or three other men who fussily tamped the poured concrete with metal rods. Twice during this whole period a shovel appeared—on one occasion it was used by a man to remove dirt that had been dropped on a sidewalk; on another occasion it was used to clean a trough down which the concrete slid." Simon concluded, "Here, before me, was a sample of automated, or semi-automated, production."

What the sample suggested was that automation is not, and cannot be, a system of machines operating without men; it can be only a symbiosis of the two. The construction site demonstrated another important fact: we may be further from displacing the eyes, hands, and legs than we are from displacing the brain. The theoretical physicist, the physician, the corporate vice president, the accountant, and the clerk, Simon suggests, may be replaced before the steam-shovel operator or the man on the assembly line.

OUR VERSATILE CHILDREN

The reasons are partly technical, partly economic. The technical have to do with man's present superiority over machines in dealing with what Simon calls "rough terrain"—the uneven ground of a construction site, the variations in materials assembled in manufacturing, or the irregularities in shape of letters, the sound of words, and the syntax of sentences. Man's versatility in handling rough terrain was never really appreciated until engineers and scientists tried to teach computers to read handwriting, recognize colors, translate foreign languages, or respond to vocal commands. The human brain turns out to be, as Herbert Simon puts it, a remarkably "flexible general-purpose problem-solving device." An adult can recognize over a million variations of the color blue. The merest child can recognize an "e" in upper or lower case, in italics or upright, in boldface or regular, in print or handwriting, in manuscript or cursive, and so on almost ad infinitum—and all of these in an almost infinite range of sizes, colors, thicknesses of line, etc. And he can catch the meaning of words spoken by a voice that is masculine or feminine, high-pitched or low, loud or soft, pronounced with an enormous variety of regional and foreign accents. In short, the central nervous system is an incredibly versatile machine.

Its versatility is equally great—perhaps greater—in dealing with activities involving the coordination of eyes, ears, hands, and feet. "Manipulation is a much more complex activity than it appears to be," Ralph S. Mosher of General Electric recently wrote in Scientific American—even the seemingly simple operation of opening a door. "One grasps the doorknob and swings the door in an arc of a circle with the hinge axis at its center," Mosher explained. "The hand pulling the door must follow an arc lying in a plane at the level of the knob parallel to the plane of the floor, and it must conform to the circumference of the circle defined by the distance from the knob to the hinge axis. In doing this the hand, assisted by the human nervous system, is guided by the door's resistance to being pulled along any other path. In other words, the human motor system responds to a feedback of forces that must be interpreted. A strong robot, lacking any means of such interpretation and free to pull in any direction, might easily pull the door off its hinges instead of swinging it open."

The complexity of the economic considerations that determine what to automate, and when, is shown in International Harvester's construction-equipment factory outside Chicago. One of the plant's three engine-block lines is "automated"—i.e., it employs numerically controlled machine tools to machine engine blocks for enormous earth-moving machines, which are produced in relatively small volume. (For any product produced in quantity, conventional machine tools are cheaper.) But the blocks are moved from one automatic machine station to the next by men, using a simple overhead crane. Right next to this automated line is a conventional machine-tool line turning out vast numbers of engine blocks for tractors and trucks. On this conventional line, first installed in the late Thirties, the engine blocks are moved from station to station by conveyers and other transfer devices. The reason is simple: the volume handled on the "automated" line doesn't justify the cost of installing and operating transfer machinery for a conveyer belt; it's cheaper to move the blocks by hand.

NEW JOBS, OLD SKILLS

Because it may actually be easier to mechanize or automate clerical, managerial, and professional work than the kinds of blue-collar work that still remain, current discussions of the labor market may be exaggerating the future demand for professional and technical workers and underestimating the future demand for blue-collar workers. The discussions almost certainly overestimate the tendency for automation to upgrade the skill requirements of the labor force. "It is not true," Professor James R. Bright of Harvard Business School, perhaps the most careful academic student of automation in the U.S., has written, "that automaticity—automation, advanced mechanization, or whatever we call it—*inevitably* means lack of opportunity for the unskilled worker and/or tremendous retraining problems." In some instances skills are upgraded; in some they are reduced.

Over-all, however, what evidence is available (and there's painfully little) suggests that automation does not radically alter the existing distribution of skills. *Jobs* change, all right, but not the level of skill, particularly as firms gain more experience with automatic equipment. When business computers first came into use, for example, it was generally assumed that computer programers needed at least a college degree. Today most computer users find a high-school education adequate, and even this can occasionally be dispensed with. There is an enormous amount of repetitive work, moreover, under automation. The work may involve a different kind of rote, but it is still rote; it's hard to imagine a much more monotonous job than that of key-punch operator.

The crucial point is that we don't have enough experience with automation to make any firm generalizations about how technology will change the structure of occupations. On the one hand, automation may tend to *increase* the proportion of the population working as mahouts and wheelbarrow pushers, in Herbert Simon's metaphor, and to decrease the proportion working as scientists, engineers, technicians, and managers, because it may prove easier to displace people at these latter jobs than at the former. On the other hand, rising incomes will tend to increase the demand for services, in which jobs typically involve ill-structured problems and "rough terrain"; the demand for teachers, psychiatrists, journalists, and government officials, for example, is likely to expand faster than the demand for ditchdiggers or light-bulb changers. (The large increase in employment of clerical and professional and technical workers that has already occurred has been due less to technological change *per se* than to the fact that industries employing relatively large numbers of such workers, e.g., insurance, education, medical care, have increased their output much more rapidly than industries employing relatively few. There has been relatively little change in the proportion of professional and clerical workers *within* individual industries.)

A QUESTION OF COSTS

Sooner or later, of course, we will have the technical capability to substitute machines for men in most of the functions men now perform. But the decision to automate would still be an investment decision—not a scientific decision. At any one point in time, businessmen may choose between a wide variety of combinations of capital and labor. Their choice is affected very strongly by the relative costs of capital and labor —illustrated quite clearly, for example, in the fact that International Harvester finds it cheaper to use men than conveyers to move the engine blocks from station to station on that "automated" engine-block line.

In the last analysis, men will not be replaced by machines because widespread substitution of machines for men would tend to reduce the price of the latter and increase the price of the former, thereby creating a new optimum combination of the two. At any given moment business firms will use capital, i.e., machinery, instead of labor in those operations where machinery's advantage over labor is the greatest, and will continue to use men in operations where the machine's advantage is the least. For the last hundred and fifty years of constant technological change, with only rare exceptions, such as in the 1930's, capital and labor have managed to combine in the U.S. so as to keep 95 percent or more of the labor force employed. This has been a remarkable record, one that has made the U.S. economy the envy of the world. It would be premature to conclude that this record cannot continue indefinitely.

Meanwhile, if one focuses on a single industry, or a single plant, or a single process within a plant, of course, he can *always* find rather frightening evidence of technological unemployment. Consider this description of technological change in the steel industry, written by an English journalist after touring an up-to-date U.S. mill. "The thing that struck me first was how few men there were about," he reported. "To watch the way in which ingots were gripped from the furnaces, laid on rollers, carried on to be pressed, rolled out with steel fingers automatically putting them into position, you would have thought the machines were human." Even more impressive, the Englishman found, was the process for manufacturing steel rails: "From the moment the ore is pitched into the furnace until the rail was finished, everything is done by machinery, and *no man has a direct hand in the work*." (Emphasis added.) The plant was the old Carnegie works at Homestead, Pennsylvania; the time of the visit was 1902.

Walter Heller
THE CHALLENGE OF AUTOMATION

. . . In a way it is surprising how reluctant we are to embrace the higher productivity levels and living standards which "automation" makes possible. Some of the more popular literature on the subject treats it as a new and frightening development. But, in fact, it is only the most recent aspect of a continuing process of technological advance that dates back to the beginning of the industrial revolution. Taking full advantage of this process, the United States has built the most productive and most remunerative economy in the world. Through time, brute strength has been progressively replaced by simple machines, mechanical power,

From testimony before the Senate Subcommittee on Employment and Manpower, 1963.

complex machines, assembly lines, and today increasingly sophisticated automatic feedback systems. At each stage of the process individuals were temporarily displaced from existing jobs, new skills were found to be needed and were acquired, and total output and employment expanded as demand increased in line with the new higher production capabilities.

Ultimately the total effect has always in the past been a higher standard of living for almost everyone—higher pay for workers, cheaper and better products for consumers, and larger profits for businessmen and stockholders. On the basis of our historical experience, automation should be recognized for what it is—an open door to a more productive economy, to higher levels of private consumption, to more effective public services, and to larger resources for the support of our international objectives.

Despite this historical record, it is occasionally argued that the newest techniques are becoming so much more productive than those they replace that we cannot possibly adjust to them as smoothly as in the past. As indicated earlier, the evidence available to date does not enable us to draw firm conclusions about the prospective rate of increase in productivity. Yet, it is clearly possible that as the newest production techniques are increasingly embodied in new capital, the future growth of productivity will speed up.

Should this possibility be a source of concern? Rather than viewing it with concern or alarm, we would argue that we should work as hard as we can for faster productivity growth—indeed, it holds the key to success of our national policies for faster economic growth and for the cost cutting that is essential to our international competitive position. It is a prime objective of this year's tax bill as well as last year's special tax stimulants to investment.

Doubts about our ability to adjust to automation seem to be based on two questions: Can we really use the enlarged output of goods and services made possible by a rising rate of productivity advance? Will the new speed and character of technological change create impossible problems of adjustment for the labor force?

Those who raise the first question sometimes argue that we cannot possibly consume all that the new techniques can produce—that the persistent high level of unemployment over the past few years is evidence of satiation, that the fantastic productivity of the American economy has outdistanced the needs of the American people. What do the facts show?

First and most obvious, it is impossible to square this notion with the persistence of poverty in the American economy. We are indeed an affluent society, by every comparative standard. Nonetheless, even in this age of affluence, one-fifth of American families still have annual incomes below $3,000; that is, they live in poverty. To them, the suggestion that we are economically satiated must seem ridiculous, if not cruel. Until our society has met the challenge of poverty in the midst of plenty, it is in no danger of being satiated with goods and services.

But, quite apart from the persistence of poverty, there is nothing in the economic behavior of even the more affluent American consumers to support the satiation hypothesis. At all income levels, except perhaps in the top 2 or 3 percent of the income wealth distribution, the ratio of consumption to disposable income is one of our most stable economic relationships. Year in, year out—ever since 1950—American consumers have continued to spend from 92 to 94 percent of their aggregate disposable income—their income after taxes—on consumer goods and services. During this period total income and average family income have both risen markedly; but there is no evidence of any growing disinclination to spend a stable and high percentage of each additional dollar of income on consumption. Even those in the upper middle income groups who are already able to meet, without strain, the basic requirements for food, clothing, housing, and transportation find that they have ample, and often urgent, uses for additional income. This may take the form of an improved quality or manner in which basic requirements are satisfied —a larger house, a newer car—or it may take the form of meeting new and different demands; longer and more rewarding vacations, better education for one's children, better medical care, more books and more concerts, and more expensive hobbies.

This does not, of course, rule out the possibility that—as in the past—some, many, or even all of us will prefer to forgo still higher income in favor of greater leisure in the form of shorter hours, longer vacations, or earlier retirements. (There are indications, incidentally, that many people find it easier to become satiated with leisure than with income.)

In addition to unsatisfied private consumption needs, there are pressing needs for goods and services which are ordinarily and in some cases inevitably provided by the public sector. Admittedly there is disagreement as to just which of these public goods most need to be increased. There are also differences of opinion as to which levels of government should undertake expanded activities. Nevertheless, almost all major segments of the American community support increases in the level of one or another of such public goods and services, whether they be, for example, urban renewal, or improved health services, or better schools, or better roads and airports, or purer water and air, or more adequate facilities in national parks. Certainly none of this bespeaks a satiated society.

In a somewhat different vein, it should also be noted that technologically advancing societies also generate high levels of investment demand, demand for producer goods like machines, equipment, buildings. In large part, of course, this reflects the favorable impact of new technological developments on the profitability of investment. During most of our history, American business has responded to such opportunities by enlarging its investment outlays. Post-war Western Europe and Japan provide examples of economies with impressive rates of productivity increase along with buoyant demand, reflecting—more than anything else—extremely high quotas of investment.

Clearly, we need not fear that the increasing productivity associated with even a speeded up rate of technological progress will founder upon a contradiction between our needs and our ability to satisfy them. As people continue to receive the extra incomes which our enlarging production can generate, they will also continue to use those extra incomes to buy the enlarged output—for private and public consumption and for investment.

The second question raised about our ability to adjust to automation concerns the labor force adjustments it necessitates.

If the advance of technological progress has speeded up, it is reasonable to suppose that, as a byproduct, the rate at which particular skills are rendered obsolescent is also increasing. But a further and different point is sometimes made; namely, that automation (in its narrower technical sense) is shifting not merely the rate but the character of skill requirements generated by technological change. Previously, it is suggested, technological change simplified the work process and hence created many semiskilled jobs, which could be filled by workers with little training. Automation, however, reintegrates the production process and thus eliminates many unskilled and semiskilled jobs.

Whether this interpretation is correct is a highly complex empirical question. Many of the jobs displaced by automation are low skilled and some of the jobs added are extremely high skilled. The design and installation of automation equipment surely requires highly trained personnel. Yet the need for these people is clearly limited, and they do not stay with the equipment long after installation. Once in operation, the equipment may actually diminish rather than raise skill requirements. Examples of highly automated installations have been cited where all of the maintenance is done by high school graduates with a fairly short trade school course in electronic repair. High skills are required for the programing function, but this also tends to be concentrated in the initial stages and "canned" programs are increasingly available in some applications. A good deal more study and experience is needed before we

can safely generalize about the impact of automation on skill requirements for the labor force as a whole.

Beyond the question of how automation (in the narrow sense)
affects average skill requirements lies the broader question of the impact
on labor markets of any general acceleration that may occur in the rate of
technological advance. This broader question involves at least two
dimensions.

A vertical dimension relates to the impact of speeded technological change on the long-term rate of increase in the average educational
content of jobs. As noted repeatedly, our past rapid increase in
educational levels has both responded to and helped bring about our
steady technological advance and rising productivity. The exact nature of
the complex interrelationships between the average educational accomplishment of the labor force, job educational requirements, and a further
speeding up of the pace of technological advance is a matter for some
speculation. But whatever the answer, more and better education will
continue to have one of the highest priorities among the values of
American society.

The horizontal dimension of our question requires less speculation. We can be certain that a speeded pace of technological change will
increase the rate of job displacement, and will require even greater
attention to measures for improving labor mobility, for training and
retraining of workers, and for an effective level of basic education to
promote adaptability and flexibility. The possibility of an accelerated
pace of technical change thus underscores an already powerful case for
stronger labor market policies to meet existing problems of displacement.

Our past economic growth has brought unparalleled levels of
well-being for all in our society. Today, we need and we actively seek
even higher levels of productivity, to help us solve both domestic and
international problems. If, as a result of our policies to stimulate
investment and improve efficiency, or as an unexpected bonus from
autonomous developments in technology, the U.S. rate of productivity
growth accelerates, we may encounter problems, but we will reap large
rewards. If we pursue appropriate policies, we can meet the challenge of
automation.

2
The Disadvantaged

In a general atmosphere of material well-being, isolated sore spots pointedly remind us that segments of our population have been untouched by general prosperity. A number of minority racial and ethnic groups are on unequal footing in the race for jobs and income. Others in our population—for example, the aged, sick, handicapped, and mislocated—are not able to compete in the impersonal labor marketing process that works so well for the qualified. The result for many in these categories is poverty.

To be sure, the blemishes on our prosperity are not caused solely by labor problems. Improvement in all aspects of their social relations is required before the minorities can rise from their lowly economic status. Some of the poor cannot be touched by the most imaginative job programs; they need other kinds of help first.

Yet, more and better jobs are still the prime requisite for minorities and the poor (there is a considerable overlap between these two groups). Education, vocational training, and social assimilation are necessary, but the extent to which these can aid the disadvantaged is finally measured by better jobs and incomes. Steady, adequately paid jobs will greatly facilitate and reinforce educational gains and social integration of the disadvantaged. Civil rights groups realize this fact, as they now turn from the excitement of awakening the nation's social conscience to the comparatively dull task of formulating specific job demands.

The first section of this chapter deals with minority-employment issues. Herman Miller's opening selection indicates the directions of change in recent Negro employment—up or down—in comparison with the rest of the population. Though it is clear that Negroes were occupationally upgraded during World War II, similar improvements in more recent times are not discernible.

The second selection deals with Mexican-Americans and the third with American Indians. (This by no means exhausts the list of ethnic groups in America that have special employment problems.) These groups often fail to receive the attention to their employment difficulties that they deserve. This is, perhaps, especially true of the Indians, most of whom derive no benefit from being indigenous to the richest country in the world.

Recognition of minority-employment problems is becoming widespread enough that issues now are focused on what to do about them. One such issue, discussed by Edward Chase, is the employment-quota system—that is, employment of minorities in proportion to their population. Employment by quotas sometimes conflicts with employment by qualifications, and herein lies the controversy.

Related to the quota issue, but also of separate interest, are the tactics of militant civil rights groups in their efforts to obtain jobs or improve job levels for minorities. Robert McKersie describes and assesses the alternative strategies employed by these organizations.

The reduction of over-all unemployment, of course, is important to minority group welfare, because the incidence of unemployment falls disproportionately on these groups. The methods of putting the unemployed back to work, discussed in the previous chapter, should be considered in the light of their special significance for minorities. Indeed, minority job improvement is tied more closely to action on unemployment than to any other current activity.

The poor represent a minority group whose only qualification for membership is lack of income. In the first selection of the section on poverty, Robert Lampman—who, along with Michael Harrington, was chiefly responsible for drawing our attention to poverty in America—identifies other characteristics of the poor.

Members of disadvantaged ethnic and racial groups are frequently poor; so are small farmers, especially in the South, as well as the aged, the fatherless families, and the unskilled workers who haven't been able to get steady employment under the protective wing of an aggressive trade union or in the paternally amiable environments of big business and government. Poverty exists because jobs are not available; some jobs don't provide decent earnings; and some persons are physically or mentally unable to work. The first two causes can be eliminated by job-creating economic growth. The other must receive special treatment, though many of those persons we now label as "unqualified" would obtain employment if the United States were to have a real, rather than imagined, labor shortage.

The selection by John Lindsay deals with one kind of "unqualified" poor. He describes the plight and reaction of coal miners who were once fully employed and proud of their place in a time-honored occupation but now cannot eke out a living in an industry transformed by technology. Economic rationality dictates migration to urban centers as a cure for the poverty of these miners, but many of these men could not face the psychological readjustments that would be required.

The South has more than its share of poverty, which falls on both whites and nonwhites. The major reason is the failure of the South to change rapidly enough from an agrarian region to one with a solid industrial base. William H. Nicholls describes how the futile attempts to preserve the traditional society of this region affected the livelihoods of those at the bottom of the social and economic hierarchy. The South is now industrializing, but poverty will persist in that region for a long time to come.

Bernard Nossiter suggests that poverty generally, not just in the South, will be difficult to eliminate. President Johnson declared war on poverty in 1964, but the impatient accuse him of fighting it with a "no win" policy, while others argue that administrative chaos will be the chief result. In the final selection of the chapter, the California State Chamber of Commerce contends that economic growth is the real remedy for poverty and that bureaucratic programs will be ineffective, especially if they are planned by the federal government.

Even much larger expenditures than are now being made would not solve the intractable problems of some of the poor. For this reason, among others, we are beginning to hear proposals for minimum-income guarantees for all citizens (see "The Triple Revolution" in the previous chapter). If poverty retains a tenacious hold as affluence continues to become a reality for many, these proposals will be issues of the future.

minority employment

Herman P. Miller
PROGRESS AND PROSPECTS
FOR THE NEGRO WORKER

Much as I am delighted to contribute an article for publication in this distinguished magazine, I feel obligated to warn the reader that I am no expert on Negro affairs. My only qualification for writing this article is that I have spent more years than I care to count at the Census Bureau where many of the basic statistics about Negro life are collected.

I have decided, therefore, to focus on the general area of employment because this is a subject of vital importance to the Negro and, also, it is one for which there is a vast storehouse of statistical data. The particular aspect of the problem that I intend to explore is the change in the occupational distribution of whites and Negroes during the past 50 years. Census information on this subject goes back to 1910. Thanks to the efforts of the Conservation of Human Resources Project at Columbia University and the work of other research organizations in this field, we are now beginning to supplant impressionistic judgments with scholarly evaluations.

In any discussion of white and Negro differentials over time it is important to distinguish between *absolute* and *relative* changes. Although this distinction is very important, it is often overlooked. If you think about the problem for a minute, the difference between absolute and relative changes will appear quite obvious and you will recognize its

Reprinted from *Challenge, The Magazine of Economic Affairs,* 475 Fifth Avenue, New York, N.Y. 10017, February 1965.
Mr. Miller is with the U.S. Bureau of the Census.

importance. There has been a general upgrading of occupational skills for both whites and Negroes as the American economy has moved from agriculture and become more complex and industrialized. As a result, Negroes who were once highly concentrated in sharecropping and farm labor have now moved up to unskilled and semiskilled factory jobs. Appreciable numbers have even moved into white-collar employment. This change has raised the skills of the Negro labor force, it has increased their productivity and it is in large measure responsible for the vast improvement in their levels of living. If we take what is perhaps the single most important aspect of life that we attempt to measure, namely life expectancy itself, we find that the Negro infant born in 1960 could expect to live 21 years longer than his mother born in 1920. This represents a gain of nearly 50 per cent in life expectancy in a relatively brief span of 40 years. Not only are Negroes living longer, but they are also living far better than ever before. Negro housing, for example, may still leave much to be desired; but the proportion living in dilapidated homes was cut in half between 1950 and 1960. The real incomes of Negroes have also shown a remarkable rise. Between 1940 and 1960 the wages and salaries of the average male Negro worker rose from about $1,000 to about $3,000, both figures measured in terms of 1960 dollars. In other words, there was a threefold increase in Negro purchasing power during this period.

I could go on and on citing the gains that have been made by Negroes in recent years. It would not take very long, however, before you would begin to wonder why I fail to mention that there has been a parallel upgrading of jobs and levels of living for white workers as well. Here, of course, we get to the *relative* aspects of the problem. It is not enough to know how much or how fast the lot of the Negro is improving. The critical question in many minds, particularly for Negroes and their leaders, is whether the relative upward movement has been as great for Negroes as for whites. Sometimes this focus on relative position blinds critics to the fact that there has been an improvement in absolute status. for example, Tom Kahn, who was Bayard Rustin's assistant in organizing the March on Washington, recently wrote, "It takes a lot of running to stand still on the treadmill of this technologically advancing society. When you know you're running hard and everyone tells you that you're moving at a fast clip, and yet the scenery around you remains the same, the most appropriate word to describe your reactions is . . . frustration." Yet, the fact is that the Negro has not been standing still and the scenery around him has been changing most dramatically. He has had tremendous increases in life expectancy, purchasing power, levels of living, occupational classification, educational attainment, and significant improvements in many other aspects of life for which objective measures are available. The only reason many Negroes feel they are standing still is that the whites, too, have had these gains and in many areas the gap between the whites and Negroes does not appear to be narrowing. It is on these aspects of the problem that I will concentrate today. How has Negro employment changed over the past 50 years? How has it changed relative to the whites? What are the prospects for a narrowing of white-Negro differentials in employment?

By 1910 the white labor force had already completed much of the transition from agriculture to industry. In the census taken in that year, only one-fourth of the white workers were employed in farming; another one-fourth worked in white-collar jobs; and the remaining one-half were more or less equally divided among craftsmen, factory operatives, and nonfarm laborers or service workers. In that same year, 1910, the Negro labor force was split 50–50 between farming and nonfarm work. The farmers were of course, largely Southern sharecroppers or laborers working and living under the most miserable conditions, even by contemporary standards. Those who were not working as farmers were employed largely as service workers (i.e., domestics, waiters, bootblacks and similar jobs) and as nonfarm laborers largely on railroads and construction gangs. Relatively few (only five per cent) had even risen to the point of semiskilled factory work, and even fewer (only three per cent) worked as craftsmen or as white-collar workers.

The next 50 years witnessed a dramatic movement out of agriculture for both whites and Negroes. This movement, by the way, must soon grind to a halt for the very simple reason that we are running out of farmers to be moved. At present, only about seven per cent of the white workers are farmers as compared with 28 per cent at the turn of the century. The biggest increase is, of course, in white-collar work. Nearly one out of two white workers is now employed in a white-collar job. At the turn of the century, only one out of four white workers was in this category.

The shift away from farming was even more dramatic for Negroes than for whites. As I mentioned earlier, in 1910 one-half of the Negro workers were employed in farming; in 1960 this proportion dropped to only one-tenth. The frequent cry of some economists for greater mobility as a solution to rural poverty has certainly been heeded by the Negro. He has shown tremendous mobility and energy in search of economic opportunity, often against overwhelming odds. The displacement of Negroes from farming has largely been absorbed by the manual and service trades. At present, about one-third of the Negroes are service workers; another one-third are nonfarm laborers or semiskilled factory workers; and the remaining 20 per cent are craftsmen or white-collar workers. Until about 1940 the occupational shift for Negroes was almost exclusively from farming into employment as domestics, factory hands and laborers. In recent years, opportunities in white-collar employment have been growing in importance.

A close examination of the decennial census data provides better insight than we have ever had before of the way in which the transformation of the Negro labor force took place. In each decade, as new industries and occupations developed, it was the white worker who moved in first.

According to one analysis by Prof. Dale L. Hiestand of Columbia University (*Economic Growth and Employment Opportunities for Minorities*), "white workers capture the newly growing fields in which labor resources are scarce, pay levels are good, prospects for advancement are bright, the technology is most advanced, and working conditions the most modern." They leave in their wake jobs in the older industries which become less desirable because the pay is not as good, nor are the prospects for advancement. Moreover, many of the jobs left behind by the whites were in industries dominated by an old technology, which when replaced, would be likely to require reduced manpower needs. Thus, in every decade, the newest and best opportunities available to the Negroes were often quite vulnerable. The jobs deserted by the whites were invariably better than the ones in which Negroes were employed at the time. They were, nonetheless, not the jobs with the bright futures. This pattern of occupational change is, as we shall soon see, of great significance in assessing the prospects of the Negro for narrowing the occupational gap between himself and the whites. It suggests that if the Negro is ever to approach occupational equality with the whites, he must seek out and somehow gain admittance to the "frontier area of occupational expansion." If he continues to get only those jobs that the white has left over, he may never bridge the occupational gap. Indeed, some would argue that if the Negro follows the traditional pattern of occupational mobility, he may find himself in a tighter and tighter job squeeze because the employment that would have normally been handed down to him is being automated out of existence.

It must be granted on the basis of the empirical evidence that the absolute position of the Negro worker, with respect to employment, has improved considerably in the past 50 years. The problem to which we shall now turn is an examination of the extent to which the relative gap between whites and Negroes has changed. In the work previously referred to, Prof. Hiestand of Columbia University constructed an occupational index which permits this type of comparison to be made. . . .

In the case of men, the index shows no significant change between 1910 and 1940. There was some slight improvement in the relative occupational position of Negro men during the past 20 years, but this is entirely due to their movement out of the South. Indexes which have been constructed on a state-by-state basis show that there were very few significant changes in the occupational distribution of Negro males relative to whites in the past 20 years.

The relative occupational distribution of Negro women relative to whites was about the same in 1940 as it was in 1910. As in the case of the males, there appears to have been some improvement in the relative occupational position of Negro women during the past 20 years, but this change may also be primarily due to their movement out of the South, with its very limited opportunities for Negro employment, rather than to any general upgrading of the kinds of jobs open to Negroes. The weight of the evidence, therefore, is strongly in support of the view that although there has been considerable occupational improvement for Negro workers during the past 50 years in an *absolute* sense, the position of Negroes relative to whites has not changed much.

Having established these facts, we may now turn to an examination of their meaning, particularly with respect to assessing their significance for future trends in Negro employment. Here we must tread with care because, as so many forecasters have discovered to their regret, past is not necessarily prologue. . . .

The weight of the statistical evidence is that the fate of the Negro worker is very much tied in with the fate of the economy as a whole. During previous periods of vigorous economic growth, white workers moved ahead very rapidly and Negro workers followed in their wake, generally picking up the jobs that were left behind. There was some movement of Negroes into the expanding areas of the economy, but the numbers were small relative to the total. Both groups moved ahead more or less proportionately as a result of the job opportunities made available by the process of growth. It is difficult to say at this point in time whether this pattern would continue if we were once again to enter on an extended period of vigorous economic growth. Of course, one might say that we are now going through such a period, having experienced growth rates in our national product of about five per cent for the past three years. Although these growth rates are considerably in excess of our long-run national average, they are associated with painfully high unemployment rates for Negro workers, suggesting that there is a shortage of job opportunities. The evidence, however, is by no means conclusive. There are many who would argue that it is still too soon to judge whether a more rapidly growing economy can provide full employment for Negroes (without inflation) despite the elimination of hundreds of thousands of unskilled and semiskilled jobs they formerly manned. The point has been made that it may take several years of vigorous growth to absorb the manpower slack that developed during the slow years since 1957. Moreover, the blind forces of the economy may have to be helped along by manpower training programs which will fit the Negro (and the displaced white workers) for new types of work.

It is understandably of great importance to the Negro not only to improve his situation, but also to narrow the gap between himself and the whites. This feeling must not be ascribed to any special perversity on the part of the Negro worker. Rather, it is a reflection of a prevalent attitude in our society which has long been recognized by economists and taken into account by them in explaining economic behavior. The British economist, Pigou, described the matter rather well around the turn of the century when he wrote that "men do not desire to be rich, but to be richer than other men."

What is the likelihood that the Negro will, in fact, be able to narrow the occupational gap between himself and the whites? This question is difficult to answer. The one thing that seems clear from the data is that the gap will not be narrowed if the traditional patterns of occupational change are maintained. In order to catch up with the whites, Negro workers will have to be propelled into promising new jobs in new industries instead of drifting into the old jobs in the dying industries, as they have done in the past. This change will come about for Negroes only if two conditions are met. They must obtain the education and training required for the new jobs, and the barriers to their entry into the better paying fields must be lowered. The prospects that both of these conditions will be met in the near future are not very good. It is unrealistic to talk about bridging the occupational gap in the modern world when one-fourth of the Negro youth in their early twenties have not gone beyond the eighth grade and over half have not completed high school. There is not much that people with so little education can be trained to do in our complex economy.

Even if the Negro showed more interest in education than the above figures imply, there is little evidence that society is willing to make the huge investments in education and training that are required if the Negro is ever to be able to compete on equal terms with the white in the labor market. Most attempts to provide effective school integration have met with hostility and "foot-dragging." Even in the prosperous North there has been more lip service than action in the improvement of the quality of education in deprived areas. Finally, we come to just plain discrimination, which may be the hardest of all obstacles to overcome because it is so deeply imbedded in our culture. We sometimes forget that about 60 per cent of the Negroes still live in the South, and according to any reasonable assumptions regarding rates of out-migration, nearly half of them will still be in that region by 1980. In view of the intensity of feeling that has been manifested by the Southern whites on racial matters, it is hard to believe that Negroes in this region will receive to any great extent either the training they need or the opportunity to move into the more promising jobs. In view of these and many other factors, I see little reason to be optimistic about the possibility of narrowing the occupational gap between the races in the foreseeable future. There are, however, offsetting forces which provide some hope.

At present, there is probably less discrimination against Negroes than at any previous time in our history. It is also likely that discrimination will tend to decrease with time because of the strong pressures being exerted by the federal government. These efforts should create new opportunities for Negro employment in federal, state and local governments, in private companies doing contract work for the federal government, and in other companies that will be under social pressure to liberalize their employment practices.

At the same time that the prospects for Negroes to obtain skilled employment have been increasing, the attitudes of the Negro leaders have been undergoing a change. In the past, the civil rights movement focused attention largely on efforts designed to publicize the plight of the Negro and to promote integration. This emphasis led to the March on Washington, demonstrations, sit-ins, picketing, and other activities that were instrumental in promoting passage of the civil rights and antipoverty legislation. Partly as a result of this success, but also because the Negro leadership may feel that the end of the line has been reached with this kind of effort, attention is now shifting to the fight for better jobs, education and housing, with only secondary emphasis on integration. This attitude was clearly expressed by Bayard Rustin when he said recently, "We have got to lift the school problem from integration to that of quality schools; which has to include, we say, integration secondarily." Implicit in a remark such as this is recognition of the importance of developing the skills and qualities that are needed by Negro workers in order to take full advantage of the job opportunities that may arise. As Nathan Glazer has pointed out very effectively in a recent article in *Commentary* magazine, the legislative gains that have been made by Negroes in the past few years make it possible and perhaps even necessary for contemporary leaders of the civil rights movement to return to the fundamental policies outlined by Booker T. Washington at the turn of the century. According to Glazer, Booker T. Washington "saw that the Negro had been denuded by slavery of the qualities necessary for building an independent and satisfying life. Primarily what concerned him . . . was the devaluation of work produced by slavery, for he felt that independent and productive work was the basis of racial respect. But Washington also assumed that the Negroes, as they gained in education and income, would be enfranchised and would be able to play a major role in politics and in the shaping of their own fate. He fought desperately against the movement to disenfranchise Negroes in the South in the 1890s. When this movement succeeded, and Jim Crow began to fasten its bonds on the Negro people, he was left with half a program. The other half became the program of 'protest.'" Glazer then goes on to state that "we now have a situation which corresponds . . . to the one Booker T. Washington first saw as his major task, the building up of the economic and social foundations of the Negro community."

The point is that so long as the Negro could see no reasonable prospect for advancement beyond the most menial jobs, he was behaving more or less rationally in assigning a low value to education, saving and the other fruitful avenues to advancement. Limited opportunities for employment in the professional fields forced Negroes to concentrate on those areas where there was a Negro market for their services—preaching, teaching and social work. Because of their concentration in these low-paid fields, the average Negro college graduate, even today, can expect to earn less over a lifetime than the white who does not go beyond the eighth grade.

In view of facts such as these, who could argue with the young school dropout who might feel what James Baldwin has expressed so well in the following words: "It is not to be wondered at that if . . . studying is going to prepare him only to be a porter or an elevator boy—or his teacher—well, then, to hell with it."

But we now have a chance to change all of this. Whether in fact we will depends upon two things: the extent to which our society opens up and takes the Negro in as a full-fledged participating member; and the extent to which the Negro is prepared to move in should the opportunities present themselves. Only time will tell whether or not we can succeed in getting both of these forces to move in the right direction at the right time.

Dionicio Morales
MEXICAN-AMERICANS IN CALIFORNIA

The problems of Mexican-Americans in California have received less recognition than those of any other ethnic group in the United States.

This is one of the striking anachronisms of our country, especially when the historical place of the Mexican-American in the Southwest is borne in mind.

The persistence of the Mexican-American, as a cultural and lingual minority, continues to form a great obstacle to the building of a strong America.

Besides the cultural and language features that distinguish the Mexican-Americans as a group, their problems are aggravated by the fact that they are sharply demarcated in economic disadvantages when compared to the rest of the American community.

It is at once encouraging and disheartening to observe the emerging interest in the community role and problems of Mexican-Americans; encouraging because it reflects a wider recognition of the needs and contribution of this community and disheartening because this recognition has been so long in coming.

Southern California alone has almost 1 million residents of Mexican ancestry—the largest minority in this area. In Los Angeles County there are about 700,000 Mexican-Americans. About 1,500,000 Mexican-Americans live in California. This is the largest single area concentration of the Nation's 4,320,000 "Spanish-speaking" people. They constitute nearly 10 percent of California's population, outnumbering Negroes, the State's next largest minority group, by about 500,000.

Their problems and their participation in the life of the community have, until now, received little attention from public officials, businessmen and educators.

Figures on the occupational distribution of Mexican-Americans in southern California demonstrate conclusively that they, like the

From a statement to the Senate Subcommittee on Employment and Manpower, 1963.

Mr. Morales is a member of the President's Committee on Community Relations.

Negroes, are now concentrated in the blue-collar job categories and are underrepresented in the white-collar fields. Even in those firms holding Government contracts, which presumably would be less discriminatory than firms not holding such contracts, the proportion of Mexican-Americans to total employed is significantly less than the corresponding proportion to the whole population of the Los Angeles area. For example, a recent survey of firms holding selected Government contracts showed a total of 61,041 workers in all categories, of whom 1,661 (or 2.7 percent) are Mexicans. Approximately 10.5 percent of the total population in the Los Angeles metropolitan area are Mexican-American.

Mexican-Americans are overwhelmingly concentrated in the manual categories. About 79 percent are in the craftsman, operative, laborer, and service categories, compared with 51 percent for all workers surveyed. More importantly, 50.7 percent of the Mexican-Americans are in the lowest three of these categories (operative, laborer, and service) in contrast with only 24 percent for all workers. These figures are corroborated by the 1960 census data on occupational distribution in the community as a whole. . . .

The median family income for Mexican-Americans in the Los Angeles area is substantially below that of the population as a whole. In 1960, the Federal census showed that the Mexican-American median income for 1959 was $5,759 compared with $7,078 for the whole population of the metropolitan area. It should be noted that the latter includes both the Mexican-American and Negro populations, and that a comparison of the Mexican-American and Anglo incomes would necessarily show an even more striking gap.

The California farmworker, 80 percent Mexican-American, generally receives about $1 an hour for his labors. His median income is $1,940.

Within the past 8 months I have had the opportunity of observing at firsthand the conditions of employment of nonunion garment workers in southern California.

Recent immigrants from Mexico are reliving the cruel sweatshop conditions, in various areas of Los Angeles County, which immigrants suffered in our country a half century ago.

Strangers in the land, unfamiliar with the language and customs, ineligible for relief or unemployment insurance, with hungry families to feed in their native land, they are desperate for any income.

A general consensus, especially in San Fernando Valley, in Los Angeles County, is that they are afraid that once fired, they will be blacklisted and never be able to find another job in the garment industry and face possible deportation if they become public charges.

If they complain, employers quickly make it known to them that they can easily be replaced by Cuban refugees, who, they allege, will even work for less. Thus, new immigrants from Mexico, Cuba, and other Latin American countries are pitted against each other and impregnated with the idea that if they become involved in anything of a supposed controversial nature, they can be repatriated immediately.

Thousands of Mexican workers therefore become victims of ruthless employers who have taken full advantage of the deep fears that go with insecurity and newness in a strange land. The psychology of fear has been so shrewdly developed that it has weakened the will of the workers to fight for better working conditions.

The result of the above described conditions is a body of frightened, unhappy people in what can best be described as "sweatshops"—1963 style—in southern California.

This is one specific illustration of an existing situation that stands out against the relentless background of abuse and exploitation. It is a picture we find in other industries in southern California employing Mexican-Americans.

There are farms throughout California on which Mexican-American families try to earn a livelihood.

The majority of these workers are not protected by social and economic legislation. They are isolated from the main stream of community life, encased in poverty, deprived of educational opportunities for their children, without adequate housing, health care, sanitation, and community services.

Serious, adverse effects created by Public Law 78 have affected the lives of thousands of Mexican-Americans in California. The most tragic figure has been the imported Mexican national himself. Millions of these workers, referred to as braceros, have displaced U.S. agricultural workers and have contributed to a horrendous unemployment problem up and down the State of California. Yes, 143,462 braceros took the jobs of domestic farmworkers, primarily Mexican-Americans, in 1962. Qualified Mexican-American agricultural workers have simply been forced out of the industry. The Mexican-American leaders have not been completely naive about the repercussions relative to the effects of Public Law 78.*
Labor leaders, religious leaders, Mexican-American organizations throughout the State of California (CSO) and every canon of justice is outraged so long as employers in a great American industry, and agencies of the American Government, extend benefits to foreign contract workers which they deny American citizens of Mexican origin. . . .

The Mexican-American finds himself in a peculiar and uncertain position as the product of two cultures. Because our society and our

* With the termination of this law at the end of 1964, use of Mexican nationals in U.S. agriculture has greatly declined (eds. note).

educational system often fail to give proper recognition to the values of his own culture, the bilingualism and dual cultural background which ought to be advantages are turned into handicaps. . . .

A bold program, therefore, is essential to eliminate discrimination, improve vocational counseling and training, promote more effective communication between Anglo and Mexican-American communities and expand the education horizons of Mexican-American youngsters.

Roderick H. Riley
UNEMPLOYMENT
AMONG AMERICAN INDIANS

In discussing unemployment of American Indians, we may begin by distinguishing between two groups—first, those Indians who comprise the Bureau's service population and, second, all others. The service population, almost all members of which live on or adjacent to reservations, is estimated at 380,000. The nonreservation population is perhaps half this size. The 1960 decennial census put the total of American Indians (including the Eskimos and Aleuts of Alaska) at 552,000, but there has been some increase in the past three years.

The reservation population of 380,000 is by no means uniform in its economic and social characteristics. It is a commonplace observation that the Indians of no two reservations are alike. What they have in common, however, is of great significance for an understanding of unemployment among them.

First of all, most Indian lands are economically depressed areas and yield incomes ranging between one-quarter and one-third those of non-Indian families of the same region. Many reservations are located in counties that also are depressed, although not so badly. These are lands to which the Indians were removed because non-Indians succeeded in getting the more desirable lands formerly occupied. Even during the early decades of this century, the loss of Indian lands continued,

From a statement presented to the Senate Committee on Employment and Manpower, 1963.

Mr. Riley is with the U.S. Bureau of Indian Affairs.

amounting to 60 percent between 1887 and 1934, when alienation was arrested as a matter of national policy. Of the 52 million acres then remaining, 45 million acres were suitable for grazing and only 4 million were farmland. It is estimated that even full practical utilization of these lands today would provide a livelihood for less than half the population now residing on them.

Second, tribal ties are strong and the Indians' emotional feeling about their ancestral land is deep and compelling. Its possession gives them a sense of security wholly unrelated to its present or prospective economic value. This psychological fact, which has its counterpart in many non-Indian depressed areas, helps explain why a population double the size that the land can support remains on the reservations.

Third, Indian cultures are not job oriented. Indians understand running livestock, but have never had a tradition of farming, much less one of industrial or commercial employment. Most Indian children grow up in families where their elders have never had regular employment, have never thought in terms of reporting for work each morning or even of rising at a regular hour. Wage work, when available, is accepted as a means of providing for the family's immediate needs, not as the basis of a family plan for the future. If income from range leases covers family needs, many Indians feel no incentive to expand it through employment.

Fourth, the education and training of Indians on the reservations lag seriously behind averages for non-Indians. Years of schooling among Indians over 25 average only about half those for white Americans. Among young adults, significantly, the gap is only one-third, 8 years as against 12. The basic requirement for success in the economic world, English language capability, is lacked by many. Progress is evident, but is being achieved slowly.

The situation on most reservations, accordingly, is one of seriously inadequate job opportunities at or near home, of inadequate education and training for jobs that may become available, of ignorance of the surrounding culture and of how to make one's way even in the nearby outside world. With respect to this third, very pervasive factor, Prof. William Gomberg, of the Wharton School, recently had this to say about the situation he found on the Pyramid Lake Reservation in Nevada:

> The standard procedures for jobseeking, so well known to most non-Indians, are not known by most people at Pyramid Lake. Application forms bewilder them; asking former employers for references embarrasses them; the bustle of the employment office frightens them.

He added that:

> Those who participated in the tests were glad the results would be kept on file at the Reno Employment Office. It was obvious they had been reluctant to visit the office in the past.

These observations are acknowledged by those familiar with the reservations as being very broadly applicable.

Under such circumstances, it is unavoidable that unemployment should be high on the reservations. The regular monthly and quarterly unemployment reports do not provide information on the reservations as such, but a special census monograph based on 1960 data is illuminating. The data, made available prior to publication of the monograph this fall, disclose an overall unemployment rate of 15 percent among all Indians in April 1960. The U.S. average during the same week was 5.1 percent. Analysis of differences between 42 Indian areas and other parts of the country supports an estimate of 21 percent for the reservation population, balanced by one of 7 percent unemployment among the non-reservation population.

An unemployment rate of 21 percent means, under the standard definition, that for every 79 persons at work there are 21 others who are unsuccessfully seeking work. This is a rate three to four times as high as the national average has run during a period of admittedly unsatisfactory economic activity. On the Indian reservations, however, even this rate is an understatement. For, located in areas of very limited employment opportunities, Indians badly needing work commonly lack the social mobility to seek it at a distance and may even not know how to seek it nearby. If jobs are brought to the reservation, on the other hand, jobseeking becomes active. This is true when factories are opened nearby and our employment assistance program is used to recruit workers; it is also true when public works funds are made available to relieve unemployment on the reservations. The typical response is galvanic; workers line up at the employment window, often bringing their tools for work in the woods. Under ordinary circumstances, however, the typical reservation Indian, aware of the shortage of job opportunities within reasonable distance of his home and unused to non-Indian jobhunting methods, is unlikely to seek work elsewhere. Those who do so—our program to assist them in such efforts will be described shortly—commonly depart from the reservation and may soon be no longer part of the population and labor force we are now examining.

Because it would be unrealistic to measure the need for employment on the reservations by the number of Indians actively seeking work without success, the Bureau has used another definition of unemployment. Our estimates of unemployment are based on a labor force estimate that includes all Indians of working age who are neither unemployable because of physical or mental handicaps nor unavailable for employment because of enrollment in school, of family responsibilities, or of early retirement. This is the definition of the reservation labor force also used, implicitly, by the House Interior Committee in the questionnaire sent to all reservations last November. The resulting survey, the first to be made simultaneously of all reservations, indicated a labor force of about 120,000, slightly more than half of whose members were employed. Half of the employment, in turn, was of temporary nature. The rate of unemployment was 49 percent. This rate corroborates the findings of earlier Bureau studies of individual reservations, which disclosed unemployment in the range of 40–45 percent of a labor force upward of 100,000.

Unemployment among reservation Indians was reported to be serious everywhere last winter. In California the rate was 20 percent, more than three times the U.S. average. At the other extreme, in our Anadarko area, comprising Kansas and part of Oklahoma, unemployment was reported at 71 percent and in five other areas it was higher than 50 percent. Among the principal reservations (population of 1,000 or more) the lowest rate was 14 percent, at Rama, N. Mex.; the highest was 85 percent, at Fort Berthold, N. Dak.

It is clear from the foregoing that 21 percent—high as this rate is in comparison with the U.S. average—understates the degree of unemployment on the Indian reservations. It is plain, too, that the more embracing definition of the labor force that the Bureau and the House committee have found it necessary to use yields levels and rates of unemployment that must include some jobless persons who would not accept regular employment if it became available on the reservation. We are confident, however, in light of our experience with industrial and public works employment on the reservations, that the overstatement of unemployment is modest. The more closely we succeed, moreover, in providing employment opportunities to match unemployment of 40 percent or more of the apparent reservation work force, the more completely may we expect to find the Indians responding to motivations typical of Americans in the general community.

Edward T. Chase

QUOTAS FOR NEGROES?

Efforts to put in practice the so-called "doctrine of compensation" are about to advance the Negro rights revolution into the difficult next stage of contention over the concrete, critical details that will measure success and failure. The doctrine holds that Negroes are now to be compensated for 350 years of discrimination by a spate of favored treatment. In practice one finds that this usually boils down to the issue of preferential hiring of Negroes, especially as it pertains to new job classifications hitherto denied them. It can also include numerical quota systems, and favoring the Negro with inferior qualifications or one with no seniority over his white competitor.

The preferential hiring issue has suddenly come to a head with the decision of prominent official advisory committees to the U.S. Commission on Civil Rights to directly support preferential treatment and even quotas. This is creating consternation among employer groups. But the issue cannot be easily evaded for long because now there are also threats of boycotts of the goods or services of those firms which employ Negroes in only token numbers or in limited job classifications. Such boycotts are now being planned on a vast scale by CORE (The Committee On Racial Equality) and other Negro action groups. These will probably make white counter-revolutions against civil rights a strong probability in some areas.

One instructive way to approach the current preferential hiring issue is to begin with a look at how the principle underlying the doctrine has been applied in the recent past. The instances are disconcerting. One finds, for example, that in 1931 Heywood Broun published a book *Christians Only* documenting in irrefutable terms that Jews (as an ethnic group) were discriminated against in admittance to U.S. medical schools on a systematic, numerical basis. Only a decade ago the American civil rights authority, Lawrence Bloomgarden, described in detail how the medical schools employed quotas to accomplish this. The dean of

Reprinted by permission from *Commonweal*, January 17, 1964.
Mr. Chase writes frequently on social and economic issues for a variety of magazines.

Columbia University's medical school had argued that "representation of the various social and religious groups in medicine ought to be kept fairly parallel with the population make-up." The dean of Cornell University medical school, too, back in the 1940's, stated explicitly that the number of Jews admitted by Cornell was to be proportionate to the Jewish percentage of the state's population (though the medical school itself was situated in New York City, where the percentage of Jews was several times higher than the State average).

Nor, one finds, have admittance quotas on Jews been confined to the Ivy League's medical schools. At the start of the Nazi era, though this coincidental fact was unknown at the time, President Lowell of Harvard openly recommended a Jewish quota on all undergraduate admissions. Bloomgarden also quotes Dartmouth College President Ernest Hopkins defending a quota system as late as 1945. Clearly these were attitudes taken on ethnic grounds.

In 1953 scholar Bloomgarden concluded bitterly that a quota policy is "never used to justify expansion of opportunity for minority groups, but only for limitation. It is never said, for example, that Negro medical students should constitute 10 percent of the total to correspond to the Negro percentage of our population." The fact that it is said now, loud and clear, throughout the U.S. press, and is applied to housing and education as well as employment, is one mark of how things have changed.

The Urban League leads the Negro movement in pressing for preferential hiring, though it sometimes rejects the phrase and so far has rejected a direct numerical quota plea. The NAACP and Jackie Robinson also condemn quotas. Governor Nelson Rockefeller and the New York *Times* have disavowed the compensation doctrine as un-American. Conservative columnists comment on the paradox of an equality drive involving a demand for inequality. Most state Fair Employment Practices Acts forbid the doctrine as discriminatory to whites. Public discussion of the issue reverberates with phrases such as "reverse prejudice," "subsidization of incompetents" and Bolshevism ("from each according to his means to each according to his needs").

Yet look what has been happening in practice. Recently an influential official body composed of business leaders, the New Jersey Advisory Committee to the United States Commission On Civil Rights, issued a militant report calling for quotas for "non-whites" in employment and also in housing, both public *and private*.

The New York City Commission On Human Rights has also now endorsed preferential treatment, claiming that "all other methods of attacking racial bias in schools, housing and jobs had failed." Commission

Chairman, Stanley Lowell, stated that Negroes should be moved to the tops of waiting lists for apprenticeship programs. "If it's found illegal in the courts," he said, "then the law must be changed."

Properly, this has made front-page news, along with the spate of rebuttals and the fence-sitting responses . . . for it marks a distinct progression in the debate. And, perhaps most important, it now has been disclosed that the Administration's "Plans For Progress" campaign (to persuade companies to hire Negroes) has already achieved an extraordinary result: of 60,000 new workers hired in the last three months by the 115 companies pledged to the program, 25 percent were Negroes, whereas previously the proportion of Negroes hired by these companies was 3 percent.

Meanwhile, in a parallel development, the drive continues in Northern cities to achieve "racial balance" in the public schools. There one witnesses official, systematic preferential treatment involving such explicit actions as transfers of students, re-zoning and exclusions, to redress the same imbalance created by ancient *de facto* geographic discrimination that has prompted the move for preferential hiring. Many schools are 90 to 95 percent all white or all colored in the big Northern cities. The courts . . . cite state education laws forbidding such expedients from being taken on racial grounds. But the pressure continues, backed by the education authorities.

The public is understandably bewildered. Both the courts and the educational authorities in the interest of integration and fair play evoke the same principles, then arrive at opposite conclusions. As an illustration of the confusion today, in one celebrated instance in housing, a block of Negro home owners banned a Negro from the one remaining vacant house on the block on the grounds this would preclude any chance for their neighborhood to escape black ghetto status.

The uproar and the moral ambiguities may yet be providential for they are stimulating new areas of public discussion and speculation, a desperate need for a public exposed mostly either to just hard news reporting or the kind of once-over-lightly commentary TV provides. Conceivably, the ordinary businessman, who ultimately makes employment policy, may be forced by the issue to question his assumption that the self-regulating American free market, magically dispensing life's goodies through the dynamic of profit, automatically makes for the best of all possible worlds—as it is being brought home to him, through boycotts, that somehow the Negro isn't being cut in on the deal.

The prospect of ever heavier taxes and social costs required to maintain a tenth of the nation in a state of extreme dependency is also a matter of increasing dismay in business circles. The amazing financial support for the Urban League by corporate giants like American

Telephone and Telegraph reflects this almost as much as it reflects corporate anxiety over a good "image" in a day of boycotts and "lie-ins."

The Urban League also has done an effective job recently in exposing the reverse preferential treatment that prevails in the trades. Nepotism, of kith if not of kin, is notoriously prevalent in American union and apprenticeship recruitment. At the recent AFL-CIO convention, Negro groups picketed with signs showing the tiny percentage of Negroes in the sheet metal workers union and similar unions.

But any widespread appreciation of the less notorious but if anything more prevalent kind of "preferential treatment" represented by featherbedding in the great private and public bureaucracies is unlikely to occur in the foreseeable future because the people are too close to it. It is as if it were a given of Nature—for instance the almost invulnerable (to unemployment) drones in the military; in the giant utilities; in the oligopolist corporations that can administer their prices; in governmental services; in certain unions, in the favored ranks of enlightened companies such as Kaiser Steel where no one can be dropped (if the job disappears due to automation, one stays on, with pay, in a pool); in the large foundations and other non-profit organizations, museums for example, that have the chummy protectionist features of social clubs, etc., etc.

And the Urban League's Whitney Young likes to cite to business-men audiences the preferential treatment given to World War II veterans in civil service hiring, where "merit" testing was modified by giving the vets 10 unearned points on their test scores. I have lately even heard preferential hiring rationalized in terms of an English precedent, the law whereby all firms of over 20 employees (in most industries) must see to it that at least 3 percent of their rolls are made up of registered handicapped workers.

All this is not to say that I believe Americans will soon agree that arithmetical quotas can be fashioned to guide them with exactitude in Negro hiring. There is hardly a chance of this. Even research surveys on the ethnic composition of government departments are still scored as somehow fostering prejudice. The *New York Times,* for one, is adamant against them. The fact is, though, that state civil service commissions are now discovering that they cannot determine whether there is discrimination in state hiring practices without them. That is why Michigan, for example, has just decided to resume the practice of entering racial identity on employment records. What is daily becoming harder to see is how, if quotas and preferential treatment are disallowed, anything much will be accomplished for Negro employment. And that failure could mean trouble, for in a wage-based, urbanized society a job is the key to practically everything.

Conceivably American opinion leaders may cease to be less squeamish on principle about a quota approach as it becomes more widely recognized that most social judgments do involve a weighing of comparative data and that the guideline in judging the progress in integration must be percentage comparisons, albeit approximate ones Americans, it is being pointed out, have acted on quotas in the past. They will be increasingly likely to do so in the future, because there is ultimately no other touchstone. Only the other day the Anti-Defamation League of B'nai B'rith charged in the headlines that there were but 328 Jews, or less than three fourths of one percent, among the 51,000 white-collar employees in Detroit plants of General Motors, Ford and Chrysler. Revelations like this are really pointless unless inferences are to be drawn from them.

The rationale ultimately invoked to win acceptance of preferential hiring may well be a combination of compassion and economics. Nothing makes principle quite so palatable as a buck; the rehabilitation concept is the key here for it embraces both good business and good will. Once restricted in its application to the physically disabled, where it achieved fame for rescuing paraplegics like the former Dodger baseball player Roy Campanella, rehabilitation is now being conceived as *the* social technique, the solution to waste and dependency. "It's just good business and common sense," runs the line on rehabilitation. The rehabilitation ideal has even been taken over in urban redevelopment thinking—you don't bulldoze slums now, because that destroys neighborhoods and relocation creates delinquency; you preserve your basic residential plant through restoration. (This is now official U.S. housing doctrine.) Rehabilitation, in the form of job retraining becomes the key manpower service in our age, when jobs [are disappearing] through automation, and when, as a recent U.S. Labor Department study revealed, "the average 20-year-old can expect to have six different job careers in his working life.". . .

This is the argument pressed as an incentive for preferential treatment and it is compelling to the pragmatic American mind. After all, American insurance companies now pool costs to underwrite auto insurance (and recently health insurance for the elderly) for bad risks, on a non-profit basis, rationalizing that they'd rather do it this way than be nationalized. The same kind of expedient is now being urged in the employment field, where, on an industry basis, young Negroes would be trained and a certain number absorbed into the employment ranks on a pro-rated, shared basis, even though they're really redundant. This is already happening on a pilot scale in the case of Negro secretaries for several national firms, like General Electric.

In an essay to be published in a forthcoming book on corporate

America sponsored by the Fund For The Republic, political scientist Andrew Hacker foresees a future USA wherein the private corporation increasingly is the beneficiary of the revolution in technology while a vast segment of the population "unneeded by the corporate machine" will be left out, what he calls the "society of losers" "the second America" (cf. Dwight MacDonald's article "The Invisible Poor" in the *New Yorker* and the book he wrote it about, Michael Harrington's *The Other America*). This second America would be the un-and-underemployed and its ranks could be heavily represented by the Negro, if they are endlessly denied any degree of preferential treatment in hiring.

Norman Podhoretz, the well known writer and editor, in his much discussed *Commentary* essay, "My Negro Problem, And Ours," sees no way out of the predicament but assimilation, what's always called miscegenation south of Washington. Daniel Patrick Moynihan and Nathan Glazer point out, however (in their new book, *Beyond the Melting Pot*), that minority groups in the past have in fact entered the main stream of American society, yet maintained their separate identities. Certainly at this point all signs point to the fact that preferential hiring of the Negro seems to be the next effort to widen this main stream. The Negro is clearly inclined to let the problem of separate identities settle itself. What he wants are jobs, good jobs, and the whole train of benefactions that come in their wake.

Robert B. McKersie
THE CIVIL RIGHTS MOVEMENT AND EMPLOYMENT

For students of industrial relations the current fight of Negroes for "freedom and jobs" is significant for several reasons. Discrimination in employment has become an important focus for the civil rights movement and has forced companies to re-examine their employment policies and to respond to the pressure for "jobs now." The activist character of the movement provides numerous parallels between its tactics and those employed by the CIO organizing committees in the late thirties.

From *Industrial Relations*, May 1964. Reprinted by permission of the author and publisher.

Mr. McKersie is Associate Professor of Industrial Relations, University of Chicago.

THE MOVEMENT

Within the movement, three groups can be clearly identified according to their primary reliance on litigation, persuasion, or direct action. The litigation approach seeks change through legislation and the courts. The National Association for the Advancement of Colored People (NAACP) has been a leader in the effort to establish and to enforce equal opportunity laws. The efforts of the NAACP before the President's Committee on Equal Employment Opportunity, the NLRB, the Department of Labor, and various state and local fair employment commissions have been well publicized and will not be discussed in this paper.

The approach that emphasizes persuasion and education, i.e., change through consensus and agreement, is best illustrated by the National Urban League. Leaders who emphasize the importance of persuasion have been termed moderates or *racial diplomats*.

The direct action approach aims at forcing change through the use of power tactics which are essentially nonviolent and often involve civil disobedience. Several groups have been closely associated with the direct action methodology: Student Non-Violent Coordinating Committee (SNCC), Congress on Racial Equality (CORE), and, in some instances, the Negro American Labor Council (NALC). The individuals who have been involved in this approach have been called militants or *race men*.

These classifications are not rigid. For example, the Philadelphia chapter of the NAACP has been extremely militant and a leader in "selective patronage" campaigns. Similarly, individuals in the Urban League have provided information and moral support to the direct action groups. Furthermore, the direct action groups in several cities are not officially connected with any national organization. In Boston, a number of Negro leaders, disenchanted with the approach and results of other groups, have formed the Boston Action Group (BAG). In Cleveland, the United Freedom Movement and Freedom Fighters, and in New York City, the Committee on Equal Opportunities, have been active on the employment front. . . .

THE DYNAMICS OF DIRECT ACTION

Most direct action campaigns pass through three phases: gathering data and selecting the target, communicating with the employer, and conducting direct action.

GATHERING DATA AND SELECTING THE TARGET.   Several techniques have been used for this intelligence operation. In Chicago, information has been gathered by posting people at company gates and counting the number of Negroes entering and leaving. Such a technique does not provide information about the occupations held by Negroes and so it is often necessary to get inside the company. In one instance, it was possible to observe the complexion of employment by walking up and down the corridors of a large office building. In other situations members of the movement have taken employment at a company in order to report on the make-up of the work force.

After information about several companies has been secured, a target is chosen. Generally, the movement has gone after the larger firms, where a breakthrough carries greater weight. A target may be chosen for its symbolic importance: for example, a chance to expand employment in the white-collar area, where relatively fewer Negroes have worked. Targets are chosen also for their high visibility: it is much more significant if a Negro is added as a salesman in a retailing establishment than as an inventory clerk in a factory.

There is also the question of whether to go after a company that is segregationist by policy or one that is so by inertia or ignorance. Where there is a choice, the movement will generally confront the latter since the chance of success is greater. Since the big obstacle to introducing Negroes into an organization is often the resistance from employees, the movement selects targets where these problems may be minimal. For example, getting a milk company in Boston to hire Negroes as driver-salesmen is easier than getting a manufacturing company in Chicago to bring Negroes into a predominantly Polish work force.

Another consideration is whether to focus the campaign on a few employers or to attack the entire white business community. Most of the campaigns in the South, where it has been important for the Negro leadership to mobilize the "will to act" on the part of the Negro community, have followed this latter approach. In the case of narrowly focused campaigns, the technique is usually to attack companies in sequence. Effective campaigns in Philadelphia have followed this approach. Where successful, this furnishes the movement with reputation and authority that results from a string of successful campaigns. Companies on the priority list often do not await their turn; they move to change their employment policies as soon as they realize the movement is headed in their direction.

Selection of a target is not always a deliberate and rational process. Emotions are involved, and a campaign can start quickly when someone is affronted or a particular group is aroused by the actions of an employer. "Spontaneous combustion" has characterized the early days of the civil rights movement as it did the early days of the CIO.

COMMUNICATING WITH THE EMPLOYER.   Once the target has been chosen the employer is contacted by letter, the "facts" presented, and a meeting requested. Letters are firm in tone and specific. For example:

Dear Sir:

On the basis of our research, we have concluded that you are discriminating against Negroes in your hiring. We note a number of Negroes in such positions as food handler, cafeteria cashier, mailboy, and janitor, but in the white-collar area, there are virtually no Negroes employed. We have only been able to locate one Negro out of the more than 80 female white-collar workers employed in your Company.

Such a low percentage cannot be explained by an absence of qualified applicants. Company X, only a few doors away and other companies in the vicinity have a dramatically different employment complexion in female staff occupations.

As soon as possible I would like to discuss this situation with you. I realize that you are busy with preparation for the introduction of a new product line, but I think it would be to your advantage, as well as to the advantage of racial equality, for us to begin initial discussions, thereby making it unnecessary for us to plan the next step: public demonstrations.

I can be reached at _____ and I would appreciate a reply by _____.

The employer's reaction is fairly predictable. He will ignore the group or, if he feels a reply is indicated, will reject a meeting. Often he will make a public statement denying discrimination. Behind the scenes a flurry of action is probably taking place. The company may move to deal with the Urban League or with other moderates in the community. As one member of the Urban League put it, "As soon as a direct action campaign is planned in the city, scores of employers come to us, asking, 'how can we be saved?'"

Most firms which refuse to meet with a direct action group do so because they fear extreme and costly demands; they wish to avoid a probably unpleasant session and uncomfortable confrontation—a likely shouting match, with more to be lost than gained. By refusing to meet with the group, of course, the company is running the risk of facing even greater militancy. A large Chicago company ignored the importunings of a group for several months, whereupon the group mounted an intensive campaign and forced the company into a meeting—with a much stronger and cohesive group than it would have met earlier in the campaign.

CONDUCTING DIRECT ACTION

The next step involves direct action where the employer continues recalcitrant. The intention is to place the employer in a situation where it is more costly for him to refuse to deal with the group than to come to terms. In many respects the power situation resembles that involved in a union organizing campaign; but there is at least one basic difference: in a civil rights campaign the pressure comes from outsiders—demonstrators, consumers, public officials, etc.—whereas in a union organizing campaign the pressure quite often comes from the employee groups. . . .

The direct approach places some form of immediate pressure on the company, be it a demonstration aimed at publicly embarrassing the company, a lie-in or mass picketing aimed at stopping production, or a consumer boycott aimed at reducing sales. The direct approach has been used in a wide variety of situations and industries.

The indirect approach attempts to reach the company through the offices of public officials. It is only feasible when the company is dependent on the pleasure of public officials. For this reason, the indirect strategy has been mainly used to reach construction companies and unions working on projects financed from public funds.

THE DEMONSTRATION. Demonstrations have been used both as preliminary and as primary tactics in a campaign. The demonstration alone, by focusing attention on the employment policies of a firm, may be all that is required to induce cooperation. Where more is required, the demonstration can be but a prelude to blockage of production or a consumer boycott. For example, in Cleveland a demonstration was organized outside a large clothing store to draw attention to the absence of Negro employees; it also induced shoppers not to enter the store. In New York City, demonstrations involving mass picketing effectively blocked trucks attempting to enter or leave construction sites.

The demonstration dramatizes feeling, for it demands considerable time, transportation cost, and public display from its participants. It can be quite effective in building group morale, as the "March on Washington for Freedom and Jobs" illustrated. It may not be as effective as the boycott in bringing a company to terms, but in putting a company or a public official on the spot it has many of the attributes of the sit-in. The success of the effort can be measured by the numbers who march. (In this day of mass-produced information, the circulation of handbills does not impress anyone.) The reputation of a leader in the movement depends on his ability to deliver numbers in response to his call for a demonstration.

THE CONSUMER BOYCOTT. The effectiveness of the consumer boycott depends on the willingness of the Negro community (and to some extent the sympathetic white community) to alter its buying patterns as the movement dictates. Consequently, the boycott is most effective when organized by ministerial groups or the NAACP, which have the attention of the Negro community.

The boycott is not a costly tactic and as a result many people participate. In a recent survey reported in the *Wall Street Journal*, the Center for Research in Marketing said 89 per cent of the Negro community indicated they would take part in a boycott if their national leaders so requested.

The boycott's effectiveness is based on the company's concern for its brand image and customer acceptance. It is effective in that it places an incentive on the employer to come to the bargaining table in order to "buy off" future damage. The demonstration and sit-in do not involve the same quid-pro-quo factor; in the latter cases the damage has been done and the employer may not stand to gain by meeting with the movement. In the case of the boycott, the employer needs the influence of the movement to restore his good name in the Negro community.

Because it is easy to participate in a boycott, the tactic does not have the same expressive value as a demonstration or a sit-in. But it confronts each Negro with a forced choice. He may not participate in a demonstration or a sit-in, but he cannot overlook the fact that he is letting the movement down when he buys certain brands.

The consumer boycott was well exemplified in Philadelphia, where it was first used during the summer of 1960 against the Tasty Baking Company. As a first step, four ministers representing an organization of 400 churches called upon the company and asked about Negro employment. Several weeks later they returned and presented demands. Negroes already were employed; emphasis was placed on upgrading them into truck driver, clerical, and icing classifications. When the company failed to meet the demands, a consumer boycott was inaugurated. After eight weeks, the company indicated it had complied with the demands of the group and the boycott was terminated. Since then, the ministers have targeted a number of oil, ice cream, newspaper, soda, supermarket, and bakery companies, with universal success. Significantly, the duration of the boycott has shortened, with the most recent campaigns running about a week.

The key problems in managing a boycott are getting word to the Negro community, and, once the demands have been met, terminating the boycott. Usually the newspapers cannot be counted on to provide publicity. For example, the Philadelphia newspapers conducted a news blackout on the progress of the boycotts. As a result the ministers passed the word through churches, handbills, and word-of-mouth intelligence. In Boston, BAG appointed block captains who spread the word from house to house when a campaign was inaugurated.

It is not easy to restore a company's good name after a boycott has been terminated; and unless consumers can be induced to shift their patronage back, once the boycott is settled, the boycott leaders lose much of their bargaining power. Some civil rights leaders are aware of this problem; Philadelphia leaders have been hesitant to institute state-wide boycotts for fear they could not effectively terminate them.

SIT-INS. The sit-in or lie-in has been frequently used in New York City. During the summer of 1963, several groups sat-in at the offices of Mayor Wagner and Governor Rockefeller and conducted a lie-in at several construction sites, especially the Downstate Medical Center in Brooklyn.

From the viewpoint of the participants, the sit-in is the most costly form of protest, since it involves personal hardship of many forms. Consequently, very few people elect to join sit-ins; and they have been employed, for the most part, by small and highly dedicated organizations such as SNCC and CORE.

It is easy for those against whom this tactic is aimed to dismiss the protest as the work of the "lunatic fringe"; but the sit-in cannot be ignored. A public official must deal with the group and in a way that does not create a nasty incident. Herein lies its great power; the sit-in, while not as drastic or dramatic as the suicide of a Buddhist monk in a Saigon square, shares with it a symbolic quality and character of protest.

The sit-in hopes to rally support of the larger population, thus bringing pressure on public officials. In an earlier era, the sit-down worked in much the same way.

> The sit-down strike arouses the widest sympathy and support among the working population because of the courage of the workers in taking "possession of the factory" and because of the self-sacrifice and hardship which such action entails.[1]

Public officials cannot remain inactive in the face of a sit-in. For example, during the summer of 1963 sit-ins and lie-ins stimulated a frenzy of activity in New York City. The Mayor appointed an "action panel" to investigate the situation, the city Human Relations Committee and the federal Civil Rights Commission conducted hearings, the unions and employers appointed a special joint committee to screen apprentices, and the city stopped construction on the Harlem Hospital—all of these efforts were designed to weaken the racial barriers in the construction industry.

But the sit-in should not be judged only for its instrumental value; it is also effective in developing commitment within the movement. A person who participates in a sit-in, and particularly if he is jailed

---

[1] Walter Galenson, *The CIO Challenge to the AFL* (Cambridge, Mass.: Harvard, 1960), p. 270.

as a result, gains an increased degree of authority. He has participated in one of the important "battles," and he refers to the event and to his "jailbird" reputation the way Reuther refers to the Battle of the Overpass and to his injuries therein received.

THE EFFECTIVENESS OF DIRECT ACTION. Evaluating the relative effectiveness of the three tactics discussed above involves a number of considerations. The boycott is probably most effective in applying direct pressure; but the demonstration and sit-in can be as effective and can be more appropriately used under certain circumstances. The *threat* of a demonstration can be particularly potent against a company sensitive to its public image. If the sit-in is directed against public officials, it may be quite effective. But the effectiveness of any protest device that seeks public sympathy cannot be gauged without examining the legality of the tactic and the posture of the larger society. . . .

THE PATTERN OF NEGOTIATIONS

An important step in any campaign aimed at expanding employment opportunities for Negroes is reaching the bargaining table. Indeed, the use of power (sit-ins, boycotts, and demonstrations) is meant to force the employer to enter into discussion with the movement. In this section we will examine several aspects of the bargaining situation: the negotiating style of the civil rights leadership, the character of the employer response, and the results of the interaction. Since these aspects are closely related, it is convenient to discuss them in a connected manner, in the context of two types of bargaining configurations which appear to characterize the negotiations that take place between the movement and management: the *militant leader*—containment response pattern and the *moderate leader*—cooperative response pattern.

MILITANT LEADER—CONTAINMENT RESPONSE

MILITANT APPROACH. Race men are basically suspicious of employers. They are convinced that peaceful methods are not effective and that progress can be made only through coercion.

In terms of personality, most of the action leaders are suited for negotiation through pressure. They have no need to be liked by employers; they have no status to maintain in the larger society. The rewards which are important to these individuals are power and personal influence in the Negro community. Consequently, they prefer hard bargaining as a way of dramatizing the fact that only they can obtain gains, and it is from these gains achieved that they draw their authority.

In a negotiation studied by the author, a leader from the activist group demanded that the company put in writing the changes it had made in the hiring and promoting of Negroes. The militant individual demanded the letter since as he said, "I need to be able to go back to my group and prove that we have won certain gains from this company."

The typical militant in negotiations presents specific demands which are not readily compromised. These demands often seem extreme, in character with the whole approach. In Philadelphia CORE demanded that 15 per cent of the building tradesmen and 60 per cent of the apprentices be Negro.

Usually the demand carries a time limitation:

> In regard to your plants in Chicago, we demand that you employ one thousand Negroes by August 1, 1964, and at least one hundred Negroes by October 1, 1963. A policy statement by you indicating compliance with these demands would be an important first step.

It must be pointed out that the extreme position of the militant possesses bargaining advantage if the employer is in a position to make concessions. To the moderate, the approach of the militant seems quite rigid and unreasonable. For instance, in Philadelphia the ministers demanded that a company hire Negroes when the firm was laying off employees for lack of business. The ministers, unfamiliar with the business world, refused to modify their demand, but were satisfied when the company agreed to upgrade several Negro laborers to the position of driver-salesmen.

However, if the company cannot make substantial concessions to meet the bulk of the militants' demands, real difficulties result. Militants are not happy with anything that might be termed a compromise. (In fact, militants do not even like the word negotiate for they say, "One cannot negotiate rights, one demands and expects to receive them.")

Compromise, or indeed any kind of flexible negotiation, is made difficult for the Negro leader by his need to develop cohesion and build support within the Negro community. The direct action leader emphasizes the importance of the Negro race, and talks about an inner culture within the United States and the "honor of being a black man." Such emphases produce problems during negotiations. Since the militant has emphasized the strengths of the Negro race, he finds it difficult to admit that there may be a dearth of qualified Negro applicants, let alone discuss steps that can be taken to alleviate the achievement gap. When an employer says, "I am willing to hire more Negroes but I can't find them," the militant is likely to say, "That's your problem."

But a more important problem is that the militants have cut themselves off from white intermediaries. Characteristically, militants shun the advice and help of whites. Hence, the race man, for the most part, has foreclosed the possibility of a solution reached with the help of human relations commissions or influential liberals.

But even if the militant leader realizes that a compromise is necessary and preferable to no agreement, he finds it difficult to "sell" the idea to his organization. Consider a dramatic example of this problem:

After considerable agitation in New York City, an agreement was reached between the Ministers' Committee on Job Opportunities and Governor Rockefeller on the problem of employment opportunities in the construction field. The Governor announced a program for enforcement of anti-discrimination laws and contracts, including the cancelling of contracts and blacklisting of violating contractors. When Reverend Galamison, the spokesman for the group, emerged and announced the settlement, he was confronted by his constituents.

> *Woman:* "They have only given promises."
> *Galamison:* "Now baby, when a man sits down and tells you this, what can you say? He is a Governor . . . he made a public commitment."
> *Young man:* "Why did you sell us out then?"
> *Galamison:* "What more do you want?"
> *Young woman:* "Reverend Galamison, what do you do if a Governor doesn't keep his word?"
> *Galamison:* "I'll be back out there on the street."
> *Young woman:* "Thank you, Reverend, that is just what I wanted to hear you say."
> *Another woman:* "Couldn't we get something we could see, Reverend?"
> *Galamison:* "What do you want to see, baby?"
> *Woman:* "I want to see something right now."
> *Galamison:* "You come back Monday, Tuesday, or Wednesday and you'll not only see people out there working but you will see them at other places too."
> *Woman:* "We had a fire going, a fire like nothing we had ever had before in Brooklyn, and now it is going out."[2]

In essence the Negro activist finds himself in a role conflict. As negotiations unfold he becomes more cognizant of the problems of the employer and comes to realize that his extreme position is not tenable. While this process of amelioration is taking place, the constituents remain adamant and demand full measure.

There are several techniques which leaders have used to resolve their dilemma. These techniques are direct analogs to those used by labor leaders.

1. In some instances they will "go through the motions," that is,

[2] *New York Times,* August 8, 1963.

act aggressively and give the constituents release for their intense feelings, but in a way that does not alienate the employer.

> The furthering of race pride and racial solidarity is a means of diminishing internal strivings in the Negro community and of lining up the community into a working unity. Whites sometimes understand this, and there is, therefore, also a certain amount of "tolerated impudence," which a trusted and influential Negro can get away with even in the presence of whites.[3]

2. A second technique is to keep the constituents in the dark about developments in the bargaining room. In a recent direct action campaign in Chicago a Negro leader, under pressure to obtain immediate concessions, spoke as a militant to the constituents but as a moderate to the employer, keeping the former in the dark about the approach to the latter.

3. A third technique is to avoid personal responsibility for a compromise by putting it before the constituency. During the campaign against the construction industry in New York City, James Farmer of CORE emerged from the bargaining room and predicted a settlement in the near future, but he added, "There will be no behind-the-door settlement; we will take it to the members for approval or rejection."

RESPONSE OF MANAGEMENT.   When confronted by a militant spokesman, the usual objective of management is to neutralize the power thrust and gain control over the direction of discussion. One approach is for the company to make some conciliatory response, but only as a diversionary tactic. Often the diversionary response takes the form of agreeing to meet with the group at the very last moment. A milk company in Boston agreed to meet just as the consumer boycott was scheduled to start, winning suspension of the boycott. During the initial meeting, the company asked for time to look into the matter. After several unproductive weeks BAG scheduled another demonstration; again the company asked for a meeting, but this time the group refused and inaugurated the consumer boycott, completely ignoring the company.

Most employers recognize that the diversionary approach creates greater problems, hence the more common approach is to "battle it out" with the movement, using power to fight power. The discussions are fraught with conflict, as Thompson has well described.

> Negotiation between Negro action leaders and white men of power are characteristically clumsy, strained, and tense. Both parties

[3] Gunnar Myrdal, *An American Dilemma* (New York: Harper, 1944), p. 771.

manifest deep-rooted suspicion, distrust, and even fear of one another. During such sessions action leaders first define the areas of racial discrimination and then proceed to outline their demands for fairer employment. Next, white officials counter by pointing to certain "fallacies" in the information the Negro leaders present, and attempt to convince them that their demands are exaggerated or impossible. They quote statistics and present information, much of which is naturally unavailable to anyone but the officials themselves. Negro leaders then counter by presenting information about the Negro community that would ordinarily be unavailable to the white officials.[4]

Usually the participants to this power game quarrel over credit and status as much as they do over substantive issues. Management strives to maintain its image of professionalism: it usually demands that all forms of direct action be terminated before deliberations begin, and the sessions with the movement are labeled "discussions" to avoid the impression that management is giving in to power.

There is also concern over who will receive credit for the changes resulting from the civil rights confrontation. Some employers and officials will not publicly admit that they are changing practices. When Peter Brennan, president of the Construction Trades Council in New York, announced that he had helped get jobs for Negroes as stationary engineers, structural iron workers, and carpenters, he added, "We have been doing this for years."

A third approach is for management to gain control of the situation through the structuring of positive attitudes and the discreet handling of concessions. In one negotiation, which the author observed, the company representative was particularly skillful in handling the militants with this strategy. The meetings were held away from the company offices and only the industrial relations director participated for the employer. Consequently, it was impossible for the militants to influence other members of management. Moreover, as the negotiations progressed he succeeded in convincing the militants that he was on their side: "I agree completely with your objectives, but you have to give me time to prepare my organization for change."

By talking frankly about the weaknesses and problems within the company, the company representative gained the respect of the militants. He also exerted every effort to develop a personal acquaintance with each leader. Between sessions the company maintained contact with at least thirty different leaders. These leaders were asked to help in recruiting qualified applicants and the company spokesman personally checked on each referral. When complaints were presented, he investi-

[4] Daniel C. Thompson, *The Negro Leadership Class* (Englewood Cliffs, N.J.: Prentice-Hall, 1963), p. 135.

gated and reported back either directly to the leader or during the joint meetings.

In effect, the company executive allowed the representatives to serve as patronage dispensers. He told them about job opportunities and gave them first chance to refer their friends and associates from the Negro community. Generally, his approach was one of emphasizing the importance of the civil rights leadership, "I've always gotten along fine with these Negro leaders; I am counting on you people to help me solve my problem in recruiting more Negroes."

Interestingly, in the case of the negotiation just cited, the company negotiator did not give in on any matters of principle. While he was pleasant and attempted to strengthen the hand of the civil rights representatives, he was careful not to jeopardize the position of the company. For example, he cleverly sidestepped the issue of releasing a joint press release about the deliberations in progress; he postponed decision about opening up an employment office in the heart of the Negro community; and he convinced the leaders that it would be impracticable for the company to inaugurate a pre-hire training program that might help unemployed Negroes qualify for the openings in the company.

MODERATE LEADER—COOPERATIVE RESPONSE

MODERATE APPROACH. This approach characterizes the individual who has had some dealings with the business community. Quite often he is a representative of the Urban League, and his orientation may reflect the approach of this institution. The leadership of the Urban League emphasizes professionalization and sophistication. They understand the problems of the business community; consequently their approach is one of concern rather than one of commitment.

The Negro moderate is concerned about his reputation in the larger community and is anxious to appear reasonable. He wants to avoid the impression of being extreme. He is more interested in solutions than in personal credit or in seeming to pressure the company into agreement.

But the racial moderate also faces a dilemma, not in his dealings with employers, nor in his dealings with his own organization, but in maintaining his position in the larger Negro community. In many instances, the militants have seized the initiative and forced the moderates into the background. The moderate becomes particularly troubled when the protest gets to the talking stage, especially when the militants have been successful in getting the attention of an employer whom the moderates have been working with for some time.

Confronted with this challenge, the moderate cannot ignore the activities of the direct action group. The threat of direct action may even work to his advantage since the company, convinced that it must do something, might rather make the changes with the help of a moderate.

However, there comes a point when the moderate must vie for control of the direct action campaign. His personal position, as well as the reputation of the institution in the Negro community, is at stake. How the moderate takes charge is a complex task, but some insights can be gained from one example:

Early in 1963 the militants took notice of Company X and gathered information about its employment situation. Since the moderates had been counseling the company on how to become an equal opportunity employer, they were in a position to provide the militants with accurate information concerning the number of Negroes at Company X. This disclosure of data was done on an informal basis and would not have been sanctioned by the leadership of the moderate organization.

By June the militants were ready for direct action. (The company had not answered any of the communications sent by the militants, although it had continued to meet with the moderates.) At this point the moderates succeeded in getting the demonstration postponed through the pressure of a city-wide civil rights congress to which both groups belonged.

Again, the militants scheduled a demonstration (partly in response to pressure from constituents who were unhappy about the postponement). This time the moderates stayed in the background, although it was reliably reported that the moderates advised the company, "The direct action people mean business; you had better deal with them." The company agreed to meet with militants and the demonstration was postponed.

A bargaining team was chosen for the first meeting with the company—the moderates were not involved. However, a key moderate joined a strategy session held immediately preceding the first meeting with the company. He emphasized the importance of taking a *hard* line with the company. (Significantly, very little progress had been made by the moderates during several years of dealings with the company.)

About a month later a second meeting was held with the company. This time the moderate leader appeared and acted as spokesman. This shift had come about since the key militant had to be absent from the second meeting and had asked the moderate to plan it. The militant had been impressed by the sophistication and resources of the moderate and his organization.

The moderate felt free to appear since deliberations had moved beyond the power stage (the demonstration had been forgotten by both sides). The moderate guided discussions in a calm and deliberate way. He moved to squelch a militant who challenged several statements by the company spokesman; he vetoed the idea of releasing a press statement; and he dodged the issue of scheduling another meeting with the company.

RESPONSE OF MANAGEMENT. Usually management responds in a cooperative fashion to the approach of racial moderates.

> Unlike meetings between race men and white officials, meetings between racial diplomats and white employers are generally conducted in an atmosphere of mutual respect and are characterized by politeness and sympathetic communication. Throughout such discussions Negro diplomats appeal to the enlightened self-interest of the employers. They persistently attempt to rationalize their contentions for wider economic opportunities for Negroes in terms of total community welfare. Their arguments are sound, persuasive interpretations of basic Christian and democratic principles.[5]

RESULTS

It appears that direct action can be quite successful in expanding job opportunities for Negroes, whereas persuasion is more effective in solving the many problems which are involved in recruiting and introducing Negroes into a work force. Direct action provides the motivation and persuasion provides the implementation.

The direct action groups can point to some very concrete gains. As a result of the Philadelphia boycotts some one thousand jobs have been opened for Negroes. In Chicago the threat of direct action against a large company provided the impetus for the introduction of 100 additional Negroes. In other situations direct action has succeeded in making a breakthrough in principle. Such was the case in Cleveland where a sidewalk demonstration prompted a large clothing store to hire its first Negro salesman. In Boston, as a result of the consumer boycott by BAG, the Continental Baking Company hired five Negroes, some of these filling the position of driver-salesman for the first time.

An attempt to measure the over-all impact of direct action involves the same sort of difficulties as are faced in an attempt to assess the influence of trade unions. One can never evaluate the future effects of establishing a principle. More importantly, one can rarely assess the secondary effects. Many employers do not wait to be asked about their employment picture; they take action to eliminate discrimination and avoid embarrassing confrontations. They may even call in the moderates.

[5] Thompson, *op. cit.*, p. 137.

Leaders of the Urban League have privately attested to the stream of employers who have contacted the Urban League for help as a result of the direct action campaigns.

The weakness of the direct action approach is that it is not equipped to handle problems encountered in the transition, or for that matter, to guarantee that a transition will take place. Since reliance is placed on coercion, each side remains wary of the other. A good example of the distrust present in the militant-containment syndrome comes from the Philadelphia situation. It was the policy of the ministers not to terminate a boycott until the specified number of Negroes had been hired; a company's statement that it intended to hire Negroes was not honored.

If the employer encounters greater pressure from another side, a whole bargain may break down. In New York City, as a result of the summer campaign and under the agreement to introduce nonwhites into the construction trades, some twenty-six hundred individuals applied for admission. Of these over three hundred were adjudged qualified, but less than 40 were actually taken on as apprentices or journeymen. As one white worker put the problem, "I've been working for five years on a permit and I'm still waiting for a union book. These people want books and jobs overnight."

The persuasion method is not as dramatic, but it is just as effective. The moderate helps the employer solve a problem, as some of the following innovations illustrate:

1. *Recruiting Negroes.* Many companies do not have Negroes working for them simply because Negroes have not applied for employment. In one negotiation the company frankly asked the movement how it could get the word out to the Negro community. The moderates advised the company in these terms, "Simply saying that you are an equal opportunity employer will not do any good; Negroes have learned over time that industry does not really want them, and hence they are not going to put themselves in the position of being embarrassed. You have to advertise in the Negro newspapers; you have to let us put the word out to the community." As a result of this advice, the company has been quite successful in generating a stream of Negro applicants.

2. *Obtaining qualified Negroes.* After it has been made clear that a company is interested in hiring Negro employees, the problem becomes one of finding qualified applicants. At this point, an organization like the Urban League with its resources can be helpful in referring qualified individuals to interested employers. But in many instances there are just not enough qualified Negroes to go around; the demand exceeds the supply. As a result, upgrading programs have been initiated to increase the supply of qualified Negroes. In Chicago, with the sponsorship of the

Urban League, the Yellow Cab Company and the Shell Oil Company have been operating training programs for unemployed workers. These types of "pre-hire" programs have been expanding rapidly around the country, and many of them have been developed as a result of the search by leaders of the movement and employers for solutions to the qualification problem.

CONCLUSIONS

We are witnessing a dramatic changeover to a new system of social relations. The mechanism for this shift has been the use of power by the direct action groups in the civil rights movement.

The meaning of the current protest can be summed up in the words which Galenson used to describe the labor protest of the thirties.

> . . . the era constituted an episode in the transition from one system of industrial relations to another; it hastened the replacement of untrammeled management prerogative in the disposition of labor by a system under which trade unions, as representatives of the workers, were to share in this function. It was perhaps inevitable that so violent a wrench with the past should have provoked management attitudes sharply antithetical to the new national labor policy. But by the same token, it is not surprising that industrial workers, having broken through on the legislative front, should seek to implement their hard won rights with whatever weapons were at hand, regardless of the law.[6]

The civil rights movement has forced management to recognize the factor of race in the same way that the labor movement forced management to recognize seniority. Recruitment and selection policies have been significantly affected. Management can no longer confine itself to hiring only those who elect to apply for work; management is compelled to search for Negro candidates. Management can no longer limit itself to selecting the most qualified; management now finds itself obligated to help the disadvantaged Negro qualify for employment and, in the actual hiring procedure, to give preference to the Negroes, other things being equal.

The direct action groups have been successful in forcing employers to take the racial issue seriously and to create additional openings. The due process and persuasion groups now face the difficult task of being just as successful in solidifying the gains and in creating attitudes of acceptance by the white majority. The work of the direct action groups is far from finished, however. In the near future we will witness many demonstrations, sit-ins, and boycotts as the social revolution spreads wider and deeper into our industrial structure.

[6] Galenson, *op. cit.*, p. 147.

poverty

Robert J. Lampman

ONE-FIFTH OF A NATION

In his State of the Union Message and again in a special message to the Congress, [1964] President Johnson called for a sustained and coordinated "war on poverty." And in his Economic Report, the President pointed out that "Americans today enjoy the highest standard of living in the history of mankind. But for nearly a fifth of our fellow citizens, this is a hollow achievement. They often live without hope, below minimum standards of decency. The per capita money income of these 35 million men, women and children was only $590 in 1962—against $1,900 per capita for the nation as a whole."

Mr. Johnson observed that in the Great Depression mass unemployment made poverty a· common experience, that since 1947 the incidence of poverty has been reduced from one-third to one-fifth of the nation, but that the erosion of poverty slowed measurably after 1957. To speed the rate at which poverty is being reduced, the President said that "the tactics of our attack on this ancient enemy must be versatile and adaptable. For the sources of poverty vary from family to family, city to city, region to region."

President Johnson's statements on poverty have historic meaning. The President associates himself with those who deny the inevitability of a mass of impoverished people. In the tradition of Jefferson and Jackson and Franklin Roosevelt, he affirms the hope and promise that wave after

Reprinted from *Challenge, The Magazine of Economic Affairs*, 475 Fifth Avenue, New York, N.Y., 10017, April 1964.

Mr. Lampman is Professor of Economics, University of Wisconsin.

wave of Americans and their children can rise from deprivation to full participation in a land of opportunity for all.

At the same time, the "war on poverty" theme signifies a dramatic shift away from a particular characterization of the American economy which flourished in the 1950s and which represented it as having arrived at a classless, homogenized state of affluence. Many critics, impressed by the explosive expansion of the economy in World War II and the virtually uninterrupted growth in the postwar period, concluded that all serious economic problems were matters for historians. Others joined a chorus of self-congratulatory celebration which highlighted the "income revolution" which Harvard's Simon Kuznets found occurred during the war (involving a drop in the income share of upper income groups), and the coming of what New York University's Marcus Nadler christened "people's capitalism" (a widening participation in ownership of the nation's wealth).

Business journals heralded the conversion of millions of low-income families to membership in the vast and growing middle-income markets. Political writers evaluated the arrival of the "welfare state" and the dominance of the security ethic. Projecting a vision of rapidly vanishing poverty, even social workers and clergymen appeared to be turning away from concern for old-fashioned poverty as an important cause of human misery and toward the idea of a "new poverty" of maladjusted individuals, a type of poverty best dealt with by psychiatrists and specialists in community organization. In short, the poor became "invisible."

It would be an interesting study in itself to uncover the factors which caused Americans to once again consider the poverty in their midst. Among such factors one would have to count the 1957–58 recession which brought to the fore such problems as chronic unemployment, depressed areas and the severe adjustment problems associated with automation. Other factors include the harsh realities of an onrushing agricultural revolution which spilled millions of poor off the farms, increasing longevity which put a national spotlight on the economic problems of the aged, and the inspirational revolt of the Negro.

In addition, there was a new emphasis on human resource development as a way to economic growth, and a gradual change in the sense of urgency related to international, nuclear and space matters. All these changes seem to have paved the way for the criticisms of American society by such writers as John K. Galbraith, Michael Harrington, Leon Keyserling and James Baldwin, who evoked a response to the ordinary needs of ordinary people that have been left behind in the rush to national riches and power. They have dramatized the fact that the poor do, as Harrington puts it, constitute the "other America," having an alienated, separatist subculture. These people remain remarkably untouched by the New Deal welfare state measures such as old-age and unemployment insurance, and are well beyond the reach of unions and cooperatives and federal programs in farming, housing and urban renewal.

In any event, President Johnson has lent the weight of his office to the school of thought which says that we have a lot of unfinished business on behalf of the poor. He underscores the view that while the poor are still with us, there are encouragingly fewer of them than there used to be, but their numbers have been dropping at a discouragingly slow rate in recent years.

President Johnson's declaration of war on poverty is an exercise in national goal setting. It calls for a new measuring rod for assessing the performance of the economy. Along with the now traditional goals of "maximum employment, production and purchasing power" specified in the Employment Act of 1946, and the less official goals of reasonable price stability, a satisfactory rate of economic growth and equilibrium in our balance of payments, the President, in appraising our national economic achievement, would have us consider a rapid reduction in the number of persons living below a stated "poverty line." No specific rate of reduction is set down as a goal, but presumably our historic experience is a good basis for selecting a feasible one. Hence, one may refer to the fact that the net reduction has averaged about 700,000 persons per year in the postwar period, with a significant drop in the rate after 1956 to a low of about 500,000 per year.

For this purpose the precise income level selected to mark off poverty from nonpoverty is not critical, so long as it is unchanged over time, except for necessary adjustments relative to the prevailing price level. The actual level which underlies the President's statement that 35 million Americans are poor is $3,000 for multiperson families and $1,500 for single individuals. It is interesting that these incomes are near the median income for several Western European nations and represent a level of living attained by only a tiny minority of the world's three billion people. On the other hand, they seem painfully low compared to the $10,000 median family income which we should reach in about 20 years.

Ideally, of course, the dividing line should adjust for differences among regions, size of cities, family size and composition, and should take account not only of current money income, but also of assets and nonmoney income of various kinds. A single income measure is, admittedly, a crude measure. Not all the people below the stated income level are in greater need than some who are above it.

How can the exodus of people out of poverty be speeded up? To answer this question we must first see who the poor are, and why they are poor.

To distinguish the poor population from the general population, one will not go far wrong by asking, "What groups are the most underprivileged, what persons have the least opportunity for making a living?" (Note that to be classed as "above the line," a family need have only one breadwinner who is fully employed at a rate of as little as $1.50 an hour.) Hence, the poor one-fifth contains more than its share of nonwhites, aged persons, poorly educated, broken families, those in low-skill occupations, and farm families.

But the two populations are not so different as one might think. There are many representatives of each of the above-listed disadvantaged groups in the nonpoor population, and the 35 million poor include persons from every social, ethnic, regional, occupational and age group. Not all of the poor are identifiably disadvantaged. Neither are all the disadvantaged poor. In many ways the poor population is only a slightly distorted cross-section of the general population. The poor are like other Americans, except that they are poor.

Two-thirds of poor family heads have no more than eight years of schooling, half are in the South, a fourth are headed by a woman, a fifth are nonwhite, one-sixth are on farms. With regard to those characteristics, the poor are notably different from the total population in which only one-third have eight years or less of schooling, one-third are in the South, 10 per cent are headed by women, 10 per cent are nonwhite and only seven per cent are on farms.

The statistics suggest that if the population could be converted to include only white husband-wife families in which the husband had completed high school, the incidence of poverty would be six per cent instead of 20. On the other hand, if the population were exclusively made up of families headed by nonwhite women over 65 with no more than eight years of schooling, 79 per cent would be poor.

However, some demographic trends seem to be working against poverty reduction. While the total number of families increased 26 per cent between 1947 and 1962, those headed by persons over 65 increased by 54 per cent; those headed by nonwhites increased by 46 per cent; and those headed by a person under 25 years of age increased by 39 per cent. The latter is particularly disturbing, since the incidence of poverty is relatively high for this group—and the trend toward more young family heads will accelerate as the postwar babies come of age.

A substantial number of families are poor because they do not have a full-time earner. In almost half of the poor families, the head is not in the labor force; in a third there is no earner in the family. This non-participation may arise out of death or disability of the principal breadwinner; it may be associated with family break-up or responsibilities for care of children.

Not all families which lack a full-time earner are poor. Many of them have been insured against the possibility of loss of earning power and have offsets in the form of property income, commercial insurance or social security.

There is another large group which accounts for at least half of the poor. These people are poor primarily because of their low productivity, because of lack of market demand for their services or because of old age or limited training. To a certain extent their low fortune is due to the present low level of over-all demand, and hence would be improved by a general rise in economic activity. But, to a considerable degree, their productivity is limited by lack of educational attainment, and to some unknown degree by physical or mental disability or lack of competence. Even in a high employment situation there will be some of the present poor who cannot add enough to an employer's product to equal the minimum wage he is constrained to pay.

The fundamental causes of poverty are numerous. In some cases it arises out of inherent deficiency, in others of a blighted family and community environment, or out of past failures to take advantage of critical opportunities for education or training. In others the salient factor is failure to plan for such contingencies as unemployment, disability or retirement. In a number of cases, the decisions or contingencies which contribute to one person's poverty may be only indirectly related to the person affected. Thus the mental illness of a mother may contribute to poverty for her children.

Hence an inquiry into causes divides into current ones and past contributory factors. Similarly, a search for remedies takes one to those that can be expected to have immediate as opposed to longer run effects. A generally strong demand for goods and services will lead to higher levels of employment in which poor family members would participate. Recall that two-thirds of poor families have at least one wage earner.

Coupled with a general rising of the demand for labor, poverty could be reduced by special efforts to (1) channel demands where the poor are—e.g., the South; (2) assist the poor to move where jobs exist; (3) assist the poor to fit themselves for potential job opportunities; (4) remove discriminatory barriers which keep them from useful work opportunities.

For those present poor who are not related to the labor market and cannot plausibly be so related, the short-run remedy would seem to lie in higher transfer payments in the form of OASDI benefits, old-age assistance, aid to dependent children, and in more extensive public provisions for such critical services as medical care and housing.

In the longer run, the remedies for poverty should be concentrated upon those children presently being reared in poverty. One of the interesting things about poverty is that relatively few people who are not born in it wind up in it. Once out, people tend to stay out. But, at the same time, the mere existence of opportunities for betterment does not suffice to bring all members of a group out of the condition of poverty. There is a self-reinforcing characteristic to poverty which renders many steps against it ineffectual. The poverty complex contributes to its own causes of ignorance and disease and stunted aspiration.

Expanded education, health, housing, recreational and cultural opportunities will contribute, or can be designed to contribute, to breaking down the resigned attitudes of those who live in a subculture of poverty alienated from the general community and its values. In the broadest sense this requires a redevelopment of the environment of the youngsters being reared in poverty. It means opening exits from poverty and encouraging and motivating them to use those exits.

This strategy, which would mix employment measures with transfer payments and educational and environmental improvement, is based upon the idea that American experience has already shown us the key to the continuing reduction of poverty. It has shown us that many poor will seize opportunities for higher earnings and take advantage of ways to improve the marketability and productivity of their labor as soon as they appear. We also know from past experience that some of the factors that contribute to poverty can be prevented and others can be insured against. Finally, we know that even the subculture of poverty and the community environment hostile to economic progress can be modified.

Full application of what we know, and willingness to learn more as we go along, can contribute to a more rapid reduction of poverty—and the wretchedness and wastefulness associated with it—than we have known in recent years. It is a goal worthy of a nation that has frequently refreshed its commitment to the value of every human being.

John J. Lindsay
WHY THEY STILL GO
INTO THE MINES

This has been a season of mining disasters—iron-mine accidents in Germany, a gold-mine accident in South Africa, a coal-mine explosion in Japan, sulphur-pit and coal-mine accidents in the United States.

The nation's attention was focused on the perils of mining when two Pennsylvania men were rescued after being trapped for 14 days 300 feet below the surface, while a third was lost. With less publicity, 287 men were killed last year in the anthracite pits of Pennsylvania and the soft-coal mines of West Virginia, Kentucky and Tennessee.

Yet thousands of others continue to go down into the mines to face the hour-by-hour threat of lonely death, maiming accidents or disabling lung diseases—risks unheard of in other industries in mid-20th century America. Why do they do it?

To answer the question one must first know the miners. Up in eastern Pennsylvania, where the mountains are low and still green, come summer, and the valleys are broad and relatively uncrowded, they are an ethnic mix, mirroring the great emigrations from Italy, Ireland, Eastern Europe and Germany of 50 to 100 years ago. To the south, in the steep, brooding hills and narrow valleys of the Cumberlands, they take pride in the purity of their Anglo-Saxon strain, unpolluted, they say, for nearly 200 years.

AN AGING LOT

Both groups have two things in common. One is that practically all of these men were, as one put it, "born to the coal." They remember that the fathers put food on their tables and roofs over their heads by rooting there in the darkness below. "When I was a young feller," said one, "coal mining just came naturally."

The other point in common is that they are an aging lot—most of them just entering the fifties. Young men don't go into the mines these

From *The New York Times Magazine*, November 24, 1963. © 1963 by The New York Times Company. Reprinted by permission.
Mr. Lindsay is with *Newsweek* Magazine.

days. Many have seen the outside world during their Army service, and have decided not to return. Anyway, there are not enough jobs in the mines even if the young men wanted them.

Coal mining is a dying industry. These statistics tell much of the story: in 1950, some 415,500 miners wrenched 516 million tons of coal from the earth in this country; last year, 136,500 miners took 422 million tons out of the ground.

Tonnage has declined because industries and homeowners have switched to cheaper, cleaner fuels—notably oil. This only partly explains the decline in employment. There are fewer jobs primarily because the high cost of mine labor—$25 a day and more in the years immediately following World War II—led operators to replace men with machines.

In strip mining—which old-timers consider not proper mining at all—a huge, five-story-high machine with a 200-foot boom and shovel literally scrapes the coal off the top of the land, leaving the hills bare and scarred. In the pits themselves are automatic tipples and giant augers, one of which can load as much coal in a day as 250 men.

A NEW BREED

Because both employment and tonnage have decreased, union dues and employer contributions to union funds have dwindled. United Mine Workers hospital and pension programs have been cut back drastically. Some men, after a lifetime of work, have seen their pensions reduced from $100 to $30 a month.

In this situation, a new breed of entrepreneur has arisen. He is the miner-turned-operator. Long-closed mines are being reopened by such men—known as "wildcatters" or "bootleggers," although in most cases they pay royalties to the companies which still own the pits. They figure they can make a profit by cutting corners. They do not pay union wages, or contribute to union funds. And because their small-scale operations are exempt from Federal regulations, they can economize on safety measures.

The wildcatter may be financed by a group of local businessmen —taking a salary and a share of the net in return for his know-how—or he may be in business for himself.

In either case, he is likely to work at the main (the face of the coal vein) alongside his men, taking all the risks he ever took before— and perhaps more. He may be put out of business by a dynamiting, or a little nighttime sniping, by unemployed union men. Or he may make more money than he ever made before. But his men hardly stand to benefit.

Roland is an east Kentuckian who works in a wildcat mine. It is what soft-coal miners call a "dog hole"—no higher than three feet at the mouth. "A man gets on his side with a pad on his elbow and a pad on his hip and loads the stuff laying down," Roland says. "A man can't make but $15 a day at the most, and half the time the mine is down."

More often than not, Roland makes less than $10 a day, and counts himself lucky if he works three days a week. When the mountain roads get gummy, the big trucks stop hauling coal, and the mine may be shut down for weeks at a time.

Conditions are no better in the hard-coal mines. Tubby, a Pennsylvania miner, recalls: "In one bootleg, I was standing in water up to my knees with the pumps working and just staying ahead of the water rise. It was coming up, and it was coming down through the roof. It was so wet I had to go outside and change my clothes three times a day.

"And I've worked mines where the main was so hot you could reach out and fry an egg on it. You could burn your face bad on it. All you could do is drive a few turns, run back and get a breath of fresh air, and then go forward and drive a few turns and back away." (The pressure of tons of rock overhead, squeezing the vein, generated the heat.)

Much of the support for an anthracite mine's roof is provided by huge columns of coal left in the galleries for that purpose. Many of the new bootleg operators, eager for a fast profit, are "stealing" this coal—i.e., cutting away more of the pillars than is safe. "Some of those birds are turning $300 a day by stealing," said one miner.

As a result, old-timers expect more disasters than ever before. In places, whole towns built above the mines are endangered.

There is not a miner who does not know the fear of a cavein: the sudden freezing horror as the coal starts "working," coming down in dribbles followed by an awesome rush as the face "pushes in," trapping him, breaking his bones or half burying him under chunks weighing hundreds of pounds, cutting him off—even if only for a few terrifying minutes—from the outside world.

WAS NEARLY KILLED

"Look at it this way," said one Kentucky veteran. "I'm laying there on my back working a jackhammer. We're putting in metal bars as roof stays. I've got me nothing but solid rock up there and it's only three feet away. The place is stinking hot and the dust ablowing back so's you can't see. Then something gives. A chunk of that there roof just slides out pretty as you please and comes down a foot away from my head. I stop the hammer and listen and, not hearing nothing stirring, I slam back into it. A man gets to thinking."

Sam, a Pennsylvania hard-coal miner, once nearly was killed in a mine slide. "Jesus, I had my teeth knocked out and was knocked cold. It battered me up quite a bit," he recalled. "They got me out all right, but I left my teeth and one boot in there." And he managed to laugh.

Cave-ins are not the only hazards. Among the worst is "the asthma," or, as it is called in the softcoal fields, "the dust," or "dust on the lungs." Its causes are many, but the chief one in the hardcoal fields is "white damp." This is the oxygen starved smoke that comes in the wake of a blast at the face of the vein.

"I worked with fellers that would go right into that stuff, breathing it in," one old-timer recalled. "Sure, they'd get home an hour earlier than I did, but often they'd have to go right to bed; they'd be sick."

The asthma is only an annoying difficulty for some, but for others it is totally disabling. The coal fields, North and South, are alive with men in their early fifties who gasp for breath as though each would be his last.

With all of this one asks: Why then, do they go back in? The romantic thing to say is that they do it because the mines are there. In a peculiar sense, this has some truth in it.

As one retired miner put it: "When I was a kid, there wasn't anything else to do. We didn't get much education then; nobody paid any attention to it. The coal was there and so were we, and we either went in or we starved. Nobody ever thought much about leaving—at least until it was too late. Then nobody wanted us."

Roland, who works in that soft-coal dog hole, explains: "I got an invalided mother and father to home, and I got to keep a roof over my head. Mining's all I know. Nobody's going to hire me for nothing else."

"I'm not good for nothing else excepting mining. That's all I know," says a Kentuckian named Ellis. "If I can't work the mines, I got no hope of working at all."

GOING NOWHERE

Ellis has five children, all but one in school. Once he was a top member of his crew, responsible for operating and maintaining a large auger. But the mine shut down. He is nearly 50 and no one wants his skills. He had thought his hand-shoveling days were over, but he is glad of the opportunity to sell "my strong back and arms for a day's pay, effen you can get one."

He is going nowhere. He tried it once and the crowded cities with their noise, danger and confusion were not to his liking. He came back.

But had he stayed what would he have done? His education is almost minimal, no more than the elementary grades in a second- or third-rate school. His kind are a dime a dozen, and the labor market—unprotected by unions for janitors and handymen, all his background qualifies him for—is ruthless, harsh, unfeeling. In the mines, for all their dangers, he is at home.

"My children have got to have an education that I didn't have," he says, "and the only way I can give it to them is to work in the mines; that's the only place I got a chance of making money."

There is the reason why men will work in cold water up to their knees; burn their bodies on the hot seams; risk being crushed by falling limestone; lie flat on their backs or bellies with their ear-drums paining from the pounding of jackhammers; inhale dust and smoke that may incapacitate them before their children are fully grown; possibly be trapped there forever in the bowels of the earth.

They will do it because they have to; most of them have no choice. The world has sped away from them with astonishing speed and their only hope lies in giving their children a chance to make the break.

Machines have all the real money-making jobs. The younger men who are in mining are running the machines. They aren't miners, though; they are maintenance men.

And even they have no guarantee of a job tomorrow.

One day recently in the hard-pressed mining town of Davy, W.Va., Frank, a 57-year-old miner, watched sadly as fire destroyed his home. "That's the last of it," he said softly as flames and black smoke shot through the roof. "That's all I have to show for 27 years in the mines. That and the dust."

It is a tragedy that will be repeated again and again—in one form or another—for a whole generation of miners now on the down side of their mining years.

William H. Nicholls
ECONOMIC EFFECTS
OF A STATUS SOCIETY

. . . The ante-bellum South increasingly hardened into a semi-feudal society which rested heavily upon the concept of status or place.

Reprinted by permission from William H. Nicholls, *Southern Tradition and Regional Progress* (Chapel Hill: The University of North Carolina Press, 1960), pp. 62–71.

Mr. Nicholls is Professor of Economics, Vanderbilt University.

During the same period, the rest of America was abolishing the last vestiges of feudalism, moving rapidly from a status society to one based on the concept of free contract. In such a free-contract society, each man, instead of being assigned a fixed and largely predetermined place in the social and economic order, was able to rise as far and as fast as his aspirations, ability, and luck might make possible. To be sure, his gain in opportunity was at first partially offset by a loss of certainty and security; but this radically new, free, and open society produced such quick and plentiful material fruits that few of its members would have willingly returned to the older hierarchical system to which the South still clung. For a time, free contract seemed to give men the freedom to starve rather than to prosper. But the consequent economic revolution also gradually produced a socio-political revolution which guaranteed that the fruits of material progress would be broadly shared and that most of the nation's business enterprise would come to accept a social responsibility which carried with it substantial certainty and security (and essentially middle-class status) to the masses of workers as well.

If the Southern aristocratic society had shown the same dynamism, social responsibility, and flexibility as its English model, the results in terms of economic progress might still have been relatively satisfactory. Instead, Southern society was relatively static, to an increasing extent brutally individualistic, and painfully slow to lose the rigidities of its social order. Of course, the pat Southern explanation for all this points to the Civil War and its vindictive aftermath. But, as modern history has made clear, ignominiously defeated nations have been able to revitalize themselves quickly enough where the dynamism and the will are there. (Admittedly, post-World War II Germany and Japan received a magnanimous assist from the United States Treasury which was far from matched during Reconstruction days.) As an excuse for Southern economic backwardness, the Civil War (like the "Hoover depression") has long since outrun the statute of limitations. Almost a century later, there seems to be more truth in Polk's conclusion that "If Southerners had been industry-minded, they would have promoted industry and become prosperous long ago, instead of sitting back and ascribing all their ills to the outcome at Gettysburg and Appomattox."[1]

Thus, not only did the South become a status society; much worse, it became a relatively static society, uneasy at any sign of change. The result was a state of mind, a personal and general philosophy, which has been both backward-looking and pessimistic. As Walter Sullivan put it: "The Southerner, faced with a questionable future, turns his eyes to

---

[1] William T. Polk, *Southern Accent: From Uncle Remus to Oak Ridge* (New York, 1953), p. 245.

the past. For the past, though often painful to recollect, is at least static and sure. . . . Like a character from one of Ernest Hemingway's novels, his hope is not for ultimate earthly victory, but for the dignity that is inherent in the bravery with which the inevitable defeat is faced." If such an outlook has been in part the effect of the South's poverty, it has also been a contributing cause as well. Certainly, so long as "The mind of the Southerner . . . is filled with the pathos of lost time," the way of regional economic progress is bound to be slow and difficult.[2]

Whatever its romantic pretensions, the South's status society largely lost those virtues of *noblesse oblige* which, as a basic ingredient of its original aristocratic ideal, had made its ante-bellum social structure at least tolerable and even rather attractive. Ellington White said, "The South is rightfully proud of its aristocratic heritage, but all too often we forget that aristocracy is a state of mind, a morality, the conditions of which are sacrifice and obligation and a concern for the welfare of others. The aristocratic mind is the mind least of all conscious of class because it is least of all afraid of losing its place in society. That fear belongs to bourgeois morality . . . which views life in terms of rights rather than obligations. . . . If this morality is allowed to maintain its control over the South, the South is doomed."[3] However, I believe that White is too hard on the Southern bourgeoisie. For all their imperfections, the latter have kept alive most of the remnants of *noblesse oblige* which are still extant in the South.

Similarly, for all their latter-day concern for the yeomen and the low-born, the Southern Agrarians showed little awareness of the concept of *noblesse oblige*. Had they left off the sneering second clause, one might find a hint of it in their declaration that "The responsibility of men is for their own welfare and that of their neighbors; not for the hypothetical welfare of some fabulous creature called society." One of their number was more brutally frank in his statement that "The inferior, whether in life or in education, should exist only for the sake of the superior"—a statement which turns *noblesse oblige* topsy-turvy. Given such a perversion of the aristocratic ideal, Odum's appraisal is more understandable, namely, that in the South there was little awareness of the "millions of marginal folk, white and black, [who] had in reality no semblance of equality of opportunity or even of living much above the subsistence level. . . . Most of the prominent folk of industry and farm never recognized the poverty and suffering level of the five million tenant

[2] Louis D. Rubin, Jr., and James Jackson Kilpatrick, eds., *The Lasting South* (Chicago, 1957), p. 123; and James McBride Dabbs, *The Southern Heritage* (New York, 1958), pp. 183–184.

[3] Rubin and Kilpatrick, eds., *The Lasting South*, p. 170.

folk. . . . There always would be shiftless poor people. There always had been."[4]

In my own contacts with leaders in the rural South, twenty years later, I have encountered with distressing frequency the same attitude, that their low-income neighbors are poor "only because they deserve to be poor." Such a point of view rationalizes a policy of inaction and obscures the fact that rural poverty is largely the result of a defective organization of economic resources and social relationships which can be ameliorated, to the benefit of the entire nation, only through vigorous public and private policies. How else can one explain the paradox that the Mississippi Delta has some of the world's richest soil but many of the nation's poorest people? How different might have been the South's present level of economic progress, despite all of its legitimate handicaps, had its leaders heeded Clarence H. Poe's warning in 1910 that "the prosperity of every man depends upon the prosperity of the average man! Every man whose earning power is below par . . . is a burden on the community; he drags down the whole level of life, and every other man in the community is poorer by reason of his inefficiency, whether he be white man, or Negro. . . . The law of changeless justice decrees that you must rise or fall, decline or prosper, with your neighbour."[5]

Instead, far too much of the South's leadership has continued to remain in the hands of those whose creed is an extreme and irresponsible individualism, almost utterly devoid of any feelings of social responsibility. Particularly as it has manifested itself in inadequate support for public-school education, this weakness of social responsibility warrants . . . detailed consideration. . . . Suffice it to say here that this lack of appreciation of the value, indeed of the essentiality, of substantial public investment in the improvement of the quality, vigor, and productivity of the South's masses of people has seriously impeded the region's economic progress. This is not to deny that in the light of the South's poverty the financing of more adequate public investments in human beings would at best have been difficult. But, as the experience of nineteenth-century Japan clearly demonstrated, even a poor nation whose leadership recognizes the importance of such public investments sufficiently to give them top priority can establish the basis for very rapid economic progress. Surely, poor as it was, the South might have achieved far greater progress if its leadership had been equally farsighted and dedicated.

---

[4] Twelve Southerners, *I'll Take My Stand* (New York, 1930), pp. xviii, 119; Howard W. Odum, *Southern Regions of the United States* (Chapel Hill, 1936), p. 213.

[5] Quoted in Edwin Mims, *The Advancing South* (New York, 1926), p. 7.

If the South's politically important planters and industrialists have shown a serious lack of concern for the welfare of the masses, I believe that they have done so far more because of their uncritical acceptance of a traditional status society than because of their selfishness or narrow self-interest. Too many social critics of the South have attacked Southern employers for "exploiting" their labor supply by paying low wages. It is not appropriate to judge such employers by national standards, according to which many of their social and economic relationships with their workers do appear to be exploitative. To judge so ignores the fact that the South's wage rates are low because of a much more fundamental economic factor—a heavily redundant labor supply with extremely poor alternative employment opportunities.

It is unreasonable to expect Southern employers voluntarily to pay higher wages or by minimum-wage laws to force them to, without attacking the basic problem of reducing the region's vast underemployed labor force. Instead of deploring the South's low wage rates on moral grounds as exploitative, it would be far sounder to look upon them as an important economic basis for attracting the additional industry needed to raise them through normal competitive processes toward national wage levels, employing ever larger numbers of Southern workers in the bargain. Policies which will more effectively promote rapid industrial development—or where such is not possible, facilitate human outmigration—are therefore clearly needed in the South.

Even though charges of exploitation against Southern planters and industrialists seem unduly harsh, it is true that they frequently do oppose such policies, in part because they feel a self-interest in perpetuating the plentiful labor supply upon which they have come to depend. Furthermore, they are not always scrupulous in avoiding an appeal to race prejudice as a means of keeping their white workers in line. However, such behavior illustrates a far more serious problem than mere self-interest, namely, their acceptance as perfectly normal and natural of a traditional social structure characterized by a very broad base of low-income people. Southern employers constituting as they so often do a major part of their community leadership, their satisfaction with things as they are is a major barrier to further regional economic progress. It is even doubtful whether their attitudes are actually in their own long-run self-interest since, however much they may resist taxation to support public services for their many low-income neighbors, they are usually forced gradually to give ground. As they do, they must carry an increasingly heavy fiscal burden, because the poor, both Negro and white, depend much more upon the public treasury than in their depleted state they are able to contribute to it. If Southern leaders concerned themselves more with raising the socioeconomic status of the low-income masses, they would benefit their entire community—including those engaged in wholesaling, retailing, banking, the service trades, real estate, and the professions—through the consequent increases in incomes and purchasing power. At the same time, they would substantially broaden the local tax base, permitting far better public services on a more efficient basis and thereby paving the way for general community progress in which they would fully share.

Such views—so commonplace as to be almost taken for granted in other American regions—still are far from winning general acceptance in much of the conservative, backward-looking, individualistic, and inflexible South. As Polk recently wrote: "Even today feudalism is more congenial than industrialism to a good deal of the South which has not yet moved all the way from status to contract. This is the South which not only likes the Negro 'in his place' but likes every man in his place and thinks there is a certain place providentially provided for him. To this South, industrialization, with its shift from status to contract and its creation of a new-rich, rootless and pushing class of people, is plainly instigated by the devil. The Southern farmer still tends to look on himself as a better and freer man than the mill worker. . . . This attitude, which is common to all classes of Southern society, is one of the brakes on the Southern transition from an agrarian toward an industrial economy."[6]

To be sure, the South has been industrializing and in the process has been undermining its traditional status society. With increasing urbanization, the South is at last giving its vigorous and hard-working middle class an opportunity to emerge from the subordinate position it held in the hidebound rural society. Nevertheless, if the Southern social structure is less rigid than it once was, it must become even more flexible if the region is to attain an optimum rate of economic progress. The Southern labor force still reflects the underlying status society from which it springs, divided as it is into a number of relatively independent "non-competing groups." Whether separated according to lines of race, class, or place of residence, such non-competing groups result in a segmented labor force which is not conducive to the achievement of maximum industrial efficiency or personal incentives.

Perhaps one of the greatest assets in the development of the matchless American industrial system was the increasing homogeneity of

[6] William T. Polk, *Southern Accent: From Uncle Remus to Oak Ridge* (New York, 1953), pp. 244–45. It should perhaps be added that in Southern industrial relations strong elements of status-conscious paternalism are frequently alloyed with an extreme spirit of free contract (particularly manifested in anti-unionism) reminiscent of the early days of the English and American industrial revolutions. However, I do not consider that a serious problem, since it reflects an early stage of Southern industrialization which will undoubtedly largely vanish as the region reaches industrial maturity.

its workers, reflecting particularly the relative equality of opportunity both educational and economic and the relative unimportance of personal attributes not directly related to doing well the job at hand. In recent decades, of course, the rapidly growing national labor unions—with their increasingly elaborate rules of seniority, feather-bedding, job security, closed shop, entrance requirements, and the like—have tended to introduce new non-competing groups into the American industrial scene. Whatever their other merits, unions have thereby erected new barriers to labor mobility which have not only at times interfered with productive efficiency but have forced American industry to reward workers of equal merit unequally. More important, as the requisite skills for industrial employment have increased, these barriers have placed late-coming Southern migrants—already handicapped by less adequate education and training—at an even greater disadvantage in finding and holding industrial jobs.

If the economies of other American regions are now perhaps sufficiently mature and financially strong to take the creation of these new non-competing groups in their stride, the South clearly is not. Instead, the South already faces enough problems in achieving optimum industrial development without substituting for, or even superimposing upon, these undesirable effects of unionism additional non-competing groups of its own making. The South must at last extend full equality of opportunity—particularly through general education, public health, and vocational training—to all of its people regardless of class, color, or location. Only thus will most of them be able to better themselves either within or beyond the Southern region, thereby destroying the remaining vestiges of the South's traditional status society. It also means that the South's upper-class whites will have to resume their traditional leadership role in order to minimize racial violence.

Given the South's social structure with its extremely large numbers of poor lower-class Negroes and whites, it is easy enough to understand why many of the region's lower-class whites remain so ready to lend support to racial violence. Their general social and economic frustration has made of the Negro a scapegoat—a deplorable situation that I believe only continued regional economic progress can significantly ameliorate. If incipient violence becomes widespread again after so many years of decline, it will seriously impede the further industrial development needed to drain off the race-oriented frustrations of lower-class whites. Surprisingly few upper-class whites in the South have yet recognized this almost self-evident fact. Instead, most of them have condoned the outspoken prejudice of lower-class whites by an acquiescence which means the abandonment of their heavy responsibilities of leadership. Dabbs expressed this problem clearly by observing, "It is customary for middle- and upper-class whites, when faced with the need for racial readjustment, to say: 'We have no great objection ourselves, but the poorer whites wouldn't stand for it: there'd be violence.' The part about violence is always said publicly—just as it [was] said publicly by Governor Faubus of Arkansas . . . —so that the lower-class whites know what is expected of them."[7]

I believe it is significant that wherever state political leadership has taken a firm stand on the side of law and order, as Governor Clement did in Tennessee, violence over school integration has been short-lived and ineffective. Equally significant is the fact that Virginia—which, according to V. O. Key, Jr., has been so thoroughly controlled by a small political oligarchy that "By contrast Mississippi is a hotbed of democracy"—ultimately capitulated on the school issue without even a hint of violence. On the other hand, Arkansas—a state which has been remarkably free of race hysteria but whose politics "is almost devoid of issue other than that of the moment"[8]—was led down a miserable trail of violence by a completely opportunistic governor. The contrast between Arkansas and Virginia is striking. If Virginia represents the South's most status-ridden society, Governor Almond at least exercised a courageous and responsible leadership consistent with the aristocratic ideal, while Governor Faubus' radical and subversive leadership was quite at variance with that ideal. As a consequence, while Little Rock has failed to gain a single new factory since Faubus took his defiant stand, Virginia's industrial development will probably continue apace.

[7] Dabbs, *Southern Heritage*, pp. 112–13.
[8] V. O. Key, Jr., *Southern Politics in State and Nation* (New York, 1949), pp. 19–20, 183–84.

Bernard D. Nossiter
IT WILL BE A LONG WAR

In what the President has called an "unconditional war" on poverty, the administration is aiming at nothing less than the destruction of the cultural conditions that cause and perpetuate poverty in the

From *The Reporter*, March 26, 1964. Copyright 1964 by The Reporter Magazine Company. Reprinted by permission of the author and publisher.
Mr. Nossiter is with the *Washington Post*.

United States. Because this is a vast and largely unexplored territory and because so many different disciplines will be called upon to penetrate it, an evaluation of the administration's program on economic grounds alone is impossible. Precisely how long it will last and what it will cost is anybody's guess. Nevertheless, some educated estimates about the program's future are worth noting. For example, Robert Lampman of the University of Wisconsin thinks that thirty years is a feasible goal. Another economist, one of the principal architects of the administration's strategy, contends that at least two generations will be needed to eradicate poverty in East Harlem alone. In sum, the most informed guesses foresee a campaign lasting several decades.

Lampman's views are entitled to special respect on several grounds. His paper in 1959 before the Joint Economic Committee was the first of the recent attempts to define and describe the dimensions of contemporary poverty. Lampman's unique contribution was to demonstrate that the percentage of the population defined as poverty-stricken fell rapidly during the first postwar decade of reasonably high employment and relatively healthy growth, but much more slowly in the next few years of a lackluster economy. This effectively rebutted the contention that modern poverty is unrelated to the economy's total health. Last spring, when Walter W. Heller, the President's chief economic adviser, first determined to spur an attack on poverty, he turned to Lampman—then on Heller's staff—for a broad design.

To gauge the progress of the campaign, Lampman has devised the concept of the withdrawal rate. This is a measure of the number who each year climb above a set level defined as the poverty line. The idea of a withdrawal rate is likely to become a fixture in the government's planning. Given the current definition of poverty as a family income under $3,000, Lampman concludes that a withdrawal rate of a million a year is within reach of the programs that a Johnson administration is likely to adopt. This rate assumes a high level of employment and some acceleration of economic growth. Since more than thirty million Americans are now below the poverty line, an annual withdrawal rate of one million implies at least a thirty-year program.

This may look like a modest pace, but it is well above the rate sustained even during the buoyant decade after the Second World War. Between 1947 and 1957, Lampman estimates, about 800,000 a year rose from the poverty level. In the next five years, the rate fell to about 500,000. This decline was the result of sluggish growth, high unemployment, and a slower gain in the payments made directly to the poor from Social Security and other channels of transferring income. The economy's recent torpor, then, has left the nation with a deficit of 1.5 million who might otherwise have escaped from poverty. Against this background,

Lampman's suggested yearly target of a million withdrawals appears more ambitious; it is in fact approximately double the recent rate.

In a recent conversation with me, Lampman discussed other proposals to transfer income. If Social Security payments were doubled, five million aged persons could be removed at once from the poverty rolls at a yearly cost of $6 billion. Lampman pointed out that in other countries, Canada and Great Britain for example, for years government allowances have been paid to families with children. These payments have helped rescue some deserted, divorced, and widowed mothers and their children from poverty. Indeed, nothing short of such direct payments is likely to do much for the impoverished aged, the fully disabled, and the poverty-stricken female heads of families. If Johnson is elected in November, his next administration probably will press for higher Social Security benefits and perhaps other welfare payments. But under the constraints of the current budget, direct payments of any significant size are simply not on this administration's agenda. A more limited program directed largely to rescuing some of those who can make a productive contribution is the most that the government economists envision now.

The long-range arithmetic of the economists follows these lines: $3 to $4 billion a year is now spent—or, perhaps more accurately, misspent—on scattered programs affecting the poor. The new programs, which will add less than $1 billion to the total effort in fiscal 1965, will be augmented by $2 to $3 billion annually in the next few years. At the peak, the Federal government will spend more than $6 billion a year on the poor. In perhaps ten years, these officials suggest, the Federal share of the costs might decline and state and local governments could be expected to pick up more of the burden.

ASSUMPTIONS AND CONCLUSIONS

The administration's strategy for its drive against poverty draws on a wide variety of sources; indeed, nobody can assert with authority what will and won't work. Even so, a set of common assumptions and conclusions underlies the whole project. Here are four essential points that guided the administration:

Because of the current budget restraints and the commitment to hold down public spending, at present the government can employ only limited resources for the huge problem it has chosen to deal with. A memorandum that circulated among the Cabinet in early November made this point explicit.

There are already a host of ill-defined programs to help the poor at the Federal, state, and local levels. They are scattered, unco-ordinated, and often duplicating. For example, in one small area of New York, ten agencies are tackling the problems of children on probation.

Poverty is found in two general settings, but only one is strongly resistant to advances in the economy as a whole. Poverty when found in the midst of plenty is relatively easy to deal with. For instance, the children of the impoverished Negroes clustered on a few streets in the comfortable Georgetown section of Washington are able to attend relatively good schools and live in an atmosphere that encourages them to look for a better life. Poverty in the midst of poverty, as in eastern Kentucky or Harlem, poses problems of a different order. Here the whole environment fosters a circular process that traps whole generations.

Some of the planners believe that the tax cut will provide job openings on a larger scale than has been officially forecast. This thesis is disputed both within and without the administration. In any event, it may never be fully tested. Next year, it is quite possible that the budget restraints will be lifted and welfare and public-works spending will be permitted to rise. This prospect will be enhanced if the administration's promise of reducing military expenditures is fulfilled.

From this blend of fact and forecast, the administration drew several conclusions. Programs must rehabilitate impoverished human beings and prepare them for more productive lives. Although direct relief is necessary for some, it won't be granted because of the budget curbs. Thus public works and those measures designed for relief alone should be minimized, and a greater effort made in education and programs that increase the ability of the poor to improve their condition.

Finally, it was agreed that direct attacks must be launched in the sectors where poverty is concentrated and institutionalized, such as the South Side slums of Chicago and the played-out mining communities of West Virginia. This attack must be launched on a broad front, against the whole environment. It cannot be limited to better housing or better schools or vocational training. The principal beneficiaries should be the young, and the principal stratagem on this sector must be to bring the present scattered programs together in some coherent fashion. Also, community leaders must be drawn into the planning. Because of the limit on resources, the campaign may be pushed in only seventy-five communities this year and twice that number the next. But such an approach will yield more dividends than thinly financed programs on a national scale.

So much for the underlying theory. In practice, of course, the administration program will take many forms. One important element consists of camps to teach basic reading and arithmetical skills to youths rejected by the draft. This is precisely the kind of program that supposedly was to be shunned, since it overrides the master plan of working through the community and applies a remedy nationally to one age group among the poverty-stricken.

But tearing apart and rebuilding impoverished environments is a slow process. The camps were accepted largely because the newly appointed director of the poverty program, Sargent Shriver, insisted on something that would bring quick and visible results. Indeed, Shriver was named in part to bring peace among the various departments and agencies with competing interests in the program, as well as to charm Congress. The Labor Department, for one, had to abandon much of its hope of contributing to the campaign by creating new jobs particularly suited to the limited skills of the poor. Labor Department officials wanted a large slice of the available resources spent on projects to clean up cities, service public buildings, and the like. In one heated session at the White House late in January, high officials from Labor and five other departments went at each other for several hours without coming close to an agreement. In the end, however, fragments of each agency's proposals will survive.

THE SANGUINE APPROACH

The public response to the President's declaration caught nearly everyone in government by surprise except perhaps Mr. Johnson himself, who is largely responsible for designating the poverty program as an "unconditional war." Before President Kennedy's death, his aides were employing bloodless titles like "Human Conservation and Development" or "Access to Opportunity." They had tentatively settled on "Widening Participation in Prosperity—An Attack on Poverty."

One day after President Johnson took office, he gave his blessing to Heller's project. By now the idea has won applause from virtually every sector but the extreme Right. In Congress, the Republican members of the Joint Economic Committee did not follow Barry Goldwater, who had suggested that poverty is the fault of the poor themselves and that the Federal government had no business worrying about it. Instead, the committee members outlined their own thoughtful seven-point program for conducting the war. For the most part, these points are incorporated in the administration's campaign. But they include one—research on the link between population control and poverty—on which the administration has so far remained conspicuously silent.

The whole enterprise is a natural for Democrats hungry to re-create some of the fervor of the New Deal days. Since the three Kennedy years were largely devoted to programs long sought by businessmen, it was especially necessary that the White House produce an issue like this in 1964. The issue came ready to hand. The rising pressure of the Negroes for a full share in the benefits of American life, coupled with a wider recognition of the damage being done to our society by neglect of the underprivileged at large, created a massive demand that cannot be met without an attack on poverty at large.

California State
Chamber of Commerce
THE REAL REMEDY FOR POVERTY

The California State Chamber of Commerce is opposed to the enactment of Senate Bill 2642 (The Economic Opportunity Act of 1964). We believe that the objectives of this bill can best be achieved by the Government encouraging local initiative and by long-range improvement of Government-business relationships aimed at stimulating the economy, rather than by the initiation of large Federally sponsored welfare-type programs that have been tried in the past and found to be unsuccessful. It is our position that the most promising remedy for the reduction of poverty and unemployment is the acceleration of general economic growth. The major role of government at all levels in this field should be to establish and maintain a relationship with business which will encourage maximum use of private capital for sound growth and the expansion of employment it affords. We, therefore, believe that this bill's tremendously expensive program, its duplication of effort, usurpation of State and local government responsibility, and unique and dangerous grant of broad and extravagant power and control to one government official will hinder and impede rather than assist and encourage the present and ongoing war against poverty that business and the States and local communities are now waging.

The enactment of S. 2642 would establish and set in motion a large number of Federally sponsored welfare programs, many of which, on an individual basis, have either been tried and rejected or turned down by Congress when first proposed. Although the stated cost of these

Statement submitted by Clark Galloway, General Manager, California State Chamber of Commerce to the U.S. Senate Select Subcommittee on Poverty, June 26, 1964.

programs for the first year is $962 million, it has been estimated that this cost would rise to $5 billion by the third year, and based upon past experience, it is reasonable to assume that the cost of the program in the succeeding years would continue to increase. Certainly, this tremendous expenditure of funds for the once rejected programs is prohibitive even if these programs were to supercede or replace other Federal antipoverty programs. However, this is not the case. On the contrary, S. 2642 will impose its programs on top of the 42 individual programs designed to combat poverty that the Federal Government is currently carrying forward. According to the Bureau of the Budget, these programs carried appropriations of $31.8 billion for the fiscal year 1964.

Under the provisions of this act, the Director of the Office of Economic Opportunity is granted unlimited power and authority. This dangerous situation stems from the fact that each of the five basic programs that the act initiates—a Youth Corps, a community action program, a rural poverty program, an employment and investment incentive program, and a domestic volunteer program—is established with very few guidelines. The Director may designate the programs that will receive assistance, select the trainees and recipients of grants, and establish the monetary amount of such grants subject to only a minimum amount of statutory direction and control. For example, under title II the Director may select for assistance any program which in his opinion is of sufficient size and scope to give promise of progress toward the elimination of poverty or a cause or causes of poverty. Under the circumstances, it is not too surprising that the Director of the Office of Economic Opportunity has been characterized as the "poverty czar."

The most significant and dangerous aspect of S. 2642 is the fact that it would foster and encourage local organizations and agencies to bypass their State and local governments. Historically, welfare and assistance programs have been administered and controlled at the State and local level. However, under the proposed act, any agency or organization may present its plan directly to the Director, and the Governor of the State or the mayor of the city could not veto the plan or even participate in the deliberations that may lead to its selection for Federal assistance. Planning and coordination at the local level is absolutely essential in any type of community health or welfare program. Without this type of coordinated effort, duplication and waste can only result. Moreover, granting the Director direct control over programs of this type could result in the establishment of a political power base that could reach unrestrained into every State, city, and rural community in America.

The California State Chamber of Commerce believes that for this effort to succeed it must remain as before, primarily a local responsibility that is locally administered and controlled. The preparation of young people for taking their places as productive citizens in the economy must be a family and local educational responsibility. In this regard, we note that many fine training programs, strongly supported by labor and management alike, are presently underway in California.

In the final analysis, however, the only real remedy for the reduction of poverty and unemployment is the acceleration of general economic growth. Unfortunately, S. 2642, the Economic Opportunity Act of 1964, is basically an attempt to substitute Federal grants and welfare programs for the cure of conditions that can best be remedied by increasing the rate of economic growth in this country.

3
Work and Leisure

Historically, the mass of population was not consciously concerned with the meaning of work. To ask why one worked was similar to asking why one tried to stay alive. Today, in the United States, to ask a man why he works and what he expects to get from his work is to ask a reasonable question. Modern industrial man has a conscious expectation of deriving more from his work than the paycheck. He is told that work is important. Employers over the past generation have become increasingly sensitive to criticisms that their offices or factories are not good places in which to work. The human-relations movement has sought to demonstrate a positive correlation between satisfaction in work and productivity at work. The continued determination of blue-collar parents to provide the means for their children to move into white-collar jobs, even when the opportunity for monetary improvement is slight or nonexistent, is significant. A person's status in society is largely defined by the type of work he does. The work people do determines to a considerable extent where they live, the clubs to which they belong, their attitudes toward politics and social problems, and their satisfaction with life generally.

Of course, not all people agree on the meaning of work or on what satisfactions can be derived from it. Nor is there agreement on the conditions necessary for people to obtain the greatest satisfaction from work activities. To illustrate, can employees in a highly industrialized society find meaning and room for creative expression in their work when the job they do consists of a few simple and repetitive operations? Is the

137

man in the "gray flannel suit" any better off? Or are we overestimating the role that work plays in the lives of people and what they expect to get from it?

Each of the writers in this chapter presents a somewhat different interpretation of important questions associated with work and its counterpart, leisure. The first selection looks at the problem of alienation in work—its causes and consequences. The writings of Karl Marx deserve much of the credit for the attention now being given to man's potential for creative expression in work activity on the one hand, and the limited extent to which man is realizing this potential on the other. The fact that Marx used "alienation" to buttress his argument for a fundamental transformation of capitalist society does not lessen his contribution. Erich Fromm, in interpreting Marx's concept of alienation in work, underscores the wider relevance of Marx's analysis—a relevance to all industrial societies. The alienation theme centers on two basic assumptions. The first is that work is the central fact of human existence and has within it the potential to help man achieve himself as a truly creative human being. The second is that the social and economic organization of industrial societies tends to reduce man to a tool of his own technology, when he should be the master. It focuses attention on the dehumanizing potential inherent in man's relationship to his technology.

In the Marxian argument, modern technology leads to subjective feelings of estrangement from job and work place. This, in turn, should produce feelings of work dissatisfaction. Robert Blauner provides a partial test of the alienation thesis by examining variations in job satisfaction among different occupational groups. His analysis sheds light on the questions of whether alienation is as universal as the Marxian argument would suggest and whether such alienation as does exist is attributable to the social organization of the work process or whether there are not other, more basic causes.

Blauner finds that most workers in modern society are not alienated. The majority of them are moderately or highly satisfied with their jobs. However, he also finds marked occupational differences in work attitudes and job satisfaction. The assembly-line worker shows the greatest degree of dissatisfaction with his job and work. But even the assembly-line worker does not experience that total estrangement implied by the Marxian analysis.

Still another perspective on the meaning of work is offered by Robert Dubin. He suggests that we not lose sight of the fact that work means different things to different people. Is it meaningful to talk about alienation in work, when work itself does not occupy a central focus in the lives of many workers? Many people view work as little more than a means to an end (i.e., the paycheck). It is possible, at least among industrial workers, that as many as three fourths do not view their work as a central life interest.

Whatever the meaning of work in the lives of people, the probability is high that more and more of them will be spending less time at work. What can or should be done to make the increase in leisure time of maximum value to the individuals involved and to society? To what extent should leisure-time activities be planned and regulated with the same care that goes into planning work activities? Sidney Lens feels that the increase in leisure provides a real opportunity to add another and deeper dimension to life, which work activity *per se* cannot provide. Lens argues for a reunification of work and education. "Under this thesis we would continue the forty-hour week but devote five, ten, or fifteen hours to adult education." He believes the work place can be put to socially beneficial purposes that extend beyond the performance of productive work activities.

Whatever the intrinsic merit in the various proposals put forth for the more effective utilization of leisure time, there remains the very difficult problem of implementation. In the last selection of the chapter, Dan Wakefield describes the perplexing nature of the leisure problem for unions. What unions would like to see happen in the use of leisure time is not happening. There is, for example, little point in unions establishing symphony orchestras when people persist in watching television. In work, there is an element of compulsion motivating people to behave productively. How do you promote productive utilization of leisure time? Unions don't have the answer. In fact, as Wakefield intimates, the union leader preaches effective utilization of leisure time to his members at the risk of losing his job. Unions want to be helpful. But workers don't want anyone telling them how to use their leisure time.

work

Erich Fromm

KARL MARX ON ALIENATION IN WORK: AN INTERPRETATION

. . . For Karl Marx, as for Hegel, the concept of alienation is based on the distinction between existence and essence, on the fact that man's existence is alienated from his essence, that in reality he is not what he potentially is, or, to put it differently, that *he is not what he ought to be, and that he ought to be that which he could be.*

For Marx the process of alienation is expressed in work and in the division of labor. Work is for him the active relatedness of man to nature, the creation of a new world, including the creation of man himself. (Intellectual activity is of course, for Marx, always work, like manual or artistic activity.) But as private property and the division of labor develop, labor loses its character of being an expression of man's powers; labor and its products assume an existence separate from man, his will and his planning. . . .

Labor is alienated because the work has ceased to be a part of the worker's nature and "consequently, he does not fulfill himself in his work but denies himself, has a feeling of misery rather than well-being, does not develop freely his mental and physical energies but is physically

From Erich Fromm, *Marx's Concept of Man* (New York: Frederick Ungar Publishing Co., 1961), pp. 45–57. Reprinted by permission. Except as otherwise indicated, all direct quotes in this selection are from Marx's *Economic and Philosophical Manuscripts,* which are reprinted in the volume from which the selection was taken.

Mr. Fromm is a psychoanalyst and author of numerous books.

exhausted and mentally debased. The worker therefore feels himself at home only during his leisure time, whereas at work he feels homeless." Thus, in the act of production the relationship of the worker to his own activity is experienced "as something alien and not belonging to him, activity as suffering (passivity), strength as powerlessness, creation as emasculation." While man thus becomes alienated from himself, the product of labor becomes "an alien object which dominates him. This relationship is at the same time the relationship to the sensuous external world, to natural objects, as an alien and hostile world." Marx stresses two points: (1) in the process of work, and especially of work under the conditions of capitalism, man is estranged from his own creative powers, and (2) the *objects* of his own work become alien beings, and eventually rule over him, become powers independent of the producer. "The laborer exists for the process of production, and not the process of production for the laborer."[1]

A misunderstanding of Marx on this point is widespread, even among socialists. It is believed that Marx spoke primarily of the *economic* exploitation of the worker, and the fact that his share of the product was not as large as it should be, or that the product should belong to him, instead of to the capitalist. But, . . . the state as a capitalist, as in the Soviet Union, would not have been any more welcome to Marx than the private capitalist. He is not concerned primarily with the equalization of income. He is concerned with the liberation of man from a kind of work which destroys his individuality, which transforms him into a thing, and which makes him into the slave of things. Just as Kierkegaard was concerned with the salvation of the individual, so Marx was, and his criticism of capitalist society is directed not at its method of distribution of income, but its mode of production, its destruction of individuality and its enslavement of man, not by the capitalist, but the enslavement of man—worker *and* capitalist—by things and circumstances of their own making.

Marx goes still further. In unalienated work man not only realizes himself as an indidual, but also as a species-being. For Marx, as for Hegel and many other thinkers of the enlightenment, each individual represented the species, that is to say, humanity as a whole, the universality of man: the development of man leads to the unfolding of his whole humanity. In the process of work he "no longer reproduces himself merely intellectually, as in consciousness, but actively and in a real sense, and he sees his own reflection in a world which he has constructed. While, therefore, alienated labor takes away the object of production from man, it also takes away his *species life*, his real

---

[1] Karl Marx, *Capital I* (Chicago: Charles H. Kerr & Co., 1906), p. 536.

objectivity as a species-being, and changes his advantage over animals into a disadvantage in so far as his inorganic body, nature, is taken from him. Just as alienated labor transforms free and self-directed activity into a means, so it transforms the species life of man into a means of physical existence. Consciousness, which man has from his species, is transformed through alienation so that species life becomes only a means for him."

As I indicated before, Marx assumed that the alienation of work, while existing throughout history, reaches its peak in capitalist society, and that the working class is the most alienated one. This assumption was based on the idea that the worker, having no part in the direction of the work, being "employed" as part of the machines he serves, is transformed into a thing in its dependence on capital. Hence, for Marx, "the emancipation of society from private property, from servitude, takes the political form of the *emancipation of the workers;* not in the sense that only the latter's emancipation is involved, but because this emancipation includes the *emancipation of humanity as a whole.* For all human servitude is involved in the relation of the worker to production, and all types of servitude are only modifications or consequences of this relation."

Again it must be emphasized that Marx's aim is not limited to the emancipation of the working class, but the emancipation of the human being through the restitution of the unalienated and hence free activity of all men, and a society in which man, and not the production of things, is the aim, in which man ceases to be "a crippled monstrosity, and becomes a fully developed human being.". . .[2]

The alienation of work in man's production is much greater than it was when production was by handicraft and manufacture. "In handicrafts and manufacture, the workman makes use of a tool; in the factory the machine makes use of him. There the movements of the instrument of labor proceed from him; here it is the movement of the machines that he must follow. In manufacture, the workmen are parts of a living mechanism; in the factory we have a lifeless mechanism, independent of the workman, who becomes its mere living appendage.". . .[3]

For Marx, alienation in the process of work, from the product of work and from circumstances, is inseparably connected with alienation from oneself, from one's fellow man and from nature. "A direct consequence of the alienation of man from the product of his labor, from his life activity and from his species life is that *man is alienated* from other men. When man confronts himself, he also confronts *other* men. What is true of man's relationship to his work, to the product of his work

[2] *Ibid.*, p. 536.
[3] *Ibid.*, pp. 461–62.

and to himself, is also true of his relationship to other men, to their labor and to the objects of their labor. In general, the statement that man is alienated from his species life means that each man is alienated from others, and that each of the others is likewise alienated from human life." The alienated man is not only alienated from other men; he is alienated from the essence of humanity, from his "species-being," both in his natural and spiritual qualities. . . .

There is only one correction which history has made in Marx's concept of alienation; Marx believed that the working class was the most alienated class, hence that the emancipation from alienation would necessarily start with the liberation of the working class. Marx did not foresee the extent to which alienation was to become the fate of the vast majority of people, especially of the ever-increasing segment of the population which manipulate symbols and men, rather than machines. If anything, the clerk, the salesman, the executive, are even more alienated today than the skilled manual worker. The latter's functioning still depends on the expression of certain personal qualities like skill, reliability, etc., and he is not forced to sell his "personality," his smile, his opinions in the bargain; the symbol manipulators are hired not only for their skill, but for all those personality qualities which make them "attractive personality packages," easy to handle and to manipulate. They are the true "organization men"—more so than the skilled laborer—their idol being the corporation. But as far as consumption is concerned, there is no difference between manual workers and the members of the bureaucracy. They all crave for things, new things, to have and to use. They are the passive recipients, the consumers, chained and weakened by the very things which satisfy their synthetic needs. They are not related to the world productively, grasping it in its full reality and in this process becoming one with it; they worship things, the machines which produce the things—and in this alienated world they feel as strangers and quite alone.

Robert Blauner
WORK SATISFACTION
IN MODERN SOCIETY

The present paper surveys research on attitudes of workers toward their work, especially those investigations commonly called job satisfaction studies. To assess the absolute level of job satisfaction in the working population is not my aim, for this is an impossible task, but rather, my purposes are, (1) to locate differences in the incidence and intensity of work satisfaction among those in diverse occupations and work settings, and (2) to discern the factors that, in accounting for these differences, seem to indicate the important preconditions of satisfaction in work. Further, the paper considers the implications of these findings for theories of work and workers in modern society, in the light of industrial and social trends. . . .

OCCUPATIONAL DIFFERENCES IN WORK SATISFACTION

Work satisfaction varies greatly by occupation. Highest percentages of satisfied workers are usually found among professionals and businessmen. In a given plant, the proportion satisfied is higher among clerical workers than among factory workers, just as in general labor force samples it is higher among middle-class than among manual working-class occupations. Within the manual working class, job satisfaction is highest among skilled workers, lowest among unskilled laborers and workers on assembly lines.

When a scale of relative job satisfaction is formed, based on general occupational categories, the resulting rank order is almost identical with the most commonly used occupational status classification —the Edwards scale of the Bureau of the Census. For example, the mean indexes of satisfaction in Table 1[1] resulted from a survey of all New Hope, Pa., jobholders in 1935.

From *Labor and Trade Unionism,* Walter Galenson and Seymour M. Lipset (eds.) (New York: John Wiley & Sons, Inc., 1960). Reprinted by permission.

Mr. Blauner is Assistant Professor of Sociology, University of California, Berkeley.

[1] In this index, the figure 100 would indicate extreme dissatisfaction, 400 indifference, and 700 extreme satisfaction.

A similar rank order resulted in a national survey when the proportions of workers in each occupational group who would continue the same kind of work in the event they inherited enough money to live comfortably were computed (Table 2).

The generally higher level of job satisfaction of white-collar over blue-collar workers is confirmed by a study of twelve different factories in 1934, in which the scores of clerical workers on job satisfaction were considerably higher than those of factory workers; by the Center's

TABLE 1

OCCUPATIONAL GROUP	MEAN INDEX	NUMBER IN SAMPLE
Professional and managerial	560	23
Semiprofessional, business, and supervisory	548	32
Skilled manual and white collar	510	84
Semiskilled manual workers	483	74
Unskilled manual workers	401	55

TABLE 2

OCCUPATIONAL GROUP	PERCENT WHO WOULD CONTINUE SAME KIND OF WORK	NUMBER IN SAMPLE
Professionals	68	28
Sales	59	22
Managers	55	22
Skilled manual	40	86
Service	33	18
Semiskilled operatives	32	80
Unskilled	16	27

national sample, which found that only 14 per cent of workers in middle-class occupations were dissatisfied with their jobs, compared to 21 per cent of those in working class occupations; and by a 1947 *Fortune* poll, which revealed that the proportion of employees who said their jobs were interesting was 92 per cent among professionals and executives, 72 per cent among salaried employees and 54 per cent among factory workers. However, a study of the Detroit area population found that only among such upper white-collar employees as secretaries, draftsmen, and book-keepers was the incidence of job satisfaction greater than among manual workers; such lower white-collar employees as clerks, typists, and retail salespeople were somewhat less satisfied than blue-collar workers.

Further evidence of the relation of job satisfaction to occupational status is provided by studies of retirement plans. Although there are a number of factors which affect the retirement decision, it is plausible to argue that the more satisfying a job is to the worker, the more likely he will choose not to retire. In a study of work and retirement in six occupations it was found that the proportion of men who wanted to continue working or had actually continued working after age sixty-five was more than 67 per cent for physicians, 65 per cent for department store salesmen, 49 per cent for skilled printers, 42 per cent for coal miners, and 32 per cent for unskilled and semiskilled steelworkers.

As has been shown in the preceding section of this paper, the majority of workers in all occupations respond positively when asked whether or not they are satisfied with their jobs. But that does not mean they would not prefer other kinds of work. The average worker in a lower-status occupation says that he would choose another line of work if he had the chance to start his working life anew. This question then, is perhaps a more sensitive indicator of latent dissatisfactions and frustrations; the occupational differences it points to, though forming the same pattern as the other, are considerably greater. For example, when a survey of 13,000 Maryland youths was made during the depression it was found that 91 per cent of professional-technical workers preferred their own occupation to any other, compared to 45 per cent of managerial personnel and farm owners, 41 per cent of skilled manual workers, 37 per cent of domestic workers, 36 per cent of office and sales personnel, 14 per cent of unskilled, and 11 per cent of semiskilled manual workers.

More detailed data for a number of professional and manual working class occupations strongly confirms these general findings. Note how for six different professions, the proportion of satisfied persons ranges from 82 per cent to 91 per cent, whereas for seven manual occupations it varies from 16 per cent for unskilled automobile workers to 52 per cent for skilled printers. (See Table 3.)

TABLE 3. *Proportion in Various Occupations Who Would Choose Same Kind of Work if Beginning Career Again*

PROFESSIONAL OCCUPATIONS—%		WORKING CLASS OCCUPATIONS—%	
Mathematicians	91	Skilled printers	52
Physicists	89	Paper workers	52
Biologists	89	Skilled automobile workers	41
Chemists	86	Skilled steelworkers	41
Lawyers	83	Textile workers	31
Journalists	82	Unskilled steelworkers	21
		Unskilled automobile workers	16

To some extent, these findings on occupational differences in job satisfaction reflect not only differences in the objective conditions of work for people in various jobs, *but also occupational differences in the norms with respect to work attitudes.* The professional is expected to be dedicated to his profession and have an intense intrinsic interest in his area of specialized competence; the white-collar employee is expected to be "company" oriented and like his work; but the loyalty of the manual worker is never taken for granted and, more than any other occupational type, cultural norms permit him the privilege of griping. In fact, it has been asserted that "the natural state of the industrial worker . . . is one of discontent." The same point has been clearly made in an analysis of the latent function of the time clock:

> The office staff does not "clock-in"—ostensibly because they are not paid by the hour, but it seems likely that at least part of the reason for this is the supposition that, unlike labourers, they do not necessarily dislike work and can be placed on their honour to be punctual. The working classes, as we have seen, are supposed to dislike work and therefore need "discipline" to keep them in order. Since "clocking-in" has been abolished in many firms, it cannot be accepted as absolutely necessary.[2]

FACTORS THAT ACCOUNT FOR OCCUPATIONAL DIFFERENCES IN SATISFACTION

The literature on work is filled with numerous attempts to list and often to estimate the relative importance of the various components, elements, or factors involved in job satisfaction. These lists do not correspond neatly with one another; they bear a large number of labels, but they all are likely to include, in one way or another, such variables as the income attached to a job, supervision, working conditions, social relations, and the variety and skill intrinsic in the work itself. The classification of these items is quite arbitrary and the number of factors considered relevant can be broken down almost indefinitely.

Whereas most studies attempt to explain variations in job satisfaction among individual employees in the same company or occupation, the interest of the present paper is to explain the gross differences in work attitudes that exist among those in *different* occupations and industries. Four factors that seem useful in accounting for these differences are discussed: occupational prestige, control, integrated work groups, and occupational communities.

[2] F. H. Harbison, "Collective Bargaining and American Capitalism," in A. W. Kornhauser, Robert Dubin, and Arthur Ross, eds., *Industrial Conflict* (New York: McGraw-Hill, 1954), p. 278.

OCCUPATIONAL PRESTIGE

Occupational prestige is the one best explanatory factor in the sense that if all occupations (for which sufficient data are available) were ranked in order of extent of typical job satisfaction, and these ranks were compared with the rank order in which they partake of public esteem, the rank-order correlations would be higher than those resulting from any other factor. This is because the prestige of any occupation depends on the level of skill the job entails, the degree of education or training necessary, the amount of control and responsibility involved in the performance of the work, the income which is typically received—to mention the most readily apparent factors. Since occupational prestige as a kind of composite index partly subsumes within itself a number of factors which contribute heavily to differences in satisfaction, it is not surprising that it should be itself the best individual measure of satisfaction.

In addition, jobs that have high prestige will tend to be valued for their status rewards even when "objective" aspects of the work are undesirable; similarly, low-status jobs will tend to be undervalued and disliked.

> . . . the lowliness or nastiness of a job are subjective estimates. . . . A doctor or a nurse, for example, or a sanitary inspector, have to do some things which would disgust the most unskilled casual laborer who did not see these actions in their social context. Yet the status and prestige of such people is generally high. . . . Above all, it is the prestige of his working group and his position in it which will influence the worker's attitude to such jobs.[3]

That the actual findings on differences in job satisfactions correspond quite closely to the scale of occupational prestige has been shown in the previous section. Professionals and business executives have the highest prestige in our society; they also consistently report the highest degree of work satisfaction. According to the most thorough occupational prestige study, doctors are the most esteemed major occupational group in the United States. It is not surprising therefore that this public esteem is an important source of their satisfaction with their work:

> [For] physicians . . . work is a source of prestige. Some doctors stated that to be a physician meant that one belonged to an elite class. It meant that one associated with important people and was in a position of leadership in the community.[4]

[3] J. C. Brown, *The Social Psychology of Industry* (Baltimore: English Pelican Edition, 1954), pp. 149–150.
[4] E. A. Friedmann and R. J. Havighurst, *The Meaning of Work and Retirement* (Chicago: University of Chicago Press, 1954), p. 161.

Among non-professional or managerial employees, white-collar workers are generally more satisfied with their jobs than manual workers. Again status considerations play an important role. Even when white-collar work does not outrank manual jobs in income or skill, office workers are accorded higher social prestige than blue-collar personnel.

Although this is so, manual work seems to be viewed with greater respect in America, with its democratic frontier traditions, than in many other nations. The historic "social inferiority complex," the "sense of social subordination" of the European industrial worker, to use the words of Henri DeMan,[5] has never been well developed in the United States. We might expect, therefore, that the level of work satisfaction among manual workers would be higher in this country than in Europe. With the rapidly increasing number of attitude surveys of European workers since the war, such a comparison would be of considerable interest.

Within the world of manual work, occupational differences in satisfaction are also related to the differences in prestige that exist among various working class jobs. The higher incidence of positive work attitudes consistently found among skilled workers is not only caused by the skill factor per se; the craftsman takes pride in the fact that he is looked on with more respect in the community than the factory operative or the unskilled laborer. Moreover, those manual workers in occupations which are particularly looked down on will find difficulty in deriving overall positive satisfactions in their work. Interviewers of coal miners have remarked on the great pride with which they are shown various home improvements made possible by the higher wages of a period of prosperity, and on the sensitivity with which some miners react to the public image of the occupation, which has been, in part, created by the hostility of the mass media to the militancy of the union.

> I don't like to strike, because people all get mad at the miners then. I wish the people would realize that the miner has to live too, and not hate him when he tries to better conditions for himself. It bothers me the way people say bad things about the miners, and makes me ashamed of my job.[6]

An attempt has been made to illustrate the manner in which variations in work satisfaction among different occupations tend to follow

[5] H. DeMan, *Joy in Work* (London: George Allen and Unwin, 1929), pp. 59–60, 208–209.

[6] Quotation from an interview with a coal miner in Friedmann and Havighurst, *op. cit.*, pp. 73–76. I do not intend to give the impression that the above is a representative quotation; the typical reaction seems to be an overt rejection of the anti-union media and public image. However, it seems likely that such feelings as the above might still haunt the average worker who would never express them.

variations in occupational prestige. Although this generalization is, to an impressive extent, supported by the evidence, it does not hold unfailingly. We can note occupations with relatively high prestige whose general level of satisfaction is lower than would be expected, whereas some low-status jobs seem to be highly satisfying. This suggests that in certain cases other factors play a role even more important than status. A good test of the approach applied here is to see whether the other factors which have been advanced as critical ones can indeed account for discrepancies in the generally marked association between occupational prestige and job satisfaction.

Control

In a perceptive passage, the Belgian socialist Henri DeMan remarks that "all work is felt to be coercive."[7] The fact that work inherently involves a surrender of control, a "subordination of the worker to remoter aims," is probably what makes the relative degree of control in work so important an aspect of job attitudes. As Max Weber, the German sociologist, suggested long ago, "no man easily yields to another full control over the effort, and especially over the amount of physical effort he must daily exert."[8]

There seem to be significant cultural as well as individual differences in the need for control and independence in work. In America, where individual initiative has long been a cultural ideal, we would expect strong pressures in this direction. And we do find that surprising proportions of manual workers in this country have attempted to succeed in small business, and that for many others the idea of running a gas station or a number of tourist cabins is a compelling dream.

Lack of control over the conditions of work is most pronounced for industrial workers.

> The very evidence of his daily work life brings home to the manual worker the degree to which he is directed in his behavior with only limited free choices available. From the moment of starting work by punching a time clock, through work routines that are established at fixed times, until the day ends at the same mechanical time recorder, there is impressed upon the industrial worker his narrow niche in a complex and ordered system of interdependency . . . a system over which he, as an individual, exercises little direct control.[9]

[7] DeMan, *op. cit.*, p. 67.

[8] E. C. Hughes, *Men and Their Work* (Glencoe: The Free Press, 1959), pp. 47–48.

[9] Dubin, "Constructive Aspects of Industrial Conflict," in Kornhauser, Dubin, and Ross, *op. cit.*, p. 43.

> The factory worker is at the bottom of the bureaucratic hierarchy; he is a person for whom action is constantly being originated, but who himself originates little activity for others.[10]

At the same time, diverse factory jobs and working class occupations vary greatly in the degree of control they permit over the conditions of work: it is these variations, of which workers are keenly aware, that are most interesting for the purpose of accounting for differences in satisfaction.

The notion of control in work, as I am using it, is, of course, a vague, *sensitizing* concept which covers a wide range of phenomena rather than a concept which is precisely delimited and identifiable by precise indicators. Among its most important dimensions are control over the use of one's *time* and physical *movement*, which is fundamentally control over the *pace* of the work process, control over the *environment*, both technical and social, and control as the *freedom* from *hierarchal authority*. Naturally, these dimensions are highly interrelated; a business executive high on the occupational ladder will tend to be high in each, whereas an unskilled laborer will have little control from any of these viewpoints. *It is possible to generalize on the basis of the evidence that the greater the degree of control that a worker has (either in a single dimension or as a total composite) the greater his job satisfaction.*

CONTROL OVER TIME, PHYSICAL MOVEMENT AND PACE OF WORK. Assembly line work in the automobile industry is a good example of the almost complete absence of this aspect of control.

> Its coerced rhythms, the inability to pause at will for a moment's rest, and the need for undeviating attention to simple routines made it work to be avoided if possible and to escape from if necessary. So demanding is the line that one worker, echoing others, complained: "You get the feeling, everybody gets the feeling, whenever the line jerks everybody is wishing, 'break down, baby!' "[11]

The consensus of the work literature is that assembly line work, especially in the automobile industry, is more disliked than any other major occupation, and the prime factor in dissatisfaction with the assembly line is the lack of control over the pace of production. Workers in assembly line plants have strong preferences for jobs off the line. A study of the job aspirations of 180 men on the line found that the

[10] William Foote Whyte, *Money and Motivation* (New York: Harper, 1955), p. 234.

[11] Ely Chinoy, *Automobile Workers and the American Dream* (Garden City: Doubleday, 1955), p. 71.

"workers' motivations were not what might normally be expected. It was not promotion or transfer in order to improve one's economic status. Rather, it was primarily a desire 'to get away from the line.'" *Only 8 per cent* were satisfied, in the sense of not preferring to get an off-line job.[12] The difference between line and off-line jobs has been clearly stated by the sociologist Ely Chinoy who worked in an automobile plant and studied automobile workers:

> Work at a machine may be just as repetitive, require as few motions and as little thought as line assembly, but men prefer it because it does not keep them tied as tightly to their tasks. "I can stop occasionally when I want to," said a machine-operator. "I couldn't do that when I was on the line." Production standards for a particular machine may be disliked and felt to be excessive, but the machine operator need only approximate his production quota each day. The line-tender must do all the work that the endless belt brings before him. . . .[13]

The greater dissatisfaction with mass production assembly line jobs is confirmed by the findings in an automobile plant that "men with highly repetitive jobs, conveyor paced, and so forth, were far more likely to take time off from work than those whose jobs did not contain such job characteristics," and that quit rates were almost twice as high among men on the assembly line as among men off the line.[14] In a study of Maryland youth during the depression, it was found that the occupation most disliked by female workers was that of operator on cannery conveyor belts. Every one of the fifty-three cannery operatives in the sample expressed a preference for different work! The control of these workers over the pace of production is at least as minimal as that of automobile workers, and in addition they lack even the protection of a strong union.

A machine operator may go all out in the morning to produce 100 pieces, take it easy in the afternoon, only putting out 50; at any rate, it is his own decision. In similar fashion a few assembly line workers may be able to build up a "bank" of automobile seats which they assemble to the oncoming bodies; a few try to get ahead and gain time for rest by working up the line, but for the great majority it is hopeless. Assembly line workers are "alienated," according to the researchers who have studied them. In their work they "can secure little significant experience of themselves as productive human beings." As one automobile worker put it a little wistfully:

---

[12] C. R. Walker and Robert H. Guest, *Man on the Assembly Line* (Cambridge: Harvard University Press, 1952), pp. 113, 110.

[13] Chinoy, *op. cit.*, pp. 71–72.

[14] Walker and Guest, *op. cit.*, pp. 120, 116–117.

You understand, if you get a job that you're interested in, when you work you don't pay attention to the time, you don't wait for the whistle to blow to go home, you're all wrapped up in it and don't pay attention to other things. *I don't know one single job like that.*[15]

According to David Riesman, what these wage earners are deprived of is "any chance to extend themselves, to go all-out." A stark example is the worker on the packinghouse assembly line who goes home after his day's work in order to "try to accomplish something for that day."[16] How do these workers stand it? Here is the deadly answer of a Hormel meat worker: "The time passes."

> Most workers are so busily engaged in pushing the flow of work that they do not *consciously* suffer from the inherent monotony of their work. They are well adjusted, because they have reduced their level of aspirations to the rather low level of the job. They coast along, keeping busy, visiting, talking, making time go by, and getting the work done in order to get "out of there" in order to get home![17]

The great dissatisfaction with automobile assembly work is an example of a discrepancy between occupational status and job satisfaction. The status of the automobile worker is not lower than that of other semiskilled American factory workers; in fact, the level of wages would suggest that it is higher than manual workers in many other industrial occupations, especially those in non-durable goods manufacturing. But the control of the automobile assembly line worker over the work process is considerably less than in other major industrial occupations, and this is a big factor in accounting for the prevalence of job discontent.

It is interesting to contrast automobile manufacturing with mining, an occupation which, though considered lower in prestige, seems to provide marked work satisfaction. Alvin Gouldner, in his study of a gypsum plant, found that although the miners had considerably less status in the community than surface workers, they showed much greater work motivation. He attributed this high job satisfaction to the fact that miners

> were not "alienated" from their machines: that is, they had an unusually high degree of control over their machine's operation. The pace at which the machines worked, the corners into which they were poked, what happened to them when they broke down, was determined mainly by the miners themselves. On the surface,

---

[15] Chinoy, *op. cit.*, p. 70.
[16] Fred H. Blum, *Toward a Democratic Work Process* (New York: Harper, 1953), p. 96.
[17] *Ibid.*, p. 85.

though, the speed at which the machines worked and the procedures followed were prescribed by superiors.[18]

Finally, the higher job satisfaction of skilled workers (documented in the preceding sections of this paper) is related to the fact that they have a large measure of control over the pace of their work. The fact that craftsmen themselves largely determine the speed at which they work gives them a marked advantage over most factory workers.

CONTROL OVER THE TECHNICAL AND SOCIAL ENVIRONMENT. In those occupations in which the physical environment or the technological work process is particularly challenging, control over it seems to be an important aspect of job satisfaction. Coal-miners have "a very personal sense of being pitted against their environment" and express "feelings of accomplishment and pride at having conquered it."[19] That steel production is found fascinating is suggested by a mill worker: "It's sort of interesting. Sometimes you have a battle on your hands. You have to use your imagination and ability to figure out what move to make."[20] Similarly, it has been noted that railroad workers derive a sense of power in "the manipulation of many tons of railroad equipment." Engineers derive more pleasure in running large engines rather than small ones; switchmen and brakeman "give the signals that move fifty or so freight cars back and forth like so many toys."[21]

A further source of the dissatisfaction with automobile assembly, then, is the fact that these jobs provide so little scope for control over the technical environment; there is little that is challenging in the actual work operation. As a man on the line puts it:

> There is nothing more discouraging than having a barrel beside you with 10,000 bolts in it and using them all up. Then you get a barrel with another 10,000 bolts, and you know that every one of those 10,000 bolts has to be picked up and put in exactly the same place as the last 10,000 bolts.[22]

Paralleling the control of industrial workers over the technical environment is the satisfaction derived by professional and white-collar employees from control over a social environment, namely, clients and customers. A study of salespeople concluded that "the completion of the sale, the conquering of the customer, represents the challenge or the

[18] Alvin W. Gouldner, *Patterns of Industrial Bureaucracy* (Glencoe: The Free Press, 1954), pp. 140–141.

[19] Friedmann and Havighurst, *op. cit.*, p. 176.

[20] C. R. Walker, *Steeltown* (New York: Harper, 1950), p. 61.

[21] John Spier, "Elements of Job Satisfaction in the Railroad Operating Crafts," unpublished paper, Berkeley, California, 1959.

[22] Walker and Guest, *op. cit.*, p. 54.

'meaningful life-experience' of selling."[23] As one salesclerk, contemplating the import of his retirement, said: "I think to be perfectly truthful about it, the thing I miss most is being able to project myself into a sphere, conquer it, and retire with a pleased feeling because I have conquered it."[24]

CONTROL AS THE FREEDOM FROM DIRECT SUPERVISION. On a slightly different level of analysis is this third dimension, which refers not to the aspects of the work process under control, but rather to the locus of control. One of the most consistent findings of work research is that industrial workers consider light, infrequent supervision, "foremen who aren't drivers," a crucial element in their high regard for particular jobs and companies.

The absence of close supervision in the mines has been considered an important determinant of the miner's high level of satisfaction. And truck drivers and railroad workers, in explaining their preference for their own trades, stress the independence they experience in these jobs where the contact between employees and supervisor is so much less frequent than in factory work. As two railroad engineers put it:

> I'd work anywhere except at a shop or in the factory. Just don't like a place where someone is watching you do your work all the time. That's why I like my job on the railroad now.
> I wouldn't last three days working in a shop with a foreman breathing down my neck. Here I'm my own boss when I run the trains, nobody tells me what to do. . . .

Such impressionistic evidence is confirmed by the more systematic comparisons of Hoppock, who found that the mean job satisfaction index of railroad employees ranked only below professional men and artists; it was higher than managers, clerical workers, small business proprietors, salesmen, and storeclerks! Although railroading is a high-status industrial occupation—railroaders have historically been part of the labor aristocracy—its occupational prestige is below most white-collar occupations. On the other hand, truck driving is a lower-status manual occupation (truck drivers are classified as semi-skilled operatives by the census, and the popular stereotypes of this occupation are somewhat derogatory), and yet in the Hoppock survey the satisfaction of truck drivers outranked all industrial occupations except railroading and was approximately the same level as that of salesmen.

It is plausible that the marked discrepancy between job satisfaction and occupational status in these industries can be explained by the

[23] Friedmann and Havighurst, *op. cit.,* p. 178.
[24] *Ibid.,* p. 106.

high degree of control, especially as reflected in freedom from supervision, which the workers enjoy.

If control in the work process is a crucial determinant of a worker's subjective feelings of well-being on the job, as I am trying to demonstrate, the question whether industrial trends are increasing or decreasing these areas of control becomes quite significant. It is interesting that Faunce's recent study of an *automated* engine plant shows that various dimensions of control may not change in the same direction. Compared to work in a non-automated, non-assembly line engine plant, automation greatly decreased the worker's direct control over his machine and pace of work, and this was felt to be a source of serious dissatisfaction. On the other hand, the increased responsibility and control over a complex technical environment of automated equipment was seen as a source of greater satisfaction and heightened status. Thus, while Faunce was able to locate the elements which made for satisfaction and those which made for dissatisfaction in these jobs (his analysis seems very congruent with the present discussion), it was rather difficult to assess the overall effect of the change on work satisfaction.

Integrated Work Groups

A third factor that is important in explaining occupational differences in work satisfaction is the nature of on-the-job social relations. The technological structure of certain industries such as steel production and mining requires that the work be carried out by *teams* of men working closely together, whereas in industries such as automobile assembly the formation of regular work groups is virtually prohibited by the organization of production. There is much evidence to support the proposition that the greater the extent to which workers are members of integrated work teams on the job, the higher the level of job satisfaction.

In a steel mill in which 85 per cent of sixty-two workers interviewed were satisfied with their jobs, Charles Walker found that "the source of satisfaction most often articulated or implied was that of being part of, or having membership in, the hot mill crew." As three steel workers express it:

> (A heater helper) We work for a while, it's like playing baseball. First one fellow is up and then you have your turn at bat. We can knock off every so often and take a smoke and talk. I like working with men I know and working like a team.
> (A piercer plugger) The crew I am in is very good. Our foreman likes to see his men on top and he does everything to help us . . . this attitude makes a lot of people put out more steel. . . . Over here it's teamwork. . . . You can have a lot of Hank Greenbergs on the team but if you don't work together, it isn't a team at all. And we like our work because we carry on a lot of conversation

with signs and the men laugh and joke and the time passes very quick.

(A piercer dragout worker) There's nothing like working here in this mill. Everybody cooperates. Every man works as a member of a team and every man tries to turn out as much steel as they possibly can. We work hard and get satisfaction out of working hard.[25]

While recognizing that close kinship ties and a small town atmosphere encouraged such cooperative spirit, Walker attributed the principal cause of the integrated work teams to the basic technological process of making steel, which requires small group operations. He compared this technology and its results with that of the automobile assembly plants in which the technological structure is such that the majority of workers perform their operations individually. There, the pattern of social interaction produced by the moving line is such that although workers will talk to the man in front of them, behind them, and across from them, no worker will interact with exactly the same group of men as any other worker will; therefore, no stable work groups are formed. Walker considered this a major element in the greater dissatisfaction he found among automobile workers compared to steel workers.

Mining is another occupation where technological conditions seem to favor the development of closely knit work groups. Since, as one miner expressed it, "the mines are kind of a family affair," where "the quality of the sentiment is of a depth and complexity produced only by long years of intimate association," it is not surprising that many miners feel that the loss of social contacts at work is a major disadvantage of retirement. The dangerous nature of the work is another factor that knits miners together:

> To be an old-timer in the mines means something more than merely knowing the technique of a particular job; it also means awareness and acceptance of the responsibility which each man has for his fellow-workers. The sense of interdependence in relation to common dangers is undoubtedly an important factor in the spirit of solidarity which has characterized miners in all countries for many generations.[26]

Within the same factory, departments and jobs vary considerably in the extent to which the work is carried out by individuals working alone or by groups; the consequences of these differences have been a major interest of the "human relations in industry" movement. A recent study of one department in a factory manufacturing rotating equipment found that the employees who were integrated members of informal

---

[25] Walker, *op. cit.*, pp. 66–67.
[26] Friedmann and Havighurst, *op. cit.*, pp. 65, 90–91.

work groups were, by and large, satisfied with both the intrinsic characteristics of their jobs, and such "extended characteristics" as pay, working conditions, and benefits, whereas the non-group members tended to be dissatisfied. Sixty-five per cent of "regular" group members were satisfied, compared to 43 per cent of members of groups which were deviant in accepting less fully the values of the factory community, and compared to only 28 per cent of isolated workers.

The classic investigations of the functions of informal work groups in industry have been produced by the "human relations in industry" school, associated most directly with the Harvard Business School and the writings of Elton Mayo, and represented by the pioneering experiments at the Hawthorne plant of the Western Electric Company. These studies have demonstrated that informal work groups establish and enforce norms which guide the productive and other behavior of workers on the job, and that such management problems as absenteeism, turnover, and morale can often be dealt with through the manipulation of work groups and supervisorial behavior. But it is striking that the human relations school has concerned itself so little with the job itself, with the relation between the worker and his work, rather than the relation between the worker and his mates. A typical human relations discussion of the conditions of employee morale is likely to give all its emphasis to matters of communication, supervision, and the personality of workers and ignore almost completely intrinsic job tasks. In a recent study by the Harvard Business School entitled *Worker Satisfaction and Development*, the only sources of work satisfaction discussed are those which directly concern workers' integration in work groups and cliques. Although creativity is a major concern of the author, it is the creativity of the *work group* to adapt to new circumstances, rather than the creative expression of an individual in his work, that he is interested in.

In its emphasis on the importance of integrated work groups the human relations approach has made an important contribution. But "a way of seeing is a way of not seeing," and its neglect of the other factors imposes serious limitations on the usefulness of this approach, at least in providing an adequate theory of the conditions of work satisfaction.

Occupational Communities

The nature of the association among workers *off-the-job* is also a factor in work satisfaction. The evidence of the work literature supports the notion that levels of work satisfaction are higher in those industries and in those kinds of jobs in which workers make up an "occupational community." One such industry is mining. Not only is the actual work carried out by solidary work groups, but, in addition, miners live in a community made up largely of fellow workers. This kind of "inbreeding" produces a devotion to the occupation which is not characteristic of many other working class jobs:

> Somehow when you get into mining and you like the men you work with, you just get to the place after a while that you don't want to leave. *Once that fever gets hold of a man, he'll never be good for anything else.*
> A fellow may quit the mines, but when they whistle, he goes back. I've had a lot better jobs, but I've always liked to work in the mines. I can't explain it, except I like being with the gang; I never could just sit around much.[27]

Such occupational communities are likely to develop in occupations that are isolated, either spatially or on the basis of peculiar hours of work. Coal mining and textile industries characteristically have grown up in *isolated small communities;* sailors, cowboys, and long-distance truck drivers are also isolated from contact with persons in other jobs. Similarly, *off-hours shifts* favor the development of occupational communities; this is the case with printers, a large proportion of whom work nights, steel-workers, who often rotate between day, swing, and graveyard shifts, firemen, and, of course, railroad men.

The essential feature of an occupational community is that workers in their off-hours socialize more with persons in their own line of work than with a cross section of occupational types. Printers generally go to bars, movies, and baseball games with other printers. In a small town steel mill, 87 per cent of the workers had spent "in the last week," at least some time off the job with other workers in their department; almost half said they had seen many or almost all of their fellow workers. However, in a large tractor plant of 20,000 people only 41 per cent of the employees said that they got together socially outside the plant with employees from their own work groups. *Occupational communities rarely exist among urban factory workers.*

A second characteristic of an occupational community is that its participants "talk shop" in their off-hours. That this is true of farmers, fishermen, miners, and railroaders has been described far more by novelists than by social scientists. The significance of talking about work off the job has been well expressed by Fred Blum, who notes that the assembly line workers in the meat packing plant he studied rarely do so.

> Whether they are with their family or their friends, rare are the occasions when workers feel like talking about their work. In response to the question: "Do you talk with your friends about the work you are doing?" only a very small number indicated that they do talk with their friends—or their wife—about their work. Quite a few

[27] *Ibid.,* pp. 70–71.

said that they "only" talk with their friends "if they ask me" or that they talk "sometimes" or "seldom." Some workers are outspoken in saying that they do not like to talk about their work. "If we get out of there, we are through with that to the next day." Another worker said, "When I leave down there, I am through down there. I like to talk about something else." *He adds to this with some astonishment: "Railroadmen always want to talk about their work."*[28]

Third, occupational communities are little worlds in themselves. For its members the occupation itself is the reference group; its standards of behavior, its system of status and rank, guide conduct.

> Railroading is something more than an occupation. Like thieving and music, it is a world by itself, with its own literature and mythology, with an irrational system of status which is unintelligible to the outsider, and a complicated rule book for distributing responsibility and rewards.[29]

We can suggest a number of mechanisms by means of which occupational communities increase job satisfaction. First, when workers know their co-workers off the job, they will derive deeper social satisfactions on the job. In the second place, an effect of the isolation of the occupation is that workers are able to develop and maintain a pride in and devotion to their line of work; at the same time, isolation insulates them from having to come to grips with the general public's image of their status, which is likely to be considerably lower than their own. Participation in an occupational community means not only the reinforcement of the group's sense of general prestige; in such worlds one's skill and expertise in doing the actual work becomes an important basis of individual status and prestige. Finally, unlike the "alienated" assembly line worker, who is characterized by a separation of his work sphere from his non-work sphere—a separation of work from life as Mills and Blum put it—the work and leisure interests of those in occupational communities are highly integrated. If the integration of work and non-work is an important element in general psychic adjustment, as some assert, then these workers should exhibit higher job satisfaction, since satisfaction with life in general seems to be highly related to satisfaction in work.

CONCLUSIONS

When we read modern accounts of what work and workers were like before the industrial revolution, we continually find that the

---

[28] Blum, *op. cit.*, pp. 96–97, my emphasis.
[29] Theodore Caplow, *The Sociology of Work* (Minneapolis: University of Minnesota Press, 1954), p. 96.

dominant image of the worker of that period is the craftsman. Viewed as an independent producer in his home or small shop with complete control over the pace and scheduling of his work, making the whole product rather than a part of it, and taking pride in the creativity of his skilled tasks, his traits are typically contrasted with those of the alienated factory worker—the allegedly characteristic producer of modern society.

It is remarkable what an enormous impact this *contrast* of the craftsman with the factory hand has had on intellectual discussions of work and workers in modern society, *notwithstanding its lack of correspondence to present and historical realities.* For, indeed, craftsmen, far from being typical workers of the past era, accounted for less than 10 per cent of the medieval labor force, and the peasant, who was actually the representative laborer, was, in the words of the Belgian socialist Henri DeMan, "practically nothing more than a working beast."[30] Furthermore, the real character of the craftsman's work has been romanticized by the prevalent tendency to idealize the past, whereas much evidence suggests that modern work does not fit the black portrait of meaningless alienation. In fact, it has been asserted "that in modern society there is far greater scope for skill and craftsmanship than in any previous society, and that far more people are in a position to use such skills."[31]

For intellectuals, it seems to be particularly difficult to grasp both the subjective and relative character of monotony and the capacity of workers to inject meaning into "objectively meaningless" work. Their strong tendency to view workers as dissatisfied suggests the idea that the alienation thesis, though a direct descendant of Marxist theory and related to a particular political posture, also reflects an intellectual perspective (in the sociology of knowledge sense) on manual work.

Surprisingly enough, business executives also tend to view manual workers as alienated. Perhaps this attitude reflects, in part, the growing influence of intellectual ideas, including neo-Marxist ones, on the more progressive business circles; perhaps, more importantly, this stems again, as in the case of the intellectual, from the middle-class businessman's separation and distance from the workaday world of his industrial employees. At any rate, such industrial spokesmen as Peter Drucker and Alexander Heron are likely to generalize much as does James Worthy of Sears Roebuck, who, in discussing "overfunctionalization," has written:

> The worker cannot see that total process, he sees only the small and uninteresting part to which he and his fellows are assigned. In a

[30] DeMan, *op. cit.*, p. 146.
[31] Brown, *op. cit.*, p. 207.

real sense, the job loses its meaning for the worker—the meaning, that is, in all terms except the pay envelope.

Thus a very large number of employees in American industry today have been deprived of the sense of performing interesting, significant work. In consequence, they have little feeling of responsibility for the tasks to which they are assigned.[32]

But, *work has significant positive meanings to persons who do not find overall satisfaction in their immediate job.* A still viable consequence of the Protestant ethic in our society is that its work ethic (the notion of work as a calling, an obligation to one's family, society, and self-respect, if no longer to God), retains a powerful hold. This is most dramatically seen in the reactions of the retired and unemployed. The idea is quite common to American workers at all occupational levels that soon after a worker retires, he is likely to either "drop dead" or "go crazy" from sheer inactivity. An English industrial psychiatrist states that this is actually a common calamity in British industry. Similarly, the studies made in the 1930's of unemployed people show that the disruption of the work relationship often leads to the disruption of normal family relations, to political apathy, and to a lack of interest in social organizations and leisure-time activities.

The studies of job satisfaction reviewed in this paper further question the prevailing thesis that most workers in modern society are alienated and estranged. There is a remarkable consistency in the findings that the vast majority of workers, in virtually all occupations and industries, are moderately or highly satisfied, rather than dissatisfied, with their jobs.

However, the marked occupational differences in work attitudes and the great significance which workers impute to being, at least to some extent, masters of their destiny in the work process, along with the fact that surrender of such control seems to be the most important condition of strong dissatisfaction are findings at least as important as the overall one of general satisfaction. Perhaps the need for autonomy and independence may be a more deep-seated human motive than is recognized by those who characterize our society in terms of crowdlike conformity and the decline of individualism.

These findings also have clear implications for industrial engineering. If industry and society have an interest in workers' experiencing satisfaction and pride in their work, a major effort must be made to increase the areas of control which employees have over the work process, especially in those industries and occupations where control is at a minimum. Charles Walker, who has written perceptively of the

---

[32] James C. Worthy, "Organizational Structure and Employee Morale," *American Sociological Review*, 15 (1950), p. 175.

automobile worker's lack of control, has advocated two major solutions for humanizing repetitive assembly line work: job rotation and job enlargement. Where job rotation was introduced in one section of the automobile plant he studied, job satisfaction increased without loss of efficiency of production. The idea of recombining a number of jobs into one enlarged job seems especially to appeal to the line workers: as one man said, "I'd like to do a whole fender myself from the raw material to the finished product."[33] But such radical job enlargement would be a negation of the assembly line method of production. Therefore, we must anticipate the day when the utopian solution of eliminating assembly line production entirely will be the practical alternative for a society which is affluent and concerned at the same time that its members work with pride and human dignity.

Finally, the findings of this paper indicate a need for considerable further research on industrial statistics and industrial trends. If the evidence shows that extreme dissatisfaction is concentrated among assembly line workers, it becomes terribly important, for a total assessment of the conditions of work in modern America, to know what proportion of the labor force works on assembly lines or in other job contexts involving little control over their work activities. It is startling, considering the importance of such data, that such figures do not exist. The situation helps maintain the conventional belief that the mechanized assembly line worker is today's typical industrial worker in contrast to the craftsman of the past.

An indication that the actual proportion of assembly line workers is quite small is suggested by figures of the automobile industry, the conveyor belt industry par excellence. If we consider total employment in the industrial groupings involved in the manufacture, sales, repair, and servicing of automobiles, we find that assembly line workers make up less than 5 per cent of all workers in this complex. There are approximately 120,000 automobile workers who are line assemblers, yet the number of skilled repair mechanics in all branches of the industry, a job which in many ways resembles the craft ideal, exceeds 500,000. In addition, the 120,000 assemblers are outnumbered by 400,000 managers who own or operate gas stations, garages, new and used car lots, and wrecking yards, and by 200,000 *skilled* workers in automobile plants. Recent developments, especially automation, have served further to decrease the proportion of assembly line operatives in the industry.

If the situation in the automobile industry is at all typical, research might well show that those kinds of job contexts which are associated with high work satisfaction and control over one's time and

[33] Walker and Guest, *op. cit.*, p. 154.

destiny, such as skilled repair work and self-employment, are more representative than is commonly believed, and are even increasing over the long run. Such a prospect should bring considerable satisfaction to all those in the diverse intellectual traditions who have been concerned with what happens to human beings in the course of their major life activity, their work. And yet, this would not necessarily mean that the problem of the lack of fulfillment in work had become less serious. For as one industrial sociologist has suggested, this problem *may become more acute,* not because work itself has become more tedious, fractionated, and meaningless, but because the ideal of pride in creative effort is shared by an increasingly large portion of the labor force as a result of the rise of democratic education and its emphasis on individualism and occupational mobility.

Robert Dubin
THE INDIVIDUAL WORKER

IMPORTANCE OF WORK

There is a curious assumption that often underlies discussions of personal adjustment to work. The assumption is that all people like to work; that all people are strongly attached to their particular work or the organization employing them. The obvious consequence of this point of view is that all workers ought to be filled with zeal for their work, displaying high morale in their employment. Furthermore, if the zeal is lacking or if the morale is low, it is assumed that something is amiss and corrective action needed. This point of view assumes that all workers are a kind of homogeneous mass of work-oriented and work-interested people.

An alternative view suggests that work, like many other routine portions of life, can have varied meaning to different people. At one extreme are the people whose work and employment are the very center of life. These job-oriented people live and breathe their work and find

From Robert Dubin, *The World of Work: Industrial Society and Human Relations,* © 1958, pp. 254–258. Reprinted by permission of Prentice-Hall, Inc., Englewood Cliffs, New Jersey.

Mr. Dubin is Research Professor of Sociology, University of Oregon.

their major satisfactions and sorrows in connection with their employment. To such people everything that happens at work, or is connected with it, takes on major significance.

At the other extreme there are people whose primary orientation towards living is outside of work. These non-job oriented people may operate in a work environment to which they can be relatively indifferent regardless of its ups and downs, and regardless of its specific content. To such people the real center of life is to be found in other areas than work, perhaps the family, the church, a hobby, or recreation. In terms of many kinds of industrial occupations, it is probable that as many as three-quarters of the workers are in the non-job oriented category, as a recent study has shown.

If the industrial scene generally reflects the results of this particular study, it is evident that there are at least two major kinds of workers. There are those who are job-oriented, and those who have a community orientation. Both of these groups of people have a significant core around which they build their lives. To the first group it is the job. To the second group it is something outside the job of vital and immediate importance to them.

There is a third type of person in a marginal category who does not have any center of strong interest, either on the job, or in non-job areas. This relatively indifferent type of person is partially alienated from all the usual centers of life interest. Such people, in general are capable of operating in routine areas of life with little difficulty. However, the extent of their emotional involvement is relatively slight. They are capable of moving from one life area into another, maintaining only superficial attachment. Indifference constitutes another kind of orientation that is found in industrial and commercial employment.

WORK-ORIENTED PERSON

The work-oriented person is an individual centering his life on his job. To him the most important single institutional unit within which he operates is the work place. He is, perhaps, best characterized as finding his major satisfactions and rewards, as well as his deepest disappointments and frustrations, in connection with his work. Being job-oriented has important implications for the way in which the individual behaves on the job, and for the systems of management that secure the most effective results from him.

The job-oriented individual is much more sensitive to the incentives of his work organization; he is likely to place high values on work incentives, if they are reasonably appropriate. Furthermore, he is likely to be highly sensitive to the rules and regulations that govern the work situation. The very sense of dedication and attachment he feels for his work is likely to heighten his attention to all aspects of his job.

The work-oriented individual has built into his own viewpoint the going demands and expectations, rewards, rights, duties, and obligations, that center on the organization and its work that he is doing. He may become the "perfect" employee, embodying the ideal image of a willing and devoted worker.

The individual whose work is the center of his life is also likely to be very sensitive to the inadequacies that usually attend any job environment. By making work the center of his life, he becomes committed to adjusting to the job environment, and also to changing those aspects of the job environment that demand too much of an adjustment. In a situation conducive to dissatisfactions, the work-oriented person is likely to feel great indignation precisely because the job is so central in his life. He is the kind of individual who may be most upset if he fails to make an adequate adjustment to work, or if he considers demands of work to be improper, unjust, or impossible. The most loyal employees, and the most bitter critics of the organization, are to be found among work-oriented people.

Greater knowledge about work is one consequence of interest in it. Workers interested in their tasks are likely to become highly skilled. This suggests that supervision of work-oriented people must take into account highly developed competence and general sense of devotion to the organization. The supervision can be relatively loose in the technological area, since a job-centered worker can be assumed to have a self-interest in establishing technical competence. At the same time it is necessary that he achieve real satisfactions from work. These satisfactions can be fortified, more or less constantly, by supervisory encouragement and recognition, and other responses to a capable job well done.

Thus the work-oriented person demands less technical supervision, on the whole, but more personal interaction with supervisors. His supervisors have to confirm actually and symbolically his wisdom in choosing this work as the central interest of his life.

COMMUNITY-ORIENTED PERSON

The community-oriented person has his life centered on institutions outside the job. From the standpoint of job performance it is more or less immaterial what is the individual's real life interest. He may be a stamp collector, detective story enthusiast, devoted family man, gardener, horse-race fan, or bridge player. These are obviously not comparable kinds of interests, but they nevertheless are all charactistically pursued outside the place of employment.

The principal fact about the community-oriented individual is that his life is focused just as intensively and just as devotedly as the work-oriented person. The difference between the two lies in the fact that one makes work the center of his life while the other chooses some non-job activity.

Community-oriented workers are likely to exhibit a distinctive kind of adjustment to work. The necessity to work is accepted as conforming to social expectations. The central meaning of work is that it provides the wherewithal to pursue real life interests. Work may represent pretty largely a source of income, necessary to pursue the things that are really important. To the community-oriented individual, then, the job is viewed as a means to an end rather than as an end in itself.

As an instrument, work can be viewed with a kind of dispassionate detachment. If there is not forthcoming from work enough payoff, for example, if the income is inadequate to pursue real interests, then community-oriented individuals may become extremely dissatisfied.

In the most extreme case the individual may have such an overriding non-job interest that he will exploit his job and his employer. Such circumstances may lead to embezzlement of company funds, for example, for purposes of gambling, though this is a relatively rare phenomenon. Ordinarily the community-oriented individual does not seek to exploit either his job or his employer to satisfy his non-job interests. He is generally willing to accept the legitimate payoff from work as the instrument for achieving his non-job satisfactions.

The community-oriented person tends to be indifferent to a total evaluation of his job, and the kinds of satisfactions it gives him. To him the major gratification the job provides is money for satisfying his non-job interests. So long as these interests are satisfied, the job is viewed as adequate. It is to such individuals that management often refers in saying that they are "not interested in anything but their pay checks." This is certainly an effective characterization of an individual who sees his work as a source of income for pursuing his satisfaction and pleasure at some other point in the society.

The community-oriented person is likely to operate at a technological level of competence somewhat below that of the work-oriented person. He can perform effectively, and certainly can meet minimum job standards. However, community-oriented workers are not moved to perfect operating techniques, nor to develop skills beyond the level of job retention. At the same time, the non-job oriented person is less upset by any technological inadequacies that may exist on his job. He will be a pragmatist, not a perfectionist, with respect to maintenance of his equipment, for example.

The community-oriented person is not emotionally involved in his work to any extent. His relative indifference permits him to accept frustrating conditions with a feeling that they make relatively little difference to him. He is likely to view inadequacies in terms of their interference with his creature comfort, not as stumbling blocks to doing a good job. The community-oriented individual is essentially materialistic toward his job. So long as his material expectations of the job are satisfied, he can tolerate many inadequacies in the job situation. Such an individual can work in a dirty shop. He can work with inadequate tools. He can accept crude and unsympathetic supervision with relative equanimity.

The community-oriented person demands little personal approval and commendation. For him the amount of personal contact between supervisor and worker is slight in comparison with interaction for the work-oriented person. Indeed, the humanly warm supervisor may find himself very much frustrated by the indifferent response of community-oriented people upon whom he lavishes praise and encouragement. This helps account for the fact that many supervisors and foremen with relatively little human relations skill can nevertheless be successful; a large majority of their subordinates, community-oriented people, do not require the finesse of subtle human relations.

INDIFFERENT PERSON

The indifferent person is an individual who has not found a central area of life that commands his interest and emotional involvement. Such an individual has shallow and temporary interests and tends to change them frequently. In the more serious development of indifference, there may be actual withdrawal from most routine social contacts and situations. The end result of withdrawal is the inability to behave adequately in any social situation.

The indifferent person is the least animated of the three types of industrial workers. He has a kind of dogged, slow system of reaction, or a degree of inattention that exemplifies his indifference. Perhaps the most important single index of the indifferent person is his relatively shallow emotional response to anything.

There are many routine jobs for which the indifferent individual is acceptable or even desirable. The very fact of his indifference prevents him, for example, from reacting with boredom or frustration to a highly repetitive job. There may also be menial tasks that are of a very low status to which the indifferent individual can adjust with minimum dissatisfaction. In general, it can be suggested that there may be important niches in the organization in which indifferently-oriented people can be used very effectively.

The supervision of people with indifferent orientation entails unique problems. Supervision can be generally oriented towards a custodial approach. That is, the supervision may involve continuous visual control over the workers who are in the indifferent category. Such workers are more likely to be adequate in jobs entailing limited responsibility, with a fair degree of repetitiveness, and a short learning period. The supervision of job performance is largely a question of maintaining standards of quality and quantity. This may be relatively difficult under the circumstances of a withdrawal from significant social relations by the indifferently-oriented person. However, it is probably best maintained by an impersonal method of supervision in which the standards expected in work performance are clearly set forth, and the individual then held to them.

For the indifferently-oriented individual, failure to meet work standards is not a consequence of the competition of another set of interests. It is simply a consequence of relative inattention to any interest. Accordingly, being forced to focus attention on work is likely to produce less of a negative emotional response on the part of the indifferent person than might be true in the instance of the community-oriented person. Because of this, supervising indifferent workers will entail less of a strain on the supervisor than any other type of person.

leisure

Sidney Lens
A SHORTER WORK WEEK?

The Wobblies, whose insurgent impulse a few decades ago made life in America a bit richer, placed high on their revolutionary banner the demand for a sixteen-hour work week—four hours, four days. America is

From *Commonweal,* April 29, 1960. Reprinted by permission.

Mr. Lens, a long-time trade unionist, writes frequently on social and economic questions.

still some distance from this inviting objective, but we have the word of Vice President Nixon that the five-day, thirty-hour week is now within our reach. Tabulating the virtues of free enterprise, Mr. Nixon sees this development as an inevitable outcome of improved technology.

Undoubtedly it is. Undoubtedly too, if we live long enough, even the Wobbly objective will approach reality. Our lopsided society has a genius for technology equalled only by its blindness in utilizing its benefits.

The question, however, is do we really want a shorter work week? . . . Are we better off with thirty-five or thirty hours of work than with forty? Is it a shorter work week we really need, or a more fruitful work week?

Just posing the question may sound like rank heresy—particularly from a trade unionist. But this is probably as good a time as any to take a more penetrating look at the whole question of work and leisure. Is leisure itself an absolute virtue? Is work itself an absolute bane? Or is it the present kind of leisure, the present kind of work?

In our established value system, work is a commodity which the worker sells his boss for a week, day, hour, minute, or second. The less of the commodity he gives for the price (wage) the better off he feels he is —this is the traditional philosophy of the marketplace. If he can receive the same payment for thirty hours as he now receives for forty hours he considers it good trading. And undoubtedly it is. . . .

It is significant that almost everyone today concedes the long term certainty of a further cut in working hours. Seventy years ago, when a new and weak A. F. of L. was mounting the struggle for the eight-hour day, the Illinois *State Register* called it the "most consummate piece of humbuggery ever suggested in connection with the 'labor question.'" The staid New York *Times* insisted that "strikes to enforce the demand for eight-hours work a day may do much to paralyze industry, depress business, and check the reviving prosperity of the country, but they cannot succeed." Today, however, with a labor movement eighteen million strong, everyone knows that a shorter work schedule is inevitable. If we are to have economic stability in an era of automation we must also have a shorter work week.

The real issue, however, is whether less work will mean a happier worker. What will the workingman do with the eight or ten hours a week additional leisure? Will it help make him a more rounded, socially-oriented human being or will it cater to the child-like desire for more escapist pleasures?

Management officials, of course, argue that workers already have too much leisure. Willard Rockwell, Jr., president of Rockwell Manufacturing, claims "that the four-day week is something to be avoided as long as possible—not only for the immediate effect on our economy, but also for the ultimate demoralizing effects on our individual and national character and strength. Over-extended leisure, we firmly believe, dulls the 'cutting edge' of a man's talents, intelligence, and pride of accomplishment."

Union officials, on the other hand, heap scorn on the traditional charge that more leisure brings in its wake more drunkenness and moral decay. "The growth of leisure," says a resolution of the United Auto Workers, "means growing recognition of man as the end purpose of economic activity, for only in his leisure time is the worker truly free to follow his own purposes. . . . With the shortening of the work week, living standards have risen and not fallen; and workers have grown in stature as cultural, intellectual and spiritual beings playing an ever larger and more constructive role in their communities and the nation."

The evidence for the union argument, alas, is not quite so conclusive. There is no doubt that the worker benefited greatly not only in economic but also in human terms when his schedule was reduced from ten, twelve and fourteen hours of daily drudgery to only eight. A century ago, certainly, when he was working seventy or eighty hours a week, he had little time to pursue a cultural or political bent, and Karl Marx predicted that once the worker won reasonable hours he would become more radical and more class-conscious.

But the introduction of the forty-eight-hour week and more recently the forty-hour week have proven that Marx and many others were wrong. There is a point at which additional leisure—unless properly utilized—becomes a bane rather than a boon for the workingman. The worker uses his extra time not to study social philosophy—but to play, to escape. He does not become more rebellious but more conformist.

Daniel Bell, former labor editor of *Fortune*, writes that the average worker masks his "to-hell-with-it-all" attitude by "constant evasion of thought about work, the obsessive reveries (often sexual) while on the job, the substitution of the glamour of leisure for the drudgeries of work." It is no accident that in our literature work is so often compared to prison. Writes Aldous Huxley: "Every efficient office, every up-to-date factory is a panoptical prison in which the worker suffers . . . from the consciousness of being inside a machine."

"What are we to expect?" asks Erich Fromm in his *The Sane Society*. "If a man works without genuine relatedness to what he is doing, if he buys and consumes commodities in an abstractified and alienated way, how can he make use of his leisure time in an active and meaningful way? He always remains the passive and alienated consumer."

Living in a society that places psychotic emphasis on consumer-consciousness, the worker succumbs to the values of the marketplace rather than culture or education. In the rubber city of Akron where a six-hour, six-day week has prevailed for some time, fully fifteen or twenty per cent of the rubber workers hold down two jobs. These "moonlighters" either work on a second shift in another rubber factory or as taxi drivers, bellhops, garage attendants, clerks, barbers or butchers. Nationally, more than one of every twenty workers, 3.7 million in all, have second and sometimes third jobs. The shorter week for them does not bring with it more meaningful leisure but only an opportunity to make more money.

If the work week is reduced from forty to thirty hours, will there be less or more moonlighters? The chances are that the number will increase considerably, for the simple fact is that the average worker does not know what to do with his time.

Melvin Maddocks, writing in the *Christian Science Monitor,* pointed out more than a year ago that "the mythical 'average adult' watches television sixteen hours a week, perhaps a third to a half of available leisure time." Our populace spends three times as much each year in buying T.V. and radio sets as on the theater, concerts, opera and books combined. "Television viewing at the saturation level virtually becomes a substitute for living."

This is the salient characteristic of leisure in modern America—it is a "substitute for living," rather than a means of better living. It results not in reading good books, going to concerts, studying sociology or biology in night classes, but in bowling, sports, television, and lurid paperbacks.

The labor movement is thus in a trap, one at least partly of its own making. It can and will eventually win the shorter work week—and it should. But based on its present philosophy it can not help the worker to convert those additional hours to "meaningful experience."

George Meany and most labor leaders still talk of "more" rather than "better." Unmindful of the fundamental changes these past few decades to bigness, centralization and alienation, they seek more wages alone rather than a better utilization of money; more leisure time rather than a better utilization of leisure time. Beguiled by the value patterns of our "free enterprise" economy they assume glibly that if you just keep adding to labor's benefits you will somehow solve all major problems. They continue to live in the past when labor was still struggling for a "living wage" and for time to relax.

Admittedly tens of millions of workers are still in need of a living wage—the two million unorganized agricultural workers, the many millions of white collar, retail and service workers. But most organized workers in the basic industries have passed this stage. . . . What they need now is some guidance on what to do with both their money and their time. It is here that the labor movement fails abysmally. It has no program for what to do next.

How, then, do you make work more palatable? Or leisure more meaningful? The Norwegian labor movement is making a special study of the subject. In Yugoslavia the Titoists argue that workers' councils and self-management of factories and other economic units are the answer. Daniel Bell in the United States suggests something less drastic: that the unions fight to end the management practice of measuring value of labor in terms of efficiency and time study. Under his suggestion we would slow the pace of production somewhat and give the individual worker more operations to perform so as to make work less monotonous.

As one contribution to the discussion I would like to suggest that the first step towards economic humanism should be a reunification of work and education. Under this thesis we would continue the forty-hour week but devote five, ten or fifteen hours to adult education.

It may be difficult to adjust our social spectacles to this "unrealistic" idea, but experiments along these lines have been going on in Europe for some years. One of the outstanding of these, Boimondau, involves a watch case factory in France. The original owner, Marcel Barbu, decided after France's defeat by Hitler in 1940 to establish a "Community of Work" with a common ethical basis. He paid little heed to the former occupation of the men he recruited for this special venture so long as they agreed to search for a system of management where the "distinction between employer and employee would be abolished." Both he and his new associates understood that common ownership and joint managership of the productive facilities was not enough. They explain their principle in the following words: "We do not start from the plant, from the technical activity of man, but from man himself. . . . In a Community of Work accent is not on *acquiring* together, but on *working* together for a collective and personal fulfillment." In discussing what they meant by personal fulfillment the first thing they listed was education. They vowed that whatever time they could save through improvements in productivity they would devote to educating themselves.

After only a few months the men of Boimondau became the most efficient watch-case makers in France. But they neither shortened their work week nor raised their wages (they were already earning ten to twenty per cent above union rates). Instead they added nine hours a week of education to their job. They continued to be present in the factory forty-eight hours (the prevailing work week in France at that time), but they put in only thirty-nine hours of physical labor. The other nine were spent inside the plant taking courses in engineering, physics, literature, Marxism, Christianity, grammar, dancing, singing and basketball.

In addition the group bought a 235-acre farm and each member and his family spent three ten-day periods each year working on the land. This too was part of the theory of "fulfillment"; no man, they felt, should be entirely divorced from the soil. Considering that the men had a month's vacation, this meant a total work year at the factory of only ten months, all of it designed to utilize more fully the worker's talents and widen his horizons.

Obviously, a small experiment such as Boimondau or that of the one hundred other communitarian societies in Europe can not automatically be fitted for broader application. Many other problems come into play when applied to large units. Yet the concept of combining work and education does seem to have universal merit. It can be an effective antidote against the consumption-mania and escapism of our times. It can rescue the individual from manipulation by Madison Avenue and big centralized institutions. It can revive his feeling of social responsibility.

In putting such a plan into practice in the United States we would have to anticipate many difficulties. At Boimondau the participants wanted to combine work and education. They didn't have to be forced to attend classes. In the U.S., with escapism so prevalent, a worker given a choice between a biology class and Red Skelton would choose to go home and listen to Skelton. How then will you get him to stay in the shop to study economics or history or biology? Will you apply compulsion? Obviously no man can learn anything if he doesn't want to.

But this problem is not as insuperable as it seems. The factory of the future might reward a worker not only for what he produces in the way of goods but for what he does to enlarge his own personality. He might be given good marks and poor marks, much like an adolescent, and if this were not incentive enough he might have to be monetarily penalized for poor study and rewarded for good. Gradually, as education and work become part of an integral process and the worker begins once again to understand both work and education in relation to the totality of life, this problem would disappear.

A second difficulty we can anticipate is who would control the education. If it were the state we might have a further intensification of the trends toward conformity. If it were the employer or groups of employers we can be certain that nothing controversial, liberal or radical would be taught. If it were the union leaders exclusively, without any checks and balances, we might also have too restrictive an educational system. The answer, it seems, is to develop a semiautonomous institution, modelled, for instance, on the Danish Folk High Schools, with representatives from the teachers, the rank and file, the unions, perhaps even the employers, guiding policy—but with the teachers given wide latitude in academic matters. This system is in effect now in many union health centers. The unions handle the administrative end of the operation, but the doctors have the final, unchallenged voice in all medical matters. This problem too would be mitigated as the values of society, labor unions, and the rank-and-file workingman make a fundamental turn in the direction of humanism.

Another difficulty that is inherent in this plan is what to do about the small factory or the small economic unit. Yet by combining small units (say by putting together the elevator operators, janitors, carpenters and office girls in a building into one group) or by organizing separate classrooms removed from the place of work and paying "travel time" to them, this problem can also be solved. Indeed, no difficulty need be overpowering once there is a reorientation of our value system.

History, I think, is completing a circle. In primitive society, under the tribal system, education and work are one and the same. Men learn about the earth, the stars, and their surroundings in the course of hunting, fishing, plowing. Their living standards in this period are very low, but—contrary to the egotistical estimate of our Western society—their social values are very high. None of our present-day societies places such emphasis on brotherhood as the tribal society. No tribesman will permit members of his clan or tribe to starve while there is any food available. He will help his kinsman in this or any other emergency as a matter of course.

As society becomes more complex, however, work and education tend to separate. Specialization begins. Society stratifies into classes and occupations. In our historical epoch, diversification and division of labor have reached their ultimate pinnacle. From this diversification we have achieved the greatest material benefits known to history, but we have paid a price for it. To stimulate "drive" we have over-emphasized individualism and individual initiative in our set of values, as against collective effort and collective concern. We have yet to find a tolerable balance between the two human drives. Every Sunday we espouse Christianity, but on Monday brotherhood flies out the window, particularly in the work shop. There, it is each man for himself and devil take the hindmost. It is efficiency that counts, not humanity.

Our educational "advance" reflects this. As the factory system matured, society found itself in need of rudimentary education. A literate working class was needed to read blueprints, instructions, safety notices on time clocks and so on. Free and compulsory education was won in America not only because of the agitation of the labor parties back in the 1820's but also because a complex society could not exist without it.

In the twentieth century, as the managerial class expands, this need has become still more pronounced. The tendency is for youngsters to go to school for longer periods if they are to make a career for themselves. A generation ago high school was considered adequate for most; now increasingly it becomes college. As Vance Packard points out in *The Status Seekers* you can hardly get a good white collar job any more unless you have a college degree.

Despite the increase in schooling, education seldom continues beyond early adulthood. For the average workingman schooling ends with high school. From that point on until he dies he does little more in any formal way to probe the mysteries of the universe. A generation ago, under the stress of unfavorable economic circumstances, many men educated themselves after leaving school. But this is a phenomenon obviously in decline as the nation enjoys a more propitious economic climate.

The tragedy of this development can not be stated in statistics. Our democracy is changing from a participative one to a manipulative one. We live in our escapist world, while we submit to direction by big politicians, big businessmen, big union leaders. We ourselves don't try to deal with the great problems of the day. We take our politics, if at all, in mild five-minute T.V. speeches around election time. We choose those men who are most "marketable," those who present the best father image, or who can put forth the most time-worn conventional wisdoms. We eschew bad news, we avoid problems. Lured by ten and one-half million dollars in Madison Avenue advertisements and public relations programs, we prefer play to education and consumption to knowledge.

The question of a shorter work-week therefore dovetails into these other and broader social problems. Merely shortening the hours of labor solves only the traditional economic problem of technological unemployment. It doesn't even touch the bigger one of human values. In that sphere it actually aggravates the problem unless more is done.

Certainly union officials ought to fight for a shorter work-week, but they ought not to lose sight of the fact that this is only a minor goal that may have to be reversed tomorrow. If the combination of education and work were to achieve its purpose we might have a situation where men actually demanded more "work"—more time for education, less time for escapism.

I am not suggesting that combining work and education is a total answer to de-humanized society, to the mass-man and organization-man. But it is an important first step.

Dan Wakefield
LABOR SHUDDERS AT LEISURE

The burden of leisure, long the exclusive curse of the rich, is now the darkest threat to the well-being of the working man and the subject of increasing concern on the part of organized labor. A recent national conference on "The Shorter Work Week and the Constructive Use of Leisure Time," sponsored by the AFL-CIO Community Service Committee, brought together union delegates from throughout the country. They heard the professional advice of cultural medicine men and grappled with the growing problem of leisure, which, as a union instruction sheet frankly warned, may turn out to be "the great emptiness." Labor's struggle with leisure has only begun, and there seems no doubt that it will prove to be a far more sinister and formidable enemy than Harry Bennett's goon squad.

For the first time in its history, organized labor is working for a shorter workweek than its leaders or its members actually want. In reluctantly adopting the goal of a thirty-five-hour week as part of its national policy in 1962, the AFL-CIO made clear that its drive was undertaken as a means of insuring more jobs in the age of automation rather than out of a desire or need for more free time for the laborer. George Meany has explained that "no one—certainly not the AFL-CIO— maintains that under ordinary circumstances forty hours a week are excessive on the grounds of health, safety or undue restriction of leisure time. On the contrary, the labor movement would be delighted if forty hours of work were available to all who wanted them." Fully aware of the problems posed by more free time, the labor movement is in the ironic position of trying to arm its members against this menace which, at the same time, it must work to bring down on them. The goal of the shorter workweek in 1963 has become the lesser of two evils, rather than a good in itself.

So far even the promise of more jobs created by more leisure, and the AFL-CIO educational campaign to win support for it, has failed

From *The Nation*, April 20, 1963. Reprinted by permission.
Mr. Wakefield is the author of *Revolt in the South* and *Island in the City*.

to inspire most people to take up the terrible burden of free time. The labor movement has to convince not only the boss of the wisdom of shorter hours, but also the workers. According to latest statistics, the majority of union men and their wives are opposed to the thirty-five-hour week: a Gallup poll showed that only 29 per cent of the population as a whole, and only 42 per cent of union people, favored it. As one speaker informed the AFL-CIO conference, leisure needs a new "image." Perhaps an appropriate slogan for the needed campaign might be: "Fun can be fun."

The union delegates dispatched to the Hotel Commodore in New York to grapple with this unwieldy problem were given a factual briefing by George Gallup, whose statistics on what people do with the free time they now have went far to explain why they don't want any more of it. The principal answer of most Americans for filling the void of their nonwork hours can be given in a single predictable word: television. "The typical family in this country uses its television set between four and five hours a day," Dr. Gallup reported. With time for working, commuting, eating and sleeping, that just about takes care of the day. Dr. Gallup elaborated: "Every seven out of ten adults tell us that they watch Westerns regularly." This ought to make clearer why people don't want more free time. Surely people see enough cowboys as it is, and the thought of having to watch more must certainly be depressing. Dr. Gallup also revealed what people *don't* do with their free time, leading us through that familiar, but somehow always surprising, terrain of our intellectual Gobi that remains so magnificently unmarked by all the talk of "cultural explosions" and the number of new symphony orchestras in North Dakota. Two-thirds of all adults in the United States have not read a book in the previous year; only one in six knows of a book he would like to read; and, in spite of all our newspapers, magazines and libraries, we still have fewer of all of them per capita than does Western Europe. Only 54 per cent of Americans who have gone to high school or college know what the Bill of Rights is, and less than half the country's voters have heard of Barry Goldwater.

Dr. Gallup was not depressed by these discoveries of his, however, and confided to the conference that "I trust I am not one who is guilty of placing too much emphasis on book learning." In the course of polling Americans for three decades, a mission which might seem to have driven a weaker man to expatriation, the pollster said he had found our people to be "wonderfully endowed by what is best described as horse sense."

Dr. Gallup suggested that this native horse sense be applied to voluntary work on community problems as a means of occupying leisure time. He revealed that his aides had asked people throughout the country whether they would "serve on a committee which would deal with some local problems such as housing, recreation, traffic, health and the like . . ." and although 39 per cent weren't interested, 61 per cent said they were. Filling up time by committee work on civic problems was hopefully pushed by a number of speakers, and Leo Perlis, AFL-CIO Community Service Director, prescribed that "public service can be the best medicine for the new leisure class—the gainfully employed with time on their hands."

But getting people to take their medicine is another problem. The union delegates who met in daily discussion groups had to face the practical matter of taking the ideas of the high-level speakers back to their own locals, and their questions about the theories and suggestions were necessarily hard-headed. As one delegate told his discussion group, "If I went home and told my union how to use their free time, I'd be out." Another delegate sympathized with this problem and asked, "How are you going to get people to do these things like public service? It's not putting money in their pockets, and its their own free time."

One of the most popular uses of free time for workers who have won shorter hours is getting another job that will in fact put money in their pockets, and this practice of "moonlighting"—frowned on by the labor movement—was explained by a number of the discussion participants. "I think what we need," said one, "is not the thirty-five-hour-week, but the seventy-hour week. Maybe then we could pay off all our mortgages." "That's right" said a man across the table, "We're mortgage-poor. We need more jobs."

But it is difficult enough these days to find *one* job, and what would doubtless be the most popular answer to leisure on the part of workingmen—more wage work—simply isn't open to most of them. Whether or not they can be persuaded to take nonpaying volunteer jobs is a tenuous question, and certainly is not the whole answer to "helping our people fill up their time," as one discussion leader put it. One of the expert speakers said it was necessary to create a kind of smörgasbord of leisure opportunities that the men could choose from, and, as one discussion leader later explained more forcefully, "We've got to create this smörgasbord that will tempt the guys to get off their duffs." But the smörgasbord so far is not very tempting.

Aside from public-service work in the community, the only other major "medicine" suggested for the pains of leisure was that great and mysterious thing variously described as "culture," "the arts" and "the finer things of life." On hand to push this highly touted, but still slow-moving, product was August Heckscher, President Kennedy's roving cultural commissar. Mr. Heckscher said that the answer to "a rewarding leisure . . . depends in no small measure upon the degree to which we can make the arts a significant part of our free time." Not only did Mr. Heckscher suggest that we all might learn to dance, draw, sing, "act with spirit" and write a poem, but that labor should take on the role of patron of the arts. "Would it not be a fitting and exciting development if we should see a great labor union sponsoring a fine orchestra or repertory theatre which would travel about the land into cities and communities hungry for the great revelations of art?"

The union men at the discussion group I attended after this speech did not seem to think so.

"Who says we have to have an interest in these so-called cultural arts?" one delegate asked with considerable fervor. "Id like to know who's behind this, saying we ought to like these continental things like art and ballet dancing. Is it because the Russians have a ballet troop in Havana now? I like the American way of doing things. I like to watch TV and spend an afternoon chasing a golf ball."

"That's right," a fellow delegate added. "They can't cram this stuff down people's throats. You have to get it in school. It's like olives— you gotta develop a taste for it."

The idea of the labor movement's actually sponsoring these "continental" pastimes—for instance by acting as patron to symphonies and theatre groups—was even more passionately opposed as a matter of pride than on grounds of preference. A delegate from Baltimore pointed out that "These architects and artists look down on the workingman just like doctors and lawyers do. And the same with the performing artists. The AGVA local didn't even join our Central Labor Council; they don't even want to brush shoulders with us. And yet we're supposed to support culture. I say let them do their own crusading in the labor movement. If the cultural arts want to make any headway with labor they better get active in the AFL-CIO."

The popular reaction against the "so-called cultural arts" at this discussion group stirred the most feeling and general agreement of any topic I had heard taken up at the conference. After the session ended, I asked the group's discussion leader about it and he explained with some discouragement that "Art is a dirty word to a lot of these fellows. It's a very touchy subject. You see, it sounds to a lot of them like getting in bed with management."

This, of course, is the feeling of many union members, but does not reflect the opinions of their own union "management." In fact, the AFL-CIO's Leo Perlis held a press conference asking for the "establishment of a United Arts Fund for the purpose of financing culture and the arts." Perlis said that such a fund in every community would "advance the cultural renaissance spearheaded by the White House."

After hearing it discussed, however earnestly and well-mean-ingly, the problem of leisure seems even more depressing than before. Faced with taking cultural "medicine" and serving on committees to solve local traffic problems, one is tempted to open a cold can of beer and turn to *Have Gun, Will Travel.*

Part Two
Labor's Involvement

4
Is There Still a Labor Movement?

In the last several years a new criticism of unions has been heard in the United States. The attack has not come from the traditional critics of organized labor—businessmen and conservative ideologists—but from friends, or at least former friends, of labor. It has come chiefly from men who were once active in unions, many of them in staff positions at high organizational levels. They are saying that unionism in the United States is no longer a major force for social progress; that, in simple language, the labor movement is dead. This view of unionism needs to be put into perspective.

The first point to be made is that the criticism rests partly on the premise that there once was a very much alive labor movement. Perhaps there was, but, if so, this fact needs more historical exposition than it has been given. Indeed, this chapter might be aptly titled "Was There Ever a Labor Movement in America?"

The aforementioned critics believe that there was, that it was born in the depression of the 1930's and existed for some time thereafter, and that its lifeblood was a zeal for sweeping social reform. If that was the actual goal of labor in the thirties, it represented an abrupt change from the bread-and-butter, here-and-now orientation which had characterized American labor previously. It is quite possible that what looked like a movement in the thirties was, in fact, just an exhilarating experience, brought about by a temporary congruence between the mood of the times and the visions of the reformers. The blending of the mood and visions was fostered by the emergence of young and vigorous union leaders, by legislation which encouraged them, and by a seemingly enthusiastic worker response. But as employment expanded, wages rose, and union leaders aged, the earlier mood disappeared and only the visions remained in the 1940's. In short, we are suggesting that American labor has never been committed to broad societal reform; and that those who believe it was possess an illusion created by their own wishful thinking.

Our second point is suggested by the first: much of the current criticism of the limited goals of organized labor stems from highly personal views held by the critics of what constitutes the "good life" in America. We mention this primarily because those writing about what unions "ought" to be doing don't always make clear their personal relationship to their recommendations. Programs for social action based on personal values are common and legitimate, but their manner of presentation should not imply that these programs were universally accepted by labor leaders before they strayed from the anointed path, so to speak.

A third point on this issue is that unions are sometimes attacked through the institution of collective bargaining. This is not surprising. It is the preoccupation of U.S. trade unions with collective bargaining that has tended to keep their attention away from broader social goals. Criticism of collective bargaining, by suggesting that it is no longer a potent force for social progress, implies that unions have misplaced this preoccupation. The criticism is inappropriate, however. One may hold that unions should have greater social consciousness, but this has little to do with the effectiveness of collective bargaining in our industrial society. As Jack Conway explains in the third article, collective bargaining is a neutral activity designed essentially to facilitate employer-worker accommodation to one another. Its role is limited. It should not be subjected to criticism more appropriately addressed to other areas of union activity or other institutions in the society.

This attempt to place the current attacks on labor unions in perspective is not meant to imply that the liberal critics of unions do not deserve some attention. On the contrary, the bulk of their criticism remains unanswered. It is alleged that organized labor has become complacent, bureaucratic, and even irrelevant to the larger society; that it is concerned only with its own members and not with the unorganized, the unemployed, or the public as consumers. Unions, it is argued, should be more concerned with minority groups, the poor, and the developing nations of the world.

We do not pretend to know whether these are appropriate, or even justifiable, criticisms. Ultimately, union leaders and members must appraise their validity. It does appear, however, that unions in this country are at an important, if not critical, juncture. Either they react to the criticism directed against them or they take a permanent place alongside many other organized groups that are prosperous and efficient but essentially limited in their roles.

Paul Jacobs and Herbert Harris, in the first two selections of this chapter, present the case for the prosecution—they argue that unions today are not meeting their social responsibilities. In the third selection, Jack Conway defends the unions and the institution of collective bargaining. Finally, Gus Tyler suggests a program for the future.

Paul Jacobs
OLD BEFORE ITS TIME: COLLECTIVE BARGAINING AT 28

Some symptoms of the breakdown of collective bargaining are obvious and attract immediate attention. Others remain obscure. But all point toward two fundamental alterations in industrial society today: first, the system of collective bargaining, which has operated successfully since the passage of the Wagner Act twenty-eight years ago in 1935, has proved less and less adequate for the solution of some basic problems now faced by unions and management, and, second, an increasing number of workers remain outside the system, with very little possibility that they will ever come into it.

Union-management collective bargaining could not and did not end the New York newspaper strike nor the dramatic strike of airline flight engineers; it cannot and will not resolve the national collision of the railroads with the railroad unions, for in that confrontation an industry with declining revenues desperately seeks relief far beyond the scope of collective bargaining: it proposes that the unions with which it deals bargain their members out of jobs and their organizations out of existence.

Excerpted from Paul Jacobs, *Old Before Its Time: Collective Bargaining at 28*, Santa Barbara, California, © The Fund for the Republic, 1963.
Mr. Jacobs wrote this essay while staff director of the Study of the Trade Union, sponsored by the Center for the Study of Democratic Institutions, Santa Barbara.

So, too, the once-proud coal miners of Pennsylvania, now learning to bend over sewing machines, and the once-skilled packing-house workers of Chicago, now sloshing suds on auto headlights in car-wash sheds, are visible and tragic human symbols of the limits of traditional collective bargaining.

Automation and the *particular* unemployment it brings to a *particular* plant are problems obviously beyond the capabilities of union-management collective bargaining. No one can reasonably expect management to continue employing unneeded workers, but no one can reasonably expect unions to concede that they and their members have become superfluous. No one can expect management to absorb all the costs of moving and training displaced workers, but no one can expect the workers to bear those costs themselves. And so the problem of automation and particular unemployment cannot be kept inside the confines of traditional collective bargaining; the government must share the responsibility for its solution, and perhaps assume the major share. True, machines have made workers unemployed before, but it has never happened at such a rate. Even if the rate were not so alarming, America has passed the point where workers who become unemployed through no fault of their own can be left to shift for themselves and somehow to scrabble out a miserable existence.

The perpetual ice age brought on by the cold war has also imposed new limits on union-management collective bargaining in the growing number of military industries. One of the first acts carried out by Arthur Goldberg after he became Secretary of Labor was to force an end to the disputes that had been plaguing production in the missile industry. In the entire aerospace complex, some form of government intervention occurs the moment a serious dispute flares up. Within the Defense Department the division to help avert labor-management disputes that threaten production of military goods or to bring the pressure of the Department to end those that do erupt has been strengthened. Only a truncated form of collective bargaining exists in these cold war industries.

Just as the permanent cold war has become accepted as a fact of our lives, so the permanent unemployment of millions seems on its way toward being accepted as natural and normal. While collective bargaining cannot be blamed for an economy that moves from "stagnant" to "sluggish" to "moderate," and back again, unemployment has the effect of weakening bargaining by taking more and more people out of its purview. The union means very little to the unemployed lumber worker of the Northwest who sits in the state employment office waiting for a job that will not come. The millions of inexperienced teen-agers leaving school today to look for jobs that do not exist never even have the opportunity to join unions, and in a few years they will be only unskilled and unemployed adults for whom the process of collective bargaining will have no significance or meaning. . . .

If unions have no members they cannot function, and if they do not function neither does collective bargaining. It is true that the shifts in the employment pattern are no more the responsibility of the unions than is unemployment. Nevertheless, unions must accept the responsibility for not attempting to overcome the dangerous consequences of the shift and for not attracting into membership any sizable number of the white-collar and technical employees who are rapidly replacing the blue-collar workers. Even apart from these professional and technical workers, an increasing number of production employees also show little enthusiasm for union membership. Just as one example, the union shop elections held [in 1962] in the aerospace industry (elections once considered so certain to be decided in the union's favor that the original provision of the Taft-Hartley Act requiring them was dropped at the suggestion of Senator Taft) ended in a defeat for the United Auto Workers and the International Association of Machinists.

These fundamental changes in the nature of the work force and in the attitude of workers toward unions have received more recognition outside the unions than inside them, despite their weakening effect on unions and consequently on collective bargaining. As late as May, 1962, George Meany, AFL-CIO president, was saying, "Some people are worrying about the future of the American trade union movement, complaining that we don't have the same zeal, the same drive we had in the early days. Well, things have changed since those early days. We are perhaps more businesslike and maybe we don't get as excited." But, he maintained, "the American trade union movement is not dying of dry rot, it is not suffering from hardening of the arteries . . . it is very much awake and very much alive."

The contrast between these sentiments and reality is startling. Meany seems unaware not only of present-day attitudes of workers toward unions but even of what is going on inside his own office building. There the social dynamism that once attracted idealistic men and women to union service has dribbled away to such a degree that recruiting union professionals becomes more difficult each year, and many of those who remain would leap at the opportunity to follow their former colleagues into the service of the government.

In retrospect, it is possible to see why the social energy that made unions so attractive in the late Thirties has now disappeared, to the detriment of the bargaining system. World War II and the cold war converted unions from a militant stance to unquestioning acceptance of the status quo. Although union membership doubled during the war, reaching more than 13,000,000 by 1945, the new members knew little and cared less about past history. Since the war, the political and economic role of the unions has been one of continuous and unquestioning alignment with the national authority. The expulsion of the Communist-dominated unions from the CIO was carried out not only because CIO leaders believed the Communists were manipulating the unions they controlled to further the interests of the Soviet Union, but also because anti-labor feeling among the public was high and the CIO felt that the Communist stigma might seriously damage its reputation. Although both reasons were good ones, an inevitable consequence of the expulsions was to bring all serious political debate inside the CIO to a standstill. In some unions it became a habit to brand as a Communist anyone who opposed the leaders, and unions could be counted on to give automatic approval to any action undertaken by the government in its struggle with world communism. Thus, ultimately, the stakes that unions developed in the economy extended to the political arena and made them prisoners of the present rather than innovators of the future.

Labor leaders show very little concern over the weakening of the links that once held liberals and labor together. Neither do they seem very troubled because the favored position unions once held among social welfare groups has been lost. This lack of social vision, as well as the change in the nature of the work force and the problems engendered by automation in a stagnant economy, have been analyzed at great length in a variety of public forums for the past five years. All three factors, developing at about the same time, have been causes for the breakdown of collective bargaining. But it is not only the failure of the unions to adapt to the new circumstances that has contributed to the present crisis: the past economic success of unions and a lag in the public understanding of the role that unions play in a technological society have also been important factors in the present failure of bargaining.

Past union success in the economic area does not mean that labor has acquired too much power vis-à-vis the employer and that the pendulum must now swing back to favoring management. In fact, unions have too little power of the proper kind. They cannot cope with automation or unemployment using economic tools. Their goals are too narrowly economic at a time when economic power is relatively useless and when a much wider spectrum of political goals is called for.

During the early part of the nineteenth century trade unions were oriented to political reform. And in 1886, when the AFL was organized, its constitution clearly demonstrated a belief in the existence of an American working class with a special identity and a special role: "Whereas," read the preamble to the first AFL constitution, "a struggle is going on in all the civilized world between the Capitalists and the

Laborers which grows in intensity from year to year. . . ." But as the economic strength and power of unions grew during the first fifty years of the twentieth century, their commitment to political goals grew progressively weaker.

It is true that because workers were often still at the mercy of employers the struggle of the unions for better economic conditions gave them moral strength even without commitment to political reform. When workers were being shot or imprisoned for trying to organize or for striking, it was not just money but justice that was at stake. Before there were unions, an employee was at the mercy of supervisors, from foreman on up to the company president. Before there were unions, a worker could have been fired for reasons that ranged from being injured on the job to not lending money to the foreman. He worked the hours set by the employer under conditions determined by the employer. Then unions came in to establish the first condition of industrial justice: bilateral determination of wages and working conditions, bilateral determination of discharges. These issues were moral issues.

By now, however, that fight is over for the most part, and the unions, having played the decisive role in bringing industrial justice to the plants, have found nothing to take the place of their moral fervor. Unions are now part of the industrial system. Once the resistance of employers to unionization ceases at the level of principles, the union, through its contracts, becomes part of the plant government, not only a force for justice but also an integral part of the system of authority needed to operate the plant. . . .

No precise predictions can be made about the long-term replacement for the obsolescent tool of traditional collective bargaining. The development of social institutions is so continuous and changing a process, so susceptible to unforeseeable pressures, and so dependent upon the imagination of man that it is impossible to do more than hazard a few guesses.

One development probably will be the replacement of crisis negotiations between unions and management, carried on under the tremendous pressure of contract deadlines, with continuous bargaining under the watchful eyes of public representatives. The process of continuous negotiation would actually be an extension of the daily resolution of conflict that takes place now at the shop level. Gradually, also, unions may give up the right to take certain kinds of strike actions against employers, but the speed and willingness with which this takes place will depend directly on how willingly corporations give up what they have always considered their sacred rights to set unilaterally the size of the work force and to determine the distribution of profits. Some national consensus about both jobs and profits will have to emerge, however, before unions or workers will ever abandon the right to certain strikes.

The place of unions in the structure of industrial justice will continue to grow smaller unless unions return to the political function that once was primary with them. They will need to design new political tools and new forms of political participation, for it is clear that future union-management relations will depend less and less on sheer economics and more and more on political instruments and political techniques. When the potential of unions was being more fully realized, it was not just the legal right to strike that made them unique. So long as their economic function brought dignity to workers like the men and women who comprise Miscellaneous Culinary Workers Local 110, unions rightly commanded the respect of the community and the allegiance of their members. Unions freed workers from worrying about being fired arbitrarily. They provided the means for many workers to hurdle the barrier raised by lack of formal education and to become eminent citizens. They instilled the principles of industrial justice so deeply in the society that no one seriously questions them any longer.

Now unions must move on from the simple economic level. In Israel, in the Scandinavian countries, in England, and in many other foreign lands unions are an integral part of the political system, not onlookers as they are in America where the simplistic AFL tradition of rewarding friends and punishing enemies in the political arena is still dominant. The tragedy of American unions is that they who did so much to create the old collective bargaining system are taking so minor and unimportant a role in developing a new one. It may mean their death.

Would it be a tragedy if American unions disappeared? Would they be missed? The answer can only be yes to both questions. Unions have the potential to be a unique political force: they are the only institutions in society that bind together men who spend an important part of their lives together, sharing the common experience of work. If unions disappear, industrial justice may survive, but their absence will be felt, not just among workers like the Local 110 "catchers" on the dishwashing machines but among all the people of America.

Herbert Harris
WHY LABOR LOST THE INTELLECTUALS

The American labor movement is sleepwalking along the corridors of history. At every step it is failing to adapt effectively to the innovations which science and technology daily impose upon our ways of work. Lacking boldness in social invention, it clings on the whole to precepts which run the gamut from static to archaic.

Typical are its responses to automation. Labor spokesmen keep pressing for the shorter work week. But this dubious palliative tends to raise labor costs and thus makes the new robotism more attractive than ever to management. Then to console the displaced worker who can rarely find anything else to do, union negotiators concentrate on larger lump sums in severance pay. This emphasis, in effect, turns the labor movement into a mortician preoccupied with arrangements for his own funeral.

In no small degree this state of affairs derives from the fact that the labor movement has been losing its minds. Ever since World War II, it has been estranging the people who produce, distribute, and conspicuously consume ideas. Intellectuals have been increasingly disengaged as labor activists and disenchanted as sympathizers. Many of them no longer regard the labor movement as protector of the underdog, pioneer of social advance, keeper of the egalitarian conscience. Merely to ask whether the labor movement has "failed" the intellectuals, or the other way round, is to start a donnybrook at any national union headquarters or university conference on industrial relations. The point may be moot and is still obscured by feelings of mutual guilt.

But there is no doubt that the cleavage between labor and the intellectuals accounts, more than anything else, for the present crisis in the labor movement, the erosion of its vitality and its membership rolls, and its prickly defensiveness toward even the friendliest critics.

The roster of intellectuals who have lately left labor payrolls for posts in government, academia, and elsewhere is formidable. . . .

In the main . . . highly qualified people are leaving the labor movement in search of more challenge and scope for their talents. Some of them need more money (union staff people are usually underpaid); others are tired of being treated like second-class citizens. The sense of disillusionment which pervades this exodus was summed up by one of this group. "When it's implied," he said, "that it's the facts that have erred, not the figures, but the social and economic facts, and that the old ways are as good today as they ever were, when nobody is listening, what can you do but bow out?"

Similarly, intellectuals who do not depend on the labor movement for income have been transferring their attention to the arts, civil rights, foreign policy, especially disarmament and arms control. Some have ruefully concluded that they were deceiving themselves when they used to think that "labor" was the hope of mankind. "The intellectual," says one such political scientist, "can identify only with certain humanist values, or with the plight of the underprivileged. But the labor movement as just another special-interest group offers nothing on either score."

Last summer when the AFL-CIO Executive Council refused to endorse the "Jobs and Freedom" March on Washington, many intellectuals were further convinced that the labor movement has become too parochial and blimpish to command their loyalty.

If the breach is not soon mended, the prospects are that, twenty years hence, the labor movement will no longer exert enough economic leverage and political influence to be a decisive force in our society. To be sure, trade unions may still be around. But unless the AFL-CIO and the rest of the labor movement can come up with new theory and tactics suited to the times, whatever unions remain will be only vendors of labor skill and energy.

"MORE AND MORE AND MORE NOW"

Conservative intellectuals, of course, have always been hostile toward the labor movement. During the entire nineteenth century they scolded it for getting born and trying to stay alive. And they have since kept whacking it for its refusal to comply with their misinterpretations of Adam Smith. But their animosity has been less important than the aid and amity of liberal and/or radical intellectuals. They have traditionally helped the labor movement to define and articulate its aspirations. They have also—at various times—explained, needled, split, glorified, and whitewashed it. Their number has included middle-class and patrician reformers as well as self-taught workingmen.

One such, for example, was the learned blacksmith Elihu Burritt, who had mastered all Europe's languages and enraptured nineteenth-century audiences with lectures on the noble need for education. After the Civil War, a former theological student and teacher turned tailor, Uriah S. Stephens, founded the Knights of Labor, which was to serve as sounding board for advocates of an industrial brotherhood that would, in effect, make every man his own employer. The Knights established some two hundred producer-consumer cooperatives in shoes, cooperage, and mining. All of them succumbed to lack of horse sense or the ungentle competition of Robber Baron capitalism. The Knights also espoused such political shortcuts to salvation as the single tax and the nationalizing of public utilities. But when the American Federation of Labor was formed in 1886 it soon discarded all such utopianism. It plumped instead for a bread-and-butter unionism, with a minimal involvement in politics and government. Determined to depend for its gains upon its own economic strength of strike and boycott, the AFL had no ultimate aims. It embraced the existing order, striving only to obtain from it "more and more and more now" in income and respectability.

The AFL majority therefore resisted far-reaching plans of political action and the formation of a labor party—proposals regularly put forward by such insider Socialists as Max Hayes of the Typographers and John Fitzpatrick of the building trades and by such outsider Socialists as authors Upton Sinclair and William English Walling. Equating socialism with intellectualism and both with "governmentalism," the AFL excoriated all three as subversive. As late as 1930, the AFL was so fearful of becoming a "ward of the state" that it opposed unemployment insurance.

From four million in 1920, AFL membership tumbled to two million in the early 'thirties. Then the AFL finally began to welcome massive federal help. It even turned cordial toward such vanguard thinkers as the young lawyer-economist Leon H. Keyserling, who drafted major provisions of Labor's Magna Carta, the Wagner Act. It was passed in 1935. In the same year a dissident faction, the Committee (later Congress) of Industrial Organizations (CIO) broke away from the AFL. The split centered ostensibly around the issue of industrial (plant-wide and vertical) vs. craft (skill-narrow and horizontal) union structure. But the cleavage also reflected profound differences as to labor's role in politics and government's role in labor affairs. Determined to go beyond AFL business unionism, the CIO was eager to extend the social and economic reforms of President Roosevelt's first term. With this agenda it became home and hunting ground for left-of-center intellectuals. (Some of their enthusiasm spilled over to the AFL in its subsequent rivalry with the CIO.)

The CIO had need for intellectuals to write, speak, proselytize, plead in the courts, organize, and administer as it sought to channel into orderly unionism hundreds of thousands of rebellious workers in automobiles, steel, meat-packing, and other mass-production industries. The intellectuals responded with religious intensity.

Many were Marxists of varying hues. There were some Stalinists among these, carefully instructed to infiltrate the burgeoning CIO. Often they fought valiantly. But they remained the agents of a foreign power. And when union interests collided with Party-line vagaries, the union always lost out. Many more were Socialists (more accurately, Social Democrats) and non-Marxist liberals in the Populist tradition. Whether on the CIO staff, or as volunteers, they prepared the pamphlets, composed the songs, collected funds, and ran the mimeograph machines turning out the endless bulletins, instructions, notices. On picket lines, they braved the cops, sheriffs, private police, the mobsters hired by employers to smash strikes, and they were rewarded with broken heads, jaws, and arms. And everywhere they talked—at faculty teas and radio forums, at dinner parties and from loading platforms. Some served as brain-trusters for young leaders coming up from the shop and others developed into union officials themselves.

During the 1920s the Communists had originated a new cult, the Adoration of the Worker. The stereotype mesmerized many intellectuals. It was visually based on drawings in the *New Masses*, which showed a larger-than-life-size wage earner, his eyes fixed on the far horizon. His martial jaw proclaimed a proletarian toughness armoring a heart that bled for all humanity. His muscular neck and bulging biceps suggested a spectacular virility. He was portrayed in effect as a combination of St. Augustine, Paul Bunyan, and a stud bull.

ABRASIVE "INSIDERS"

It was not until the 1940s that the mystique of the worker began to evaporate. The intellectuals discovered by means of personal contact that he was pretty much like everybody else; that, indeed, the son of toil they had romanticized at a distance could be anti-Catholic, anti-Semitic, a white supremacist, a rancorous xenophobe; that his favorite reading was the sports page, comic books, and detective magazines, and that this diet did not endow him with a profound grasp of national and international issues.

They discovered also that the CIO and AFL (they did not merge until 1955) were concentrating on business or market unionism, intent on taking care of their own, and downgrading social or national-interest unionism.

Critical reports and articles began to appear as labor's intellectual friends found, for example, that union "democracy" was not always of the New England town-meeting variety and that the corruptions of commercialism were infecting unions. Perhaps they were naïve. But above all, these intellectuals did not want the labor movement to become merely the mirror of a society in which everybody sells out to everybody else. Workers, they believed, should use some of their new ease and leisure to pursue things of the mind and spirit.

Within the labor movement the new criticism was more sophisticated. It was spearheaded by two of the foremost union-made intellectuals of the century. The first was J. B. S. Hardman, a former editor of *The Advance,* official organ of the clothing workers, and a man whose incorrigible optimism is tempered by a wry and even mordant wit. Under CIO auspices he established in 1946 a "Union Institute for Labor and Democracy." His right hand in this venture was Solomon Barkin, then research director of the Textile Workers (CIO) and perhaps the most incisive and even abrasive "insider" analyst of the modern labor scene. The Institute and its publication, the bimonthly *Labor and Nation,* were created to foster candid and independent examination of the labor movement and its missions.

But after six years this enterprise foundered for lack of support. Mr. Hardman observed that the place of the intellectual in the labor movement was to make a philosophy of no philosophy and went on to coedit with Professor Maurice Neufield of Cornell the symposium *The House of Labor.* Mr. Barkin kept warning the labor movement that it faced stagnation unless it became the champion not just of its own adherents but of slum dwellers, migrant workers, and other Americans in the lower depths. Mr. Barkin left the Textile Workers last year to join the Office of Economic Cooperation and Development.

His counsels have been largely ignored. Indeed, the labor movement stopped listening to such apostasy in the first few years after World War II when it was riding high and enjoying unprecedented growth. During the 1935–45 decade alone, union membership rose from a scant four million to a staggering 14.3 million. For this achievement union chieftains quite humanly credited their own perspicacity and sweat. . . .

Nor did the union chieftains recognize that special circumstances of depression and war had enabled them to fashion a new design for union living out of the economic autarchy of Samuel Gompers and the political favoritism of Franklin D. Roosevelt. They had forgotten, too, that the labor movement, in bringing to millions of workers a new sense of economic self-determination and psychological self-respect, had performed as a vehicle of social reconstruction; that it was to this image of its function that it owed public acceptance and support, without which it would lose its thrust. But the intellectuals who said this were arguing against success, with its heady aroma. And since there are limits even to their masochism, they began, one after the other, to give up and slip away. As early as 1948 the union protagonist and Columbia sociologist, the late C. Wright Mills, pointed out that union leaders as "new men of power" were proving to be either unwilling or unable to cooperate with the "men of intellect" on any viable basis.

"OUT IN LEFT FIELD"

Why has the latter-day labor movement been largely impervious to the critiques and recommendations of intellectuals? The answer lies in the character of the typical labor leader, his background, his style, the way he sees his job. He is a blend of political boss, evangelist, military chieftain, and salesman. Above all, he is a self-made man. He is the Siamese twin of the versatile entrepreneur who has built the business from scratch, is reluctant to delegate authority, and yearns for the old days when he could call everybody in the shop by his first name. Moreover, the labor leader has had to claw his way up in a bruising competition that makes even the high-tension cabals of the executive suite seem genteel. He is manipulative and practical in all his dealings and it is in accord with these criteria that he measures the extent to which the intellectuals are useful to him.

Among the latter are the staff economist who prepares a presentation to justify a wage increase; the lawyer who argues the union case before labor-relations boards and commissions, and in the courts; the industrial engineer who figures out how the union can benefit from a new time study for production norms; the publicist who puts together a speech or Congressional testimony; the actuary familiar with the intricacies of pension funds.

All these assist the labor leader to crystallize, express, dress up what he wants to do. (The Michigan professor, Harold L. Wilenski, who a decade ago conducted the only full-scale sociological survey of union intellectuals, thinks that their overriding function is that of "Verbaliz-ers.") The labor leader thinks it is up to him to create and coordinate policy while the experts implement it, rather than do much to formulate it. He regards such aides as his men just as he regards the union as an extension of his psyche. Even though he may respect the abilities and attainments of intellectuals, his attitude remains ambivalent, especially toward the university scholar, the foundation researcher, the writer turned social critic who concerns himself with union affairs. Labor leaders usually refer to the member of this genus as "pedantic," "an ivory tower guy," or as "out in left field, hell, further, out in space," or as a "pipe-smoking long-hair" (labor leaders cherish their cigars only more than their barbers).

Labor leaders are not impressed by the intellectual's inclination toward objective inquiry; they have felt too long beleaguered for that. They are even less impressed by his individualistic propensity to dissent from the prevailing values and mores of "the system." For the labor leader is gregarious, one of the boys, regards himself as chief of a tribe for whom he gets what he can out of the system which he accepts more than it accepts him.

THREATENED BY BRAINPOWER

Within the labor movement there is still a tiny handful of intellectuals who play a key role in formulating and initiating union policy. . . . But this dwindling remnant can scarcely begin to meet the labor movement's need for brainpower at a time when leadership in our society is being everywhere transferred to people with intellectual training and capability. The labor leader who in most cases has only a high-school education is not unaware that the intellectual may one day threaten his own ascendancy. This fear explains his insistence that intellectuals be kept in their place and his lack of pronounced grief when they depart. He can then more comfortably rely on the old concepts and techniques of which he is master and which hasten labor's decline.

Today trade unions have not only stopped growing; as a percentage of the total labor force they are not even holding their own. Between 1960 and 1962, they lost nearly half a million members, and the rate is accelerating. Only a few years ago, one out of four persons who had a job or was looking for employment belonged to a union; now the ratio is edging toward one out of five and all indications are pointing downward.

Some apologists absolve the labor movement from responsibility for this predicament. They blame, among other factors, technological change; the guile of employers who forestall union organization by pretending to offer union-won benefits "for free"; the restrictions imposed by Taft-Hartley, Landrum-Griffin, and the state right-to-work laws; the unfriendliness of the press, radio, TV; the extent to which the McClellan disclosures on labor racketeering and corruption have been falsified into national folklore; the lavish anti-union propaganda and lobbying of the National Association of Manufacturers and the John Birch Society.

Yet it seems almost comic to ascribe all of labor's troubles to external conditions. After all, union members with their families still comprise nearly a fifth of the entire population of the United States, hardly a fragile potentiality in terms of economic and political strength.

The labor movement in fact is in a bad way chiefly because the bulk of intellectuals are not affirmatively on its side, and because it is no longer making use of that theoretical-pragmatic "mix" demanded by the ecology of the space age.

The discourse between analyst and administrator produced during the past generation our finest achievement in domestic policy, the Tennessee Valley Authority, and perhaps our finest achievement in foreign policy, the Marshall Plan.

Similarly, the State Department can hardly begin to function until its policy-planning staff has sifted the reports, the insights, the proposals of both the "pros" and the "professors" in international relations. The Pentagon's adroit use of its "military intellectuals" explains, in no small degree, the readiness of our defense posture.

Industry, likewise, regularly has its judgments checked by management consultants, the free-lance intelligentsia of the business community. And within many companies the intellectual who was formerly regarded only as specialist is being brought closer to the policy center. The word has gone out to business recruiters on campus to search for fewer conformist organization men and more independent eggheads.

But the labor movement has little truck with such newfangled notions. The AFL-CIO headquarters has no policy-planning staff. It has no clearinghouse for the regular exchange of views between intellectuals and labor leaders. It has no equivalent, in terms of its own requirements, of alternative position papers, gaming theory, operations or market research and analysis. Among its affiliated unions, only a handful have management training and development programs. There are, of course, research, legislative, legal, editorial, and public-relations people. All are overworked. All are immersed in immediacies, and play little part in basic decision making.

Yet the practical men who, by and large, are leaders of labor cannot by themselves reverse the movement's downward slide. It is not a question of intelligence. In native sagacity, or at least shrewdness, they are the equal of any comparable group in industry, government, the professions. But today's issues transcend their lore of collective bargaining, of building and running a union, of grasping intimately the problems of a particular company or industry. The dominant issues are now matters of national policy. To blame automation as they do for causing unemployment, for example, is like blaming armaments for causing war. The answer to automation will be found in a national policy which can modify the socioeconomic framework to enable the computer to create more jobs than it destroys. And similar considerations of national policy on prices, wages, taxes, investment, manpower retraining, foreign trade are intertwined with any attempts to organize the unorganized, blue-collar or white-collar; to educate the unionized; to improve channels of communication between leaders and rank and file; to determine whether the labor movement should be politically something more than the tail of the Democratic party kite; whether the very structural forms of unionism should be revised.

In all these areas the labor movement has no logical choice but to draw, more positively and consistently than ever before, upon the talents and disciplines of intellectuals. In no other way can Big Labor test prevailing assumptions, explore new directions, and adjust to pivotal developments in Big Business and Big Government.

At the AFL-CIO convention last November, Walter Reuther argued cogently for the establishment of a National Planning Agency to coordinate by democratic means our human and material resources to achieve full employment and full production. He pointed out that, over the next decade, we must come up with some forty-one million new jobs if we are merely going to maintain an unemployment rate of around 5.5 per cent; that only an "economic moron" believes that we can any longer rely exclusively upon the "blind forces of the marketplace" to provide the opportunity to earn a living for everybody who needs to do it.

On past occasions Mr. Reuther's disquisitions in like vein have been perfunctorily received. Delegates would rush to the nearest bar to recover from so much cerebration. This time he was warmly applauded.

PLANNING WITHOUT A PLAN

The AFL-CIO majority, however, is unlikely to take the initiative in advocating national economic planning unless the present sub-crisis of unemployment shows signs of erupting into fourteen to sixteen million jobless. Some forecasters say this may happen within the next three to four years. Meanwhile, Mr. Reuther and his supporters are determined "to get across the idea that public planning for people is compatible with private planning for profits."

But they can hardly advocate planning without a plan. While it need not be a detailed blueprint, final and frozen, it must be something more than a pencil rough. Yet to put any such document on paper exceeds the intellectual resources currently on tap not only for the UAW and the Industrial Union Department but the entire AFL-CIO. Such an undertaking would entail the counsel and direct participation of additional economists—political, mathematical, or merely sensible—along with philosophic and practical thinkers in other fields.

Trade unions and corporations, as systems for the accumulation of power, are not only economic organizations. They are also private

governments. Their relations with each other and with the public
government, under national economic planning, must be seriously pon-
dered and spelled out. This is no pastime for some rainy Sunday
afternoon, as Mr. Reuther is the first to perceive. And this is only one
among many reasons impelling him to establish a "new working alliance"
between intellectuals and labor leaders. If he and others of like mind
cannot get this kind of cooperation started soon within the higher reaches
of the labor movement, the 1960s may prove to be the Gettysburg of its
Confederacy.

Jack T. Conway
IDEOLOGICAL OBSOLESCENCE
IN COLLECTIVE BARGAINING

The question I have undertaken to answer in this paper—Can
Collective Bargaining Do the Job?—can only be answered prophetically.
I cannot cut the future to the measure of my predictions. I can only try.

When it was first proposed that I discuss this question of the
relevance of collective bargaining, the New York newspaper strike was
still in progress. Major strikes on the docks and the railroads were in
suspension at the moment. Editorials in the newspapers throughout the
country were suggesting these crises indicated that collective bargaining
and unions were obsolete, without recalling that before these activities
became obsolete in their judgment, they had routinely offered other
reasons for doing away with them. The *Wall Street Journal* had, over a
period of time, published articles, news analyses, and stories whose
central theme was that technological change in many industries, especially the newspaper industry, but not excluding transportation and
manufacture, had gone so far and so fast, that the traditional forms of
enterprise were obsolete, the traditional skills were obsolescent where
they are not already obsolete, and that in a normal lifetime men and
women could naturally expect that they would have to acquire two or
three competences to keep current with developments, if they could keep

An address to the Industrial Relations Conference, Institute of Industrial
Relations, University of California, Berkeley, 1963. Used by permission.

Mr. Conway has held several union and government positions. At present he
is with the Industrial Union Department, AFL-CIO.

pace at all. It was suggested that unions had already passed their time, and that it was now necessary to devise other institutions and methods for performing the service which unions once provided.

The *Wall Street Journal* is too useful a newspaper to be singled out for pillorying in this connection. Actually it only accurately summed up the spate of views and observations which are still appearing in magazines and books, that are skeptical not only of unions, but of the government, and of people. There are suggestions, for example, that human beings are also superfluous and that the task now is to reorganize the society of man to exclude people.

These judgments, which come from the ringside and not from the ring, while fashionable, are not profound, and in my experience, embody no great wisdom. They are manifestations not of institutional obsolescence, or human obsolescence, but of a combination of ideological obsolescence and personal senescence. In the case of unions, for example, the people, frequently relics of the 1930s, who are publishing articles which purport to describe the demise of the labor movement are using exhausted concepts and illusions which blind them to what is actually happening today.

What has been written by these people about my own recent career in a sense is an anecdotal illustration of the inadequacy and irrelevance of this sideline and uninformed interpretation of the evolution of the labor movement. When I left the UAW two years ago to work in the Administration in Washington, it was said, falsely, that I was disillusioned, that I was part of a parade of people leaving the labor movement because it had come to a deadend where there was no longer any function for collective bargaining. Recently, after two very satisfying years in a Federal Agency, when I returned to work in the labor movement, the same people said, "Aha, he is disillusioned with the government."

What this incident, and altogether too many other comments on current events, reveal about these professional intellectuals who proclaim their concern about society is a shallow cynicism in connection with the very agencies and instruments, governmental and nongovernmental, that are operating most effectively to deal with injustice, inequality, and insecurity.

Government, parties, and the labor movement are decried for going too far, not going far enough, for being timid, or arrogant, for overriding individual rights, or for paralysis, for activism, or inactivism.

Moreover these denigrations characteristically carry an emotional charge and almost invariably embody a moral judgment. Not only is it said that collective bargaining is inadequate to some purpose that is never defined, it is also implied that the people who engage in collective bargaining are committing an undefined wrong, or are engaging in something that is unspecifically immoral, and are betraying some ideal ethical principle which once distinguished the labor movement in better, happier times.

These expressions of outrage, of course, mistake the essential nature of collective bargaining, which is a neutral operative activity that is used socially as an instrument for arriving at particular kinds of decisions. A complex apparatus which has evolved in this country over one hundred and fifty years, it incorporates the experience of at least six generations of American employers and employees and works rather well when it is operated and maintained competently. Like any piece of machinery, whether it is a court or a car, the performance quality depends upon its operators. Collective bargaining is neither magic, nor automatic. For the best results, it demands intelligence, integrity, courage, and work on both sides of the bargaining table, and a reasonable regard for the traffic rules which regulate economic flow.

Judgments of the success or the failure of bargaining, and there are comparative failures from time to time, as there are successes, imply a measurement against some standard, which most often is called public interest. Unfortunately, the public interest is nowhere precisely defined. Indeed, as the history of labor legislation in the United States demonstrates, it has been impossible to define, at least until now.

Even if there were an adequate, limiting, and accurate description of the public interest, the specification would not be a criterion for judging the effectiveness of collective bargaining. What is better or worse in a particular situation depends not on comparison with an ideal solution but on the contrast with the actual alternatives. It is for this reason, than when a negotiation is over, the people on both sides of the bargaining table cannot guarantee that the agreement reached was an ideal solution. All they can reply to critics is that they came up with the best solution they were able to reach. These imperfect decisions have served and continue to serve the country rather well, in spite of occasional crises which have their own uses and value.

At this moment, collective bargaining has a larger claim to vitality and utility than ever before in the history of the American society. Neither side of the American bargaining table is haunted by an uneasiness over what has been called the end of ideology or the exhaustion of the uses of collective bargaining. In the American unions, it has been estimated that there are about 250,000 men and women in leadership roles and there is no credible indication that these people believe that the labor movement has entered into a decline or that it has become universally infected by cynicism or corruption. Similarly, it is obvious that the extent to which people—wage earners and employers—

in every community in the nation are daily engaged in some form of collective bargaining and are by their efforts giving direction to the economy represents a total refutation of the silliness that this movement of some sixteen or seventeen million American wage earners is barren of leadership.

Taking into account the fact that bargaining also comprehends the people on the employer side of the negotiations, it is not an exaggeration to say that bargaining is actually the most widely pervasive democratic activity in the nation and is more widely accepted than ever before in American history. This development alone indicates that it is nonsense to suggest there really was an inspiring labor tradition in some glorious past which somehow has been ground to dust and lost to this generation through the operation of an iron law of bureaucracy.

Most of these capsule summaries of the situation in the American labor movement are captious, capricious, and, in reality, anxiety projections by people who are describing something within themselves rather than the exciting—even though disturbing—variety of developments in the factories and workplaces as well as the neighborhoods and the legislatures of the nation. They recall the Kentucky politician whose constituent conceded that the candidate had gotten the man a job, had arranged for a variety of services for a long list of relatives, but still asked what had been done for him lately. Actually, the labor movement has been performing and is providing an astonishing assortment of essential services to the American people not only lately, but now.

But the actuality should not be exaggerated either. No one in the labor movement would insist that the American unions are without fault, that union leaders all qualify for the Sir Galahad medal, or that the unions are the front ranks of a marching band entering paradise. But what organization or movement in the United States does meet this specification?

If you examine what the American labor movement has accomplished in the last fifteen years, it is impossible to talk of the end of collective bargaining and to speak intelligently. Paid holidays, improvement in vacations, pensions, the establishment of bargaining as an operative feature of the economy, the extension of health and sickness insurance to a majority of union wage earners, the virtual end of violence on the industrial relations scene, the supplementary unemployment program, the adoption, however imperfect, of ethical practices standards for the labor movement, the genuine advances being made against discrimination; very lately, the provisions dealing with automation, the new sabbatical vacation plan set forth in the Steel agreement, the cost-sharing plan between the union and Kaiser Steel, the American Motors Progress Sharing Plan with the UAW, whose innovating features have not yet been properly understood; and most recently, the inauguration of what could be a profound alteration in the collective bargaining process itself in steel and in the automobile industry. There is hope that a year or two from today it will be possible to add to this list the realization and the mastery of new organizing methods appropriate to the demands of the changed industrial topography. Nationally, unions, utilizing a variant form of collective bargaining have had some role in the enactment of certain features of the Trade Expansion Act, of the Area Redevelopment program, and of the Manpower Retraining Act. Except for the initiative of the labor movement, the Fair Employment Practices effort, however far it is from where it should be, would not be operating as well as it is, and the civil rights movement would be more nearly a whisper in the distance, instead of the most challenging development in the nation today.

So, it can be expected that people will rejoin to this recital, sure you have done all these things, but how come you have not established equality in American life, ended nuclear testing, and restored democratic government to Cuba? Nor is this anticipation facetious, for actually, it is clear that most of the criticism of the American labor movement today is based on what has been called the Free Tom Mooney fallacy. During the historic depression it was reported that a tenants' committee met with a landlord over a list of demands and that the landlord finally said he would paint the halls, reduce the rents, turn the heat on at seven o'clock instead of eight, and provide new gas stoves, but, "Tell me," he concluded, "how can I free Tom Mooney?"

When the alienated and rather well-provided intellectuals who today choose the American labor movement for their target (this is not a reference to the people in the civil rights movement who are making proper, if uncomfortable, demands on unions for far more speed and far less deliberation), when these critics aim their spitballs at the unions, essentially they are looking at bargaining and other union activities through unfocused glasses, under a number of disabling misconceptions.

Actually the blur and the badly aimed spitballing are due to the multiple roles unions play in our society:

Their primary activity as bargaining representatives of the people in a particular workplace; their activity as a moral spokesman in the community for wage and salary workers, and the dispossessed, and the alienated, and the persecuted, and the mistreated, and the victims of whatever automatic social trend happens to be running; and their activity, as a political institution, not a party, rather an effectively organized, but by no means omnipotent, interest group, but nevertheless a big one.

While in practice, unions as collective bargaining agents can be influential factors in the determination of wages, hours, working conditions—conditions of employment in the enterprises where they have been standing—unions in fact have no effective control, and not very much influence at any particular time, over the operation of the total economy or the broad society. Unions are never in a position to Free Tom Mooney, about the most they can do is to join other people on a petition.

Unions as bargaining agents, for that matter, have little control over the context of the bargaining situation, that is, the movement of the economy, demand changes, alterations in the society, which can and do change the nature of bargaining, and have in the past in some cases simply eroded the basis for bargaining.

Critics of unions, failing to distinguish among the various functions of unions and the varying powers of unions:

1. make demands on unions they cannot possibly fulfill, and

2. criticize unions for failures in the society or in the economy that are no more the responsibility of the unions than they are of the church, or the Congress, or the President, or the companies, or history itself.

Critics thus ask of unions what they intend to do about:

a. poverty in the United States, that is, the 20 per cent of the people who live outside the national economy, and another 20 per cent who, while they live in the community, live largely as the deprived and not as participants,

b. discrimination in the United States one hundred years after the Emancipation Proclamation,

c. automation and the accelerating technological displacement which is discharging workers from the production process at one end with the speed that doughnuts, or engines, or soft drinks, or cans are released at the other end, and

d. the disappearance of traditional democratic activities in favor of institutional and bureaucratic procedures as the pressure of size and technology move the nation toward computer, vending machine, and information storage methods.

Nowhere in the society is there more concern with these developments than in the labor movement. In most of these areas, the labor movement has been primarily responsible for making the original demands and proposals for dealing with these failures in the society. But what unions are asked to do in connection with these problems is far beyond the competence and the powers of the labor movement, and in some cases beyond the competence and powers of any society or government that is known. Here, it should be acknowledged the demand on the unions to be more effective and to exert powers they do not have also comes from union members, for understandable reasons.

Yet, while unions are taunted for failing to undertake tasks which would require far greater powers, responsibilities, and bureaucracies than anyone has ever proposed for what are essentially voluntary organizations, simultaneously they are targets of a contradictory charge. Ignoring the changes taking place in the big society, which have compelled unions to institutionalize and organize their activities, people who cherish memories from a time when unions were very often only protest groups, insist that the labor movement return to a primitive state of informal grace that survives nowhere else in the community.

Unions, like any other major human activity, need criticism, from inside and outside; the more important they are, the more criticism they need. But some of the criticism that is misdirected at the unions tends to interfere with specific indictments which should be aimed at other institutions. It is easier, for example, to direct fire against unions for their participation in discrimination, than against the companies responsible, or the cities, or the political agencies. Similarly, it is easier to ask what are unions doing about automation than to call attention specifically to the failure of companies in some instances to incorporate plans for the human use of human beings in their long-range programs, or to the failure of the government to implement the public policy set forth in the Employment Act of 1946.

All this having been said, it should be acknowledged that unions, as bargaining agents, as quasipolitical activities, as institutional centers for agitating on moral grounds, are only now emerging from one of their less creative and less responsive periods. In partial extenuation, reference can be made to the difficulties of accommodating to federation unity and to drastic economic and social changes in the society; union leaders, unfortunately, often tend to share the smugness and the complacency of our business-oriented society itself. But no one should fail to take into account the possibility that if the labor movement should slip back into unimaginativeness, into a lack of resilience (which is not likely because of political pressures which will not tolerate immobility), it is indeed conceivable that it will play a less important role in the future.

But even in this circumstance what the labor movement now does—successfully sometimes, less successfully at other times—needs to be done, and will be done, in one institutional form or the other.

Actually, however, the labor movement is beginning to make the adaptive changes that will enable it to contend with those problems with which it is competent to deal and to associate itself with other groups in the society to deal with those problems with which it is concerned but not capable of solving by itself.

No discussion of this question should fail to enumerate the very many different forms that collective bargaining assumes today, involving it in concerns, activities, and decisions which nowhere have been described adequately, certainly not in the texts and treatises dealing with collective bargaining. Indeed what actually happens is complex and varied to a degree that falsifies the conception most people hold of union negotiations.

For example, as the result of the advances made during the last two decades, bargaining proceeds less and less frequently (as in the newspapers) in a hotel meeting room, at midnight, two minutes before a strike deadline, over a new contract. Bargaining goes on continuously in the joint committees which administer the pension programs, the supplementary unemployment benefit funds, and the medical, hospital, and sickness funds. During recent years unions have, it has seemed, been negotiating on a five-day-a-week basis with the Blue Cross-Blue Shield state organizations and other suppliers of health services. Union committees have been compelled to negotiate on actuarial and related problems with the insurance companies. Funds created to deal with personnel changes arising from automation have provided a new bargaining place, have presented opportunities for unprecedented new research into the possibilities of the bargaining process, and have created the need for union leadership training of a kind never attempted before in the labor movement.

But although bargaining is an expanding activity, it certainly cannot do the job, if what is understood to be the job is the provision of full employment, job opportunities for young people, and true security for wage earners throughout their lives. These are public policy questions which require action *outside* the essentially bilateral bargaining process. However, within the limits of what can be done by dealing directly with employers or with associations of employers, something significant and enduring will be established.

Unquestionably, within the next few years collective bargaining will routinely begin to concern itself with the investment of the enormous sums of money which are accumulating in the pension funds, in the SUB funds, and, most recently, in the allocation of money from the progress-sharing funds of the American Motors Corporation or from the economies realized under the Kaiser contract.

This very hasty survey of where collective bargaining is today is intended only to indicate that collective bargaining is not a bankrupt enterprise, but that it has evolved into one of the critical decision-making activities in the economy. Moreover the simpler, less evolved forms of face-to-face collective bargaining will also undergo decisive changes that will be dramatic even if they do not produce picket lines, strike violence, and shrieking headlines. Here, of course, I refer to the move in steel and autos—and it will not stop in these industries—to take bargaining out from under the headline and to make it a cooperative inquiry into economic advance and adaptation. Already the table pounding, the violent language, the masculine vocabularies which were a hallowed if slightly ridiculous feature of the bargaining process of yesteryear have gone by the way.

But beyond the bargaining within plant limits and with specific companies and groups of companies, unions and employers must inevitably—and soon—begin to engage in a three-sided negotiation over the operation of manpower training programs, or tariff problems, and eventually investment and fiscal policy as they relate to jobs and full employment. Moreover, when full employment is an established and continuing feature of our national economy as it must inevitably become, bargaining will necessarily continue within plants and with companies in the customary dialogue, but the crucial decisions will probably be made regionally and nationally as is beginning to be the case in England, in France, and less obviously, but with far greater effect, in Sweden.

Ultimately and inevitably under full employment conditions in the United States, the traditional demands of the union movement will undergo transformations. Already in the highly developed European countries—as in the United States, for that matter—union members with union responsibilities do not conform to the public picture of them as men walking up and down in front of a strikebound shop or factory, with or without picket signs, crying unfair. No one has counted the many thousands of workers in factories and shops and offices whose union duties require them to meet with city, state, and national governments over complicated technical problems which bear vitally on the operation of the society, employment, health administration, housing, city planning, traffic, investment, education; the list of items on the agenda includes every community concern. What should be kept in mind is that the men and women who are now engaged in making these decisions democratically in the community and the broad society only a generation ago were hired hands, people across the railroad tracks with no rights in the plant, no voice in the community, and no meaningful vote in the large social questions which shaped their lives.

Out of this almost invisible but dramatic process will come new institutions in our society, which, far from isolating and alienating human beings, will restore them to the governing process and give more and more of them increasing responsibilities. The new agencies will generate new politics whose issues will be alternative programs for full employment, alternate ways of investing to maintain the dynamics of a growing economy, alternate devices and agencies for facilitating the movement from a manual, largely uneducated working class to an educated society of wage earners. Here one statistic invites examination: in 1930, for all the jobs available in the economy, 32 per cent were unskilled and 25 per cent were either semiskilled or service jobs. Thus 57 per cent of all jobs required relatively little education. By 1970, it has been predicted that instead of a demand category of 32 per cent for unskilled labor, only 5 per cent of available jobs will be unskilled; from 25 per cent, the proportion of semiskilled and service jobs will have shrunk to 21 per cent. Seventy-five per cent of all jobs available will, we are told, require a rather high degree of education. These developments have a significance for the society which is by no means confined to their impact on collective bargaining or the structure of the trade union movement. Trade unionists, however, cannot help but wonder at the influence these developments will have on the structure of unions, local and national, and on the types of personality possessed by those who will become union leaders in the future. In any event, the union structure, the union processes, and union activities, which have already changed more than is generally acknowledged, will inevitably undergo a further dramatic metamorphosis.

For we are, above everything else, a dynamic, mobile, and protean society. The rate of change in the technology, however much it confounds the people caught in the process, does produce equilibrating accommodations. Even when the intellectual reaction to change is apparently out of date and seems to be an effort to solve today's problems with yesterday's answers, the community, making use of a common experience, does adjust and emerge, painful though the adjustment may seem to be.

When one describes the growing participation of the union in the industrial and social economy and the evolution of collective bargaining into an increasingly bureaucratic activity (for the very reason that the society itself is increasingly organized rationally), one runs the risk that critics will be encouraged to cry out, "I told you so, unions *are* becoming one vast bureaucracy."

But the administering bureaucracy that has necessarily evolved in the union is not the bureaucracy critics talk about. They complain, and their complaints would be valid if their description were accurate, of a deadening, self-serving, insensitive bureaucracy lodged comfortably in affluent recumbency on the backs of wage earners. What actually operates in the unions, however, is a rational reconstruction of some features of the economic process to admit more democracy, more flexibility—so that if there must be crises they will not come from blundering, from stupidity, or from inefficiency, or because the proper briefs, or forms, or petitions have not been filed. In contemporary society, where measurements are in millions, hundreds of millions, and billions, there is no escaping the use of efficient administrative machinery. This is bureaucracy, but it is a creative procedural process that organizes and facilitates democratic procedures.

Admittedly, there are dangers from this development, which have not altogether been evaded in Sweden or Israel, two places where the evolution is well advanced. But if some bureaucratization in its invidious sense cannot be escaped, it can also be said that even tribal societies have their flyspecks. The movement will not be from an ideal society to an imperfect one, but rather from one kind of less efficient society to a more efficient but still imperfect endeavor. Bureaucracy will be easier to bear as an imperfection than unemployment or insecurity.

It has been said that politics is the art of the possible. This implies exclusion of the impossible but not of the improbable. Historically, the labor movement—both its political and economic wings—has on occasion played both "practical" and highly improbable politics; it counterpointed obviously possible demands against demands that were not obviously possible. It can be taken for granted that unions, which inevitably carry on their work under a number of countervailing political pressures, will not abandon the element of unreasonableness in their demands (even in the new society) which often make them so exasperating to employers, to governments, and to right-thinking academicians who know perfectly well that what the unions are demanding is impossible, or impractical until the demands are ultimately won. The agitator element in the makeup of the union movement will, as it has in the past, continue to preserve the morality of the labor movement, which is fundamentally not only the justification of unions but also a specific antidote against rigidity in the society. What seems unreasonable to employers may be the basis of moral responsibility to the rank and file.

Can Collective Bargaining Do the Job? If it can't, something else will have to be invented to do what collective bargaining is doing. When it is invented, what will come off the assembly line will not be a computer, but collective bargaining. Even employers who have sought to escape it, at great cost to themselves and the community, have discovered that.

More than anything else, now there is needed, not wailing about the bankruptcy of collective bargaining, or the exhaustion of vitality in the unions, or the end of ideology, but careful, closely focused examination of function and responsibility and potentiality—an approach that is scientific in its integrity, moral in its responsibility to human needs, and practical without complacency in its realism.

Gus Tyler
A NEW PHILOSOPHY FOR LABOR

. . . A new philosophy for labor can easily spell out the highest order of ethical conduct, but in the long run it will become just a scrap of paper unless it is accompanied by a new order in the real—not the alleged practices of the American community, especially at the business and governmental level.

Toward this new philosophy for labor I would propose six major patterns:

1. SOCIAL UNIONISM ON A PURE-AND-SIMPLE BASE. The most immediate tie of the union with its members is still the old pure-and-simple nexus: working condition as embodied in contract. The protection and progress of the worker on the job must remain the broad, continuing base of effective trade unionism. But if this bread-and-butter duty is not to deteriorate into business unionism or worse, if it is not to result in an uninspired, even corrupt, leadership with an inert, even fictional, membership, then the trade union needs a greater goal than the contract, a broader religion than the dollar sign. It must be concerned with industry as a whole, with the economy, with the nation, with democracy. The social view has a double value: it makes the union an integrated and contributory force in the community; and it raises the spiritual level of both the leadership and the rank and file.

The current fad of trying to limit unions to being collective bargaining agencies is dangerous. One of the great forces for democracy would be numbed. What is more, if this idea were carried to its logical conclusion against all the organized forces in the community, it would lead to the disintegration of our society. Imagine religion limited to prayers on Sunday, newspapers limited to reporting, advertising limited to the peddling of wares, economists limited to economics, and politi-

Reprinted with the author's permission from Gus Tyler, *A New Philosophy for Labor*, an Occasional Paper of the Center for the Study of Democratic Institutions, Santa Barbara, California, 1959, pp. 10–14. © by The Fund for the Republic.

Mr. Tyler is Assistant President of the International Ladies' Garment Workers' Union.

cians limited to politics. Who then would worry about man as man? Could man find his way without benefit of the many "experts" in our society—editor, businessman, economist, politician, trade unionist?

Unions should be *urged* to develop a broad and sensitive social interest and conscience. Many of the weaknesses and evils of present-day trade unionism arise from the fact that too many unions and union leaders and members have been solely interested in the narrow, selfish aspects of the union, with a minimum of concern for the community, for ethics, for moral standards of public behavior. A dedication to enduring ideals, a sense of duty to the community, an economic program, a concern for democracy—these broad involvements can do much to lift the level of trade union behavior.

The community itself has a responsibility in helping to form the philosophy of the trade union. If the community wants business unionism, it should not be surprised if the union leader conducts himself according to prevalent business practices. If the community insists that it wants trade unionists who will stick to the narrow job of collective bargaining, it should not be surprised if they show no interest in the community at large. If the community insists that it does not want trade union leaders with ideas about social reform, it should not be surprised if they demonstrate no interest in civil liberties, civil rights, the United Nations, or clean government. The business community cannot expect to create trade union leaders in their own image and then be annoyed when the unions fail to exhibit an ethic any nobler than that of the run-of-the-mill entrepreneur.

2. POLITICS WITH A SOCIAL PURPOSE. It is fair to say that the present interest of the unions in politics was not of the union's own choosing. The Taft-Hartley law did more to politicalize the more conservative American trade unions than several decades of socialist-minded propaganda in the American Federation of Labor. But even if labor were not goaded into political action by labor-management legislation, it would still have to maintain a continuing interest in politics in order to protect the economic standing of its members.

The American economy of the second half of the twentieth century is much too much of a legislated economy for the unions to believe that they can defend the economic status of their workers solely through contract. A worker's real income and real standard of living are immediately and directly affected by the cost of living; by monopoly price-fixing; by publicly controlled utility rates; by public policy on rents, housing, building subsidies; by tariffs on competing manufactures or on consumer items; by the tax law; by the unemployment insurance and social security payments; by the vast complex of legislative and administrative activity that may flow from the full employment act; by the minimum wage law; by price supports on farm products; by the award of government contracts and the determinations about prevailing wages in those contracts; by regulations and laws concerning discrimination in employment. All these forces of legislation and public administration are just as important as the money wage a worker gets in his contract in finally determining his real wage and his family's standard of living. To give the worker more than make-believe protection, a modern union must be concerned with influencing the legislation that goes to make up our legislated economy.

In its political work, the trade union must place primary emphasis on social purpose rather than personal power, on program rather than patronage. This is not only morally desirable; it is also the most realistic way to proceed, because the only way a trade union leadership can "deliver" the votes of its membership is by convincing its membership that a program or a candidate is desirable. The key to those votes is understanding: the workers must know why they should vote, for what they should vote, and for whom they should vote. Concentration on the political education of the worker would not only keep labor politics on a high plane but also revolutionize American politics, by teaching millions of voters that politics is a struggle of ideas and ideals and not just a contest among labels, faces, names, and prejudices.

3. PROFESSIONALIZATION WITH DEMOCRATIC CONTROLS. The modern union needs "professional" leadership in the same way that modern government needs "professional" guidance. The unions of the twentieth century are not the simple little clubs of one hundred years ago. The modern union is not only large; it is complex. Its contracts are long and complicated. Its methods of wage determination, piece rates, incentive payments involve mathematical, engineering, and statistical skills. Its internal administrative machinery, run correctly, parallels that of most corporations or banks. Its finances require intelligent investment. Its buildings and properties must be managed; its staff and personnel selected and trained and directed; its offices administered. Unions run health centers, summer camps, rental units, co-op stores. Unions must operate within the framework of federal, state, and local law. They conduct public relations campaigns, consumer education bureaus, union label drives. They publish papers, run huge mailing operations. They engage in intensive economic research, prepare legal briefs, hold classes in the humanities and citizenship. They run social welfare clinics. They conduct political campaigns and legislative drives.

The proper conduct of so vast an operation is not a job for the amateur, rising from the ranks without training and returning to the ranks after a brief term of office. To do the job well requires "career" people whether elected or appointed.

In our government, we recognize the realities of its structure and turn over about ninety-nine per cent of the jobs to "professionals." Our army, navy, and air corps, our post office, our foreign affairs, our departments, bureaus, and agencies are run by career people. Even the top people—Secretaries of State or Defense or Labor—are appointed and not elected. This huge career mechanism, involving hundreds of thousands of people, exists side by side with a democratically elected legislature and presidency consisting of exactly 536 officials.

Traditionally, unions have another kind of attitude about who should be elected. In some unions, the membership elects not only the top managerial official but also all the other full-time officers, the Executive Board, the sergeant-at-arms, the financial secretary, the organizer, the corresponding secretary, the shop steward, the various shop committees, and even—in some cases—the office workers. This tradition stems from the early days of trade unionism just as the Jacksonian tradition of allowing anyone and everyone to become a bureaucrat stems from the first days of American government.

Finding the proper relationship between professional administration and democratic control is a necessary part of a new philosophy which seeks trade unions conducted along efficient, ethical, creative lines within the framework of a vigorous democracy. The relationship certainly cannot be established by counting the number of career officeholders as compared with the number directly elected by the membership. Nor can a proper test be the length of time people continue in high office. Consider the tenures of the men holding top administrative posts in government, universities, churches, medical societies, or as chairmen of legislative committees. The real measure is the responsiveness of the administrative machinery to the needs and will of the membership as expressed through periodically elected officials, legislative bodies, and bargaining committees. The structural devices for democratic direction and control must vary from trade to trade, union to union, but the form is less important than the spirit: namely, professional performance under democratic controls.

There are still further considerations in structuring a union. A union is constantly involved in conflict: collective bargaining, organizing strikes, grievance settlements. Whatever the form of the conflict, a high degree of discipline is required. Reconciling this need for discipline with democratic procedures is difficult, as many a democratic nation has discovered in time of war or severe crisis. Much of the answer lies in the kind of officials who head a union: how selected, how trained, how promoted. The fact that a man is popular with his buddies or can gather their votes in one way or the other is no guarantee that he is knowledgeable, efficient, democratic, or honest. The best guarantee of ethical conduct is his sense of dedication; the best guarantee of efficiency is his intelligence, training, and experience. And the best method for obtaining leadership of this calibre is a system of selection, training, testing, maturing, and promotion that combines the best features of West Point, a theological seminary, and ward politics.

The central point is this: ethics and efficiency are more a product of the kind of people who head an institution than of its forms, although a sound structure is a means for good men to rise and for the rank and file to run a continuing check on their leadership.

4. REGULAR INCOME WITH PUBLIC ACCOUNTABILITY. American unions can enjoy regular income through the union shop and through the maintenance-of-membership clause. The advantages of this stable income, in terms of superior service for the membership of the union, have been described. There is also a public good derived from stable unions resting on stable income and financing; namely, more stable industrial relations.

Advocates of laws to illegalize the union shop and the maintenance-of-membership clause too often fail to calculate their long-range effect on industrial relations. When a union has a security clause it is able to interpret its contracts with a degree of objectivity: processing a proper grievance, rejecting an improper one, halting a wild-cat, mediating a flare-up. It can act as a stabilizing influence because it need not fear that its acting with restraint will lose the union. But where the security clause is illegalized, the union is in constant fear that an irate member or membership will whimsically withdraw from dues payment. To keep the membership in line, the union needs issues, hot issues, daily issues. It can no longer afford to be moderate, statesmanlike, conciliatory—because the member who is irked by this objectivity may simply withdraw and get his shopmates to do likewise. Hence, the union leader will be driven to magnify and multiply each grievance, to process all of them no matter how unfounded, to keep tempers high, to perpetuate a battle atmosphere as a means of holding the ranks united.

From the point of view of both servicing the member and maintaining civilized industrial relations the union security clauses with their predictable flow of income through dues are highly desirable. However, because of the large sums of money involved, because they are to be held and used in trust for the membership, and because dues payments are obligatory, there must be public accountability of union finances. Preferably, this should be complete and voluntary. Failing that, it should be compulsory, under legislation that allows freedom of action

for the union while protecting the membership against theft, misappro-
priation, or malfeasance of funds.

5. AUTONOMY WITH COLLECTIVE RESPONSIBILITY.   Unions require
autonomy—in structure, in policy. It is necessary because of the wide
variety of circumstances in the crafts, trades, and industries to which
different unions must make adjustment. It is also required because of
local customs, ethnic attitudes, traditions. The continuing autonomy of
national and even local unions also contributes towards a pluralistic
distribution of power centers without which internal democracy is considerably weakened.

If antonomy were carried to its extreme, however, a union could
do anything it pleased without any need to account to anyone outside the
union. If the leadership effectively suppresses internal democracy, it does
not have to account to the membership. Then, enjoying unlimited
autonomy, it need not report to anyone, above or below. This kind of
autonomy is anarchy.

Although this situation actually prevailed in the old AFL for about
two generations, the labor movement in recent years has felt the need to
modify the old concept. This feeling arose from the fear that the good
name of labor would be blackened by the behavior of some unions and
unionists. Although labor as a whole had no legal responsibility for every
part thereof and lacked the constitutional means for correcting the
behavior of any part thereof, it nevertheless recognized that it had a
collective responsibility for each of its constituents before the public.
This realization created a concept of modified autonomy: If you want to
carry the family name, you must not disgrace the family. A minimum
standard of conduct is established and the Ethical Codes are enforced
with warnings, requests for reform, and ultimate expulsion.

The expulsion of a union from a labor federation does not mean
that the union goes out of existence. It can live—even grow—on its own.
And if its actions continue to be anti-social, the problem is no longer
simply one for the labor movement but, logically, for all of society and its
law enforcement agencies. It is at this point that confusion arises about
the handling of labor racketeering. Suppose a group of gangsters move
into the home of a respectable citizen and his family, terrorize the
household, spend the family's money, hold everyone in bondage by
violence. Would it be proper to put the family in jail for harboring
criminals? In the same fashion one might ask if labor should be held
responsible for the violent seizure by underworld elements which have
moved into some unions—unwelcome, uninvited, unwanted—just as they
have moved into business, sports, politics.

Labor can expel unions so dominated, but it cannot do the whole job. American society—with its vast governmental and non-governmental powers—must assume collective responsibility for handling illegal and anti-social elements within its midst. To do less is not only hypocrisy but indicates tacit approval of anarchy and violence. . . .

6. FREE TRADE UNIONISM WITHIN A FRAMEWORK OF PUBLIC LAW. Free trade unionism is one of the pillars of a democracy. The right to organize, to choose officers, to strike, to voice political opposition to the existing government—these are the hallmarks of free trade unionism. They are the first rights to be wiped out in dictatorial countries.

In the United States, the labor movement has been wary of governmental intervention in union affairs. This has been a firm tradition of both pure-and-simplers and social unionists. Clearly the former would be against state intervention. But, during the 1930's, when some locals that had been strongholds of social unionism were invaded by gangsters, using straight gangster methods, the socialists refused to go to the District Attorney, the police, or the courts to complain about beatings, sluggings, and rape of the union constitution. That the social unionists, with their interest in state intervention in the total economy, should oppose governmental codes dealing with unions would seem contradictory until one realizes that these people looked upon existing government as the "executive committee of the ruling class." By different avenues, both pure-and-simpler and social unionist came to the conclusion that the state should keep its hands off the unions.

In the light of some of the major problems facing the labor movement today, however, this attitude is antiquated. To begin with, the trade unions now enjoy official governmental recognition. Both the Wagner Act and the Taft-Hartley Act recognize collective bargaining as proper national policy and extend official recognition to the union that is able to win a majority of the votes in craft, shop, or industry election. The union shop and maintenance-of-membership clauses, with their guarantees to the union of stable membership and regular income, are also recognized by federal law. The law also defines unfair labor practices, theoretically guaranteeing to unions a reasonable climate within which to exist.

Because of this body of explicit law—and an even larger body of legal decisions that compose implicit law—a union, while voluntary, is only quasi-so, and, while private, is only quasi-so. This does not mean that law or the courts *created* any union. We do not have compulsory unionism such as exists in New Zealand. But neither do we have the kind of purely voluntary unionism that exists, let us say, in Italy or France where the union shop and majority rule are virtually unknown. American unions hold a *mid-position* as basically voluntary organizations that, at a given point of strength in a given situation, take on quasi-compulsory and quasi-public character because of the status granted the union at this level by law and by courts.

As such quasi-public institutions, deeply and immediately affecting the public interest, unions cannot hope to escape and should positively seek some degree of public regulation. They should demand a body of public law that would make union officers accountable not only to the membership but to the public for proper handling of finances and conformity with a union's democratic constitution. Such a body of law would establish a new plane of union existence, just as the various state laws determining and regulating the existence of political parties marked a new and higher level than obtained in the days when parties functioned as self-appointed clubs and caucuses totally outside all law.

This would mean a new and more intimate relationship between the unions and government. For, as unions pass into the area of governmental regulation, it is inevitable that labor will become more and more concerned with the nature and personnel of the prevailing government. State intervention in unions must stimulate union intervention in state, in exactly the same way that governmental interest in farm prices, in public utilities, in the rights of Negroes, in railroad labor conditions has stimulated farmer, utility, Negro, and railroad labor interest in government.

The alternative to proper legislative regulation of unions is no legislation. This is acceptable and feasible if there is no misuse of funds or power by trade union leadership. But so long as there is any sizable or well-publicized abuse—a probability made more likely in the absence of public regulation—the national temper will ultimately turn against unionism to demand not just that the abuses be eradicated but that the unions themselves be destroyed.

Such extremes can be avoided if there is a body of public law that would oversee this semi-public institution called the union; and it can best be drafted by those most intimately acquainted with the nature of the institution; namely, the trade union.

Can these six strands of proposed policy be woven into a pattern of balanced rights and responsibilities?

A union has the right to protect, advance, and champion its dues-paying members against all and any. But it has the responsibility to understand how its activities affect the total society of which it and its members are a part.

A union has the right to security: a union shop and a regular income. But it has the responsibility to guarantee internal democracy and to provide a proper accounting of its funds.

A union has the right to autonomous action. But it has the responsibility to join with its fellow unionists to establish and enforce a collective code of ethical, democratic, and socially-minded behavior.

A union has the right to develop methods and personnel that will provide a professional level of operation. But it has the responsibility to place this professional machinery under democratic controls.

A union has the right to political action. But it has the responsibility to turn its political power to high social purpose.

A union has the right to free action within a democracy and to establish legal status. But it has the responsibility to work within that democracy to define and regulate its legal status so as to give further strength and moral purpose to democratic society.

Is this philosophy new? Yes, it is new, in the sense that it discards the evil, the dying, and the dead; that it makes a selection of the good, the living, and the growing; that it conceives what has been non-existent out of existing creative forces that are worth preserving and multiplying. It represents no abrupt break with the present; it foresees no future without past. Is this not the way of living things?

5
Must Union Membership Decline?

The dialogue over the question of union growth has some very ironic aspects. In sheer numbers, the American labor movement is the largest of any in the western world (some 17 million in 1964). Union membership has the same meaning for millions of working men and women that membership in the professional association and junior chamber of commerce has for white-collar and professional workers. The influence of unions reaches into the very highest levels of economic and political decision-making. There is hardly a community in the country where unions have not made their influence felt. Few politicians at any level can afford to ignore the union view except at their own peril. Employers, of course, have long appreciated the vigor with which unions pursue their collective bargaining objectives. To be sure, there is opposition from many sources to the goals and conduct of specific unions; and from a number, albeit a dwindling number, of sources to the principle of unionism. But in the aggregate, American unions are no longer weak or poor. They exert wide influence and have at their disposal large resources of money and manpower.

It is ironic, therefore, that the question of growth in membership should be viewed as one of the most significant and difficult problems confronting the unions. In the opinion of many labor leaders, membership expansion is the single greatest problem confronting American unions. Does this concern reflect merely the thirst of powerful labor leaders for even greater power? Or do unions, in spite of their many achievements, face a problem in maintaining a rate of growth commensurate with the growth in the labor force. The answer is apparent. Unions do have a problem. Their general success in attracting millions of workers and obtaining benefits for them is dimmed by a parallel failure to extend union organization in significant numbers to the traditionally unorganized groups. It is these latter groups, particularly white-collar and government employees, who constitute the most rapidly expanding sectors of the American labor force. Although some of these workers are in unions, their proportion is far below the potential membership and far below the proportion of manual workers who are in unions.

Can American unions organize the growing armies of white-collar workers within the framework of the present trade union structure? Or will fundamental changes in union structure and method be required to accomplish the job? Or indeed, will unions stagnate, no matter what they do, as traditional sources of new members continue to shrink?

Those who are pessimistic about the prospects for union growth base their predictions mainly on changes in the composition and distribution of the American labor force. These arguments were stated in their sharpest form by Daniel Bell in an article written some ten years ago. Bell argues that the occupational and industrial groups which unions can organize are, for the most part, already organized to the saturation point. These traditional fields of union growth are declining in importance; and he sees scant evidence that unions can organize the growth sectors of the labor force.

Such arguments have been attacked by Irving Bernstein and others who conclude that there are no really valid reasons for assuming that unions will not continue to grow in the future in much the same way and for most of the same reasons that they grew in the past. The fact that unions have not expanded rapidly in recent years is, in Bernstein's judgment, not to be attributed to the special characteristics of the presently unorganized, but to a network of forces (especially economic ones) that have always controlled the ebb and flow of union growth.

Only the passage of time will tell which hypothesis is right, but the question is of considerable importance right now. At least in the white-collar sector, the evidence would seem to lend greater support to Bell's hypothesis. Although unions have been active among white-collar workers for a good many years, Solomon and Burns are able to show that in 1960 (6 years after the Bell article was written) only 2.7 million, or 15 per cent of all union members in the United States, were white-collar workers. Although there is high organization among certain white-collar groups (e.g., airline pilots, musicians, and railway clerks), only 13 per cent of the white-collar potential is organized. This degree of organization does not augur well for the union movement as a whole.

A bright spot in the Unions' horizon appeared in 1962 when

President Kennedy issued Executive Order 10988. It established the framework for a more effective system of employee-management cooperation in the rapidly expanding federal service. Unions generally applauded the Order. John Macy, the chairman of the U.S. Civil Service Commission, who has been involved in all steps of the program, assesses the system after one year of operation. Prior to the Order, the proportion of federal employees who were members of employee organizations was approximately the same as that of the Nation's nonfarm work force generally. It is still too early to say whether Executive Order 10988 will stimulate large-scale new organization, as unions hope, or whether its net effect will be simply to streamline and structure existing relationships.

Union activity in the federal service will require a modification of the traditional functions and methods of unions. It might be argued that this is due solely to the special nature of public employment. But this is only part of the reason. It is also probable that the major unorganized sectors generally (white-collar, professional, and public employees) require a different kind of protective organization.

Archie Kleingartner makes the point that, at least among salaried professional workers, the issue of growth cannot be defined simply as a question of whether these workers will join unions or be without any representation. In a number of these groups, the traditionally staid professional associations have assumed the characteristics and functions of unions. It may be an oversimplification to equate the absence of unionism among the salaried professions with an absence of representation.

The last two selections of the chapter present two sharply contrasting analyses of the role of unions among engineers and teachers —the two largest salaried professional groups in the country. In the first, the National Society of Professional Engineers, which wants it understood that it has "consistently, openly, and aggressively opposed the unionization of professional engineers," presents unionism among engineers as an aberration that is on its way to extinction. The NSPE views unions as completely irrelevant to the situation of engineers. In fact, the NSPE maintains that the continued presence of unionism constitutes a major stumbling block to full professional recognition for all engineers.

The Krider selection presents a vivid account of how one salaried professional worker made the decision to join a union. In doing so he rejected the viability of the dominant professional organization in teaching, the National Education Association. Krider makes it clear that his motivation for joining the teachers' union "was not directed by any zeal for labor unions *per se*." But once a member, he came increasingly to see unionism as a necessary instrument for giving teachers a greater voice in dealing with work and professional problems.

Daniel Bell
PROSPECTS FOR UNION GROWTH

. . . An assessment of the potentialities of union growth must stand, primarily, not in an analysis of the causal factors in the past but on the possibilities of those causal factors repeating themselves in the present and in the future. Take, for example, the causal hypothesis of social unrest, ergo union growth. Obviously, it was not social unrest *per se* that led to union growth, but social unrest among a particular type of worker, the industrial worker. But the industrial worker is organized. The white-collar worker is not. Would social unrest among white-collar workers lead to the same type of response as the industrial worker? I doubt it. In any event, an analysis of the causal role of "social unrest" should be based on an assessment of the make-up and social characteristics of the *present* unorganized work-force of the country. Looking at that work force I see little warranty, certainly in the sweeping conclusion that "if . . . the nation should experience another social cataclysm, we might soon thereafter expect to see a great expansion of union members." Why not?

Labor organization in the U.S. has proceeded—to use an alliterative device—by *eruption, extension* and *enforcement.* The most important is *eruption.* Here we see, as in the late thirties, a large-scale willingness on the part of workers to join unions. *Extension* takes place when, after a break-through, competitive and comparable firms are forced into line. This comes in a climate in which unorganized firms feel that they too should cease to resist unionism, and a feeling on the part of unorganized workers that perhaps unionism is not a bad thing. The stability and growth of union membership in the wartime forties, through National War Labor Board maintenance-of-membership represents the legitimation of extension. *Enforcement* takes place when through closed shops, union shops and other contractual and legal devices minority workers are "blanketed" into union membership. This has been the most characteristic form during the war and after, of the growth of the

Reprinted by permission of the publishers and the author from a discussion by Daniel Bell in *Proceedings of the Seventh Annual Meeting,* Industrial Relations Research Association (Madison, Wisconsin, 1955), pp. 231–236.
Mr. Bell is Professor of Sociology, Columbia University.

A.F. of L. Building Trades, and represents, probably, one of the chief elements in the recent growth of sections of the A.F. of L. Other unions may yet grow in the same fashion; the railroad unions, for example, will enlarge their membership once they obtain a union shop.

What are the prospects for the three processes? The most significant means of union growth are through the first two. . . .

Union membership in the last seven years or so, I have argued in *Fortune*,* has been on a plateau. In individual instances where growth has occurred, it has been largely through enforcement. . . .

My conclusions are based on present-day institutional considerations and their sociological consequences. Each of these could be elaborated to the full extent of a paper. For the sake of sharpening the argument, let me state them schematically:

1. In manufacturing (with the exception largely of textile and chemicals), and in mining and rail transport, most industry is about 80 to 100 per cent organized. Proving the degree of saturation is difficult, but, I accept, in the main, the B.L.S. statements in that regard. The problem of union growth is primarily one of *extension*.

2. Certainly, the big business firms in the economy are in the main unionized. A *Fortune* survey of 102 (out of 150) manufacturing firms who employ more than 10,000 workers, showed that fifty-five were between 80 to 100 per cent organized, and another thirty between 50 to 80 per cent organized. Only three dealt with no union at all. (A check of thirty-seven additional firms of this size showed thirty unionized to some degree, *Fortune*, June, 1952.)

3. In these areas, unorganized segments are almost completely supervisory and white-collar workers. The former have legal barriers to organization, the latter, as a prevalent practice, are given "tandem" increases and have little incentive therefore to join unions.

4. In manufacturing, the major unorganized areas are largely small size. The U.A.W. survey showed that 97 per cent of the still unorganized plants within the union's jurisdiction have less than 250 workers and 63 per cent have less than fifty. These plants are difficult and costly to organize. Social relations prevailing in these plants (identification with employer, etc.) are vastly different than in large plants. The size makes them costly to organize and service. Moreover, and here the trend even more sharply accentuates the problem, these plants are located in smaller towns, and in the South where the atmosphere is often distinctly hostile. Many of these plants—and the town's welfare consequently—live on their ability to cut union wage corners. The political atmosphere in these towns makes organizing more troublesome.

* "The next American Labor Movement," *Fortune*, April 1953 (ed.).

5. To sum up, in existing highly unionized industries the degree of further extension may be increasingly difficult. Unionism, here, may be said to have reached the top of the asymptote and is levelling off.

In the large remaining, unorganized areas, the areas where *eruption* would have to be the mode of union growth, there are a variety of institutional barriers. These can be indicated variously:

1. In trade and service lines, the small size of the units again becomes the major obstacle. Not only are the social relations different than in large plants, and organizing costly, but turn-over of personnel is higher, and union structure itself becomes a barrier. The most successful unions in the trade and service fields are, like District 65 of the Retail and Wholesale Workers, "amalgamated locals" embracing a wide variety of shops. For many unions, however, "amalgamated locals" create constitutional and structural barriers.

2. In office and financial institutions unionism has failed to take hold because its language and actions are cast in the mold of the industrial worker and unions have failed to find a language appropriate to white collar workers. A large majority of these workers are younger females with few expectations of permanent position and turnover again is high.

3. Management has learned considerably since the thirties, and its new personnel practices and benefits, its research into morale . . . its willingness to change supervisory practices tend to reduce an explosive atmosphere once conducive to unionism.

4. By social ideology, outlook and character, therefore it is unlikely that these workers in any *eruptive* manner will accept unionism.

Modern unionism, the unionism of the last two decades, has flourished largely in the hot-house area of government protection. Its growth in the last decade, as I have argued, has come, in large measure through various government-sanctioned *enforcement* devices. Here too, the picture has changed.

1. Government, on the national and state levels, is no longer favorable to unions. If anything, unionism today is conducting a holding operation. It was the National Labor Relations Board, in its rulings, which gave unions a firm seat at the bargaining table. As Professors Cox and Dunlop have shown (63 Harvard Law Review, 1950), the Board, by interpreting the clause "duty to bargain," successively brought into union purview not only wages and hours, but holiday and vacation pay, work schedules, merit increases, and finally pensions as subject of compulsory bargaining. Yet "there was not a word in the hearings, in the committee reports or the debates to suggest that the [Wagner] Act could define the subjects for collective bargaining or give the Board power to resolve issues in disputed cases." Given the political balance of the country, it is

doubtful whether any National Labor Relations Board, even under a Democratic administration, will lean heavily in a labor direction.

2. Public opinion, that amorphous and highly manipulable animal, is today distinctly edgy about unions. Talk about "Big Labor" . . . has had its effect in a suspicion of union purposes.

3. The barriers against the closed shop, against the hiring halls, etc., ineffectual as they may be, probably will remain. Union growth, as a reflection in the growth merely of the labor force, comes about through "enforcement." Again, except in places where the practices are deeply embedded, as in the building trades, a rise in union membership through enforcement may be nil.

Beyond these, other sociological factors which militate against union growth can be adduced. One is the bureaucratization of the labor movement. Many union leaders today fear a sudden growth in union membership, especially if such a growth might threaten existing power relations. Many union leaders have lost their élan; there is no will or ability any more to begin large-scale organizing drives. Evidences of corruption, particularly in welfare funds, and most often in the Teamsters union, undoubtedly sour a number of workers against unions and deepen the cynicism that unionism is merely a racket. And finally, one can point to the basic changes in the composition of the labor force—the growth of quaternary and quinary areas, primarily research, semi-professional, government, teaching employments, which for various reasons resist unionization.

In this analysis, I have borne down heavily, if schematically, on factors which will hinder real union growth. There are counteracting tendencies: the mechanization of the office and the stimulus, therefore, for some white-collar workers to join unions; the willingness of some employers, particularly in the distributive trades, to sign with unions rather than run the costs of harassments by the Teamsters. There will be significant internal changes in the composition of union strength as changes in technology and markets affect unions: electricians will expand, bricklayers contract; machinists will grow, textiles will shrink.

The question, however, is one of balance. My feeling, documented as well as I can, analytically and impressionistically, is that the tide of unionism has reached a high-water mark and that in the next five years—*as in the last five*—unionism will not advance significantly.

Irving Bernstein
THE GROWTH OF AMERICAN UNIONS, 1945–1960

During the past decade students of the American labor movement have differed sharply over its rate of growth. There have been two schools of thought. The "saturationists" have stressed structural factors. By the end of World War II, they have argued, unions had penetrated the readily organizable segments of the labor force—male, blue-collar workers employed mainly by large firms in the manufacturing, mining, transportation, and construction industries in the larger urban centers of the North and West. Labor organizations now faced the virtually impenetrable sectors—women, white-collar workers, employees in wholesale and retail trade, the service industries, the professions, government, and in agriculture, little firms, small towns, and the South. Further, the labor movement is disadvantaged by the contemporary labor force shift from blue- to white-collar employment.

The historical school has adopted a broader frame of analysis, emphasizing that many factors in addition to the structural have been at work in determining the rate of union growth. The labor movement is seen as increasing its size in two ways—at a modest pace over long spans of time and in sharp spurts at infrequent intervals. The forces that have caused secular growth are the expansion of the labor force, the increasing social acceptability of unionism, the growing homogeneity of the working class, and the extension of union security provisions in collective bargaining agreements. In the short run unions have increased their memberships dramatically as a consequence of wars and major depressions, in both of which government tends to intervene to protect the right to organize.

Fifteen years have now elapsed since the end of World War II. It is time to examine the course of union growth during this era in order to determine which of these analyses is correct.

This controversy seems preposterous on its face. The answer is a

From *Labor History*, Spring 1961. Reprinted by permission.
Mr. Bernstein is Professor of Political Science and Associate Director, Institute of Industrial Relations, University of California, Los Angeles.

matter of fact: during this period union membership has either increased or it has stagnated. One need only examine the figures to learn what happened. But the rub is in the statistics. There is no internally consistent series for the years 1945–1960.

Ultimately, all measurements of membership depend upon figures submitted by trade unions. The basic difficulty is that unions differ sharply in their definitions of a member. Some count only those who have paid dues; others employ the criterion of "good standing." This affects persons who are unemployed, on strike, in the armed forces, in apprenticeship, and in retirement. The definition significantly influences the count. In 1958, for example, the Bureau of Labor Statistics found that 62 international unions out of a total of 186 had 933,000 "members" who for various reasons did not pay dues. Another difficulty is that some unions do not report accurately. They either inflate the figures to show greater strength than they actually have for institutional reasons, or they inflate or deflate their memberships to avoid payment of per capita taxes to federal bodies or to raise or lower representation at federal conventions. There is, of course, no way of knowing how much of this goes on. In addition, many "international" unions have members outside the continental United States and show them in their statistics. The main concentration is in Canada, while others are located in Puerto Rico, Hawaii, Alaska, and the Canal Zone. In 1958, according to BLS, 1.2 million were in this category, of whom 1.1 million were in Canada. Finally, the agencies that count members nationally rely upon the international unions as sources and do not include the members of organizations confined to one employer or to one locality. BLS estimated that in 1958 over 500,000 persons were members of these smaller organizations. Thus, the reader should bear these qualifications in mind in evaluating the data that follow. That is, they exclude many persons in good standing who do not pay dues, contain some inaccurate reports, include foreign and territorial members, and exclude members of organizations limited to a single locality or employer.

For the purpose of this paper it is necessary to have an annual membership series for 1945–1960 with reasonable internal consistency. . . .

Table 1 shows the actual membership of American labor unions for the period 1945–1960. . . . It also reveals . . . "real" union membership, that is, actual membership expressed as a per cent of the civilian labor force. Since some students of union growth prefer the employment over the labor force series in calculating real membership, Table 1 also gives these data. In my judgment they are not satisfactory because unions have both unemployed and self-employed members as well as farm workers who are not counted in the nonagricultural employment statistics.

For the period as a whole the actual membership of unions rose 5,228,000, or 39.1 per cent. Viewed historically, this is a formidable absolute achievement. The number of members added during these sixteen years exceeded the total size of the labor movement in any year prior to 1937. The percentage of growth is also impressive when one considers the high base. That is, a 1 per cent increase on the 1945 base yielded 133,790 members; for 1930 it was only 29,730, for 1900 but 8,685. Real union membership, however, advanced only modestly, 2.5 per cent between the terminal years of 1946 and 1960. (Here it is advisable to disregard 1945 because the disproportionately large number in the armed forces in that year depressed the size of the civilian labor force.)

There were, of course, significant internal differences within this sixteen-year span of time. Seven phases are notable. The first is the post-World War II boom, which lasted from 1945 to 1949, in which American unions added 1,581,000 members, a gain of 11.8 per cent. During these years real membership was fairly steady at about 24 per cent. This was a time of full employment and of marked increase in consumer prices, both of which contributed to union expansion.

The recession of 1949–1950 formed the second period, which saw

TABLE 1. *Union Membership, 1945–1960*

		"REAL" MEMBERSHIP		ALTERNATE "REAL" MEMBERSHIP	
YEAR	ACTUAL MEMBERSHIP (THOUSANDS)	CIVILIAN LABOR FORCE (THOUSANDS)	UNION MEMBERSHIP AS PER CENT OF CIVILIAN LABOR FORCE	NON-AGRICULTURAL EMPLOYMENT (THOUSANDS)	UNION MEMBERSHIP AS PER CENT OF NONAGRICULTURAL EMPLOYMENT
1945	13,379	53,860	24.8	40,037	33.4
1946	13,648	57,520	23.7	41,287	33.1
1947	14,845	60,168	24.7	43,462	34.2
1948	14,916	61,442	24.3	44,448	33.6
1949	14,960	62,105	24.1	43,315	34.5
1950	14,751	63,099	23.4	44,738	33.0
1951	16,211	62,884	25.8	47,347	34.2
1952	16,730	62,966	26.6	48,303	34.6
1953	17,884	63,815	28.0	49,681	36.0
1954	17,757	64,468	27.5	48,431	36.7
1955	17,749	65,847	27.0	50,056	35.5
1956	18,477	67,530	27.4	51,766	35.7
1957	18,430	67,946	27.1	52,162	35.3
1958	18,081	68,647	26.3	50,543	35.8
1959	18,452	69,394	26.6	51,975	35.5
1960	18,607	71,056	26.2	53,135	35.0

a decline in membership of 209,000 in 1950, or 1.4 per cent. Real membership dropped to 23.4 per cent, the lowest point of any year between 1945 and 1960. At this time joblessness was quite severe and consumer prices fell slightly.

The Korean War of 1950–1953 was the third phase and witnessed the most notable advance in union membership—3,133,000, or 21.2 per cent. Here real membership rose to 28 per cent, the peak for the whole period. Conditions were highly favorable for union growth: more than full employment and a sharp rise in the cost of living.

The fourth phase occurred during the succeeding recession of 1953–1955, which saw a decline of 135,000, or 0.8 per cent. Real membership dropped one point to 27 per cent. At this time there was a good deal of joblessness and prices were steady.

During the capital goods boom of 1955–1956, the fifth period, membership rose by 728,000, or 4.1 per cent. In 1956 real membership recovered to 27.4 per cent. At this time there was substantially full employment and a modest rise in prices.

The sixth phase took place during the recession of 1957–1958, when membership fell 396,000, or 2.1 per cent. Real membership declined a full point to 26.3 per cent. This downturn saw severe unemployment and, interestingly enough, some increase in prices.

The final period was the recovery of 1959–1960, in which membership rose by 526,000, or 2.9 per cent. Real membership, however, did not recover, remaining at a fraction over 26 per cent. While unemployment diminished, a significant amount of joblessness remained and the size of the civilian labor force leapt upwards in 1960. Further, employment lagged in two sectors in which unions are relatively strong— manufacturing and mining. At the same time prices rose modestly. . . .

I shall now turn to an intensive examination of the "saturationist" analysis. Before doing so, however, I must stress the importance of the fact that we know little in a systematic way of how unions organize. The only method that is charted is the election procedure of the National Labor Relations Act. It is hazardous to draw general conclusions from this information. Unions in many industries lack legal recourse to the NLRB; other organizations which are eligible to use the Board prefer other methods; the United Mine Workers during much of the period under examination refused to qualify itself under the Taft-Hartley Act. For these and perhaps other reasons only a limited number of labor organizations normally seek to organize through the election procedure of the NLRB and they are heavily concentrated in manufacturing industries. From 1946 to 1959 the factory segment of NLRB collective bargaining elections fluctuated between 64.1 and 78.4 per cent of all such elections.

There are many other methods by which unions organize, some acting through the employees, others through an employer, and still others through another labor organization. The union may conduct an organizational drive, sign up enough members to demand a contract, and persuade the employer either voluntarily or after a strike to begin collective bargaining. In an expanding bargaining unit covered by a union or closed shop new employees automatically become members. In the case of a corporation already under agreement which opens a branch plant the union may extend the existing contract to the new unit, often with the consent or even active support of the employer. Similarly, a master agreement in a multi-employer unit may be extended to a new or hitherto unorganized firm. Or the union may disregard the employees and organize the employer under a union security provision which automatically makes his people members. Finally, unions may add to their ranks from the membership of other unions by raiding or by merger; or a powerful organization, frequently the Teamsters, may compel an employer to deal with a weak union. There is little firm knowledge on the incidence of these techniques or their distribution among industries and unions.

With this qualification, I shall now turn to an assessment of the roadblocks to union growth stressed by the saturationists. They point out, first, that women are less well organized than men and that the prospect is for a larger female proportion of the labor force. Both points are valid. In the mid-fifties, according to BLS, only about 16 per cent of the females in the labor force were union members in contrast with 31 per cent of the males. Further, the proportion of women has been rising secularly—17.7 per cent of the labor force in 1900, 21.9 in 1930, 25.3 in 1940, 30.3 in 1955. Ewan Clague, the Commissioner of Labor Statistics, anticipates a figure of 33.4 per cent by 1965.

In fact, we know nothing about the comparative propensity of men and women to join unions. In the abstract there is no reason to anticipate a difference, because the economic and social forces that shape the decision work on both sexes. Women, that is, tend to be as indifferent or as militant as men. The difference in the membership rate, rather, is to be explained largely by the fact that women work primarily in industries and occupations into which unions have not made a deep penetration, primarily office, sales, and services. In those areas both sexes are relatively unorganized. . . .

The second saturationist argument is that unions, which have in the main organized large corporations, now face the tougher small firms. Here there is no certainty as to fact in general, although it is the case in manufacturing. A big anti-union employer, obviously, has greater resources than a little one; the UAW had more trouble organizing General

Motors than the typical parts supplier. The great majority of NLRB elections that unions have won have been in units with fewer than 100 employees—83.8 per cent of the total in 1959. Union representatives in both manufacturing and services have informed me that their organizations could unionize many more small units if they wished. The question is only in part whether the job can be done; more often it is whether it is worth the expenditure in time and money in view of the potential return. In recent years the labor movement seems normally to have answered this question in the negative. Many unions, as well as the AFL-CIO, have been operating under restricted budgets.

The saturationists, third, make the same contention about small towns. Again, it is not an assured (though a probable) fact that big cities are better organized than little ones. Exceptions come readily to mind. In California, for example, Fresno and Bakersfield are more highly unionized than Los Angeles. In that state between 1954 and 1957 the three leading areas in rate of union growth—the Southeast, Santa Barbara-Ventura, and the Sacramento Valley—had no great cities. In California, and I suspect elsewhere, the industrial spillover from cities to satellite communities in expanding metropolitan areas has brought unionism to small towns.

On the other hand, the atmosphere of a community can influence the propensity to unionize. Historically, for example, this factor made the difference between "closed-shop" San Francisco and "open-shop" Los Angeles. For all practical purposes, there are no longer large cities in which anti-union sentiment predominates. Some small cities of this sort remain, largely in the South and in the Plains states. However, this does not in itself prove that small towns are harder to organize.

The fourth roadblock to union growth, the saturationists argue, is agriculture. It is, of course, a fact that virtually no farm workers belong to labor organizations and that they are denied the benefits of the National Labor Relations Act. The obstacles to unionization are formidable. Even here, however, there are long-term forces at work—mechanization, a rising skill level, and a rapidly shrinking labor force—that suggest that some day organization may come. It is not without significance that, as this paper is written, the most serious campaign in a generation to unionize California's farms is underway.

The fifth saturationist contention is that government employees are hard to unionize. It is true that public workers are not as highly organized as those in manufacturing, mining, and construction. Yet . . . both actual and real union membership among government employees have been rising in the United States and in California. There are many reasons for this development: the narrowing of historic fringe benefit differentials between private industry and government, the growing variety in public employment, the increased willingness of government instrumentalities to experiment with collective bargaining systems, and the shift of some properties, especially in local transit, from private to public ownership. . . .

Sixth, the saturationists argue that the South is a formidable regional bar to unionization. Here analysis is hobbled by the virtual absence of membership statistics. The latest estimate is Troy's, which showed that the South Atlantic, East South Central, and West South Central areas lagged far behind the rest of the nation in 1953. A study by H. M. Douty of manufacturing workers covered by collective bargaining agreements in 1958 suggests that the gap may have narrowed in recent years. He found that 46.1 per cent of southern factories had bargaining agreements covering a majority of their workers in contrast with 67.9 in the Northeast, 72.6 in the West, and 76.5 per cent in the North Central. Douty also concluded for the nation as a whole that the number of workers covered by agreements was the same as the number of union members. Frederic Meyers has found significant unionization in Texas not only in manufacturing but also in nonmanufacturing industries: virtually 100 per cent in telephone and telegraph and on the railroads, 80 per cent in transit and interstate trucking, 50 per cent in construction, and 25 per cent in electric utilities.

It is popular to conceive of the South as a monolith; in fact, there are significant internal differences. Douty discovered for manufacturing a high degree of unionization in primary metals, petroleum and coal products, transportation equipment, paper, tobacco, stone, clay, and glass, machinery, chemicals, and printing and publishing. The low incidence industries were textiles, lumber, furniture, and apparel. In general, both Meyers and Ray Marshall have emphasized that unions have been most successful in organizing newer and larger units (notably branch plants of nation-wide corporations) and have found the going tougher in the older and smaller establishments (especially in textiles). As the South has industrialized, the proportion of the former has risen and unions have thereby gained.

In the light of these findings, fragmentary though they are, it would be incorrect to regard the South as the Sahara of the labor movement. Unionism, though still markedly behind in that region, has made notable gains. This is confirmed by the regional distribution of NLRB collective bargaining elections: prior to the Korean War the South accounted for less than 20 per cent; in the late fifties its share rose to about 25 per cent of these elections. Certain unions, especially the Teamsters and District 50 of the United Mine Workers, have invested in vigorous organizing campaigns in the South with not insignificant success. As the region industrializes, one might reasonably anticipate the further growth of union membership.

This is not to say that the saturationist hypothesis is wholly invalid. It seems to explain those industries into which unions have failed to penetrate deeply—textiles, hosiery, lumber, and furniture. In all probability it also explains the weakness of unionism in some southern communities.

Finally, and with great emphasis, the saturationists stress the white-collar bar to unionization. The American labor movement in membership, leadership, and tradition is predominantly blue-collar. In 1958, according to BLS, only 2.2 million trade unionists, just 12 per cent of the total, were in nonmanual occupations. Of the twenty-nine members of the Executive Council of AFL-CIO at that time only two— the presidents of the Railway Clerks and the Retail Clerks—were from white-collar organizations. In addition, the labor force is undergoing a secular shift away from manual to nonmanual employment. In 1910 professional and technical workers, managers, officials and proprietors, clerical and sales workers accounted for 22 per cent of the labor force; by 1956 this share had risen to almost 40 per cent and for the first time exceeded the number of manual workers. "The most important occupational development that we foresee," Ewan Clague has written, "is a more rapid increase in employment among white-collar workers than among the blue-collar workers."

There is a tendency to lump all white-collar workers together. In fact, they have significant differences. A professional engineer, a motion picture star, a railway clerk, a telephone operator, a postal clerk, a checker in a food market, a secretary in the central office of a large corporation, and a secretary in a lawyer's office have as little in common with each other as they have with manual workers. They are divided by differences in education, income, employment regularity, status, and relationship to the employer, all of which shape their propensity to unionize. Further, the shift to white-collar employment has been uneven. Within the manufacturing group, for example, the percentage of manual workers declined sharply between 1944 and 1959 in aircraft, petroleum, and chemicals; fell moderately in machinery, steel, paper, stone, clay, and glass; and dropped only slightly in rubber, shipbuilding, and textiles. Thus, it is hazardous, if not impossible, to generalize about the organization of white-collar workers as a whole.

This conclusion is reinforced by an examination of the distribution of union membership within nonmanual occupations. They are strongly organized on the railroads and in telecommunications. In public agencies extensive unionization exists in the postal service, with much less in other federal agencies and in state, county, and municipal employment. There is uneven organization of the clerical staffs of manufacturing firms. Virtually no unionism exists in banking, finance, and real estate, although there is some in insurance. In retailing, unions have made significant penetrations into department stores, into food, drug, and variety chain stores, and into mail-order houses, but into little else. Professional people in the entertainment field are almost completely organized, as are the air line pilots. A substantial number of newspaper reporters and editors are union members. Only a slight percentage of school teachers, nurses, engineers, scientists, architects, draftsmen, and technicians are in labor organizations.

It is precisely in the white-collar area that union growth has made impressive strides in recent years. The expanding organizations . . . have been the Air Line Pilots, the Railway Clerks, the Teamsters (with a substantial membership in retail and wholesale trade as well as in clerical occupations), the Retail Clerks, the Retail, Wholesale, and Department Store Union, the Musicians, the Screen Actors, AFTRA, the postal organizations, and the State, County, and Municipal Employees. Few serious students of the labor movement regard the present low level of organization among white-collar people as permanent. Jack Barbash has recently written, "When the white-collar person becomes a baby sitter for an automated machine, pride of work gets drained out of his job, and he is going to try to join with his fellows. . . . Once the white-collar worker gets over the initial trauma of being in a union, he behaves like a bricklayer."

This is not to say that the organization of nonmanual workers on a massive scale is likely to come about either quickly or dramatically. In all probability the growth will occur differentially by continuation of those expansionist tendencies already evident and by the gradual emergence of new ones. Certain areas, for example, banking, finance, real estate, and office employees in very small units, will be organized in the distant future, if at all. In order to achieve the unionization of white-collar people it will be necessary for the labor movement to adapt itself in structure and in outlook and for Congress to amend the National Labor Relations Act, which presently denies certain nonmanual workers the benefits of the statute. The organization of these workers is presently and prospectively the Number 1 challenge to the American labor movement. There is no reason to regard it as insurmountable.

Daniel Bell wrote in 1953: "In 1946 U.S. unions had organized about 15 million workers—48 per cent of the 31 million potential members. . . . Since 1946 the working population has expanded but union membership has remained stationary." As Table 1 demonstrates, his figure for 1946 was more than 1 million too high and his estimate for 1953 was almost 3 million too low. In fact, between 1946 and 1953 American unions added 4.2 million actual members and their proportion of the labor force advanced 4.3 per cent. In the entire period between the close of World War II and 1960 the American labor movement grew in size by more than 5 million and real membership rose 2.5 per cent. As the discussion in the preceding section indicates, I do not believe that the saturationist arguments taken together have general validity. Only a handful deserve any weight and that in relatively narrow sectors: small towns in the South and the Plains states; the textile, hosiery, furniture, and lumber industries in the South; some white-collar areas—banking, finance, real estate, and office employees in small units.

Thus, I think the saturationist analysis must be dismissed as a general proposition. There is no difficulty in fitting the period 1945–1960 into the historical theory. It was an era dominated by the slow, secular rise of union membership, actual and real. There was a secondary war which stimulated the growth rate, and no major depression occurred. In these features this period paralleled the years 1897–1914. In that earlier era union membership, actual and real, grew gradually except for the acceleration given the rate by the Spanish-American War, and there was no deep economic downturn.

In one respect the years since 1945 constitute an aberration: in no prior period in the history of the American labor movement has so large a proportion of its constituency worked in manufacturing industries. This has made membership more sensitive to fluctuations in employment than at any other time, at least during the twentieth century. This is because employment in manufacturing is more sensitive to the cycle than is employment in nonmanufacturing. The decline in the manufacturing share of total union membership, which became evident in the late fifties, constitutes, I suspect, a permanent resumption of the pre-World War II pattern. If this proves to be the case, union membership in the future should be less sensitive to employment fluctuations than it was in the recent past.

This shift from manufacturing to nonmanufacturing unionism suggests several probable aspects of union growth in the future. First, it is likely to come quietly, in a fashion unlike the great manufacturing breakthrough of the thirties. The pattern has already been laid down by such organizations as the Retail Clerks and the State, County, and Municipal Employees, which grew rapidly in the fifties without major strikes and with little public attention. Second, there are likely to be significant changes in the centers of power within the labor movement. The relative gains of the Teamsters, the building trades, the Hotel and Restaurant Employees, the Railway Clerks, the Meat Cutters, and the Retail Clerks at the expense of the industrial unions in manufacturing and mining have been noted. This trend should continue to the advantage of most of these nonmanufacturing organizations. They may well be joined in size by such presently modest unions as the Building

Service and the State, County, and Municipal Employees. Third, we may expect the leadership of the labor movement increasingly to reflect its growing white-collar base. In some nations in which nonmanual organization is highly developed, notably the Netherlands and Germany, the white-collar group supplies a disproportionately large share of labor leadership.

Finally, it is necessary to note and explain the fact that between 1956 and 1960 actual union membership did not grow and real membership fell. As already indicated, I do not think the saturationist hypothesis offers a useful explanation. This was the time when the revelations of the McClellan Committee blackened the public's "image" of the labor movement. While this factor, undoubtedly, explains the stagnation in part, I think it is only in small part. The Teamsters, who suffered most from the exposures, actually expanded during these years. Far more fundamental, in my judgment, was the failure of the American economy to grow. Output did not advance significantly and there was a persistent and large lump of unemployment. The growth of the labor movement is inextricably linked to the growth of the economy. If union membership expands in the future, it will do so only as part of an expanding economic system.

Benjamin Solomon
Robert K. Burns

UNIONIZATION
OF WHITE-COLLAR EMPLOYEES

In recent re-examinations and "agonizing reappraisals" of the status and "decline of the labor movement," the possibility of unionization of white-collar workers is being given increasing attention. . . .

In 1960, the over-all union potential totaled 47 million, of which

Reprinted from Benjamin Solomon and Robert K. Burns, "Unionization of White-Collar Employees: Extent, Potential, and Implication," *The Journal of Business*, Vol. 36, April 1963, by permission of The University of Chicago Press. Copyright 1963 by The University of Chicago.

Mr. Solomon and Mr. Burns are both affiliated with the Industrial Relations Center, University of Chicago.

20.8 million, or 44 per cent, were white-collar employees and 26.2 million, or 56 per cent, were blue-collar employees. Of the white-collar workers, an estimated 2.7 million, or 13 per cent, are union members. These comprise 15 per cent of all union members in the United States. . . .

CLERICAL AND KINDRED WORKERS

Approximately 5.4 million of the 9.1 million clerical and kindred workers in the 1960 union potential are "office workers" as contrasted with peripheral and kindred groups such as railroad clerks, letter carriers, telephone operators, clerical workers in plants and warehouses, and the like, who account for the remaining 3.7 million. Of the 5.4 million office workers, about 70 per cent, or 3.8 million, are estimated to be located in urbanized areas (central cities and their fringes). A major part of the office workers in urbanized areas are concentrated in central business districts or outlying business or manufacturing districts.

Office workers are the largest of the white-collar groups and represent perhaps the most widely accepted image of the white-collar employee. It is interesting to note, therefore, that the number organized is probably no more than 500,000, less than 10 per cent of the total. There is little apparent concentration of organization, whether by union, by geographical location (such as the central business district of a large city), or by industry. The union with the primary jurisdiction in the field, the Office Employees International Union, had only 65,000 members in early 1962. A more substantial segment is held by a number of industrial unions in manufacturing fields and by unions in the telephone industry. In important fields such as finance, insurance, and real estate (with some 1.25 million office employees in 1960), there has been little organization of office workers by any union. The unions operating in the government field (not including post office) are estimated to have less than one-sixth of government office employees in their ranks.

In the peripheral and kindred groups, the several postal unions have a high degree of organization of the clerical workers in post offices. The same is true for unions among railway clerks, railway telegraphers, and commercial telegraphers. There is substantial organization of telephone operators. Industrial unions have organized some significant numbers (though not large proportions) of plant clerical workers. The retail unions and the Teamsters have organized small sections of the clerical employees in stores, warehouses, and mail-order houses. All told, the peripheral and kindred group account for about two-thirds (or about 1.1 million) of the total union membership among the 9.1 million clerical and kindred workers.

PROFESSIONAL, TECHNICAL, AND KINDRED WORKERS

The Census Bureau lists sixty-nine separate occupational titles in the professional, technical, and kindred worker category. Any discussion of unionism in this field will necessarily reflect this high diversity, though the decisive questions relate to a few large occupations.

Professional workers in the entertainment services are highly organized, and there is substantial unionization in the smaller fields comprised of reporters, air pilots, and technicians in radio communication. Important unionization efforts exist in two large fields, engineers and scientists and schoolteachers, but on a scale that is small compared to the size of these fields. There is limited organizing activity in the professional nursing field. Beyond this, there are a variety of professional or technical occupations, mostly of medium or small size, for which there is no union whose major jurisdiction is in the field, though one or more unions may organize some of the members of the occupation.

Unionization of engineers and scientists by the American Federation of Technical Engineers (AFTE), which has the AFL-CIO jurisdiction among engineers, is negligible. In 1960, there were over 1 million engineers and scientists, of whom some 850,000 were in private employment. Of those in private employment, 70 per cent were in manufacturing, with concentrations in electrical equipment, aerospace and ordnance, and chemicals. A good part of the small membership of the AFTE is at subprofessional levels and is in the state and local government, construction and railroad fields. The largest share of organization among engineers and scientists is that held by the local, non-affiliated unions, with the major concentration of these in the West Coast aerospace industry. Some of the large industrial unions affiliated with the AFL-CIO have sought to organize engineers and scientists in their respective jurisdictions but with limited results so far.

Out of a total of 1.8 million schoolteachers in 1961, almost 1.5 million worked in public elementary and secondary schools in 31,700 school districts. An estimated 600,000 of the public school teachers are concentrated in 800 to 900 school districts in cities of about 25,000 or more population. The American Federation of Teachers (AFT), the chief union in this large occupation, had a membership of 70,000 in early 1962.

Though the jurisdiction is vast, the future extension of unionism among teachers will be decisively influenced by the headway the AFT is able to make in a small number of large city school systems. A high proportion of AFT membership has historically been concentrated in the large northern and western cities, but most of these locals have not been able to win a majority of teachers as members. While the union has gained steadily during the post-World War II years, its progress has been slow despite the favorable climate for new organization provided by inflationary pressures and demand-and-supply conditions. However, the winning of collective bargaining rights for the 40,000 teachers in the New York City schools following a brief strike in 1961 may provide a new impetus for AFT growth.

The new fluidity in teacher unionization arising from the possibility that other school boards may be persuaded to grant collective bargaining may also affect the policies and tactics of the AFT's traditional rival, the National Education Association. The NEA, by vigorously advocating the doctrine that teacher unionism is unprofessional, has been a major force in limiting the progress of the AFT. But with the growing likelihood of the spread of collective representation and negotiations, the role of the NEA and its state affiliates may undergo significant change in the coming years. It appears likely that the NEA, while still eschewing unionism, will strive to develop approaches that it can describe as "professional" and that will enable it to establish itself as the representative of teachers in negotiating salaries and working conditions with school boards.

SALES WORKERS

Of the total union potential of 4 million in the sales occupations, 2.6 million, or 65 per cent, are retail sales workers. The largest single retail group, totaling 0.5 million, are in the food lines, while the remaining 2.1 million are in the various other retail merchandise lines. Some 1.4 million sales workers are in non-retail fields, such as insurance, advertising, or selling at the wholesale and manufacturing levels.

The major base of sales-worker unionization is in the retail sector. The Retail Clerks, by far the strongest union in the retail field, has about half its strength among food supermarkets and the other half among the other retail lines. The much smaller holdings of the Retail, Wholesale and Department Store Union include department stores and specialty lines such as shoe and drug stores, mainly in New York City. In some sectors the Meat Cutters have extended their organization to the grocery departments of supermarkets, while the Clothing Workers have some retail strength in men's clothing stores and, more recently, in discount stores. The Teamsters have established something of a foothold through their organization of a large part of Montgomery Ward.

As with other major white-collar fields, such as office employees or schoolteachers, the focus of organization has been in the urban areas and large cities. Points of concentration are food chains, mail order chains, large department stores and department store chains, and chain systems in other retail lines. On a geographic basis, the downtown shopping districts of large cities, neighborhood shopping districts, and suburban shopping centers offer concentration of retail salespeople. Most organization is along trade lines within a particular city or larger region.

The organization of retail sales personnel has moved forward steadily as indicated by the approximate doubling in membership since 1949 of the leading union in the field, the Retail Clerks. However, the greater part of the jurisdiction still remains unorganized. Progress in the last decade has been slow among department stores, a sector of both numerical and strategic importance. A little under one-half of white-collar retail union membership consists of supermarket employees. From the standpoint of the amount of salesmanship required by grocery sales clerks in supermarkets, these employees can best be viewed as a peripheral white-collar group.

Organization among wholesale salesmen is minor and is practically nonexistent in other sales lines such as manufacturing salesmen, real estate agents, or advertising salesmen. In the insurance field, there is strong organization among only one category of insurance agent, the sellers of industrial insurance. . . .

John W. Macy, Jr.
EMPLOYEE-MANAGEMENT COOPERATION IN THE FEDERAL SERVICE

For the first time in its history the civilian service of the executive branch of Government has a uniform, comprehensive plan and policy for cooperative relationships between employee organizations and management. What are the objectives of this program? How did it come about? How does it differ from the systems of employee-management relations in industry? An appreciation of the answers to these questions is essential

From *Personnel Administrator,* January–February 1963, Society for Personnel Administration, Washington, D.C. Reprinted by permission.
Mr. Macy is Chairman of the U.S. Civil Service Commission.

to an understanding of the impact which this program is expected to have on relationships between employees and their supervisors in the Federal Service.

THE SETTING FOR THE FEDERAL PROGRAM

Although there has been a long history of formal union-management relationships in American industry, the Federal Government has lagged in the development of a systematic policy governing relationships with its own employees.

This does not mean that unions have not been active in the Federal service nor that there has been a complete absence of organized relationships with management.

As early as 1830 some craftsmen engaged in Federal industrial activities were affiliated with unions. In 1861 Government employee unions persuaded Congress to enact the first of the "prevailing wage" statutes which laid the basis for agency wage board systems under which some 700,000 Federal blue collar workers are now paid. Unions of postal employees became active in the late 1800's. More recently, negotiations of a rather highly developed nature were to be found in segments of the U.S. Interior and Post Office Departments and the Tennessee Valley Authority.

However, in spite of these evidences of a gradually increasing role for employee organizations and a demonstration of their ability to participate responsibly in the cooperative programs established in some departments, there was no clear, Government-wide policy for their recognition. Lacking guidance in this area, most agencies had made little progress towards establishing active programs of their own. To an increasing extent there was public and Congressional interest in the development of a Government-wide policy which would bring the Government up to date with industry in relationships with its employees.

It was in this setting that President Kennedy issued a memorandum on June 22, 1961, designating a special task force to advise him on employee-management relations in the Federal service. The Task Force consisted of the Secretary of Labor as Chairman, the Chairman of the Civil Service Commission as Vice Chairman, the Secretary of Defense, the Postmaster General, the Director of the Bureau of the Budget, and the Special Counsel to the President. This Task Force made an extensive study of the state of relations between management and employee organizations both in and outside of the Federal Government. The findings of the Task Force clearly confirmed the need for a consistent, Government-wide policy.

On November 30, 1961 the Task Force presented its report and recommendations to the President. The recommendations were accepted and given effect by the issuance of Executive Orders 10987 and 10988 on January 17, 1962. . . .

THE NATURE OF THE PROGRAM

Executive Order 10987 provided for a more uniform system of appeals within the agencies and the extension to non-veterans in the competitive service of the same adverse action rights as veterans already had. This was of itself a highly significant accomplishment; however, it was Executive Order 10988 which focussed greatest attention directly on the question of employee-management cooperation.

The program conceived by the Task Force and established by Executive Order 10988 is not an exact duplicate of programs found in private industry. Rather, it is one which has been very carefully tailored to the special needs of the Federal service.

The differences between the Government's program and those found in industry are traceable to the differences in applicable laws and to the basic principle of the public interest in the successful accomplishment of the functions of Government. The laws governing labor relations in the private sphere do not apply to the Federal scene and conversely there are special provisions of law and policy—such as the principle of the merit system—which must be taken into account in the Federal program.

Thus, for example, it has been established by law of Congress that there may be no strikes against the Federal Government. Other acts of Congress, such as the various pay laws, provisions for annual and sick leave, retirement and insurance statutes, etc., limit the areas of personnel policy which are subject to negotiation. Many matters relating to the basic personnel structure, basic benefits, and basic employee rights which would be established in industry through collective bargaining, are thus established for Federal employees by law and regulation.

The principle of the public interest and the unique character of Government programs are reflected in provisions such as the following:

All agreements are subject to approval by the head of the agency concerned.

Management officials retain the right, in accordance with law and regulations, to assign and direct employees, to hire and fire, to reduce staff, to determine methods of operation, and to take any action necessary to carry out the mission of the agency in emergencies.

If, after full discussion, agreement is not reached on any matter under negotiation, there is no provision for third party arbitration and the decision of the agency prevails.

Provision is made for adoption of procedures for arbitration of grievances, but this is limited to advisory arbitration.

The program is not applicable to any office performing intelligence, investigative, or security functions. Agency heads may suspend the application of the program to activities outside the U.S. if necessary in the national interest.

There is strict management neutrality on the question of forming organizations of employees. Management may do nothing to hinder or assist the organizing of employee groups.

The closed shop is prohibited.

The freedom of employees to join or not to join lawful employee organizations is maintained.

Another feature which contrasts with labor relations practice in industry is the provision for three levels of recognition (namely: informal, formal and exclusive) to accommodate varying levels of employee interest in programs of consultation and negotiation. The official recognition of employee organizations does not alter the special consultative relationships which Government agencies have maintained with veteran organizations.

The Task Force estimated that about one-third of all Federal employees were members of employee organizations, approximately the same as the extent of union affiliation in the Nation's non-farm work force. However, outside the Post Office Department where 84% of employees are members of employee organizations, only about 16% of Federal employees are members. The extent of membership in these remaining agencies ranges from some 82% in the TVA to less than 10 members of employee organizations on the staffs of each of 17 agencies, most of which are relatively small in size.

The *informal* form of recognition does not require that an employee organization have any minimum number of employees as its members. It entitles an organization to express its views on matters of interest to its members, but it can claim no right to be consulted. This form of recognition may be granted without regard to the granting of recognition to other organizations, provided that the organization concerned meets certain basic requirements of ethical conduct and meets the basic definition of an employee organization.

The *formal* type of recognition is appropriate where an organization has at least 10% of the employees in a unit or activity as its members and where no organization has been granted exclusive recognition. This form of recognition carries the affirmative right to be consulted on matters of interest to the members of the organization.

Exclusive recognition may be granted to an organization that is chosen by the majority of the employees in an appropriate unit. Exclusive recognition carries the right to enter collective negotiations for the purpose of reaching an agreement in writing, applicable to all employees of the unit.

In addition to the provision for varying degrees of recognition, in proportion to the degree of employee interest within units determined to be appropriate for purposes of representation, the program is sensitive to the special needs and interests of supervisory and professional employees. Units established for exclusive recognition may not contain both professionals and non-professionals unless a majority of the professional employees votes for inclusion in the unit. Where exclusive recognition is involved, units may not include managerial officers nor the supervisors of the employees concerned. Professionals and supervisory groups are free to establish organizations of their own and, where appropriate, separate units may be established and such organizations granted recognition.

The policy established by the Executive order precludes dealings with any organization which imposes an obligation on its members to assist or participate in a strike against the Government, advocates the overthrow of the Government, or discriminates in its terms of membership because of race, color, creed, or national origin. Likewise recognition cannot be granted to an organization regarded as subject to corrupt or non-democratic influences.

Thus, it can be clearly seen that the various provisions of the policy and program established under the Executive order contain abundant protection to ensure that the vital functions of Government are not impeded and that the special requirements of a personnel system founded on the merit system are preserved.

In spite of the special conditions which apply, there are numerous and substantive areas for consultation and negotiation between Federal agencies and employee organizations. Generally these areas are concerned with local issues of working conditions and local policies on such matters as promotions, shifts, grievances, safety, and training, within the framework of broader agency policy. The agencies have been urged to structure their respective programs in a way which leaves freedom for decentralized consultation and negotiation in appropriate subject matter areas.

Because the Government as an employer is different from other employers, and because the program has been tailored to reflect these differences, the program does not re-create within the Federal service a carbon copy of the "adversary situation" commonly regarded as characterizing labor relations in industry. Instead, the program draws on some of the best features from industrial experience, and combines these with proved features of previous Governmental experience. The result is a program which is not wholly new, but which places central emphasis on cooperation.

The program calls on both management and employee representatives to share more than the usual amount of responsibility for settling differences of opinion and reaching agreement, without resort to some of the techniques customary to the resolution of differences on the industrial scene.

THE ROLES OF THE COMMISSION AND THE AGENCIES

Although both the Civil Service Commission and the Department of Labor have been given certain responsibilities to assist or instruct the agencies, no special assignment has been made to any agency to *direct* the program or to serve as an intermediary between employee organizations and management. The program rests primarily on the shoulders of each agency. This fact, plus the emphasis which agencies are being asked to place on decentralization, will result in a new slant in the role of most Federal agency personnel programs.

The Department of Labor has been given responsibility under the order for nominating arbitrators in connection with issues of unit determination and employee representation. This service is provided at the request of the agencies or of employee organizations seeking exclusive recognition.

The role of the Civil Service Commission is to develop a program of guidance to the agencies, to provide technical advice, to assist in developing programs for training agency officials in the discharge of their responsibilities in the public interest, and to provide for continuous study and review of the program and the making of recommendations to the President for its improvement.

Together the Civil Service Commission and the Department of Labor were made jointly responsible for preparing standards of conduct for employee organizations and a more detailed code of fair labor practices in employee-management relations in the Federal service, which have now been issued by the President. . . .

The ultimate success of the program depends on how well these parties undertake and accomplish their new joint responsibilities.

Our hope is for a more effective system of employee-management cooperation in the Federal service, and at this point we have every reason to believe it will be achieved.

Archie Kleingartner
PROFESSIONAL ASSOCIATIONS:
AN ALTERNATIVE TO UNIONS?

The growing proportion of salaried professional workers in the American labor force is alternately cast as an ominous shadow or a bright new frontier for union growth and expansion.

Between 1950 and 1960, the white-collar sector of the labor force grew by 28 percent, but its professional-worker component expanded by 47 percent. This expansion has been accompanied by the concentration of salaried professional workers in large work organizations. For example, in 1962, 54 percent of all engineers and scientists worked in establishments employing 1,000 or more.

Union leaders are encouraged by this evidence of concentration. They contend that the mass employment of salaried professionals in large bureaucratic organizations generates a need for the type of protection which unions are uniquely qualified to provide. They claim that salaried professionals, like manual workers, require a strong voice to deal with job and employment problems at the work-place level.

But if this is so, why have unions had so little success in recruiting salaried professional workers? This essay will examine that question from an angle that is seldom given much attention.

There is sufficient evidence to consider the hypothesis that the normally conservative, employer-dominated professional associations may effectively obstruct the growth of unionism among the salaried professions, no matter how rapidly these occupations expand or how much their work situation becomes like that of manual workers. Even though the need among the salaried professions for a trade union approach to their job and professional problems may increase, unions probably will not be the form of organization to which these occupations will turn for assistance. It is an oversimplification to view the choice for salaried professionals as simply one of unionism or no organized representation. There is considerable evidence that professional associations, often accused of structural rigidity and of wearing ideological

This paper is published here for the first time.

Mr. Kleingartner is Assistant Professor of Industrial Relations, University of California, Los Angeles.

blinders, do in fact have the capacity to adapt to the changing needs and situations of the professions they represent.

The main lines of evidence supporting this assertion can be found by examining the trends among nurses, engineers, and teachers— who constitute the three largest salaried professions in the country.

NURSES

The nurses in the United States, who number 582,000, provide an example of a group where a professional association has moved significantly in the direction of collective bargaining in response to pressure from within the profession. This the American Nurses Association, with 152,000 members, has done without developing any formal alliances with organized labor, and while taking the official position that it should not be considered a labor union.

The present ANA collective bargaining program goes back to World War II, when low salaries and a shortage of nurses made hospital working conditions extremely difficult. During that period, the California Nurses Association (CNA), an ANA affiliate, became the collective bargaining agent for a number of nurses employed in hospitals. The California experience provided the impetus for the ANA to explore the possibility of collective bargaining by its other state affiliates. In 1946, the ANA convention gave overwhelming approval to a nationwide collective bargaining program.

Today, almost all of the ANA's state affiliates have prepared themselves to serve as collective bargaining agents. Many state affiliates have negotiated contracts, and in their main headings, these contracts are the same as those negotiated by traditional trade unions.

To those critics who claim that collective bargaining by professionals is unethical the ANA replies that, far from being unethical, its collective bargaining program is an ethical imperative to help nurses achieve the professional status to which they are entitled.

The expansion of the ANA collective bargaining program is hampered by inadequate legal protection, by the resistance of employers, and, in many cases, by the lack of economic sophistication on the part of nurses themselves. But it is significant that a professional association such as the ANA was able to establish a realistic and dynamic collective bargaining program, largely in response to dissatisfactions at the work place. The program was established against the wishes of hospital administrators as a group, and without the support of the organized medical profession. Although the economic and working conditions of nurses have improved substantially, nurses still are the lowest paid group among the recognized professions. So long as this situation prevails, collective bargaining will continue to gain adherents. The sentiment within the profession appears to be for more, not less, militancy in its demand for recognition and in its negotiations.

There is little doubt that collective bargaining under the aegis of the professional association has become a permanent instrument for the improvement of both the job status and professional status of nurses. Nurses have shown virtually no interest in traditional unionism. The ANA draws no distinction between its functions as a professional association and those as a collective bargaining institution. It seeks to perform the functions of both as a single professional organization for nurses.

ENGINEERS

No single professional organization for engineers has as much influence among its members as the ANA has among nurses. However, like the ANA, some engineering societies have demonstrated the ability to give a collective response at the work-place level. It has been estimated that there are well over one hundred separate engineering societies.

The passage of the Wagner Act in 1935 precipitated a reevaluation by the major engineering societies of their attitudes toward unionism and collective action. There were two major reasons for this. First, the Act did not explicitly provide against the possibility of industrially employed engineers being engulfed, against their wishes, by the burgeoning labor unions. Even though the National Labor Relations Board, as early as 1937, gave engineers the options of joining a production bargaining unit or their own unit or having no union representation at all, the fear persisted that engineers would end up having their salaries and working conditions determined by manual-worker dominated unions. Secondly, there existed substantial unemployment and low salaries among engineers in the 1930's. Even during World War II, the economic position of engineers declined in relation to that of unionized manual workers, who were able to exert pressure for wage increases and overtime payments.

Against this background, a number of professional engineering societies decided that perhaps collective bargaining for engineers wasn't so bad, provided the societies did the bargaining. The American Society of Civil Engineers and the American Chemical Society went the furthest in adopting complete collective bargaining programs. However, the programs they adopted were hampered by a defensive attitude and unrealistic rules. The basic reason for establishing the programs was to ward off unionism. Even though the societies were not committed to the principle of collective bargaining, it is significant that they responded to the union threat by assuming some of the characteristics of unions.

With the passage of the Taft-Hartley Act in 1947, which specifically ruled out the possibility of engineers being absorbed by large production unions, and postwar improvement in the economic situation of engineers, the union threat began to disappear. Almost at the same time, the collective bargaining programs of the engineering societies became defunct.

Today trade unions have only a fingertip hold on the 800,000 professional engineers. Almost no new organization has occurred since 1950, and a number of unions established during the 1940's have been decertified. Only some 40,000 engineers are represented in collective bargaining by unions of all types. Engineers, while not without problems, enjoy generally high salaries and good working conditions. Perhaps all of this will change in the future, but today engineers view collective bargaining as having little relevance to their own situation. Most of them probably believe that unionism and professionalism are incompatible. The professional societies reflect the decline in the fortunes of engineering unionism, and the improvement in the economic situation of the engineers. They oppose unions, and they oppose collective bargaining.

The 62,000-member National Society of Professional Engineers (NSPE) has emerged as the most active engineering society concentrating on job and professional problems. The influential, but more technically oriented, founder societies (such as the American Society of Mechanical Engineers) describe the NSPE as an effective action organization in the economic and professional areas. The NSPE openly and aggressively opposes unionism among engineers. In its view, collective bargaining is both irrelevant to the situation of engineers and unprofessional.

What would happen if the economic situation and working conditions of engineers should again deteriorate to the point that engineers would press for corrective action, and possibly start joining unions in large numbers? The survival instincts of the engineering societies suggest that they would not complacently pursue their present course of complete opposition to collective bargaining. It is conceivable that the various engineering societies would unite behind the NSPE, which would adapt its purposes and structure to cope with the changed conditions. It is probable that the opposition of the engineering societies to unionism goes considerably deeper than their opposition to collective bargaining.

TEACHERS

The National Education Association (NEA), with a membership of approximately a million, is the dominant professional organization among the more than one and one-half million teachers. The NEA portrays itself as an organization broad enough to give expression to the interests and needs of all of the institutional elements which make up our educational system—classroom teachers, school administrators, and school boards. Though the bulk of the NEA membership is composed of classroom teachers, the policy-making apparatus of the NEA has traditionally been dominated by interests representing the numerically much smaller group of school administrators.

Union activity among teachers has been provided by the American Federation of Teachers (AFT), which was chartered by the American Federation of Labor in 1902. In 1950, the AFT had a membership of only 50,000, and, until quite recently, the NEA paid little attention to it. However, in 1961, the AFT's New York City affiliate scored a decisive triumph as the exclusive bargaining representative for that city's 40,000 teachers. The victory served as a boon to teacher unionism throughout the country. Frustrated AFT locals in Detroit, Chicago, Los Angeles, and many other cities took on new life and renewed their efforts to obtain exclusive representation elections. However, in almost every community, school boards, PTA's, news media, etc., remained solidly opposed to teacher unionism.

The New York election and its aftermath had a profound impact on the NEA. Its national officers tried to explain the New York situation as a special case of a school system with more than average problems, composed of teachers having more than average union sentiment. The NEA also acknowledged that its attention to the job and work problems of teachers in the large cities had not been fully adequate. The NEA state and local affiliates saw deeper forces at work. They saw the deep dissatisfaction of many teachers with salaries, working conditions, and school administrators. Perhaps most important, the local affiliates saw the growing interest of teachers in what the union had to offer. The realization that the AFT victory in New York could not be brushed aside as the result of a unique set of circumstances soon permeated all levels of the NEA.

At its 1962 convention, the NEA responded by passing two resolutions, one on "professional negotiations" and a second on "professional sanctions." The NEA took pains to distinguish between "professional negotiations" and collective bargaining, but the National Association of School Boards equates them. Similarly, the NEA declared a distinction between "professional sanctions" and strikes, which the AFT allows under certain conditions. However, the critics of strikes condemn "sanctions" as just a fancy term for a strike.

Since 1962, many NEA affiliates have negotiated contracts with school boards. Sanctions have been invoked in a number of places, including statewide sanctions in Oklahoma and Utah. The argument is sometimes made that the contracts negotiated by NEA affiliates cannot be construed as equivalent to the inclusive contracts negotiated by the AFT and that sanctions do not really have the force of strikes. This argument has some merit. Nevertheless, professional negotiations and sanctions may provide teachers with a viable alternative to the AFT.

The AFT has continued to grow, attaining a membership of 100,000 in 1964, but the NEA has also continued to expand. More significantly, some NEA affiliates are going far beyond what is implied by negotiations and sanctions in meeting the union challenge at the local level. In Milwaukee, for example, the NEA affiliate was certified as the exclusive bargaining representative for Milwaukee teachers after it defeated the union in an election conducted under the provisions of a recent Wisconsin labor law. Its conduct is governed by the same law that governs other public-employee unions. Other NEA affiliates have even participated in strikes. Many NEA affiliates appear quite willing to do whatever is necessary to meet the AFT challenge while camouflaging their activities in the terminology of professionalism.

What can be concluded about the capacity of professional associations as alternatives to unions from this examination of nurses, engineers, and teachers? First, the specific policies and methods adopted by professional associations typically represent measured adaptations to the pressures for direct action from the members of the profession and to the union threat to the primacy of the association.* Since the salaried professions differ in terms of both forces, the postures of associations (at any given time) quite naturally differ from profession to profession. Second, all of the associations discussed share the determination to preserve their dominant position in the profession. They try to make unionism appear unnecessary, and they are prepared to behave like unions if such is required.

The willingness of the associations to become "union-like" has blunted union organizing efforts and will continue to do so. The probable future success of this strategy is enhanced by certain other built-in

* In the U.S. there is little evidence that a union and professional association can live in harmony, serving complementary functions within a single profession. In those professions where both organizations are present, they are generally in bitter opposition, with both claiming the capacity to represent the entire spectrum of needs and interests of the members of the profession.

advantages enjoyed by the associations, three of which seem of particular importance.

First, in deciding between the two forms of organization, salaried professionals feel it is more respectable to join the association. There are many reasons for this. Associations are free of the manualist image of unions. They are not affiliated with organized labor. Membership in an association often constitutes a mark of status while the reverse may be true of union membership. Professional colleagues in colleges and universities are members of the same association. Employers would rather see their professional employees in an association than in a union, and salaried professionals are concerned with what their employers think. For many salaried professionals, the status costs associated with union membership could not be repaid by any gains the union can provide.

A second advantage is the feeling among professionals that unions have little ability to perform many functions that the associations have traditionally performed. This includes such things as protection of work standards, professional education, determination of standards for entry into the profession, and relations with other professions. Many unions have gone to great lengths to demonstrate their interest and effectiveness in these areas. Yet salaried professionals continue to feel that unions are not truly competent to deal with these purely professional interests.

A third advantage is that, in most salaried professions, the associations already enjoy a big edge in membership. The challenge for unions is not only to attract the unorganized but also to take members away from the associations. With only a few professions as exceptions, unions have not had notable success in either area. Nor does the problem appear to be entirely one of inadequate union know-how or a lack of money and manpower. The associations profit from the fact that unions often do not show a real will to organize.

SUMMARY

The main conclusion is that the professional associations among nurses, teachers, engineers, and, in all probability, other salaried professions as well, appear to have the capacity—by adapting to the changing needs and conditions of the professions—for discouraging large-scale unionization in the foreseeable future. Even while eschewing any identification with labor unions, these associations appear quite willing to act like unions to protect their dominant positions in the professions.

It cannot be said that unions do not have the ability to help salaried professionals achieve both their job-related and their professional goals. Indeed, the fact that the associations are adopting many of the methods of unions suggests the basic effectiveness of their approach. In the final analysis, the real challenge of the associations is not to unionism as a method but to unions as organizations.

The National Society
of Professional Engineers

THE ENGINEERING UNION— DINOSAUR IN THE SPACE AGE

Western Electric engineers vote resoundingly for "no union," in a national election representing nearly 7,000 engineering employees.

At Minneapolis-Honeywell Regulator Co., engineers and technicians choose "no union," in preference to both UAW representation and representation by an all-engineer/scientist bargaining unit.

Engineers and Scientists of America, a Federation theoretically banding together engineering unions in a national alliance, slips quietly out of business.

Engineers and technicians at Speery Gyroscope Company, in a decertification election, vote 1724 to 1509 against the union which has represented them for fourteen years.

Since 1952—nearly ten years—no major group of engineers has indicated that they wanted union representation. Where there have been elections, with any significant number of engineers involved, the vote has been consistently "no union."

In a profession comprised of some half a million registered and nonregistered engineers, less than ten per cent—under 50,000—are currently represented by collective bargaining units. In regard to these, the comment of one former union executive is significant: "With one possible exception, I think any of these groups could be crushed by management in a matter of weeks. For the one exception, the only difference is the amount of time it would take. By and large, all of these units exist at the sufferance of management, and for that reason alone."

Certainly the foregoing suggests a fairly clear trend. The obvious

Reprinted by permission from *American Engineer*, July 1961.

The NSPE is strongly opposed to the unionization of engineers. It admits as members professional engineers from all branches of engineering, including those who are in management positions (ed.).

implication is that the engineering union is going the way of the Dodo and the Great Auk, slowly but inevitably into extinction. Why is this so? There are probably several basic reasons that could be applied in general, and there are also specific reasons that have come up in connection with specific instances of union rejection.

The most fundamental reason that engineering unions are vanishing seems to be simply that they don't offer the individual engineer enough in the way of benefits to make them worth his while. From a professional standpoint, certainly the engineering union is in direct opposition to the individual's interests. From an economic standpoint, there seems to be no reasonable indication that union membership improves the position of the individual engineer. In terms of such intangibles as prestige, harmony in working relationships, and intracompany communications, there seems to be a tendency on the part of unions to work directly against the interests of the individual engineer.

Harold A. Mosher, P.E., past president of National Society of Professional Engineers, sums up the situation this way: "We think it is fair to say that the advancement of the welfare of engineers employed in industry through the union method has been given a fair trial and has been found wanting. In more recent years, the union approach has been rejected in virtually every known case in which the engineers had a full and free choice."

One former union man's comments reflect the same feeling in regard to the Western Electric election. "The biggest single factor we had working against us was that many engineers who voted didn't think the union was powerful enough to do more for them than they could do for themselves." The union in question was the Council of Western Electric Professional Employees—National, and when it was defeated, it was eminently clear that the engineers who had voted had done two things. First, they had realigned themselves with the vast majority of professionally oriented engineers in the Nation. Second, they had dealt a serious, and perhaps fatal, blow to the only national association of engineering and scientific unions as such—Engineers and Scientists of America.

Perhaps *coup de grace* would be a better term, for since its founding in 1952, ESA* steadily lost members and affiliates until it quietly went out of business last winter. In many ways the dissolution of ESA is symbolic of the decline of engineering unionism in the past decade, for steadily and surely the unions have lost ground in practically every situation where they have been put to a test.

At first glance, it would seem paradoxical that during this same time period, the engineering profession has in fact come into its own—for

* The Engineers and Scientists of America was established as a federation of professional engineering unions (eds.).

this implies a directly inverse proportion between the strength of the profession and the strength of its unions. However, this is exactly the case. Given the impetus of exploding technology in the past ten to twenty years, the engineering profession, as a profession, is stronger than it has ever been. It has achieved this position through professional methods, and putting the paradox in its proper perspective it is little wonder that engineering unions simply don't offer the individual engineer enough to justify themselves.

There is one other basic factor connected with the explosion of technology that bears directly on the engineering unionism question. This is the growing reliance that industrial management places on the engineer, and the resultant responsibility accruing to the engineer. Perhaps more than ever before the engineer must necessarily be a part of the management team and accept the professional status that is implied in this position. Where in the past management placed reliance on the comptroller, the production specialist or the sales/marketing functions to produce profits, the technological nature of today's economy has placed this responsibility on the engineer. More and more, management includes strong, top level engineering representation. To maintain a competitive position, they simply must.

The result of this situation is perhaps best summed up by NSPE Past President Mosher: "The engineer in industry wants an opportunity to share in and be a part of the company, to know what the company is doing, how they are working toward their goals, and what his responsibilities and prospects are in that plan. In short, the engineer in industry wants to be a part of the team, not an outsider looking in. For this purpose, the engineer in industry wants the opportunity to earn the confidence and respect of his employer, and to deserve a place on the team, not to be a part of an opposing group which wants to lick the team of which he is a member." More pointedly, it is probably true that from a professional standpoint, the engineer has an obligation to accept the foregoing as his responsibility, for if he does not, there is the definite chance of his falling short of professional fulfillment on his job.

"Professionalism" and "unionism" are certainly general and relatively abstract terms. In an actual election situation, does the engineer make his decision on such an idealistic plane? Apparently, the answer is "yes," particularly if the engineer chooses in favor of professionalism. It is interesting to contrast two opinions on the matter, particularly in the light of the positions of those commenting. A member of the decertification committee at Minneapolis-Honeywell states categorically, "The decision here was in favor of professionalism, as abstract as that may seem. The idea of union membership on the opposite side of the ballot was rejected as unionism, and I think it would be very difficult to accurately narrow the reasons for the vote down much more than that."

On the other hand, take the comments of one union worker: "It's been said that simply setting up a good employee insurance program would make the difference in many cases." Perhaps the best measure of who is right is the results that have come in at the polls in the past. There can be little question that one of the basic mistakes that has been made by the unions in the past is their failure to realize that they are dealing with people who are a notch above the production worker in terms of education, professional concepts and general sophistication.

Take the comments of Jack Barbash, now a labor economist with University of Wisconsin, and formerly with AFL-CIO: "Once the white collar worker gets over the initial trauma of being in a union, he behaves like a bricklayer." Referring to the Air Line Pilots Association, Barbash continues: "What are they doing? They are engaging in jurisdictional disputes with the flight engineers—an old weapon in Detroit and other places . . . they are calling quickie strikes and wholesale strikes. In short, they are behaving like trade unionists."

Even assuming that these pilots qualify as professionals under the Taft-Hartley definitions (an unlikely assumption in the light of NLRB case decisions) their degree of true professional awareness and responsibility is not founded in the same way as is the case for doctors, lawyers or engineers. And whether or not behaving "like a bricklayer" is a legitimate aspiration of professional responsibility would also seem open to question.

Another indication of the union approach is offered by picking a pair of quotes from *Engineering News,* published by International Union of Electrical, Radio and Machine Workers, AFL-CIO, District 4:

"It is not American wage rates which are putting American manufacturers at a competitive disadvantage, but excessive executive salaries, says Cameron Hawley, industrialist-turned-novelist. . . ."

Or "Professional and technical unions . . . are the only means of providing the protection which allows an engineer to place his conscience and public trust above his loyalty to his employer—the only mark of a real professional. . . ."

The first quote is a blatant example of the "management bogey-man" approach to union organization. It seems strange that so naïve an argument would be used as a tool to sway professional men towards unionism, and yet this is one of the unions' favorite devices.

The second quote is a clear implication that some ninety-plus per cent of the American engineering profession are unable to "place confidence and trust above . . . loyalty to . . . employer." In addition to being outright distortion, it again implies a healthy amount of naïveté on the part of the person it is supposed to influence.

Perhaps one result of this sort of an approach to the organization of engineering unions is best summed up by a former union official who worked closely with the Western Electric election. "You would be surprised how much trouble we had with wives who simply were against having their husbands in unions. For many people there is a sort of stigma attached to union membership."

Certainly there are broader factors that work in this same direction. If the end of rampant monopolistic big business came with the rise of unionism and the trust-busting actions in the early part of this century, it is probably true that unions are facing much of the same thing at the present time. The most obvious example of this is, of course, the McClellan hearings regarding Jimmy Hoffa's Teamsters. Rightly or wrongly, this sort of exposé must necessarily create a bad picture of unionism as a whole in many people's eyes. Whether or not the "management bogeyman" approach is the best way to counteract this sort of an impression seems to be worth a good bit of analysis.

Certainly a strong case could be made for the fact that the unions have never really put forth an organized and concerted National effort to create strong engineering unions. As an AFL-CIO official points out, "There are other white collar areas which we consider more important, and more immediately profitable." A good measure of the divisiveness involved is shown in an IUE comment on the demise of ESA. Commented an IUE newspaper, "Doomed from the beginning by its self-imposed isolation from the rest of the American labor movement, ESA was dissolved. . . ."

On the one hand, ESA's approach was slanted to a "professional union," whether or not this appears to be a contradiction in terms. The union attitude is summed up by Everett M. Kassalow, research director of the AFL-CIO Industrial Union Department. "I am convinced that one reason why some of the white collar engineering unions of the past decade collapsed was their failure to develop among their members a clear-cut acceptance that a union must act and regard itself as a union. Attempts to cover this with the notion that the organization is of a purely professional character and/or an arm of management will not stand up in the long run before aggressive management." Kassalow's conclusion is that stronger maintenance and production unions will eventually be the source of any successful organizing of engineers.

But the facts of the matter are that neither approach seems to be palatable to the engineer; both have failed when put to the test of an election. Ironically, the underlying reason for this failure is contained in Kassalow's words: "Whether it calls itself a 'professional' group or not, a union is a union, and as such is rejected by the professionally oriented engineer." If this is true, as it certainly appears to be, the eventual hope of evolving a foundation for engineering unionism from the production and maintenance labor organizations seems remote indeed. Having stated so unequivocally their feelings regarding quasi-professional organizations such as ESA, it seems more than remote that engineers would allow themselves to be amalgamated with production and maintenance employees in unions dominated by nonprofessionals.

In a 1959 convention, the United Auto Workers, AFL-CIO made this sweeping statement: "Organizing engineers, technicians and office workers is the most essential organizing task facing the trade union movement in the United States and Canada now and in the years ahead. . . ." The basic reason for such a statement is that the ratio of white- to blue-collar workers is steadily increasing. The unions offer other arguments along the same lines. They point to the ever-increasing concentrations of engineering talent in single companies, and point to the impossibility of each individual engineer being able to demand enough of management time to state his individual case. They point to the dependence of engineers on ever-changing defense contracts, and the wholesale layoffs which can result in such situations. They indicate that median age for engineers in the Nation is low—about 32—and say that many engineers, because of their relative youth consider themselves headed for managerial positions, when in fact they are not.

Certainly, as is true in any profession or other line of work, the engineer must face a fair amount of economic instability and a less than secure future. And in a strong, national, wholly professional organization, there obviously will be protection for the engineer, individually and as a member of a profession. As other professions have proven, such a system can work most effectively.

In the summer of 1960, the Association of Professional Engineering Personnel struck five Radio Corporation of America plants in the Camden, N.J., area. Affiliated with ESA, the organization was out for six days. Production workers refused to cross the picket lines to be paid, and demanded paychecks be handed out outside the plant. The end result was a snake-dancing, egg-throwing melee in which seven engineers were arrested, charged with, among other things, disorderly conduct and assault and battery of a police officer.

To these methods of violence and coercion, the engineer has said, "No." It is a measure of over-all professional responsibility that the engineer has said, in election after election, "No union." Professional development through professional responsibility has been the choice in the past, and there is every indication that it will continue to be in the future.

Donald Krider
A TEACHER AND A LABOR UNION

My first teaching position, in 1941, was in a small industrial Wisconsin community in the Fox River Valley. Early in the school year I was informed that I was to pay my membership fees for a teachers organization to the principal's secretary by a given date. I was not asked; I was directed, and I resented the high-handed manner. The pressure was so constant and direct that I felt it necessary to pay my fee and help earn a 100% membership certificate for the school. I lacked the strength of conviction and the ability to go without eating to take a positive action against the situation. Similar membership recruitment prevailed throughout the nation—and it still is evident in many schools. My aggravation with myself led to a general resentment of the teachers organization which promoted and exercised such coercion. I am certain this experience tainted my outlook on teacher associations.

Later, in the Madison school system, the approach was less objectionable. I was informed that the principal's secretary would collect my dues for "professional membership." However, I received no pressure from the administration nor was a 100% membership certificate framed in the teachers' room. I joined the local and state teachers association without hostility and served this group as a school representative and as a member of several city-wide committees.

Then I became aware of a minority group of teachers in the school who were members of another organization: The American Federation of Teachers. The knowledge that such an organization existed came to me after four years of college and two years of teaching. A well kept secret. At no time did an educator mention such a group to me in college nor did I read a book that considered teachers in labor unions. I received my Bachelors degree from a state college in 1941. The American Federation of Teachers affiliated with the AFL in 1916. I was unsophisti-

Reprinted from *The Wisconsin Review,* Vol. 2, No. 2 (Summer 1963), by permission of the author and the editor.

Mr. Krider is Assistant Principal at a Madison, Wisconsin, high school, and is a past president of the Madison Federation of Teachers and the Madison Labor Council.

cated but not unwilling to learn. Apparently the news had not sifted down to the teachers college I attended or I was being insulated from it. I was fortunate to find teachers who had learned of the organization.

The senior teachers in our school in Madison were members of the AFofT. Their local number 36 was one of the oldest in the nation. These people were respected in the school by pupils, their colleagues, and by the administration. They served on policy-making committees with other teachers meeting with the Board of Education and with the Superintendent of Schools. They were well informed on matters of concern to me as a new teacher in the system. They were able to explain our insurance plan, the salary schedule, and matters of teaching procedure. They were willing to help and they impressed me as people of quality.

I was also impressed that they did not knock other teachers organizations, nor did they pressure me to join theirs. When I asked about membership in the Federation, they gave answers. In 1949—eight years after graduation and after four years of teaching—I became a paying member of the ranks of Labor.

It was the intent of this brief biography to point out that my motivation for joining a teachers union was not directed by any zeal for labor unions *per se*. I chose to belong and participate with a group of people I admired in a friendly and functional local organization that happened to be a labor union.

Consideration of why people choose, or do not choose, to affiliate with any social group requires a complex study of social-psychological motivation. I have not undertaken such a study, but I feel that I can begin to understand my own motivation in seeking membership in the American Federation of Teachers.

My generation of teachers in Wisconsin have not joined teacher unions for many of the same reasons that kept me from joining earlier. First, many of us came to teaching from small non-industrialized or non-unionized communities. We lacked a background of tradition and experience of family and community participation in the labor movement. I observe that this is changing somewhat and more young people from urban areas are training to teach. This may bring some changes in the future.

The training we received in the State Colleges tended to emphasize the professional obligation of teaching above and beyond other considerations. Teaching methods, educational psychology, and philosophy were our learning tools. Unless a person majored in the social studies, the total world of man was somewhat neglected. Even in the social studies we did not suffer from an overexposure to radical ideas.

Some of my teachers were sympathetic to the "plight of the worker" and even supported the New Deal, but teachers were not laborers, nor to be so considered.

To some of the sons and daughters of the middle class and lower middle class the prestige of professional status seems to have been more important than a just wage, good working conditions, or even the right of behaving like adult humans. I was frequently informed in my neophyte teaching days that all I might aspire to was genteel poverty and a chance to kick up my heels once a year at the state convention. I was even admonished once by a principal for the unprofessional act of smoking in public. This was in 1941—not in the Dark Ages. The cataclysmic social changes following World War II and the increasing need for teachers has changed the accepted social mores for teachers, but the desire for professional status still hangs on. The fact that the medical profession in the American Medical Association and the lawyers in their Bar Association have well organized and functional organizations working in behalf of their economic and political well-being barely seems to dent the consciousness of many of my teaching associates. To them the nobility of our task of educating children transcends the fact that we are civil servants, hired by and receiving our directives and pay from a unit of government. We do not, certainly at the classroom teachers level, receive the homage that our society gives to doctors or lawyers—and, perhaps, we don't deserve it.

Many of my teaching colleagues were appalled by the recent New York teachers' strike. They regarded such action as neglect of a professional responsibility. They fear the possible power of distant national labor authority to intervene in local educational affairs. It is generally understood that the success of the efforts of the American Federation of Teachers in New York City has sparked a concerted effort to maintain a more conservative and professional position on the part of the teachers associations. I am not aware of any notable increase in membership in the teachers union in Wisconsin as a result of the successful action of labor union teachers in New York. There is no flocking to the banner.

Many young women who flock to teaching are a deterrent force against greater union growth. Teacher training gives them a license to earn a living at a relatively good starting salary for single women. They are engaged in a task which is socially acceptable for women and they are economically functional should their future husbands and families need their assistance. The large turnover of young teachers is primarily from this group of women who are passing through teaching on the way to the altar. Many are not sufficiently concerned with long term issues to give their support to controversial issues and organizations. Their interests in education are in short term social and economic security.

Perhaps teaching tends to attract a personality type that is not aggressive or competitive. One of the major virtues in teaching is patience with human behavior. As an occupational group, teachers have been patient.

Teachers will join the teachers union when and where there are crises of sufficient import that are not being met adequately by other teacher organizations. Labor unions in all occupations find membership growth when there is an important issue at stake. Teachers join unions when they are experiencing a specific hurt and want assistance. They appeal for help against unfair treatment in salary and assignment; against something that hurts the pride and/or the pocketbook.

They join when there is security in membership. Communities in which there is strong labor organization which will support unionized teachers have growing teachers unions. Oddly enough, there are communities in Wisconsin with strong labor unions where the teachers are not well supported or are ignored. Security also comes with a permissive attitude on the part of the local school administration. When such an attitude is expressed by the administration, granting all teachers' groups equal access to the policy-making power, where there is no fear of being fired or passed over because of union membership, teachers unions do prosper—or at least survive.

Teachers join unions, just as I did, with a desire to associate with a group of compatible and interesting people who share similar occupational problems and social interests. I think there are other reasons why teachers should join and support the teachers in the union movement.

The minority, with freedom to express intelligent opposition to directions taken by the majority, is basic to our concept of democratic social change. Through the teachers union this minority can formulate a policy and express it with greater freedom from coercion by supervisory authority than is the case in the teachers associations. These associations are frequently controlled by education administrators rather than by classroom teachers. Even where no real coercion exists, the presence of administrators may reduce the willingness of teachers to speak up against the established order.

In most Wisconsin communities where teachers are unionized, the union is the minority organization. It is a flea on a dog. But it can be a stimulating and initiating flea, keeping the dog from lethargy and complacence. A small membership of sincere teachers willing to work and study is able to do a more efficient job of membership education on specific issues than is the bigger group with many belongers and few workers. Minority action has often prodded the majority to follow along or even to find a better alternative.

As teachers, we educate the children of the entire community and we should seek support of the entire community through affiliation with its many organized parts. It is as necessary that we communicate with AFL-CIO members as it is that we be able to communicate with members of a prestige service club. City-wide educational problems of bond issues for school construction receive one vote per person regardless of the person's affiliation.

I have been pleased with the audience the Madison City Labor Council has given delegates of our teachers union. We are members—not outsiders. At a recent City Council hearing on teachers salaries two groups supported the Board of Education request for increased funds; the PTA and the AFL-CIO. The union arrived at its decision to support the position after three hours of careful examination of the teacher delegates from the teachers union. They wanted to know why they should give them support. Without a teachers union who would have had the audience of this large portion of our community? Who would have been present to answer the "Why's"? It was desirable that a teachers union exist.

From what I have observed as a participant in public education in Wisconsin, I see no great immediate organizational triumph for teachers unions in this state. Specific communities failing to meet the needs of teachers may find a rush of its teachers to union membership. Money and organizational personnel from the AFL-CIO may stimulate some new locals and give a shot in the arm to some existing groups.

But teachers associations are also changing to meet the needs of teachers. They too have alert and intelligent personnel and a good treasury. Perhaps more important, they have in their favor generations of educators serving in the schools who are either strongly anti-labor union or at most, not against unions except for teachers.

This group will have a continuing effect on teachers and teacher organizations for some years to come. We know, however, that change is inevitable and collective bargaining action by teachers in their own behalf and in the interests of education will persist. Education associations are currently seeking to be recognized as bargaining agents under state labor laws. They have advocated boycotting school districts unfair to teachers. They have always acted in the collective name of those employed in education in reaction to legislation at all levels of government. Given time we may not be able to distinguish between teachers' union and teachers' association.

6
Inside the Unions

Few institutions in America can match unions in the careful attention they pay to the quality of their internal life. Perhaps this merely attests to the vital role played by unions in our society. The public generally expects much from unions and is quick to condemn misconduct. At the same time, unions themselves set high standards by which they ask to be judged.

The environment in which unions operate is not always friendly. Unions, like all other organizations, have to worry about institutional survival; this fact frequently affects the courses of action they pursue. Organizational survival, which must come first, is frequently in conflict with other demands made upon unions.

Unions represent a broad segment of American society and assert their right to be heard (and heeded) on vital issues of the day. They claim that unions articulate the interests and aspirations of working people everywhere. It is not surprising, therefore, that unions are frequently asked that bothersome question: "Is your own house in order?" Is there a serious discrepancy between the ideals proclaimed by unions and their actions? If so, is it of the unions' own making? Unions accept being judged on these matters, but they ask for fair judgments based on full knowledge of the nature of unionism and the environment within which unions operate.

While the interest in union internal problems never wanes, the specific points of interest do change. In the late 1950's, for example, corruption in labor unions seemed to be the overriding issue. Today, other (and perhaps more fundamental) problems are at the center of the stage. Three of the most pressing problems are examined in this chapter: relations between unions and disadvantaged minorities, especially Negroes; union security and the "right-to-work" controversy; and the issue of union democracy and membership control.

The question of relations with Negroes causes great pain to the nation's top union leaders. Long the victims of societal discrimination, they are hurt by charges that they themselves discriminate against others who presumably have the greatest need for the type of protection that unions can provide. No responsible labor leader denies that a real problem exists, however. But this problem wears many faces, as the Marshall selection makes clear. For one thing, union leaders at the national level have taken steps to eliminate racial discrimination that are far in advance of what many local unions are willing to accept. The revered principle of local union autonomy has slowed efforts to eliminate racial discrimination at the work place. The critics of union racial practices sometimes forget that unions are not monolithic organizations. The article by Marshall and the report of the New York State Advisory Commission describe union racial practices at the national and local levels. Both selections end on a note of cautious optimism regarding the ability of unions to deal with this problem.

Herbert Hill, Labor Secretary of the NAACP, is very critical of the union record in dealing with racial discrimination. He argues, essentially, that the entire labor movement has lost whatever zest it might once have had to deal with the problem, that it has become conservative in its maturity, as if mesmerized by the restrictive practices of certain craft unions who have always followed discriminatory policies. Are Hill's criticisms fair? Lipset thinks not. The whole problem is enormously complicated, as Raskin documents in his article on the union role in civil rights legislation. Raskin's analysis speaks well for the sincerity of the leaders of American labor with respect to this issue.

Three selections are presented on the issue of union membership as a condition of employment. Ever since the Taft-Hartley Act was passed in 1947, unions have been pressing for repeal of Section 14(b), which permits individual states to pass laws prohibiting union-security agreements. George Meany, speaking for organized labor, makes a strong plea for repeal. Reed E. Larson supports the answer of those among the opposition who are the best organized and most vocal. "At the heart of it all," he states, "lies the question of individual freedom of choice. Forced association or forced financial support of any group is not consistent with the American ideal."

In 1965, nineteen states had constitutional or legislative prohibitions on the negotiation of union-security agreements. Of these, Texas is the largest and most industrialized. Meyers studied the effects of the Texas "right-to-work" law and concluded that both sides to the controversy have been overstating their case. In his view, the issue is largely "symbolic."

The way unions are affected by and react to such issues as civil rights and "right-to-work" laws is, to a considerable extent, a function of the quality of union government. Unions, as they gain acceptance and security, become less and less distinguishable from other institutions in the community. A parallel development, which Lester discusses, is a shift in function, power, and decision making from the local to the national headquarters of unions and a blurring of differences between the union leader and business executive in their activities and living standards. Perhaps this is an inevitable outcome of successful unionism in an affluent society. But it also raises some perplexing questions. Have union leaders become so respectable and so successful that they cannot afford to dampen their image by dealing with difficult and controversial problems?

Thomas Brooks feels that union members are alienated from their leaders, and that a good many successful unions are ripe for rank-and-file revolt. The defeat of David McDonald as president of the United Steelworkers Union by I. W. Abel, a "craggy-faced, white-haired man" who, according to one local leader "has attended about every affair my district has had for the past several years," is only the most publicized instance of rank-and-file dissatisfaction with the top leadership.

In the last selection of the chapter, Stieber describes how the United Automobile Workers pioneered in the establishment of machinery to open the internal operations of the union to outsiders. The UAW Public Review Board constitutes, according to Stieber, "the broadest grant of authority over its internal affairs ever voluntarily given by a labor organization—or any other organization for that matter—to an outside body."

All of the selections in this chapter deal ultimately with the question of how the large and complex labor organizations can best accomplish their formal goals—honor often ambiguous standards of internal conduct, deal effectively with opposition from within and without—and, at the same time, not lose sight of their broader societal obligations and opportunities.

the right-to-work issue

George Meany
ARE RIGHT-TO-WORK LAWS
DESIRABLE?   NO

. . . It is the position of the AFL-CIO that the Congress should revise the National Labor Relations Act to make its provisions as to union security clauses the supreme law of the land, just as its other provisions are. We ask that the Congress repeal section 14(b), the unique and peculiar provision which permits State so-called right-to-work laws to override the national act in this respect. . . .

Collective bargaining presupposes, and Federal law provides, that the bargain made with the employer by the union binds all the employees in the unit. If individual employees are free to make their own deal with the employer, that is the end of collective bargaining. If individuals can undercut the union wage to get work, that ends the union wage.

Under collective bargaining, the contract which the union negotiates determines all the major conditions of the worker's industrial life. It determines what he gets paid; what hours he works; whether he is subject to discharge only for cause, with the right to go to arbitration, or subject to discharge at the whim of the foreman; whether layoffs are made according to seniority or favoritism; whether or not retired employees receive pensions, and all the rest.

A right-to-work law carves out a single exception. Where a right-

Statement before the Special Subcommittee on Labor of the Committee on Education and Labor, House of Representatives, May 1965.
Mr. Meany is President of the AFL-CIO.

to-work law is in effect, the collective bargaining agreement may cover every phase of the worker's industrial life, except that it may not provide that he shall join the union or pay dues to it.

As a citizen of the industrial community the worker is still bound by whatever agreement the union negotiates, but the law gives him the option of declining membership and refusing to pay dues. His life as a worker is lived under the terms of the union contract. By law he enjoys whatever benefits the union wins, but he may not be required to join or pay dues.

This is so grossly inconsistent that it persuaded the late Senator Taft to preserve the union shop in the Taft-Hartley Act. But the inconsistency goes deeper.

As a matter of philosophical consistency, it is not possible to advocate a right-to-work law on the purported ground that compulsory membership violates the freedom of the individual worker, and at the same time declare a belief in collective bargaining, which gives the union the power to negotiate a contract affecting every aspect of the worker's industrial life.

I believe in collective bargaining, and so I believe in union security. I also believe in democracy, and so I believe that when the majority of the employees join a union, they should be entitled to negotiate a union security agreement with their employer, if they want to and if they can.

The standard argument of the right-to-work advocates is that they are concerned about the freedom of the individual worker to hold a job without belonging to a union. Some of those who express this concern are probably sincere, but that is beside the point. They simply do not understand or take into account the employment conditions in urbanized, industrialized, 20th century America.

They seem to be unaware that there is no true right to work. The first and most arbitrary requirement a worker must meet is to find an employer who will hire him. Once hired, he is subject to many other arbitrary regulations, from punching a timeclock to a "no smoking" rule. Every workplace has a long list. These regulations are set by employers. Why are they more acceptable than a union shop requirement, jointly agreed to by the employer and the union? Why is this the one regulation, among all the others, from which workers need to be "liberated"?

The right-to-work advocates never seem to wonder why—if workers want this kind of "liberation"—these right-to-work laws have won the most acceptance where union membership is smallest. And they seem to pay no attention to the rights and interests and wishes of the majority.

These advocates of right-to-work laws are nostalgic for an earlier and simpler day, when farmers owned and worked their own subsistence farms, and industry was embodied in the village blacksmith.

Well, for better or for worse, that sort of society has pretty much disappeared, and will never come back. The village blacksmiths who once ran their own shops work at racetracks now, as employees. They have a union, and they bargain collectively.

The option today is not between having unions and collective bargaining, and having an agrarian society of independent owner-producers. Big industrial plants will grow bigger; and huge corporations will grow larger. The options today are between giving the managers of these great enterprises the unilateral right to decide what they will pay, who they will lay off, and whether they will grant pensions, and so forth, and assuring a voice in these decisions to workers acting together in a union. Surely the latter alternative is the more democratic, and the one which preserves to workers the greater degree of individual freedom. . . .

Reed E. Larson

ARE RIGHT-TO-WORK LAWS DESIRABLE?   YES

. . . In opposing repeal of section 14(b), the National Right to Work Committee is presenting the view of the American people. Like the vast majority of Americans, we believe that union membership should be voluntary, not compulsory. We represent the grassroots of the Nation— the workers, the small business people, the professional people who understand and are concerned about the damage being done to our country by the excesses growing out of compulsory union membership. While labor union representatives profess to speak for the American worker, the fact is that less than one-fifth of the people comprising our country's work force have chosen to join or be represented by a labor union. Although every employed person is guaranteed by law the right to join or form unions, more than 80 percent have chosen not to do so. Further, even among the remaining one-fifth of workers now represented

Statement before the Subcommittee on Labor of the Committee on Labor and Public Welfare, U.S. Senate, June 1965.

Mr. Larson is Executive Vice President of the National Right-to-Work Committee.

by unions, a substantial number are opposed to the efforts of their unions to make membership compulsory.

Our committee came into being through the initiative of a group of rank-and-file union men, members of the railway brotherhoods, who, although loyal to their unions, opposed the demands of brotherhood officials for compulsory union shop agreements in the railroad industry. Since its formation in 1955 this committee has attracted the support of additional thousands of union members in all industries and in all parts of the country. . . . Notwithstanding the efforts of union officials to brand this committee as a front for big business, we are in fact the voice of the worker, and we are here to speak in his behalf.

You have heard . . . union representatives give their reasons why they want section 14(b) repealed. Although the arguments of these proponents of repeal are able and eloquently presented, they remain, in the final analysis, abstract arguments far removed from the hard, realistic fact of compulsory unionism as it is experienced by the individual workingman who is its captive or, if you will, its victim. He is the one whose rights are at stake when a union forces him to join or pay dues and fees in order that he may be permitted to work at his job or trade. He is the one whose personal dignity and moral convictions are affronted when he is locked into a corrupt or immoral or subversive union. He is the one whose individual and constitutional rights are sacrificed when his money is thus taken from him and spent for political action, for propaganda, and for ideological causes to which he is personally opposed. . . .

While these deprivations of the political rights of individuals are of great importance, they represent only one aspect of the problem. Even more serious is the tyranny and fear to which rank-and-file employees can be subjected under compulsory union shop contracts. You no doubt recall the extensive testimony heard by the McClellan committee describing the flagrant corruption which exists in a number of the largest unions in the country, and the abuses of individual rights by those unions under "sweetheart" deals obtained by intimidating employers. The Senate has also received extensive testimony and reports regarding control of major unions by Communists, and the use of union funds to promote subversive activities and movements. In these hoodlum and Communist controlled unions the rank-and-file worker is at the mercy of the union hierarchy, and any failure to stay in line brings sharp reprisals against him. . . .

Section 14(b) is one of the few protections these people have against abusive, unfair, and discriminatory treatment. It gives them the right, in those States which have adopted right-to-work laws, to refuse to join or support corrupt unions and Communist controlled unions, and to withdraw from any union which exalts the power and privileges of the union officers instead of the rights and general welfare of the rank-and-file members.

Freedom of association is a precious right. In our society no group should have the power to compel any person to join, to obey or to conform to their rules. We believe that the average American citizen, the man in the street, is firmly committed to this idea and opposes any program of forced association or forced financial support to any group. The Government alone should have the right to tax the citizen or to require him to conform to its laws and regulations. No private organization, whether it be labor union, a church, a fraternal body, or any other type of organization, should have such power. . . .

We share the view of many union members that a union is stronger and healthier when it earns the support and loyalty of the rank-and-file workers on a voluntary basis. Like any other organization, if a union provides effective service, it will receive the deserved support, freely given, of its members, and when it does it is incomparably stronger than a union composed largely of coerced dues payers who have little interest in or loyalty to the union. . . .

There are many other arguments and many other points which we could make in defense of voluntary unionism and in opposition to repeal of section 14(b). At the heart of it all, however, lies the question of individual freedom of choice. Forced association or forced financial support of any group is not consistent with the American ideal. . . .

Our opposition to repeal of section 14(b) can be summed up in the observation made by one union member that "good unions don't need compulsory unionism—and bad unions don't deserve it."

Frederic Meyers

MYTH AND REALITY IN THE RIGHT-TO-WORK CONTROVERSY: THE CASE OF TEXAS

. . . A "Right-to-Work" statute was first introduced into the Texas legislature in 1945. It failed of passage then only because of the

Excerpted from Frederic Meyers, *"Right to Work" in Practice*, A report to The Fund for the Republic, © 1959 by The Fund for the Republic, Inc.

Mr. Meyers is Professor of Industrial Relations, University of California, Los Angeles.

adjournment of the Senate while it was still on the calendar. In the following session, in 1947, the law passed by a wide margin in both houses of the legislature and was signed by the Governor. . . .

For eleven years now, the "Right-to-Work" law in Texas has been a powerful symbol. To management it stands for the political power it has held and hopes to retain; to the labor movement it marks another in a series of disappointments in the area of state legislation. The actual workings of the law do not bear out the claims or anticipations of either side—"Right-to-Work" does not guarantee individual freedom, nor does it destroy the union. Perhaps some businessmen have taken the statute seriously and decided to locate, or not to locate, in Texas because of it, but if this is true the motivation was a response to the symbol and not to a law that makes Texas so different from the rest of the United States.

It is my considered conclusion that the "Right-to-Work" statute in Texas, taken by itself and apart from the body of state labor legislation, has had minimal direct effect.

In the traditional areas of the closed shop, particularly the construction industry, the old practices remain in force and violate not simply the state law but federal legislation as well. In the industries in which the union shop is a normal mode of operation, the law does not directly inhibit new organization since it only becomes operative after recognition is gained. However, there is no doubt that the statute has had an indirect effect here because it has so changed the climate of organization in some marginal situations that campaigns which would under other conditions have been won have been lost.

In the situation for which the law was designed—that of forbidding union security clauses after recognition has been achieved— "Right-to-Work" apparently has not had any decisive impact. In many units, membership is effectively 100 per cent. Indeed, the only areas where the law might be a crucial element are those in which there are enough union members who could win a union shop if they were allowed and thus bring a significant minority into the union (or face them with the loss of their jobs). But this kind of balance of forces potentially affects only about 6 per cent of the eligible employees in the state. Thus, whatever the peripheral, indirect, and difficult-to-measure aspects of the law's operation, it has not transformed labor relations in Texas or, for that matter, affected either its partisans or its foes in a decisive manner.

The impact of the statute on the rate of union growth has probably been minimal. Existing unions have not been destroyed. Their bargaining power has not been materially impaired, since those with power to negotiate a union shop are not those whose strength is insufficient to face up to management. On the other hand, the inability to negotiate "compulsory unionism" has apparently not freed many workers from a union tyranny objectionable to them since the vast majority are members because they want to be. Nor, even, has it obliterated compulsion and coercion. Loyal members of strong unions have expressed their resentment against those they regard as "free riders" in ways at least as objectionable, morally, and nearly as effective as if union membership were a requisite to employment.

In the case of grievances, the law *has* had a demonstrable effect. It has made the unions not more responsible but more responsive to the demands of a tiny vocal minority of the membership. It has consequently caused issues to be pressed through the grievance machinery which, under conditions of union security, would not and should not have been taken up. The union leader without security is often most responsive not to the majority of loyal union members who will remain, but to the small minority, often irresponsible, whose continued membership is doubtful.

The absence of union security has forced unions into bargaining positions conditioned by minorities and indefensible on any grounds other than the necessity of survival. Rather than freeing managements of "excessive" demands and policies, as the preamble to the statute foresaw, it probably faced some managements, both in grievance procedures and over the bargaining table, with more objectionable demands than would have been the case if a union shop had prevailed. It may be that some of the managements would prefer this situation to the necessity of bargaining about union security, but it seems doubtful that the law should make the choice for them. Furthermore, in the few instances in which the statute served to abet deliberate management policies to keep a union weak and ineffective, it is doubtful that the law should serve these purposes either.

These are, in my view, clearly undesirable consequences of the statute, affecting not only the individual employees who choose to refrain from union membership but all employees, and managements as well. The restrictions placed on the most responsible functioning of unions by making it impossible for them to achieve security affect everybody's interests, individually and collectively, and narrow the range of choice at the point where it should be broadened—in the direction of greater long-term responsibility.

In the sense of increasing the range of alternatives available to some individual employees, the prohibition of union security agreements has undoubtedly increased their freedom. This could have been said *a priori;* this study only adds the fact that, at least in Texas, the number of employees to whom the exercise of this choice is important seems to be small. It is also true that a large number of jobs that do not require union membership, either because the employment is unorganized or because the negotiation of a union shop is unlikely, will continue to exist for a long time.

Yet if these facts about the limited range of the statute are converted into arguments against it, this does not seem to me to be persuasive. Those who say that the rights of only a few people are involved are guilty of disregarding minority rights. And the statement that there are enough non-union jobs available for the small group who are opposed to membership is only an inversion of the familiar anti-union argument: "If you don't like your job, go find another."

It is significant that the abstainers from membership can be divided into two basic groups, a rather large group who do not object to unionism and union membership as such but reject the particular union representing them, and a rather small group of conscientious objectors. But the statute which forbids compulsory membership for the latter also prevents the free negotiation between union and employer of agreements that would require union membership of the former.

The uniquely American device of exclusive representation implies a duty of the union to all represented employees, members or non-members; it likewise seems to me to imply a correlative duty on the part of employees to participate at least minimally in the policy-making processes of the institution that represents them and, secondarily, to provide their fair share of the funds to carry forward union functions effectively.

The law provides devices through which rival union issues can be disposed of by a majority of the employees in the bargaining unit. It seems not unreasonable to require those who feel their interests would be better represented by a rival union to remain in the recognized union until they can convince a majority of their fellow employees of the desirability of membership in the other union. The law already protects such persons, in their job tenure at least, against reprisals by the recognized union. In any event, with merger of the federations, gradual mergers of competing unions, and the increasing effectiveness of no-raiding agreements, rival union problems are likely to be less and less important as the basic reason for abstention from membership. Objection to the internal policies and practices of particular unions, already very significant, is likely to become more so.

The pure and simple free rider—the employee who recognizes benefits he derives from representation by a union but who refrains from membership simply to save the financial cost of membership—is probably relatively rare. But certainly many of those who object to some particular aspect of union policy or activity—be it refusal to handle a specific grievance, the distribution of wage gains, or some problem in the application of seniority—recognize other benefits personally derived from other aspects of union membership. And they cannot, even if they would, leave the sweet with the bitter.

We have made industrial democracy a national policy goal through our recognition of collective bargaining. Consequently, the industrial citizen can reasonably be required to assume the responsibility of citizenship. Provided that appropriate agreements are arrived at in collective bargaining, those who object to particular aspects of union policy can reasonably be required to put themselves into a position to influence the decisions of the union representing them by participating in union processes.

The fact that the processes of democracy have been stultified and perverted in a few unions does not remove the duty of participation. In the first place, continued autocratic control is abetted by non-participation. Second, legislation permits those who would avoid this responsibility in democratic as well as autocratic unions to escape. Third, the democratization of undemocratic unions is a problem susceptible of separate treatment. This process is, indeed, proceeding, as the labor movement itself develops judicial doctrine giving increasing protection to the individual member in the exercise of his right to object and to voice his objection, and as the efforts of Congress give some promise of statutory relief to the victims of autocratic labor leadership where it exists.

Though denying to all unions the right to negotiate freely for union security is no proper solution to the problems of undemocratic control in some, the suggestion that it might be should serve as a further stimulus to labor both to redouble its efforts to clean its own house and to accept the efforts of legislators to provide reasonable protections to the democratic process in the labor movement. In its maturity and strength as a social force, labor can no longer live by the shibboleths of its youth— national union autonomy and complete freedom from regulation.

The problem of the conscientious objector to unionism is rather more difficult. If it were possible to distinguish him from those who do not join for other reasons, a strong case might be made for legislation to protect him against compulsory union membership. If there were no other material consequences, it would seem clearly wrong to require membership of a worker who either recognizes no benefit to himself from union membership or is willing to forego those benefits as the price of not joining in an organization whose very existence violates his principles. Yet, if there are benefits from union action in a shop, it is impossible for the individual worker to forego many of them voluntarily, even if he wishes to do so. Furthermore, abstention from membership affects, though perhaps in small measure, the free exercise of the rights of others, who are usually the large majority. The union survives because of the attachment of the majority, who believe not only that they derive benefits from the union but that abstention, even by a few, weakens the common cause. A device like prohibiting strikes in pursuit of union security clauses, while it protects the right of the conscientious objector, restricts the right of the majority to refuse collectively to work beside the non-member.

Still another consideration, though obvious, must be reiterated. Absence of a "Right-to-Work" statute does not impose a requirement that union security be negotiated; it merely frees the parties to do so if they wish. It would be quite another situation if union membership became a governmental requirement—a difference the War Labor Board recognized in refusing to go further than to require existing members to continue their membership for not more than a year, while admitting the right of the parties to collective agreements to impose membership themselves as a universal condition of employment.

Legislatures must make a choice, not between legislative restriction of the freedom of one group or another but between no legislative restriction of anyone and legislative restriction of the freedom of one group to protect that of another. Some freedoms are so clearly important that we have, constitutionally and legislatively, chosen the latter course. It is doubtful that those involved here are of that order of importance.

It remains my feeling that "Right-to-Work" proposals are of much less importance than either side to the controversy has been willing to admit. The issue is a symbolic one. What is at stake is the political power and public support of management and of unionism. The groups supporting the proposals, in Texas in 1947 as well as in other states more recently, wish essentially to make a public demonstration of the power to defeat the labor movement in the political arena. "Right-to-Work" proposals have become a convenient symbol for this purpose, perhaps because, in effect, they do mean so little, and perhaps also because vested interests in organizations formed to promote the statute have served to keep it as a symbol. The labor movement can do little but respond with the most strenuous efforts to have it rejected.

The issues raised by both the partisans and the opponents of "Right-to-Work" are serious ones because they involve the question of how we are to achieve freedom in a complex industrial society. And yet, as this study indicates, the claims of either side as to what will happen if the law is enacted have little to do with actual practice. This does not mean that we are freed of our obligation to consider the issues. It does mean that we must confront them on a more relevant level, so that we may free them from the passions and exaggerations of the "Right-to-Work" debate.

unions and minorities

F. Ray Marshall
UNION RACIAL PATTERNS

. . . In discussing union racial practices, we shall emphasize racial exclusion from unions by formal and informal means, segregated local unions, discrimination in the building trades, and the ways unions influence economic opportunities of Negroes. . . .

FORMAL EXCLUSION

The number of national unions with formal racial restrictions has declined significantly in the last 30 years. In 1930, at least 22 unions formally barred Negroes from equal membership.[1] By 1943, mergers and changing racial practices had reduced the number of restrictive unions to

Statement before the Subcommittee on Employment and Manpower of the Committee on Labor and Public Welfare, U.S. Senate, September 1963.

Mr. Marshall is Professor of Economics, University of Texas.

[1] The following unions are known to have had formal race bars in 1930: Brotherhood of Railway Carmen—AFL (BRC); Switchmen's Union of North America—AFL (SNA); Brotherhood of Railway & Steamship Clerks—AFL (BRSC); the Order of Sleeping Car Conductors—AFL; Masters, Mates & Pilots of North America—AFL (MMP); Railway Mail Association—AFL (RMA); Wire Weavers Protective Association—AFL (WWPA); Commercial Telegraphers—AFL; Boiler-makers—AFL; International Association of Machinists—AFL (IAM); the Order of Railway Telegraphers—AFL (ORT); the Brotherhood of Dining Car Conductors; the American Federation of Railway Workers; Brotherhood of Railway Station Employees & Clerks (BRSEC); American Train Dispatchers Association; Railroad Yard Masters of North America; Neptune Association; Brotherhood of Locomotive Engineers (BLE); Brotherhood of Locomotive Firemen and Enginemen (BLF); Brotherhood of Railway Conductors; the Brotherhood of Railroad Trainmen (BRT); and the Railroad Yard Masters of America.

about 13, 7 of which were AFL affiliates (SNA, BRSC, IAM, MMP, RMA, WWPA, and the ORT).[2] In 1949 there were at least nine unions with formal race bars, two of which were members of the AFL (WWPA and ORT). The ORT removed its race bar in 1952 and the WWPA merged with the United Papermakers & Paperworkers. After the AFL-CIO merger in 1955 there would have been no major national affiliates with race bars if the BRT and the BLF had not been admitted to the merged federation. The BRT removed its race bar in 1960, leaving only the ORC, the BLE, and the BLF with formal restrictions. The BLF, the only one of these unions affiliated with the AFL-CIO, removed its race bar in 1963.

The following forces caused unions to abandon exclusion by formal means, or to adopt more subtle forms: Expansion of Negro employment into jurisdictions covered by these unions, especially during World War II; competition between unions for Negro votes in representation elections after the passage of the Railway Labor Act; the embarrassment of exclusionist union leaders at conventions and in the press by criticism from Negro and white union leaders; action by such governmental agencies as the wartime and State FEP committees, especially the creation of the New York State Commission Against Discrimination in 1946; and fear of the loss of exclusive bargaining rights, union shop provisions or other legal privileges under the Railway Labor Act or the Taft-Hartley Act.

INFORMAL EXCLUSION

The decline in formal exclusion by international unions does not mean, however, that discrimination declined by the same degree because of local variations from official policies. Unions with formal race bars frequently have accepted Negro members and the locals of some international unions with no formal bars, particularly in the building trades and on the railroads, have excluded Negroes by such informal means as agreements not to sponsor Negroes for membership; refusal to admit Negroes into apprenticeship programs; refusal to accept applicants from Negroes, or simply ignoring their applications; general "understandings" to vote against Negroes if they were proposed (for example, three members of the BRT or BRSC lodge may bar an applicant for membership); using examinations to refuse Negroes journeymen status which either were not given to whites or were rigged so that Negroes could not pass them; and by exerting political pressure on governmental licensing agencies to see to it that Negroes failed the tests. An examination of union racial practices in various building trades unions throws more light on this problem.

[2] See *Ibid.* for names of these unions.

BUILDING TRADES

The pattern of racial exclusion in the building trades has been second only to the railroad industry in its rigidity. The craft locals of the International Brotherhood of Electrical Workers (IBEW) and the Plumbers & Pipe Fitters (UA) have had an almost consistent pattern of discrimination throughout the United States, but the following other building trades unions are also prominent in the list of unions regularly charged with racial discrimination: Granite Workers, Flint Glass Workers, Structural Iron Workers, and Asbestos Workers. In addition, locals of the following organizations less frequently have been charged with discrimination by various civil rights organizations: Bricklayers, Masons & Plasterers (BMP); Plasterers & Cement Masons (PCM); United Brotherhood of Carpenters & Joiners (BCJ); International Union of Operating Engineers (IUOE); Lathers International Union; Painters, Decorators & Paperhangers (PDP); International Association of Sheet Metal Workers; and Elevator Constructors. Some of these latter unions, like the BMP, the PCM, and the Roofers are in occupations with relatively large Negro memberships, and the Bricklayers International Union seems consistently to have sought to abolish discriminatory practices—except segregated locals—whenever these have been brought to its attention. The unions in the so-called trowel trades and the Roofers have many Negro members in integrated or virtually all-Negro locals in the South, but there have been charges of segregation in the South and other forms of discrimination in many places in the non-South. Other organizations like the IUOE and the Teamsters have had reputations for barring Negroes in some places and accepting them in others.

INTERNATIONAL UNIONS

We should note the distinction between the policies of international unions and their locals. Both the Plumbers and the IBEW internationals have become concerned about the adverse publicity they are receiving, which has caused their actions to be carefully scrutinized by civil rights and Government agencies and which threatens to jeopardize their control of the trades. The Plumbers established a committee in 1959 to study charges of racial discrimination against their locals throughout the United States and in 1962 the international union included a nondiscrimination clause in its national agreement covering large contractors, which could be significant for some Federal contractors. Similarly, the 1958 IBEW Convention adopted a resolution on civil rights, which resolved that it was the "enduring goal of our brotherhood to assure to all workers their full share in the benefits of union organization without regard to race, creed, color, or national origin." In 1963, 18 building trades internationals agreed to take more vigorous action to eliminate discrimination, and the powerful Brotherhood of Carpenters & Joiners adopted a nondiscrimination program, including the elimination of segregated locals. Moreover, building trades unions throughout the United States have recently responded to the widespread charges of discrimination against them by admitting some Negroes to membership. It remains to be seen, however, whether these equalitarian measures will produce significant changes in racial employment patterns.

CONCLUSIONS ON UNIONS WITH INFORMAL EXCLUSION

The evidence seems to support the following conclusions concerning unions that bar Negroes from membership by informal means:

1. Racial exclusion by informal means is not restricted to any particular geographic area. Though restriction is undoubtedly more rigid in the South, unions in the following trades probably have more Negro members in the South than some other places: the trowel trades, longshoremen, teamsters, roofers, hod carriers and common laborers, and hotel and restaurant employees. These trades have been practiced by Negroes in the South because they have been regarded as "Negro work" and because Negroes have sufficient supplies of labor to protect their interests and to protect their employers, who might be boycotted by whites. These occupations also are relatively old and have stable techniques, making it difficult for unions to exclude Negroes by monopolizing the latest technology.

2. While some craft unions have had egalitarian racial policies and some industrial union locals have refused to admit Negroes to membership, as a general rule the unions which practice exclusion are craft organizations. The members of craft locals have the ability to exclude Negroes from membership and from the trade if they can control the labor supply. Industrial unions on the other hand are forced to organize workers hired by the employer, while the craft unions determine in many cases whom he hires. In addition, craft unions at the local level consider it to their advantage to exclude workers, while industrial unions consider it to their advantage to organize extensively.

3. The foregoing factors are not, however, sufficient to identify the general character of excluding unions. Some other factors include: because of the egalitarian trend in race relations, those unions which are older, other things being equal, seem more likely to exclude than newer unions; in many cases the employer determines the hiring policy; whites are likely to attempt to exclude Negroes from certain status jobs like

airline pilots, stock wranglers, locomotive engineers, white-collar and supervisory jobs; and, in some cases, exclusion is directed against all except a particular nationality group. (It has been common practice in the building trades for instance, for locals to be made up entirely of a particular nationality.)

AUXILIARY AND SEGREGATED LOCALS

A number of international unions which did not bar Negroes from membership restricted them to auxiliary locals controlled entirely by whites; about the only thing Negro members of these locals were allowed to do was to pay dues. Auxiliary locals were weakened by attacks from the wartime FEPC court decisions which prohibited the closed shop where auxiliaries existed, NLRB decisions that the auxiliary could not be coupled with the checkoff of union dues, State FEP laws, the Taft-Hartley and Railway Labor Act amendments making the union shop unenforcable if all workers are not admitted on equal terms, and the Landrum-Griffin Act of 1959 which makes it possible for Negro employees to bring action to abolish auxiliary locals. A few auxiliary locals remained in 1959, but had become relatively unimportant by that date.

Segregated locals are theoretically different from auxiliary locals in that the Negro and white locals are equal and have separate charters. This distinction sometimes is more theoretical than real, however, because the white local might in fact represent the Negro local in dealings with employers. We must note, though, that there are actually relatively few truly segregated locals in the sense of separate unions for Negroes and whites in the same plant or craft. . . .

While it is extremely difficult to generalize about segregated locals, the writer's experiences suggest several broad conclusions:

1. Negroes in the South frequently favor a continuation of segregation because they would usually be in the minority and know that whites might discriminate against them; Negroes have their own buildings and other property, as well as their own officers and representatives, and thus have a vested interest in perpetuating segregation; some Negroes believe they can engage in nonunion matters of interest to Negroes better if they have their own locals.

2. Whether or not Negroes oppose integration depends partly upon the effects of segregation on their economic opportunities. Some unions, like the Bricklayers, Musicians, Longshoremen, Barbers, and others, feel that their economic opportunities would not be improved if they integrated because they have protected territories.

In other cases, however, Negro workers are extremely unhappy with segregation because they are denied equal job opportunities. Almost everywhere, for instance, Negro Carpenters' locals in the South have virtually atrophied because they cannot get adequate job opportunities. The Painters have a number of segregated locals in the South and have had experience similar to the Carpenters. As noted above, however, the Carpenters adopted a policy in 1963 to merge these locals.

3. The ideological and philosophical positions of Negroes will also influence their attitude toward segregated locals. Some Negro leaders are opposed to segregation on principle and feel that the AFL-CIO should deliver an ultimatum to its segregated locals to integrate or be expelled. On the other hand, a majority of the Negro leaders in segregated unions in the South probably oppose integration. Younger Negro workers are more likely to insist on integration, but older leaders fear Negroes will suffer short run losses from integration.

4. The proportions of Negroes in unions will influence the ability to merge segregated locals. If there are very few Negroes, whites will agree to merge, but if the Negroes are in the majority the whites will frequently oppose integration.

5. Negro resistance to integration has been reduced by special arrangements to make it possible for them to continue to have some control over their affairs when they integrated.

Finally, we may note the following developments concerning segregated unions in recent years:

a. The practice of establishing segregated locals has been almost completely discontinued. Observers also detect tendencies for Negroes and whites to segregate themselves in union meetings less than they did 20 years ago. There are, moreover, increasing examples of integrated union social affairs in the South.

b. A number of international unions have agreed to establish no more segregated unions (Painters; Tobacco Workers; Pulp, Sulphite, and Paper Mill Workers) and other organizations have taken measures to integrate segregated locals (International Ladies' Garment Workers, the National Association of Letter Carriers, the International Association of Machinists, the International Brotherhood of Teamsters, the American Federation of Musicians, the Carpenters, and the American Federation of Teachers). Most of the organizations with segregated locals in the South, however, have refused to integrate locals on the grounds of local autonomy, especially opposition by the colored members (Bricklayers, Longshoremen, Molders, Paper Makers, Railroad Clerks, Maintenance of Way Employees, Railway Carmen, Railway Trainmen).

c. The AFL-CIO has taken a formal position against segregated locals, but has refused to invoke sanctions or to establish a time by which segregated locals must integrate.

We should note, however, that to say a local is "integrated" might not mean very much. It could mean that one or two Negroes belong to the organization but never participate other than by paying dues. "Integration" might also mean that Negroes are members of the industrial union and if they attend meetings they segregate themselves or are segregated by whites.

CONTROL OF JOB OPPORTUNITIES

Craft unions influence job opportunities for Negroes by controlling entry into the labor market through closed-union, closed-shop conditions, job referral systems, apprenticeship programs, and pressure on employers to hire or not to hire Negroes. Industrial unions affect job opportunities through control of hiring, transfer, promotion, and layoffs. Many employers are convinced that if they transfer Negroes into previously "white" occupations the white workers will strike, and there is sufficient historical precedent to validate this belief, though it is rarely possible for a group of rank and filers to block the employment or upgrading of Negroes without the aid of either the employer or the international.

Finally, unions have positively influenced employment opportunities of minorities by promoting civil rights legislation, including nondiscrimination clauses in contracts and adoption of companywide seniority agreements to make it possible for Negroes to break out of "Negro" jobs.

While our attention has been focused on problems of racial discrimination within unions, we have noted that unions also have contributed to the improvement of the Negro worker's position. In spite of these positive measures, however, racial discrimination is still a serious problem within the labor movement and probably cannot be solved by the unions themselves. This conclusion is based on the belief that those unions and leaders who want to change union racial practices do not have sufficient power to do so. . . .

CONCLUSIONS

We may conclude by noting some of the main changes in union racial practices in the last 30 years.

1. The number of international unions with formal racial bars has declined from at least 22 in 1930 to 2 major unions today; and none of these is affiliated with the AFL-CIO. Moreover, informal exclusion has declined considerably, and recently some of the most intransigent craft locals have accepted Negro members for the first time.

2. Negro union membership has increased from about 56,000 in 1930 to between 1.5 and 2 million today.

3. The AFL-CIO has adopted a stronger equalitarian racial position than either the AFL or the CIO, though the federation really has little other than moral power to enforce its policies against offending locals. While implementation of the federation's racial policies has been impeded by difficulties within the federation and its civil rights committee and department, there is evidence that the AFL-CIO is moving with increasing vigor to abolish discrimination in its ranks; the external pressures being exerted on the labor movement by civil rights organizations have strengthened the federation in its dealings with its affiliates.

4. Negroes occupy official positions within the labor movement. Two Negroes were elected to the AFL-CIO Executive Council, though one of these (Willard Townsend) died and was not replaced by a Negro. At least 17 international unions have or have had Negro vice presidents or executive board members. There are also many Negroes in positions of responsibility within local unions.

5. The level of the debate over union racial policies has changed in the past 30 years. Thirty years ago discrimination was defined largely in terms of unions which would not admit Negroes to membership and the prevalence of racial wage differentials. Where Negroes were admitted, it was commonly to auxiliary locals. Today, the racial wage differential has almost disappeared in jobs covered by union contracts and auxiliary locals are almost nonexistent. The main areas of conflict today involve the exclusion of Negroes from some craft locals, abolition of segregated seniority rosters, the election of Negroes to international executive boards and overcoming Negro and white opposition to the desegregation of local unions. While many building trades and railroad locals continue to exclude Negroes from membership, and Negroes continue to be concentrated in the lowest job categories, segregated seniority rosters have been changed considerably in many industries. Moreover, while segregated locals exist in all sections of the country, it is rare to learn of the establishment of new segregated locals, and several international unions are taking measures to abolish Negro locals where they exist.

6. Thirty years ago, Negro leaders frequently encouraged colored workers to act as strikebreakers. Today, in spite of the growing public split between the Negro community and the labor movement, many Negro organizations remain prounion and Negro strikebreakers are rarely heard of. Moreover, Negro labor political alliances continue to be important forces in most industrial cities.

7. A considerable body of law has been developed in union

racial practices, and a number of organizations have evolved to which aggrieved workers can take charges of discrimination against unions. Indeed, one reason union racial practices have not been changed more than they have is the paucity of verifiable charges filed with these agencies.

There is ample evidence of discrimination against Negroes by unions, but it would be false to allege either that there has not been a significant lowering of racial barriers in unions in the past 30 years, or that the union movement has not made significant contributions to the Negro's welfare.

A Report of the New York
Advisory Committee

DISCRIMINATION
IN THE BUILDING TRADES:
THE NEW YORK CITY CASE

BUILDING CONSTRUCTION IN NEW YORK CITY

. . . At 6:16 on weekday mornings a train leaves Bridgeport, Conn., carrying a group of commuters relatively unknown to the general public. They are men with skills in the building trades who arrive in New York City at 7:30, and report to construction jobs. It costs about $15 a week to commute from Bridgeport to New York, but a union electrician earns $200 per week, and the work is steady.

These blue-collar commuters represent one of the many indications of the obvious fact that New York City is in the midst of a continuing boom in large construction. There is presently more office space in New York City than in the next 15 largest cities combined. Despite rows of office towers like those north of Grand Central on Park Avenue and rows of residential towers like those all along Third Avenue,

Reprinted from "A Report of the New York Advisory Committee to the U.S. Commission on Civil Rights," in Vol. 3 of *Selected Readings in Employment and Manpower* of the Subcommittee on Employment and Manpower of the Committee on Labor and Public Welfare, U.S. Senate, 1964.

The field work for the study was directed by Donald Shaughnessy of Columbia University.

there are estimates that the backlog of needed construction in New York City may take decades to fill.

How do these buildings get built? With wide allowance for over-simplification the process can be summarized as follows:

When the architect has completed his design and specifications, general contractors competent in the size of job being undertaken submit bids to the owners. Subcontractors (electrical firms, plumbing firms, and the like) have previously submitted bids to the general contractor upon which his bid, in part, is based. The contract is then awarded to a general contractor, who engages subcontractors, and men begin to appear to perform the work in the specialized trades. First the excavation, then the other trades in their turn appear on the job.

Most firms in the building industry are not large; they do not steadily employ a large number of skilled workers. These firms build a product that is immobile. This product must be built in the city, essentially by local contractors and subcontractors, and in particular by a locally based labor force.

The men who build New York City's buildings are recruited from labor pools controlled by the unions in the building trades. The union is the employment agency and the men who appear on the construction job, whether they be local or out-of-town men, are the men whom the union permits to appear. Since a building cannot be erected in Detroit or Atlanta and shipped to New York and since the unions regulate the local use of out-of-town labor, the labor supply is rigidly controlled.

The construction worker tends to identify with his union for a number of reasons. He is rarely on any job for a great length of time. He may well have five or six employers in 1 year. He is not likely to develop an attachment for a particular firm or to have steady fellow-workers from year to year, and, of course, he has no fixed place of work. His job security comes from the local union. The local union is not only his hiring hall but the place where his friendships are formed and the continuing stable element in his employment. Local unions may or may not be ethnocentric but their members are likely to be united against outsiders. In one local outsiders may mean people not of Italian ancestry, in another it may mean Jews. For most unions in the building trades, as for many other institutions, color is the most readily identifiable badge of nonmembership.

With these economic and social bonds to his local union, the man in the building trades is little concerned with the labor views on the subject of race relations. George Meany, once a plumber, now President of the AFL-CIO, concedes that local unions can effectively disregard the resolutions opposing discrimination that are regularly adopted by feder-ated bodies in the labor movement. On the bread-and-butter issues it is not the international or any council that delivers, but the local union.

This is not to say that the building trade unions lack the ability to unite in support of their common interests. In the building and construction trade department of the AFL-CIO there are 19 international unions. New York City locals of these unions form the New York City Building and Construction Trade Council. This council serves as a very effective spokesman for the building trade unions in city and State legislative halls and executive departments. While the council is active and effective in speaking to the outside world on behalf of its constituent locals, it has not traditionally exerted effective internal pressures. . . .

In brief, the economic structure of the building industry tends to concentrate in the local unions the decision as to who obtains employment and, even more important, who gets admitted to the craft. The dominating role of the union in construction employment affords to contractors the opportunity to disclaim all responsibility for discrimination in the building trades. The employers seem to welcome the opportunity, which accords with their consistent tendency to avoid rocking the boat. Our study found no instance in which an employer sought to promote equal employment opportunity in the building trades.

APPRENTICESHIP

Current apprentice programs provide from one-half to two-thirds of the skilled workers needed simply to replace craftsmen who retire, die, or leave the trade. By fixing the number of apprentices in accordance with a ratio of apprentices to journeymen (the mean ratio is 1 to 6), and not in accordance with present or future demand, the building trades unions continue to maintain an effective shortage of labor. One way that this shortage is preserved in the face of continuing high demand is in the use of commuters like those from Bridgeport who represent an auxiliary source of manpower that can be cut off at any time.

While 120-mile-per-day commuters have found steady employment for several years, a local source of skilled manpower is ignored. New York City has 22 vocational high schools in 5 of which are taught skills used in the building trades. These schools are financed by Federal, State, and city funds. The best qualified graduates of the vocational schools often take low-paying nonunion jobs, or jobs outside the trade. Federal and State apprenticeship agencies have not been heard to complain that Negro youngsters, taught a trade at public expense, are consistently deprived of the opportunity to practice it.

New York State law on the subject is clear and precise. Section 296 of article 15 of the Executive Law prohibits discrimination by employers in hiring, compensation, employment privileges, working conditions, and discharges, prohibits union discrimination in membership, and bars discrimination by employers and unions in admission to apprentice training, on-the-job training, and the like. This policy is also reflected in the existence of agencies such as the State commission for human rights, the New York City Commission on Human Rights, and the civil rights bureau of the State attorney general's office. The last-named agency is largely responsible for the fact that, in the State of New York, there are now two Negroes in the apprentice training program of the Plumbers Union.

The national agency in the field of apprenticeship is the Bureau of Apprenticeship and Training in the U.S. Department of Labor. The Bureau has an essentially passive role in certifying and registering apprentice training programs. This role is of no great importance since less than half of the apprentice programs in the city are certified by the Bureau. The Bureau appears to have been neutral in the matter of racial discrimination, an inappropriate posture the abandonment of which is recommended, at the end of this report.

First, let us review the practice of several of the unions in New York City:

Local 28, International Sheet Metal Workers Union

There has been no significant change in the size of this local in the past 10 years, despite the fast increase in construction. There are no Negroes among its 3,300 members nor among its 75 apprentices. Admission to the apprentice program of the Sheet Metal Workers Union is on the basis of a personal interview with a joint committee. The applicant is usually sponsored by a union member, sometimes by an employer. The union states that there are four applicants for every vacancy but gives no indication that any applicant sponsored by the union has ever been rejected. The apprentice committee maintains no liaison with vocational schools. Its apprentices attend a union school which obtains no Government support. Various requirements are listed for admission to the apprenticeship program, but they are not applied to sponsored applicants. In March 1963, the Civil Rights Bureau of the Attorney General's office charged local 28 with discriminatory practices.

Local 2, United Association of Journeymen Plumbers & Steamfitters

The Plumbers Union says it has four applicants for apprenticeship for every apprentice who can be accepted. On the other hand, the union admits that there are 1,000 out-of-town plumbers working in New York City. Of 3,300 members of local 2, none are Negroes. While there are requirements that theoretically apply to admission to the apprenticeship program, the main practical requirement has to do with bloodlines;

80 to 85 percent of those admitted to membership are sons or nephews of local 2 members. Members of this union consider that the right to nominate apprentices is among the important benefits of union membership.

District Council of United Brotherhood of Carpenters & Joiners (42 Locals)

The council has 34,000 members of whom over 5,000 are Negroes. While there tend to be predominantly white and predominantly Negro locals, the Carpenters Union has provided the only substantial employment opportunity for Negroes in the building trades.

Local 60, Operating Plasterers & Cement Masons International Association

In this union there is a larger ratio of Negroes presently employed in the trade than in its apprenticeship program; 300 of 2,000 members of local 60 are Negroes, as compared to 5 of the 80 apprentices. In local 60's apprenticeship program, as in most others, no aptitude tests or objective standards are applied in the admission of apprentices.

Locals 14 and 14B of the International Union of Operating Engineers

This union trains its members through apprenticeship local 15—a 3-year program. Unlike most other union members, the operating engineers must take an objective examination, administered by the New York City Department of Buildings. The examination is open—not limited to union members. After passing the examination, an apprentice must obtain two sponsors (members of locals 14, 14B) in order to be admitted to the union. Thus far only 23 Negroes have been admitted to the 1,600-member union.

Local 3, International Brotherhood of Electrical Workers

Local 3 recently won fame in securing a 5-hour day. This union has different levels of membership, the most important of which is "A-card construction worker." These men (who won the 5-hour day) comprise 9,000 of the 30,000 members of local 3. The number of Negroes who hold the A-card and earn $5 per hour is small, estimates ranging from 300 to 400. There are about 2,250 men from outside New York City working in electrical construction, filling jobs from which qualified vocational school graduates are excluded. On the lower level of local 3, members work for the lamp and lamp-shade manufacturing industry and are paid about $2 per hour.

In the spring of 1962, Mr. Harry Van Arsdale, president of local 3, announced that the union would recruit 1,000 new apprentices, on a nondiscriminatory basis. The Urban League forwarded the names of 51 qualified Negroes and the NAACP forwarded 57 names. Negroes and Puerto Ricans were recruited from other sources and a total of 1,600 apprentices were screened by a nonunion committee of 3 men, one of whom was a Negro—1,020 apprentices were admitted to the program including about 140 Negroes and about 60 Puerto Ricans. This dramatic result and local 3's broad recruiting effort is, so far as we know, without parallel in any building trades union in the country.

In the course of its inquiry, the New York State Advisory Committee became aware of undocumented charges to the effect that the approximately 200 Negro and Puerto Rican apprentices have not entered into regular apprenticeship channels, but are being utilized to perform unskilled labor. This issue was raised by Committee Chairman Sachs in a meeting with Mr. Harry Van Arsdale, business manager of Local 3, IBEW, and Mr. Theodore W. Kheel, director of the Office of Impartial Review of the Electrical Industry. Mr. Sachs received unequivocal assurances from both Mr. Van Arsdale and Mr. Kheel that these charges are unfounded, and that the 200 apprentices in question are undergoing regular apprenticeship training leading, in the course of 4 years, to full journeyman status and a class A union membership card, on the same basis as all other apprentices.

The six examples listed above illustrate that control of apprenticeship programs gives the building trades unions a potent weapon against the possibility of future unemployment. By restricting the apprenticeship program, the union can continue to maintain a chronic labor shortage and to assure reasonably full employment for their members. Entry into such a well-protected, high-paying career is an outstanding employment opportunity. These employment opportunities have, in effect, become union patronage. A union leader who is not skillful in dispensing this patronage may lose his position. They and the rank-and-file members consider that their power at the bargaining table has won them control of apprenticeship opportunities.

The unions have maintained a tight rein on apprenticeship openings despite the current widespread projections of a continued high level of new construction. Earlier projections by the Department of Commerce indicated that for every 100 skilled in the building trades in 1955, 122 would be needed in 1965 and 145 by 1975. Current apprenticeship programs not only fail to provide for this growth but, as noted above, fail to produce enough journeymen to replace those who retire, die, or leave the trade.

In keeping with this static philosophy of apprenticeship, Negro participation has remained relatively constant. In 1950, Negroes constituted 1.5 percent of the apprentices and 13 percent of the population of

New York City. In 1960, Negroes constituted 2 percent of the apprentices and 22 percent of the population of New York City. It is estimated that by 1970 Negroes will constitute about 33 percent of the population of New York City. If Negro participation in apprenticeship programs continues to bear no relation to the size of the Negro population, then larger and larger numbers of Negroes will be obliged to compete for the dwindling supply of unskilled jobs.

The alternatives are essentially three:

1. Retention by the building trades unions of presently prevailing practices. This is likely to result in no substantial increase in Negro and Puerto Rican apprenticeship.

2. Voluntary adoption by other unions of programs like that of Local 3, IBEW, with positive efforts to recruit Negroes and Puerto Ricans and an objective body to screen and approve apprenticeship applicants.

3. Adoption by public authorities of regulations, contract policies, and other practices which provide objective criteria for apprentice selection and enforce compliance by the manner in which public funds are expended and withheld.

While our study was limited, it was sufficient to reject the first alternative as intolerable and to conclude that while the second alternative may be more desirable, the third is required for prompt and effective action. . . .

Our recommendations follow:

RECOMMENDATIONS

The New York State Advisory Committee recommends to the U.S. Commission on Civil Rights that steps be taken to bring about the following changes in present practices:

1. (a) That the Federal Bureau of Apprenticeship and Training be authorized and empowered to require that all apprenticeship programs in the construction industry be registered by the Bureau; that it establish, in consultation with representatives of unions and management, objective criteria for admission to apprenticeship programs; that it determine the number of available apprenticeship openings in each program, giving consideration to the skilled manpower needs of the Nation as well as to those of the industry and the immediate locality; and that it establish a meaningful and effective evaluation system for each of the trades; (b) That the Federal Bureau of Apprenticeship and Training be authorized and empowered to require that all notices of acceptance and rejection to apprenticeship programs be filed with the Bureau, and that acceptances and rejections be accounted for in terms of the established objective criteria of admission; (c) That the Federal Bureau

of Apprenticeship and Training be authorized and empowered to conduct systematic apprenticeship recruiting programs, in part by means of uniform vocational guidance procedures in public schools, and to investigate, on its own initiative, apprentice training programs which are, or are believed to be, engaged in discriminatory practices.

2. (a) That departments, agencies, offices, and bureaus of the Federal Government be required to withhold all financial support from apprenticeship programs which fail to admit qualified Negro applicants or fail to comply with the requirements of the Bureau of Apprenticeship and Training described above; (b) That departments, agencies, offices, and bureaus of the Federal Government be required to withhold all financial assistance from any contractor and from any building project employing the labor of any union or local thereof which cannot give satisfactory proof that it does not follow discriminatory practices.

3. In the event that the foregoing procedures are found to be ineffective, we recommend that Congress enact legislation declaring that admission to apprenticeship in the construction trades is a matter affecting interstate commerce and that such admission be vested in a suitable agency empowered to adopt and enforce procedures analogous to those employed by the Civil Service Commission.

Herbert Hill
ORGANIZED LABOR AND THE NEGRO WAGE EARNER: RITUAL AND REALITY

In the late nineteen thirties and early forties during the phenomenal rise of the Congress of Industrial Organizations there was a great hope for Negroes within organized labor.

With the rapid growth of industrial unions in the basic mass production sectors of the economy where tens of thousands of colored workers in steel, automobile, rubber and packinghouse plants joined CIO unions on the basis of equality, there was reason to hope that the "old line" AFL craft union tradition of racial exclusion and segregation would

From *New Politics*, Vol. 1, No. 2, Winter 1962. Reprinted by permission.

Mr. Hill is Labor Secretary of the National Association for the Advancement of Colored People.

be thrust aside in the forward surge of the new industrial unions.

But, unfortunately, the course of events in the past decade, and especially since the merger, clearly indicates that the social consciousness of the industrial unions with their sensitivity to the problems of the Negro wage earner have now all but totally vanished. Instead, trade unions are responding like other conservative institutions in American society to the new demands of the Negro for full equality and recognition of individual ability.

In the early years of the 1940's the leadership of the CIO repeatedly joined with the Negro community in publicly condemning the vicious racism of several major AFL unions when they abused Negro workers. This occurred, for example, when the International Brotherhood of Electrical Workers, upon becoming the collective bargaining agent at the Bauer Electric Company in Hartford, Connecticut, demanded that all Negro electricians be dismissed from their jobs, as Negroes could not be admitted into membership; when the Boilermakers Union forced Negro workers out of their jobs in several shipyards, and the similar action of the International Association of Machinists at the Boeing Aircraft Company plant in Seattle.

In its time the National CIO filed *amicus curiae* briefs in support of litigation initiated by Negroes and assisted in a variety of ways the protests of colored workers against the operating railroad brotherhoods and other discriminatory labor organizations.

But this has long since come to an end. The industrial union bloc in the AFL-CIO hardly differentiates itself from Meany and the Building Trades Council on racial issues. The leadership of the Industrial Union Department remained silent when Randolph, as the spokesman for Negro trade unionists, was repeatedly attacked by Meany and they voted with the rest of the AFL-CIO Executive Council in denouncing Randolph and in rejecting proposals to eliminate discrimination and segregation in affiliated unions. In addition, many of the former CIO unions have themselves compromised, especially in the South, with anti-Negro practices.

It appears that on racial issues the industrial unions have made their peace with the narrow and bigoted AFL craft tradition. There was a time when they challenged that tradition, but today, they remain silent and acquiesce as organized labor becomes more conservative and rigid, unable to organize vast new industries and basing itself upon an increasingly small and limited section of the work force in the United States. The AFL-CIO has greatly compromised the social objectives declared at the time of the merger in 1955 and in addition has not realized the basic collective bargaining goals it set for itself at that time.

Thus, today, the militant Negro worker is confronted not with a trade union movement that is a force for social change but on the contrary, with a national labor organization that has become a very conservative and highly bureaucratized institution, closely allied in many cities and states to reactionary political forces and defending that status quo which is now directly attacked by the Negro in virtually every area of American life.

A significant manifestation of organized labor's conservatism on non-economic issues is the rigidity of anti-Negro practices in many important unions. The refusal to yield on racial matters, to bitterly resist change in the status of Negroes, is responsible for the fact that today many trade unions lag behind the progress made by other institutions in the community. In East St. Louis, Illinois, and Tulsa, Oklahoma, for example, Negro children attend integrated schools during the day but their parents attend segregated union meetings at night, if they are admitted into labor unions at all. Recently, A. Phillip Randolph called "for a crusade to desegregate the Southern AFL-CIO State Conventions and City Central bodies," and stated that, "this is a problem probably not less significant or difficult than the desegregation of public schools in the South."

There is a deep distrust among many Negro wage earners and others within the Negro community toward trade unions. It is a distrust well founded on experience. For today, as in the past, there is a profound disparity between the public image presented by the national AFL-CIO and the day-to-day realities as experienced by many Negro workers. This is true in the North as well as in the South. There are some few exceptions, especially in the mass production industries where, historically, there has been a large concentration of Negro workers, and in some unions such as the United Automobile Workers (UAW) and the United Packinghouse Workers (UPW) where there is an ideological sensitivity to the "Negro question."

But for the Negro in major areas of the economy, in the building and construction trades, the railroad industry, among the boilermakers, oil and chemical workers and machinists, in pulp, tobacco and paper manufacturing, in metal working, in the printing trades and in many other industries highly unionized for a long period of time, trade union practices are characterized by a broad pattern of discrimination and segregation.

The pattern of union responsibility for job discrimination against Negroes is not limited to any one area of the country or to some few industries or union jurisdictions but involves many unions in a wide variety of occupations in manufacturing industries, skilled crafts, railroads, and in maritime trades as, for example, the Seafarers International Union which operates union controlled hiring halls on Great Lakes ports such as Duluth, Chicago, Detroit, Buffalo and Cleveland. Over the years, Negro members of the Seafarers International Union have repeatedly protested the systematic practice of dispatching Negroes for menial jobs only, as mess boys in the galley, but to no avail, as the union continues discriminatory job assignments in its hiring halls.

On occasion, after much protest, one or two Negroes have been admitted into an all-white local union as token compliance with a state or municipal fair-employment practices law as with the International Brotherhood of Electrical Workers in Cleveland, the Bricklayers in Milwaukee, the Railway Clerks in Minneapolis. But this is essentially a limited and strategic adjustment to community pressure and represents very dubious progress. After six years of protest and the threat of legal action by the Attorney General, IBEW Local 26 in Washington, D.C. gave one Negro a temporary work permit. The IBEW in most cases excludes Negroes from membership in the key local unions having jurisdiction in construction installation. Thus, because IBEW Local 26 in Washington refuses membership to non-white persons, Negroes were prevented from working on the construction of the AFL-CIO national headquarters building, the new House of Representatives office building and other public and private construction in the nation's capital. Local 26 remains a "lily-white" union.

There are also many instances where unions have removed the "lily-white" exclusion clause from their constitution as a public relations gesture but continue to exclude Negroes from membership by tacit consent.

As long as union membership remains a condition of employment in many trades and crafts and qualified Negroes are barred from union membership solely because of their color, then trade union discrimination is the decisive factor in determining whether Negro workers in a given industry shall have an opportunity to earn a living for themselves and their families. This is especially true in the construction industry where AFL-CIO building trades unions exercise a high degree of control over access to employment. . . .

Soon after the merger of the AFL and CIO in 1955, two international unions were admitted into the Federation with "lily-white" exclusion clauses in their constitutions although this action was clearly in violation of the policies announced at the time of the merger agreement. They were the Brotherhood of Railroad Trainmen which later removed the clause and the International Brotherhood of Locomotive Firemen and Enginemen which did not.

In November, 1958, the Brotherhood of Locomotive Firemen and Enginemen successfully defended its exclusion of Negroes from union membership in a suit brought by Negro firemen against the union in the

Federal District Court in Cincinnati, Ohio (Oliphant v. Brotherhood of Locomotive Firemen and Enginemen). Despite many appeals the National AFL-CIO refused to intervene or make any public comment and this union continues to exclude all Negroes from membership.[1]

On October 10, 1961, Negro workers in St. Petersburg, Florida, and Memphis, Tennessee, filed affidavits with the President's Committee on Equal Employment Opportunity against the Brotherhood of Railway Trainmen (AFL-CIO). In these complaints it was charged that the Trainmen's Union conspired with the Atlantic Coast Line Railroad and with the St. Louis-San Francisco Railroad Company, as well as with other railroads to have all Negro brakemen classified as "Porters," that competent Negro railway workers are consistently denied opportunities for promotion and advancement, that because of improper job classification they are discriminated against in wages and that "The Brotherhood of Railroad Trainmen, a union that is authorized and recognized by the Atlantic Coast Line Railroad is a 'lily-white' union and that said union accepts only white employees as members."

Obviously, when the Brotherhood of Railroad Trainmen removed the "Caucasian Only" clause from its Constitution in 1959, this was done mainly for public relations purposes since the union continues in most cities to exclude qualified Negro railroad employees.

Separate lines of seniority promotion constitute yet another injustice to the Negro worker. These are negotiated into collective bargaining agreements, effectively denying Negroes equal seniority rights with white workers, and preventing them from developing skills. The result is that Negroes are unable to rise from unskilled and menial jobs into more desirable classifications.

Negro workers employed at the Sheffield Steel Company in Houston, Texas, were forced to initiate litigation against the United Steelworkers of America and the Company and as a result succeeded in eliminating the most extreme features of the separate seniority lines in the union contract. Very slow and isolated progress has been made in a few other instances as a result of protest by Negro workers and action by the NAACP.

Nevertheless, the fact remains that the pattern of such discrimination remains practically intact in Southern industrial operations where trade unions hold collective bargaining agreements. Many thousands of Negro workers who are members of AFL-CIO unions in Southern paper mills, chemical plants, pulp works, oil refineries, steel plants, and in tobacco factories suffer the acute disadvantage of separate lines of progression. In Lake Charles, Louisiana, for example, the Metal Trades

---

[1] The Brotherhood of Locomotive Firemen and Enginemen removed its formal race bar in 1963. See p. 281 (eds.).

Department of the AFL-CIO is directly responsible for negotiating such clauses in its union contracts with several major oil and chemical refineries.

Collusion with management in regard to unequal seniority rights is common. Typical offenders in the rapidly growing paper manufacturing and pulp and sulphite industry in the South are to be found at the huge Union Bag-Camp Paper Corporation, Savannah, Georgia, where all the Negro workers are limited to membership in two segregated locals, Locals 601 and 615, affiliated to the International Brotherhood of Pulp, Sulphite and Paper Mill Workers. All white workers hold membership in Locals 388 and 435 of the same union and Local 408 of the United Papermakers and Paperworkers Union. Similar conditions exist at and in virtually every plant organized in the South by the United Papermakers and Paperworkers Union and the International Brotherhood of Pulp, Sulphite and Paper Mill Workers.

In these and many other paper mills throughout the South these two unions hold joint collective bargaining agreements and maintain a rigid pattern of racially segregated local unions with separate seniority lines limiting Negro employment to laborer classifications.

The harmful consequences of rapid technological change and automation upon the unskilled Negro wage earner is compounded by the exclusion of Negroes from apprenticeship training programs. Because there exists a disproportionate number of Negroes in the unskilled labor force, a disproportionate number of Negroes are being permanently dismissed from jobs as a result of automation and other technological change. It follows that the plight of these unskilled Negroes can become an economic disaster for the entire Negro community where these workers are not permitted to learn new skills, i.e., where they are excluded from apprenticeship programs and other forms of technical training. Such exclusion is widespread in the North as well as in the South. According to recent studies no significant breakthrough has been made by Negroes in those craft unions in the building trades or in the Railroad Operating Brotherhood, which have traditionally excluded non-whites.

In the ten-year period from 1950–1960, in the State of New York, the increase of Negro participation in building trades apprenticeship training programs rose only from 1.5% to 2%. In most of these programs the role of the labor union is decisive because the trade union usually determines who is admitted into the training programs and, therefore, who is admitted into the union.

Almost equally exclusive are the printing trades unions with exceptions being found in some areas of the Assistant Printing Pressmen's Union and the Lithographers Union. Open access to plumbing and pipe fitting apprenticeships controlled by the Plumbers Union is a rare experience for a young Negro in the North as well as in the South. Similarly, Negro youth are almost completely excluded from apprenticeship programs operated by the Sheet Metal Workers Union, the Ornamental and Structural Iron Workers, the Glass Workers, the Tile Setters, the Machinists and the Bricklayers Union.

The exclusion of Negroes from apprenticeship programs, controlled by AFL-CIO craft unions, prevents thousands of young people from realizing their full potential and dooms them and their families to a marginal existence. It is in this area of apprenticeship training that the disparity between the public relations pronouncements of the AFL-CIO on civil rights and the day-to-day reality for Negro workers is most sharply delineated.

Many traditional sources of Nego employment (the nation's railroads and mass-production industries, for example) are rapidly disappearing as a result of automation and other technological changes in the economy. Today the status of the Negro wage earner is characterized by drastic change and crisis. Thus, the virtual exclusion of Negroes from apprenticeship and other training programs forces them to remain as marginal employees in the economy. They are the ones who are hired last and who can be dispensed with easily with the added advantage that their displacement can be rationalized in terms of lower attainments in craft skills.

The concentration of unskilled, low-paying jobs with a lack of employment stability, together with other income limitations such as denial of access to union hiring halls in the building trades, and separate racial lines of seniority promotion in collective bargaining agreements, all contribute to an explanation of why Negroes constitute a permanently depressed economic group in American society.

Seymour M. Lipset
NEGROES AND
THE LABOR MOVEMENT:
A REPLY TO HERBERT HILL

There can be little doubt that Herbert Hill is correct when he points to various facts which indicate that large sections of organized labor are sustaining racially discriminatory practices, and that those segments which oppose such discrimination are not doing very much to bring their recalcitrant or prejudiced brethren into line. The facts are not at issue, but the causes and prospective solutions to the problem are.

In so far as Hill suggests a cause, it would seem to be the growth of bureaucratic conservatism, especially among the leaders of the old CIO unions who seemingly no longer strongly care about or support the liberal or radical objectives of their earlier days. The blame is placed on a change in the perspectives or situation of the leadership. I would question this interpretation.

All the available information gathered in diverse surveys indicate that on both economic (welfare state, government planning, social policy) and non-economic (civil rights, civil liberties, internationalism) issues, the *leaders of organized labor are more liberal or radical than are their members.* For example, when comparing the opinions of leaders and followers, the officials are less likely to be Republicans, more likely to favor the need for a labor party or systematic labor political action, more disposed to support government medicine, government planning, public ownership of natural resources and utilities, support of trade unions abroad, and so forth. The leaders are also more prone than their members to favor civil liberties for unpopular minorities even Communists, and are more favorable to equal rights for minority groups, particularly Negroes. The greater liberalism of the leadership would seem to be derivative from aspects of the leadership position itself, the fact that it involves them in many activities which lead them to understand the relationship between the needs of organized labor and these political policies, as well as a certain degree of self-selection for union leadership posts of those

From *New Politics*, Vol. 1, No. 3, Spring 1962. Reprinted by permission.
Mr. Lipset is Professor of Sociology, University of California, Berkeley.

who initially are more disposed to believe in the social movement values of the labor movement.

Although former CIO men are somewhat more liberal than former AFL men, the difference is not as large as it is between each group of leaders and their followers. Far from the image of conservative leaders restraining a progressive rank and file, the true picture more clearly resembles the opposite. This is not to deny that in many unions there is an active minority of rank and filers who are more liberal or radical than their officers. This more leftist minority is often disproportionately represented among the union activists, those who attend meetings, and hence sometimes create an illusion of a more radical membership. And it is, of course, also true that some unions are led by men who can properly be described as reactionaries.

The fact that the members generally are more conservative or bigoted than their leaders ironically often means that the more democratic unions exhibit more prejudice. For example, if one compares the behavior of the two sailors' unions, there is no question that the former CIO affiliate, the National Maritime Union, has a much better record on Negro rights than do the units of the Seafarers International Union, which belonged to the AFL. But the origin of this difference lies in the fact that the NMU was dominated for many years by a powerful dictatorial Communist apparatus which instituted the practice of racially mixed crews without giving the membership the option of objecting.

The Sailors Union of the Pacific, the major founding unit of the SIU, on the other hand, was led by an old Wobbly, Harry Lundeberg, who believed in frequent consultation of the membership as well as in few paid officers, and low pay for them including Lundeberg, himself. The membership of the SUP refused to adopt policies requiring racially integrated ships. A major difference between the CIO and AFL unions rested in the fact that the former were largely industrial unions which bargained nationally, while the AFL unions were in large measure craft organizations with decentralized local bargaining and authority. Thus the very fact of a strong national administration with tremendous power over local unions meant that the leaders of the industrial unions could ignore membership sentiment as expressed in the locals or plants, while those organizations in which local unions retained a great deal of power more clearly reflected membership sentiments and prejudices.

It is a well known fact that union government is much more democratic in the local than in the national administration. There are many more contested elections and turnovers in office on the local than on the national level. The Carpenters' Union, one of those cited for an unsavory race relations record by Hill, is oligarchic and dictatorial nationally, but many of its affiliated locals are extremely democratic. The same is true for others of the generally prejudiced building trades unions. The International Typographical Union which is democratic on both the national and local level has very few Negro members. The paucity of Negro printers reflects the fact that admission to the union sector of the industry is largely in the hands of the union members, themselves. Men generally become apprentices through being brought into the shop by union members, and the white members of the union, whether consciously prejudiced or not, are not likely to bring Negroes into the trade.

The supporters of Negro rights must face up to the fact that unions remain one of the more discriminatory sectors of American life precisely because they are one of the more democratic sectors, particularly on the local level. Union leaders are relatively free to express their generally liberal personal sentiments in public policy resolutions at state and national federation meetings since such resolutions do not affect what goes on in the shop, or at the local union meeting. But those dependent on support in the shop or local feel inhibited about trying to force union members to change their behavior. An employer sometimes can be more liberal precisely because legally he is a dictator, he is not up for re-election in the local.

If the general tenor of my argument is correct, then it follows that any basic solution is not to be found within the structure of organized labor acting unilaterally. Unions and union members must be forced to accept job rights for Negroes by public action, by legislation, by strong enforcement of Fair Employment Practices legislation. And here, of course, is the rub. For obvious reasons, unions generally oppose any legislation which gives government agencies power over union admission policies as well as other aspects of their internal affairs. In the past, liberal and radical intellectuals, generally favorable to unions as the largest single force sustaining the redistribution of privilege to the larger society, have supported the unions' resistance to government interventions. But the fact remains that as in the case of serious violations of union democracy, often little can be done to reform unions from within to make them effective instruments of integration.

It must be admitted that the suggestion that the struggle to modify union exclusion policies should be carried on primarily on the level of government action is not one which offers much hope for effective reform in the immediate future. The Democratic Party is today the primary partisan political instrument for improving the lot of the Negro. But the two largest groups within the Democratic Party are the trade unions and the Southerners. While differing on most issues of social policy, these two groups unite in opposing legislation which would force unions not to discriminate. And Democratic administrations in the North as well as in the Federal government are reluctant to get involved in direct fights with union leaders on whom they must rely for strong support on Election Day. The Republicans, although not loath to embarrass unions and desirous of winning Negro votes, also find themselves incapable of taking action in this field. It would be difficult for them to strongly support the rights of Negroes to union membership without also favoring Fair Employment legislation, policies opposed by their businessmen supporters and Dixiecrat Congressional allies.

All this would seem to imply no alternate except the traditional remedies of organized pressure tactics and public exposes. Democratic Party and trade union leaders alike must be subjected to a barrage of criticism for their failings on the supreme domestic moral issue of the mid-twentieth century. Leaders, whether union or political, react to pressures. And at the moment the pressures to which they are subjected, both within unions and in the general polity, make inaction on this issue seem most appropriate. The labor movement and the Kennedy administration are basically led by men of good will with respect to civil rights issues. To embarrass them into acting is the best thing which those who want more effective trade union action or political realignment can do to foster these objectives. Picket lines should be at least as effective outside union halls or Congressmen's offices as they have been outside of Woolworth's.

A. H. Raskin
CIVIL RIGHTS: THE LAW AND THE UNIONS

"We worked harder than anybody except the NAACP to get the Civil Rights Act through Congress; now our problem is to get it through our own unions." That is the essence of organized labor's predicament in this year of Negro progress toward full equality, as viewed by a top official of the AFL-CIO. It is a quandary made more worrisome by the fact that this is also a Presidential year—one in which the Republican nominee is a man whom labor's leaders are more eager to sweep into overwhelming defeat than any major party candidate in this century.

From *The Reporter*, September 10, 1964. Copyright 1964 by The Reporter Magazine Company. Reprinted by permission of the author and the publisher.
Mr. Raskin is on the editorial board of the *New York Times*.

The federation's official position against bias in jobs, promotions, apprenticeship programs, and every other form of economic opportunity could not be firmer. "The AFL-CIO is for civil rights—without reservation and without delay," said its president, George Meany. "Mere acknowledgment, mere lip service to equal rights is not enough. The labor movement is committed to a positive program for translating principle into reality on every front."

Yet private polls taken under union auspices in several Northern centers indicate that the white backlash against Negro pressure for faster integration draws much of its strength from rank-and-file unionists in the mass-production industries as well as from those in the exclusionist skilled trades. The most tangible evidence of the extent of this disaffection came in the heavy primary votes Governor Wallace of Alabama received last spring in the workingclass districts of Gary, South Milwaukee and East Baltimore.

More recent samplings have shown that this segregationist sentiment has led many workers into the Goldwater movement despite the fact that even the traditional Republicans in labor's high command have joined with the Democrats in backing President Johnson. David J. McDonald of the United Steelworkers of America told the President at a recent White House dinner that a check of the union's members in Indiana pointed to a majority for Goldwater. And a poll in one large Teamster local in New York showed a 7–3 margin for the Republican Presidential nominee, with civil rights as a major factor.

Part of the union backlash, of course, stems from such conventional worries as housing and schools and the status-consciousness of families that have achieved a modest degree of financial security and community recognition. In Polish, Hungarian, and Italian neighborhoods, where ethnic ties remain strong even though the flood tide of immigration stopped almost two generations ago, the walls of worker districts are especially hard to breach.

But the root of the special union problem is anxiety over jobs during a period when automation is taking its heaviest toll of work opportunities in the fields where most union members work and where most Negroes want to work. There are fewer jobs and more workers competing for them. In an effort to intensify ill will between whites and Negroes on this issue, segregationists seek to convince white unionists that their seniority, hiring halls, and all the other elements of job control on which their high wages and security depend are imperiled by the fair-employment practice provisions of the Civil Rights Act. At the same time, Negroes are being told that they ought to get behind the drive for enactment of state "right-to-work" laws as a means of ending the union shop and thus breaking down union-imposed barriers to fuller employment in construction, printing, and other fields where "white only" is still the predominant practice. Thus far the drive has not affected the top-level co-operation between the AFL-CIO and the chief Negro organizations, but the signs of friction below are prevalent enough to cause concern in both groups.

WHO CAN YOU TRUST?

The cultivation of apprehensions among white workers is clever, direct, and well financed. The Coordinating Committee for Fundamental American Freedoms, which receives much of its funds from the tax-supported Mississippi State Sovereignty Commission, has mailed an analysis of the rights law to every local union in the country. The document is designed to instill fear that the new law will mean the wholesale displacement of white workers in the interest of "racial balance."

Also widely circulated is a speech made by Senator Lister Hill of Alabama in the course of the civil-rights debate. Hill denounced the bill as a "blow to labor union freedom" and a death knell for the seniority system. Since Hill has been the sponsor of much pro-labor legislation and has always been highly regarded in union ranks, the Hill strictures have caused more dismay than the more blatant propaganda of those who could readily be disregarded as apologists for anti-labor racist sweat-shoppers.

A memorandum prepared by the AFL-CIO legal staff and sent to all unions does a comprehensive job of demolishing the Hill arguments. It notes that twenty-five states already have fair-employment practice laws of their own, and that none of these has undercut unions, impaired seniority systems, or compelled the discharge of white workers because there were not enough Negroes on the payroll. In addition, the federation's field representatives have been trying, with only moderate success, to erase the various misconceptions about the bill.

Actually a reading of the act would provide considerable reassurance to any worker anxious about being pushed out of his job to make way for a Negro. The fair-employment section does forbid unions or employers to withhold any job right on the basis of color. But it likewise specifically states that it is not illegal to apply different standards of pay or protection under the terms of a bona fide seniority system, provided there is no intent to discriminate on racial grounds. The law is just as explicit in disavowing any requirement that unions or management grant preferential treatment to rectify racial imbalance or to establish quotas in line with community race ratios.

The enforcement provisions are mild, not because the AFL-CIO wanted it that way but because of pressure from Southern Democrats who did not want any fair-employment clause and from some Northern Republicans who were not much more enthusiastic. The President is to appoint a five-member Equal Employment Opportunity Commission, which is to stress conciliation as a means of eliminating discriminatory practices. Where there are state fair-employment laws, the commission must defer to the state for at least sixty days before initiating any formal Federal proceedings. If all efforts at voluntary compliance or state action fail, the aggrieved worker has the right to bring a court suit to compel the union or employer to take him in. Direct government participation in the suit is limited to cases in which the Justice Department certifies that "a pattern or practice of resistance" exists to an extent that makes the matter "of general public importance."

Experience with the fair-employment laws in many industrial states, most of which are stronger than the new Federal statute, makes it plain that they represent no instant solution to union bias. In New York, for example, the State Commission for Human Rights has the power to enforce its cease-and-desist orders through the courts, and district attorneys are authorized under the Penal Code to seek jail sentences and fines against employers or unionists who exclude Negroes from jobs. Since 1935 a ban on discrimination by any contractor doing state or city work has been part of the New York Labor Law, but no contract has ever been canceled for that reason.

In general, the effort in New York State has been to proceed slowly on legal crackdowns, even in the most flagrant cases. One of the few in which the state finally decided to act involved Local 28 of the Sheet Metal Workers International Association, which for three-quarters of a century never admitted a Negro to membership or apprenticeship. After the efforts of the AFL-CIO, a complaint by the State Attorney General, and a variety of other pressures had proved ineffective, the state commission ordered the local to discard its Jim Crow waiting list for apprentice training and to compile a new list based on objective standards of qualification. The union went to court to fight the ruling, but late last month it gave in and agreed to a new system, with enough safeguards against bias to make it a model for the building trades.

The probability is that the Federal program will operate along similar lines of slow rather than meteoric progress. Yet there is already an undercurrent of unease among some secondary leaders in the crafts that the end result will be to put outside "do-gooders" in the role of judges over every aspect of union apprenticeship and assignment procedure, thus smashing the tight little monopolies that many locals have been able to insulate against the inroads of the Taft-Hartley Act.

The fear that the civil-rights drive will weaken the structure of union job control has been strengthened by recent actions of the National Labor Relations Board. One was its decision that it was an unfair labor practice under the Taft-Hartley Act for an independent union at a Houston tool plant to discriminate against Negroes. The union was stripped of its bargaining certification, thus making it vulnerable to raids by other unions. Labor leaders in the forefront of the desegregation effort looked with some disquiet on the ruling—not because they objected to the penalty for dealing unfairly with a Negro but because they feared a flood of complaints to the NLRB whenever workers felt their unions had not represented them fairly in any kind of grievance, with or without racial overtones.

Another source of union concern is a complaint issued by the regional office of the NLRB in New York against Local 2 of the Plumbers Union, Meany's home local. The case grew out of a strike by white plumbers that occurred when three Puerto Ricans and a Negro reported for work last spring on a municipal market project in the Bronx. The NLRB complaint accuses the striking local of having forced an employer to discriminate against the quartet because they were not members of the union.

Meany himself played a leading role in settling the strike, even though he was convinced that the placement of the four non-white plumbers on the job was part of an attempt by some elements in the civil-rights movement to embarrass him for reasons of personal malice. In cooperation with Mayor Wagner, Meany worked out a formula under which the four men could be given qualifying tests under impartial supervision. Factional troubles inside the local, plus the hostility of many of its members to authorizing special treatment for Negroes or Puerto Ricans, delayed the settlement. Finally, the tests were given—and the men failed. But before Meany broke the log jam over even letting them take the tests, he rankled the civil-rights groups by voicing unreserved support of the refusal of the local's members to work with nonunion men. He said he would tear up his own card if the local ever departed from that stand.

This was precisely the reverse of the position Meany had taken in 1960 when Local 26 of the International Brotherhood of Electrical Workers in Washington was refusing to take in Negroes. At that time the AFL-CIO chief said he would personally recruit nonunion Negro electricians to work on Federal office buildings if the local did not end its defiance of anti-discrimination recommendations made by the Eisenhower administration. The ensuing struggle involved a political "Who's Who" that included Vice-President Nixon, Secretary of Labor James P. Mitchell, Meany, and the contractor, Matthew H. McCloskey, then treasurer of the Democratic National Committee. Meany and the two high government officials put so much pressure on McCloskey to break the electrical local's lily-white pattern that the contractor sought to bring in Negro members of a Philadelphia electricians' local. When this brought a threat by all the Washington construction unions to strike, Meany said he would stall the job with nonunion men and lead them to work himself. The administration followed with a warning that it would sue Local 26 for its ban on employment of Negroes on Federal works. The parent union also exerted pressure. The result was the same as in New York. The local reluctantly agreed to let five Negroes take qualifying tests—and all failed. Later, a small breakthrough was made and the all-white hiring design ended.

What is involved in the New York plumbers' case, however, goes far beyond the issue of discrimination. It brings into challenge the sub rosa closed-shop arrangements many unions of skilled craftsmen have managed to retain, even though those have technically been illegal since the passage of the Taft-Hartley Act seventeen years ago.

The building-trades employers, seldom disposed to question the unions' ironclad rule over jobs, have been content to leave old relationships undisturbed. Some modifications have been made under legal pressure to avoid too obvious inconsistencies with the law, but a full-dress challenge by civil-rights groups could compel a basic dilution of union job monopolies in many areas.

There is no real wish on the part of the NAACP or other large organizations to undertake such a drive without giving the federation adequate opportunity to bring its own dissidents into line. The NAACP is as conscious as organized labor that the result could be a weakening of unions on a scale that would seriously impair their capacity to fulfil their function as guardians of pay scales and job security. Though it initiated the Houston decertification case, the NAACP's general policy on court actions to upset discriminatory union practices is one of caution.

This is chiefly because it is now persuaded of the sincerity of the approach of Meany and most of his associates in the AFL-CIO Executive Council in using voluntary action to abolish union bias, which Meany describes as a "bootleg product sneaked in by the back door and nowhere condoned."

One reason for the civil-rights leaders' new confidence in Meany's earnestness—quite apart from the stern lectures he has given laggard unionists in the privacy of his own paneled office a block from the White House—is the knowledge that the new Federal civil-rights law would not contain any fair-employment section if it were not for him.

When President Kennedy sent the original draft to Capitol Hill, it did not have a section covering discrimination in jobs. The administration signified its support for fair-employment bills already pending in

Congress, but it was clear to everyone that any such proposal separated from the omnibus civil-rights bill would never stand a chance of passage. The section was inserted in the administration bill only at the strong insistence of the AFL-CIO.

AN AYE FOR AN AYE

The federation took the view that the threat of legal action was essential if the most intractable holdouts in organized labor were to be forced to comply with the pledge in the AFL-CIO constitution to extend the full benefits of unionization to "all workers without regard to race, creed, color, or national origin." The alternative to legislation was the ouster of Jim Crow unions from the federation, a purification device that failed when it was used to discipline the Teamsters for domination by corrupt elements.

Throughout all of the long fight in both the House and Senate for the full Civil Rights Act, union lobbyists worked in close co-operation with those of the NAACP, CORE, and other rights groups. Indeed, there was no item of purely union interest on which anything like the same amount of effort was expended by the AFL-CIO legislative staff.

The civil-rights organizations were equally vigorous in opposing the passage of state "right-to-work" laws. Twenty states, most of them in the South and Southwest, now have such legal prohibitions against any form of compulsory union membership. A major drive was made to add Oklahoma to the list last May, and much of the sponsors' appeal was addressed to Negroes and Mexican Americans, all on the basis that the law would open skilled jobs in fields controlled by Jim Crow unions. The NAACP and its allies waged such an effective rebuttal that Meany gave them primary credit for the defeat in the statewide referendum.

But the genuineness of the rapport at the top offers scant guarantee that the spirit of co-operation will penetrate all levels of either the union or the civil-rights structure. This is not merely because unionists reflect all the passions and prejudices of the general population and are no more disposed than any other Americans to have their attitudes dictated from above. It is because the crucial rounds in the civil-rights struggle are being fought in a period when the age-old concern about job security is made more acute by the impact of technological change and the inability of our society to guarantee anything approaching full employment.

"How can we take in Negroes when we haven't got enough jobs for our own?" is the cry in unions from one end of the country to the other. Even the argument that apprenticeship systems should be opened up on a nondiscriminatory basis gets a cold reception. "I'm no Rockefeller. I've got no fortune or no business to leave to my son; what's so bad if I get him first crack at an apprentice's job?" asked a New York building tradesman. And his question is echoed in a thousand other locals.

In the mass unions, where outright discrimination has been practiced much less than in the skilled trades, automation is generating new hostilities. These are bound to increase because the essence of the union response to the problem of technological displacement is the defense of the jobs of those who already are in. The man who has a job is protected against forced layoff. But the man who is outside wanting to get in—especially if he has been excluded through years of discriminatory hiring practices—is not likely to believe there is anything equitable about building a wall around the workplace to protect the early arrivals. It is this competition between the "outs" and the "ins" that is liable to cause a polarization of hostilities in many areas. It is one reason that in cities like Gary, white men rake up memories of nearly a half century ago, when Negroes were called in as scabs in the steel mills. Or in Detroit where similar memories are dredged up of the times when Negroes were used to keep out the union at Ford.

The big question is whether the labor and civil-rights alliance can survive the pressures it must meet at its birth—the virulence of the white backlash in many unions, the insistence of the Negroes on much faster progress toward a full breakthrough in jobs, housing, and education and, most stubborn of all, the shortage of new job openings—for white youth and Negro youth alike. What both sides want is a solution in which the test will not be whether a white American or a black American walks the streets jobless, but where there will be enough jobs for all. And nothing in the platform of either major party makes full employment certain enough in this period when the onsurge of automation makes itself felt more in fear of unemployment than in promise of abundance.

leaders and members

Richard A. Lester

THE CHANGING CHARACTER
OF AMERICAN UNIONISM

Since the mid-1930's, unions in this country have experienced certain internal changes. Many, especially the newly formed industrial unions, have been shedding youthful characteristics in the process of settling down or "maturing."

Some support exists for the theory that institutions tend to pass through stages of development, that organizations like unions, which aim at altering the balance of rights and privileges, experience a natural evolution of organizational life, particularly if they are successful. In their early stages such organizations will be militant and turbulent, with internal factionalism and vigorous external opposition. At first they must fight for existence as well as for goals that generally are considered radical. Under the circumstances membership participation is likely to be high and leadership positions in the organization are apt to be won by the agitator and the table-pounder.

Later on, as the organization gains acceptance and security and succeeds in establishing new rights and other aims, a transformation tends to occur not only in the organization's goals but also in the nature of its leadership, in its internal operations, and in the distribution of

Reprinted from *As Unions Mature* by Richard A. Lester by permission of Princeton University Press, pp. 21–29. Copyright 1958 by Princeton University Press.

Mr. Lester is Professor of Economics, Princeton University.

power and functions among different structural levels. Instead of being simply an opposition or anti-body, the new organization becomes more and more integrated into the life of the community. Instead of pursuing a crusade against the "enemy," it cooperates increasingly with other groups in industry, government, and society. As some of the organization's initial goals are achieved, its objectives tend to broaden and become more complex, so that they are increasingly difficult to define and delimit. As the organization grows in size and its activities and responsibilities enlarge, it faces new problems of administration, discipline, and public relations. The need for specialists becomes more pressing, a hierarchy and bureaucracy tend to develop, and the relationship of top officials to the rank-and-file grows more impersonal. Some functions and decisions shift from the local to higher levels in the organization. And, as the top positions come to require more administrative and manipulative talents, the oratorical agitators are superseded by skillful managers.

Of course, every organization, even every one for improving the lot of labor, does not have the same life history. There is no one inevitable pattern of metamorphosis, no single evolutionary route. Each organization is influenced by its own circumstances and experience—the way it was formed, the traditions it has developed, the industrial challenges it has faced, the sort of opposition it has encountered, and the character of the growth it has achieved. Certain general factors may, of course, affect all organizations, albeit unevenly. For instance, within a large organization with officers selected by ballot, a political machine tends to develop, but that does not mean political parties and unions inevitably end up controlled by a ruling clique as postulated by Robert Michels' "iron law of oligarchy." Not only must one recognize that various underlying forces may not all push in the same direction but also that considerable deviation from any trend is to be expected in the case of institutions with diverse historical experiences such as trade unions. . . .

CENTRALIZATION OF FUNCTIONS AND CONTROL

A number of factors have been instrumental in shifting some functions, decisions, and power from the local level to the national headquarters of unions.

In the first place, expansion of the size of the national union, by means of growth in the number of locals and perhaps by merger also, serves to reduce the importance and influence of a particular local within the union. Furthermore the larger the national union, the more patronage there is by which to build up a political machine with control from the top, and the more union communications (including publications) are likely to be centrally controlled. Also, large unions tend to have comparatively large staffs of specialists and experts, upon whom locals come to rely for guidance. Indeed, the assumption generally is made that, with unions, large size means more effectiveness, efficiency, and power. That assumption stems partly from the notion that a larger union can hire a bigger and better staff, partly from the gain to be achieved from central pooling of resources such as strike funds, but partly also from the naïve notion that size and power are directly correlated.

Expansion in the area of collective bargaining and enlargement of the spread of bargaining patterns have also contributed to central determination of union policies. The national seeks a common program for the whole industry or area of competitive production. Bargaining strategy necessitates some central control of demands, along with headquarters' approval of settlements negotiated by locals and of strikes by locals. In short, union-wide programs increase the influence and authority of the national headquarters.

A change in the character and subject matter of negotiations has likewise added to the dependence of the locals on the top echelon of the union. Collective bargaining has tended to be increasingly factual, statistical, and full of economic reasoning, so that the amateur negotiator feels himself at a disadvantage. But it is particularly the technical nature of the new subjects in negotiations that has increased the role of the national headquarters and the staff. Subjects like job evaluation, time-and-motion study, pensions, medical and hospital care, and supplementary unemployment benefits, are generally beyond the training and know-how of persons at the local level. For guidance in such matters, the union may need to rely upon the advice of staff experts.

National labor legislation, intervention in industrial relations by Federal agencies, and reliance upon arbitration also increase the dependence on experts, especially lawyers and economists, attached to the national headquarters and appointed by the top officials. The Taft-Hartley Act is a complex piece of legislation, on many aspects of which legal advice may be necessary before a union makes a decision. Appearances before Federal agencies (National War Labor Board, Wage Stabilization Board, Atomic Energy Labor-Management Relations Panel, etc.) are generally a function performed by the national union. In addition, national union officers or staff members are likely to play a dominant role in significant arbitration cases, including grievance arbitrations.

The role of local union leaders has been reduced with the shift of the center of union activities from organization to disciplined administration of the agreement and with the newer methods of organization and dues collection: namely, certification by the National Labor Relations Board, the union shop, and the check-off of dues.

Prior to World War II, much of the time of the local union leaders in the mass-production industries was taken up with maintaining and increasing the membership and collecting dues. Now employers do most of that for the union, by enforcing the union shop and deducting the dues from workers' wages for the union. On the other hand, the union helps the management to enforce the shop rules and plant discipline by insistence on no violation of the agreement. Such a partial swapping of functions has resulted in a reduction of the power and authority of shop stewards and other local leaders. No longer can they call men out on strike without the national union demanding that the strike be revoked as a violation of the agreement, the union's constitution, or both. In the case of grievances, which now are likely to be the bulk of the local's business, not only must they be handled in an orderly and businesslike fashion, but the national union may have a hand in them at a fairly early stage because it assumes responsibility in the final steps of the grievance procedure. Thus, compared with the 1930's, local unions now generally serve less as independent centers of leadership and decision-making and more as the administrative agencies of the national union.

The No-raiding Pact, the AFL-CIO merger, national union mergers, and other restrictions on change of local-union affiliation have also helped to reduce the independence of action and the bargaining power of the locals within their national unions. With rival national unions and national federations, the locals of any union could threaten to leave it and affiliate with a rival union, if the national disregarded the local's wishes or sought to restrict and dominate it. No longer is that a possibility for most locals. Higher authority denies them freedom of affiliation.

Although in recent decades the centripetal forces have tended to expand at the expense of centrifugal factors in most unions, some have succeeded in maintaining a balance between them. For the most part, however, only unions in local-market lines with numerous small firms, like the building trades, have been able to do so. Other unions, such as the Teamsters, have experienced a strengthening of the regional or district units at the expense of the locals, but with comparatively slight gains in headquarters power and control. Along with the character of the industry, the traditions of the union and its historical development may help to determine the location of union control and decision-making power and the extent to which they have been moving toward and into the union's national headquarters.

ALTERATION IN TOP LEADERSHIP

As unions expand and become accepted by the community, subtle changes tend to occur in their top leadership. The founding fathers and the early recruits with a missionary zeal die or retire with the passage of time. They are replaced by a second or third generation of leaders, who personally have not experienced the bitter struggles for existence in the union's early days and who are less likely to have had the influences of an immigrant background or socialist convictions in their youth. As already indicated, such successors tend to be, not the crusading agitator, but the skillful political operator and level-headed administrator able to manage a large organization and to perform the necessary desk duties. The president of a union has a variety of administrative responsibilities. Among other things, he is the employer of a staff, the head of a political machine, and the highest union authority in the enforcement of collective agreements.

As unions settle down, the path to top leadership tends to be a steady climb through the various levels of the hierarchy. Stratification in organizations generally increases with their size and age. In mature organizations, the selection and training of leaders at the lower levels are likely to be controlled from the top. High union officials are organization men, who are prone to stress unity and to frown on insurgency. The prospects for advancement may also discourage insurgency. Mobility within the labor movement is largely vertical in one national union; seldom do union leaders transfer from one union to another, which might imply some lack of loyalty to the union's administration. Yet as unions mature, their growth curve tends to flatten out, which means that advancement is largely confined to replacements in the hierarchy, and such replacement openings are reduced by the absence of a specific retirement age similar to that in British and Swedish unions. This organizational development, of course, affects attitudes at various levels in the institution.

The promotional outlook is, however, but one aspect of the psychological change which is likely to occur. The gap between the members' wages and the salaries of the presidents of the larger unions has increased relatively during the 1940's and 1950's. The heads of the dozen largest unions have salaries ranging from $18,000 to $60,000 a year, plus ample expense accounts and frequently other perquisites. That union presidents sometimes urge conventions not to increase their salaries does not alter the fact that it is possible for them to live on a scale equivalent to that of business executives and that, in the newly-built union headquarters, the presidential offices are as impressive as those of high corporate officials.

Nowadays the presidency of a union carries a wide range of duties and responsibilities. The concept of the office has broadened as union presidents have increasingly held positions on community, industrial, educational, and governmental boards. The president of a sizable union may be expected to make pronouncements on national economic policy, foreign policy, domestic politics, and all sorts of legislative proposals as well as the problems of his industry. Many of his activities might be considered extraunion, and in connection with them he associates with leaders in all walks of life.

As full-time union officials progress up the union hierarchy their interests and perspectives tend to broaden. Over the years, the scope of union activities has been enlarging, which has meant an increase in the "sobering responsibilities" of the presidency. For instance, he may shoulder the ultimate responsibility for the investment of the growing union and joint funds. Their financial interests have led unions to participate in the banking, insurance, and real estate businesses, to say nothing of investments in stocks and bonds.

Many union leaders in the past have been unconventionally motivated—men with a mission to alter the economic and social order, with little thought of personal gain. There are indications that the concept of the successful union president may have been changing somewhat in the 1940's and 1950's, even in the minds of many holding that office. As their interests and associations have broadened, they may place more stress on their reputations with the general public.

Of course, the union official is a politician with a definite constituency. To continue in office he has to be reelected by the membership or their chosen delegates in convention assembled. He must, therefore, be sensitive to membership views and discontents. The leadership of a union is under pressure to achieve material gains for the membership, to make a "breakthrough" that will increase the prestige of the union compared with other unions.

The role of the union president is, however, somewhat ambivalent. At the same time that he desires to negotiate noteworthy gains, he also strongly wishes to achieve a settlement without a strike that could threaten the security of the present leadership or of the union itself. Part of the union leader's job, therefore, is mediating and working out satisfactory compromises. Above all, he assumes responsibility for enforcing agreements, for upholding the sanctity of contracts even though that means disciplining malcontented elements within the union membership. By insisting on the use of orderly settlement procedures and preventing wildcat strikes, he joins with management in maintaining discipline within the plant.

Changes in the concept of union leadership at headquarters do, of course, work their way down the line. Not only are union presidents spending more time in community and governmental activities but so are full-time officials in the lower ranks. And conceptions at the lower levels are influenced by the fact that those seeking to advance into the charmed circle at the top tend to conform to the aims and viewpoints of their superiors.

In discussing the tendency for union leadership to evolve in certain directions it should be clear that there is no compulsion for all union headquarters to conform to a single pattern. However, factors have been at work which are influencing the evolution of union leadership. Unless new factors—such as a severe business depression, upsetting internal crises in particular unions, or perhaps a war—arise to alter the direction of the drift, the differences between union executives and business executives in living standards, in daily activities, and in business interests, are likely to continue to diminish. . . .

Thomas R. Brooks
LABOR:
THE RANK-AND-FILE REVOLT

Angry, frustrated and haggard from lack of sleep, Thomas W. ("Teddy") Gleason, president of the 60,000-member International Longshoremen's Association, slumped behind his desk in a downtown Manhattan office one gray morning last January, mulling over a chain of disasters. Only a few days before, he had jubilantly initialed an unprecedented four-year contract with the New York Shipping Association that would mean an 80-cent-an-hour package increase for 24,000 New York dockworkers. And since New York's contract traditionally sets the pattern for settlements in other ports, it was hardly surprising that

Reprinted by special permission from *Dun's Review & Modern Industry,* March 1965. Copyright 1965, Dun & Bradstreet Publications Corp.

Mr. Brooks has recently written a history of American labor entitled *Toil and Trouble.*

Gleason buoyantly predicted an early national settlement. After all, as the ILA leader saw it, the contract was "the greatest in the history of the union."

The union's members thought otherwise. New York longshoremen rejected the contract, sparking a strike that closed every port from Maine to Texas. With that, the power of Teddy Gleason eroded by the hour. He watched impotently as Assistant Secretary of Labor James J. Reynolds and David A. Stowe, a Department of Labor consultant on waterfront problems, ignoring him, set out from Washington to parley with local union leaders in each strikebound port. He swallowed his pride and sent an urgent call for help to his friend, President George Meany of the AFL-CIO, but Meany merely sent a public relations man who drafted a four-page explanatory leaflet on the details of the rejected contract. The final indignity came when Gleason had to spend ten hours licking stamps, stuffing envelopes and trudging three blocks to the local post office with the mail. Asked what had happened, Gleason could only mumble: "It was a misunderstanding."

It was the understatement of the year. For Gleason, like many a union leader these days, in feeling the full force of a wave of resentment that is sweeping through the rank and file of the American labor movement. In some cases the rebellion takes the form of a demand for local autonomy in bargaining. In others, it is a planned series of unauthorized strikes that embarrass and discredit the national union. There are cases where workers either break away to form their own independent organization or invite another union to stage a "raid." By the time the revolt has run its course, many union presidents and their policies will be overthrown, and the present methods of collective bargaining will be altogether changed.

A decade or more in the making, this surge of discontent has already toppled the administrations of three unions—the Textile Workers, the United Federation of Teachers and the State, County and Municipal Employees union. On the West Coast, 20,000 papermill workers left their international union, made an alliance with the International Brotherhood of Teamsters, then proceeded to call their first strike in thirty years. Disgruntled members of the United Mine Workers of America have already skirmished with President William A. Boyle, the hand-picked successor of old fire-eater John L. Lewis, and are regrouping for another battle. Even the strike of the New York welfare workers was sparked by a splinter group of militants who broke away from the parent union. As if all this were not enough, the Teamsters, although outlawed by the AFL-CIO, has taken advantage of this feuding to mount successful recruiting campaigns among the disenchanted and the unorganized.

Why has the labor movement foundered precisely at the time when its policitical influence has seemingly reached an all-time high? Why are blue collar workers, the backbone of labor, becoming more and more cynical about unions? And why are embattled union leaders, most of whom rose from the ranks in the tough organizing days of the Thirties, the current targets of this rank-and-file revolt?

The answer, in a fashionable word, is alienation. No longer can union members identify themselves with a distant, and often authoritarian, figure. To Detroit autoworkers, bored and weary with the daily grind of a monotonous task, the lofty generalizations of Walter Reuther about such topics as the problem of recreation for the elderly seem ludicrous. The endless stream of hortatory leaflets and booklets, urging union members to concern themselves with the broad issues of national and international politics, contrast sharply with the crude maneuverings of intra-union political squabbling. More important, grievances on matters apart from wages are either ignored or lost in the limbo of union bureaucracy.

The explosive content of the rank-and-file rebellion is high indeed. A rebellious streak within the United Automobile Workers, for example, shut down General Motors Corp. for 30 days and Ford Motor Co. for 28 days last fall. The issue: local working conditions. The walkouts took place despite a favorable national agreement wrapped in a 60-cent package, enclosing, among other gains, pensions of nearly $400 a month and inducements for early retirement. Significantly, in the year preceding last fall's auto talks, there had been an almost complete turnover in the leadership of UAW locals at GM plants. "The strike," a UAW official concedes, "was another expression of the rank-and-file dissatisfaction with the leadership and inability to correct plant conditions."

Some spokesmen for labor attribute the grass-roots rebellion to the protection afforded dissidents by the Landrum-Griffin Act, which, among other things, attempted to check the power vested in union officials. But it is much more than that. For along with the disenchantment of the workers, there is increasing evidence that most major unions are split by struggles between the incumbent administration and local leaders, who are using the militancy of the rank and file to propel themselves to power.

The waterfront strike is a good example. ILA President Gleason's first proposal to the industry was a one-year contract that would postpone such controversial issues as the size of the work gang and flexibility in work assignments. Immediately, Gleason's rival, smooth, articulate Anthony Scotto, who heads Brooklyn local 1814, seized this opportunity. Along with other local presidents he devised a formula for a four-year contract that would allow employers to whittle down the work gangs from twenty to seventeen men, but this bitter pill was sweetened by an annual wage guarantee and a provision for stable employment. Although reluctant, Gleason agreed to go along with his plan, principally because he was assured that the New York members would approve the contract.

When the contract was rejected, Gleason, as the union's top officer, had to accept responsibility for the ensuing national strike. His power and prestige diminished, he watched helplessly as local leaders in other ports demanded the right to negotiate their own contracts rather than follow the New York formula. The attitude of the dissidents was best expressed by Willie C. Wells, president of the ILA'S Houston local. Said Wells: "We have been getting pushed around for a long time by the international union to go back to work after the locals in the East settle. The men are going to be rough about it this time, and we are going to stay out until we can get enough to help us catch up with the conditions in the East."

STEEL UNION BATTLE

This interrelationship between the struggle for power and the discontent of the rank and file is also clearly evident within the United Steelworkers of America. The roots of the present steel union difficulties go back to 1957 when an unknown millworker, Donald C. Rarick, rolled up a surprising vote of 223,516 to President David J. McDonald's winning total of 404,172. At that time, the 38 district directors of the USW stood behind McDonald, even though many of them had been hostile to the president. This coalition quelled the Rarick rebellion, without, however, dampening the growing dissatisfaction of the rank and file.

While the silver-haired, ruddy-faced McDonald has won praise from management and the public for his labor statesmanship, steelworkers are stinting in their praise of his achievements. "We've been without a raise for four years now," a husky Indiana steel roller said in explaining his opposition to McDonald. Some steelworkers, too, are critical of McDonald's alleged "high living." When gossip columnists linked his name with Zsa Zsa Gabor, McDonald explained that "We were merely introduced" when he sat at a nearby table in a New York restaurant. "I believe, as John L. Lewis and Philip Murray taught me," says McDonald, "that you travel first class."

Possibly the union members do not resent the high life as much as they do McDonald's absence from the union hall. "Abe [I. W.] Abel has attended about every affair my district has had for the past several years," says William J. Hart, director of a 36,000-member Pittsburgh-area district. "We've invited McDonald, but we haven't been able to get him here for any of them."

Steelworkers are also suspicious of what they call "the secrecy" of the Human Relations Committee. "The committee," charged Walter J. Burke, Milwaukee district 32 director and an anti-McDonald contender for the USW secretary-treasurership, during the election contest, "has usurped the prerogatives of the negotiating committees."

Criticism of McDonald came to a head last September at the steel union convention in Atlantic City. Behind the scenes, his "palace guard" attempted to pressure the 61-year-old McDonald into retirement. But McDonald was not so easily separated from his $50,000-a-year post. He succeeded in pulling together a semblance of unity, simply because the dissident directors were reluctant to undertake a major intra-union battle in public prior to negotiations with the major steel companies. However, the convention did establish a mandatory retirement age of 65 for union officers.

There matters might have rested, with McDonald's rivals content to wait out the years until he retired. Rebellion, however, rumbled within the ranks, and leaders of the big steel local unions were advocating the right to strike over individual plant problems, citing the UAW experience. In steel, unlike the UAW, once the national contract is signed, a strict no-strike clause goes into effect. Dissatisfied local unionists, however, wanted a change to something roughly equivalent to the auto locals' right to strike over matters affecting health and safety.

When some district directors sounded out the larger steel locals, they found considerable support for a challenge to McDonald's leadership. They decided to throw their strength behind I. W. Abel, a craggy-faced, white-haired man who was secretary-treasurer of the international union.

For steel management, it made little difference who won on February 9, the day of the steel union referendum. Once battle lines were drawn, both sides became ultra-militant in the effort to win supporters. The difficulties of the winner would lie not so much in securing a raise in wages as in settling local plant working conditions. So, for the first time in years, a national settlement in steel is no guarantee of labor peace.

CHANGING BARGAINING METHODS

Leadership fights, such as those in the USW, tend to obscure the real significance of the current rank-and-file rebellion within the unions. Its genesis is in the factory, and its lasting impact is likely to be on the methods of collective bargaining. In the past, the growth of giant corporations made the formation of strong national unions almost inevitable; the national agreement was a consequence. It was useful to corporate management as a means of manpower discipline, while for union members it was a device to equalize wages and work standards. However, in recent years corporations have been decentralizing while labor management has not.

The rank-and-file rebellion, turning as it does on local plant work issues, runs counter to the centralizing tendency of the standard national labor relations contract. UAW local unions, for example, used their right to strike as leverage against both corporate management and the national leaders of the UAW. In effect, during the negotiations last fall, they told UAW President Walter P. Reuther and Louis G. Seaton, GM vice president in charge of personnel, that a national agreement would not preclude their right to settle local plant problems.

It is true that union members are divided over the issue. Some believe that plant problems cannot be solved on a plant-by-plant basis. Striking just one plant, they say, does not bring to bear the power of a company-wide or industry-wide strike. Others, however, believe they can solve local problems if freed from the restraint imposed by the national union.

This conflict, too, can divide union leadership. For example, General Electric Co. and the International Union of Electrical, Radio and Machine Workers have a national agreement that permits "local understandings." GE also encourages its local management to make its own decisions. For more than a year now, GE management in Lynn, Massachusetts and IUE Local 201 have been battling over wage-job classification issues. Last January the union brought the issue to a management study team in New York. But the management group backed its own local people in Lynn. Then Local 201 called a strike, protesting the imposition of the new job rates, claiming that they would lead to a wage cut.

But in Schenectady, Local 301 of the same international union accepted a wage cut for a group of its members. As a result, the local, under the leadership of Leo E. Jandreau, its business agent, is battling IUE President James B. Carey over a "local understanding" that the Schenectady IUE members feel saved their jobs, but which Carey has termed a "sellout."

Whatever the outcome of such specific local situations, it is clear that there has been a decided shift in the locus of decision-making. No longer can the leadership of a national union impose its will on the rank and file. Even more important, the power structure within the unions must be reconstructed, even to the extent of granting autonomy to local unions at the bargaining table.

Does this mean an end to the national agreement? By no means. It does indicate that national agreements may become more like an umbrella shading a variety of "local understandings" or local agreements, rather than a master plan imposing uniform conditions throughout. The settling of wages and benefits will continue to be spelled out in national agreements. But local agreements will include an ever-widening range of plant job problems. After all, as the ILA strike has shown, such issues have already taken precedence over wages.

Jack Stieber
THE UAW PUBLIC REVIEW BOARD

The UAW [United Automobile Workers] Public Review Board, established by the 1957 constitutional convention of the union, represents the broadest grant of authority over its internal affairs ever voluntarily given by a labor organization—or any other organization for that matter —to an outside body. It goes much further than either the Upholsters' Union experiment, which predated it by four years, or the more recently established United Packinghouse Workers' Public Advisory Review Commission. Also, unlike these other boards which have decided only one case between them, the UAW Public Review Board has had enough experience to permit an examination and evaluation of its accomplishments so far.

THE ORIGIN OF THE BOARD

There are differing versions of the origin of the idea of the UAW Public Review Board. Walter Reuther, President of the UAW, is generally credited with initiating the proposal early in 1955. At that time the idea was discussed among top UAW officials and staff but did not

From Jack Stieber, "The UAW Public Review Board: An Examination and Evaluation," in *Democracy and Public Review*, A report to The Center for the Study of Democratic Institutions. © 1960 by The Fund for the Republic, Inc.

Mr. Stieber is Director of the Labor and Industrial Relations Center, Michigan State University.

find sufficient support to warrant bringing it before the union's constitutional convention. Like many other Reuther ideas, this one was too far in
advance of traditional union thinking for immediate action and was put
on the "back burner" to await a more opportune time for presentation.

That time came in 1957. The AFL-CIO merger in December
1955 had given the UAW some bedfellows whom it did not particularly
relish. The McClellan Committee hearings, though barely under way in
early 1957, had already begun to promise sensational revelations regarding the odorous malpractices of some union leaders. While the UAW had
nothing to fear from this investigation and had, in fact, urged the
establishment of a Congressional committee to investigate "corruption
and racketeering in all phases of American life," its leadership recognized
that, in the public mind, all labor was likely to be indicted for the sins of
a few unions. With this setting, the international executive board, which
two years earlier had been unenthusiastic about the idea, was now
prepared to accept Reuther's suggestion for a Public Review Board. . . .

The UAW international executive board unanimously approved
the establishment of the Public Review Board early in 1957, and the idea
was first presented to the union membership in the report of the
president to the UAW convention in April of that year. Reuther proposed
two changes in the union's trial machinery. First, he proposed the
selection of local union trial boards by lot rather than by election to
prevent the administration of justice from becoming a local political
issue. Second, he proposed the creation of a Public Review Board as an
alternative—at the member's choice—to the established procedure of
having the convention serve as the final step in certain disputes between
an individual or subordinate body and the international union.

At the convention, discussion on the motion to adopt the latter
constitutional amendment centered around the question of whether the
UAW needed an outside body to help it regulate its own internal
government. One delegate said that his caucus had debated this question
for hours the previous night and added, "I am opposed to anybody who
doesn't belong to our great organization coming within this group and
laying down laws and saying that we have to do this or that." Another
delegate favored the Board because it was necessary to guarantee fair
trial procedures at the local if not at the international level. Others feared
that this action would be interpreted as an admission that "there is dirt at
our executive board level" and that "the McClellan Committee has got
something to come in here for." The expense of such a Board was also
brought up, as was the belief, on the other side, that it would help
counter the bad publicity the labor movement was getting as a result of
the McClellan Committee hearings.

In his report to the convention Reuther expounded on the idea that "more and more the leadership of the labor movement must be prepared to have their stewardship . . . subject to public review." He told the convention delegates: "You ought to recognize that this is the real thing, there are no ifs, ands, buts, or loopholes. . . . I think . . . you ought to recognize that this gets into an area that we are either going to have to deal with voluntarily or the government will deal with it for us." The amendments were adopted overwhelmingly—Reuther, chairing the convention, estimated a 97 per cent vote in favor of the proposal.

THE BOARD'S JURISDICTION, PROCEDURES, AND COMPOSITION

Under the UAW constitution there are four paths by which cases may reach the Public Review Board:

1. Appeals from decisions of the international executive board in cases involving alleged violation of an appellant's rights as a member of the union (subordinate bodies, including local unions, may also appeal to the Public Review Board);

2. Appeals from decisions of the international executive board in cases involving alleged violations of the AFL-CIO ethical practices codes;

3. Board review, on its own motion and in the absence of an appeal, of any complaint of an alleged violation of the ethical practices codes which, in the Board's judgment, the international executive board has disposed of without adequate action;

4. Complaints related to alleged violations of the ethical practices codes may be submitted to the Board by majority action of the international executive board of the union.

The most common routing of an appeal proceeds as follows: Except in cases where direct appeal to the international executive board is specifically permitted by the constitution, a member's complaint against any action, decision, or penalty of his local union must first be passed upon by the membership of his local; if he is dissatisfied with this decision, he may appeal, within thirty days, to the international executive board; if he is still dissatisfied, he may appeal, within an additional thirty days, either to the UAW convention, which meets biennially, or to the Public Review Board, but not to both. The decision of the Public Review Board is final and binding.

The Public Review Board does not have jurisdiction over cases involving official collective bargaining policies of the UAW. In grievance cases, the Board's jurisdiction is limited to those situations in which it is charged that the grievance was improperly handled because of fraud, discrimination, or collusion with management. The Board may not be regarded as a substitute for the local union grievance machinery. Where a grievance case is taken to the Board and dismissed for lack of jurisdiction, the appellant may then take his case before the international convention.

The Board is authorized to consider cases through panels of three or more of its seven members, but it may dismiss a case without a hearing if a preliminary investigation indicates that the allegations are not "sufficiently serious and substantial to justify a hearing" or cannot possibly be substantiated. In order to discourage groundless and malicious charges of ethical practice code violations, the Public Review Board is authorized to fine the accuser up to $500 if it finds that he acted "in bad faith or with malicious intent and in a willful effort to divide and disrupt the union." All parties have a right to counsel before the Board. Hearings are public and all expenses are borne by the Board. The Public Review Board is required to submit an annual report including a summary of all cases handled during the year to the membership of the UAW, drawing attention to any improper activities of the union and commenting on any steps taken by the union to correct such situations. The annual report must be carried in full by the UAW official publication, *Solidarity,* which goes to all members of the union. Board decisions are often reported in the newspapers, especially in areas where affected local unions or members are located.

Members of the Public Review Board are appointed by the UAW president, subject to the approval of the international executive board and ratification by the convention. Members' terms run until the next convention. Vacancies between conventions are filled by the president from a list submitted by the remaining members of the Public Review Board, subject to the approval of the international executive board.

The original members of the Board included clergymen from each of the three major faiths, a Negro judge, a Canadian magistrate, a university chancellor, and a professor of economics. . . .

THE RECORD OF THE BOARD

As of the end of March 1960, the Board had decided twenty-nine cases, upholding the international executive board twenty-three times and reversing it in six cases. This is in contrast to the record of UAW conventions, which constituted the last resort of an appellant prior to the establishment of the Public Review Board. The 1953, 1955, and 1957 conventions reversed the executive board in only two of the thirty cases appealed to the delegate bodies. During its first two years of operation, the Public Review Board also dismissed seven additional cases because it lacked jurisdiction; two were abandoned by the appellants before the Board could act; and one was returned to the international executive board at its request to be disposed of in accordance with previous decisions.

The cases submitted to the Public Review Board have originated in the following kinds of situations:

1. Refusal of six local union officers and five international representatives to cooperate with the Senate Internal Security Subcommittee investigating communism in unions;

2. Local union factionalism and internal political disputes. Specific issues included charges of irregularities and fraud in local union elections; alleged use of union mailing lists for political purposes; suspension from local union office due to alleged misappropriations of union funds; resort by members to a civil court to seek damages for alleged libel during a local union election campaign; alleged violation of local union by-laws in reducing stewards and committeemen after a plant lay-off;

3. Charges of improper handling of shop grievances by officers, stewards, or committeemen. Most of these cases were dismissed by the Public Review Board without a hearing because the appellants did not allege fraud, discrimination, or collusion with management and, therefore, did not come within the Board's jurisdiction. The Board did consider a few cases which charged that union officers or plant committeemen had deliberately discriminated against a member in the handling of his grievance;

4. Discharge of a member because of complaints by fellow workers that she used loud and abusive language;

5. Dispute over who was entitled to be president of a local union —the elected president, who had resigned after he was nominated to an appointive state job but who reasserted his rights to the office when his appointment was disapproved by the State Senate; or the vice president, who had succeeded to the presidency when the elected official resigned;

6. Dissolution of skilled trades councils and reorganization of the skilled trades structure of the UAW;

7. Alleged violation by the appointed administrator of a local union of the AFL-CIO ethical practices code, which assures each member the right to full and free participation in union self-government and the right to voice his views without fear of retaliation;

8. Suspension of a member for dues delinquency because his employer failed to check off his dues both during his attendance at the union's convention and when he was absent from work because of injuries sustained in an automobile accident;

9. Challenge of grounds and procedure followed in establishment of an administratorship over a local union.

COMPLAINTS

The Board's policy has been to make its services available to members of the UAW concerning any problem within the union structure. The Board describes this aspect of its function as a combination complaint department, inspector general, and conciliation service. While not expressly provided for in the constitutional provisions governing its jurisdiction, the Board considers the handling of informal complaints, as distinct from cases reaching it through formal channels, to be one of its important functions. Through its executive director, the Board receives informal complaints presented by letter, telephone, or personal visit.

During the first two-and-a-half years of its existence, the Board received approximately 100 complaints, some involving two or more union members. In each of these, the executive director has made an effort to understand the member's problem and to determine what he has tried to do about it before coming to the Public Review Board. If the member has made no attempt to obtain help through his local union or regional representative, he is advised to do so and is invited to contact the Board if he runs into trouble in trying to be heard. If, on the other hand, he has taken the obvious preliminary steps without satisfaction, his complaint is referred by the executive director to an administrative assistant in the office of the UAW president. Such a referral involves no determination as to the merits of the complaint. The executive director simply calls the grievance to the attention of the international in some detail and is thereafter kept informed as to the outcome.

Complaints received have involved such charges as prejudicial handling of shop grievances; political reprisals; undue delay in processing appeals; failure of local unions to abide by constitutional provisions and by-laws; election irregularities and excesses; denial of democratic rights at membership meetings; discrimination in the application of seniority; union-management collusion. A typical complaint often covers several of these charges.

The Board's second annual report presents a summary of one such complaint. Two members came to the Public Review Board headquarters and complained that they were constantly thwarted by local union officials in their efforts to exercise their membership rights. They said they were not recognized at meetings, were denied a copy of the collective bargaining agreement, were refused copies of the local union by-laws, and in general were dealt with in a discriminatory fashion. They felt that this treatment was not unrelated to the fact that, as gauge and layout inspectors, they represented only about thirty-five of the 3000 members in the local union. The complainants wanted an opportunity to be heard on the question of seniority at local membership meetings considering the ratification of a new collective bargaining agreement.

The Public Review Board's executive director arranged for the complainants to meet with one of Reuther's administrative assistants. As a result of this meeting, the international contacted the local union officers and the complainants were given an opportunity to be heard at the next membership meeting. Despite the very small minority of the total membership represented by the group involved, the meeting voted overwhelmingly to uphold their point of view. This experience led the two complainants to write the following letter to the Public Review Board's executive director:

> *We are very sorry that we have not contacted you before this time. The last time we were in contact with you we were still fighting to get date-of-entry seniority in our department. After about three months of hard work we have succeeded on this problem. We have taken your counsel and gotten active in our local politics. We can tell you that our group was instrumental in having our opposition defeated in the primaries and finals. Mr. _____, myself, and all the boys in our department will be indebted to you and your office for the help we have received. The boys in our department became more alert and active in our union since they knew that your office is in existence, and knowing that any individual or minority group has a place that they can be heard and helped.*

> *We Thank You Wholeheartedly.*
> *(Signatures)*

· · · ·

CONCLUSION

The creation of the UAW Public Review Board evoked varying fears, expectations, and sentiments. Some union leaders and friends of labor were fearful of granting such broad jurisdiction over internal union affairs to a group of outsiders on the ground that their decisions might affect collective bargaining policy, encourage dissident elements within the union, and even weaken the union in its dealings with employers. Others, including some UAW delegates who spoke against the establishment of a review board at the convention, felt that a union like the UAW, whose democratic processes, ethical standards, financial affairs, and existing appeals procedures had never been seriously questioned, needed no outside body to pass final judgment on decisions of its international executive board. Enemies of labor and the UAW dismissed the Public

Review Board as nothing more than a public relations stunt and "rubber stamp" for Walter Reuther and his executive board. The UAW leadership and most commentators stressed the Board's role as "the censor of the union's moral conduct" and as a "public watchdog" to keep the UAW free from corruption, racketeering, communism, or other unsavory elements. The more important role of the Board, as a body to which any union member could appeal an adverse decision of the international executive board, was almost lost sight of in the sea of high-sounding rhetoric which accompanied its creation.

The Board's record to date has not borne out the fears of labor's friends, the expectations of its enemies, or the fondest hopes of the UAW leadership. The Board has scrupulously refused to exercise jurisdiction over cases that might even remotely impinge on collective bargaining policies or interfere with the control of the UAW leadership over its own staff. If anything, it interprets its function much more narrowly than does the UAW leadership. Its record of reversal of executive board decisions, its questioning attitude toward certain constitutional provisions, and its sharp criticism of union procedural lapses in the handling of appeals cases have silenced the skeptics and reactionaries and, at the same time, have demonstrated that violations of member rights can and do occur even in a union as clean and basically democratic as the UAW. Its respect for the union's own constitution has caused it to be criticized by two groups: by union leaders who complain that the Public Review Board has been too technical and too legalistic in its insistence that constitutional procedures be strictly followed without regard to the merits of the particular case; and by those who think that the Board should look beyond the union's own constitution in order to assure fairness and equity in cases that come before it.

With regard to this last criticism, it must be noted that the Board, while hewing to the existing constitution of the union, has not hesitated to question the "wisdom or desirability" of constitutional provisions that might be considered inconsistent with fair and equitable appeals procedures. In such cases the union has amended the constitution to meet the Board's explicit or implied criticism. Equally important is the fact that the union has not amended the constitution to permit it to continue long-standing procedures that the Public Review Board has held to be violations of the constitution. By adhering to existing constitutional provisions, while at the same time calling public attention to its defects, the Board has chosen to sacrifice justice in the individual case in the interests of giving the union an opportunity to fashion its own law according to its own procedures for amending the constitution. Whether the Public Review Board would continue to follow this approach if the union showed less willingness to accept its suggestions one cannot say with certainty. However, there is a strong presumption that the Board would regard the union's refusal to follow its suggestions as a signal to exercise its broad authority to go beyond the union constitution, if necessary, to assure members fair and equitable treatment.

Perhaps the Board's greatest contribution has been the creation of an increased awareness and respect, on the part of the UAW leadership, for the importance of due process as set forth under the union's own constitution. The international executive board had tended to regard the Public Review Board as a super appeals body which would double-check union decisions in appeals cases to make sure that members were not treated unfairly. The members of this tribunal, while mindful of the constitutional requirements in appeals cases, were more concerned with administering justice on the merits of each case than with the procedures through which such justice was obtained. They fully expected that the Public Review Board would approach its task in the same fashion. When the Board refused even to consider the merits of cases in which constitutional procedures had been violated, the union officials were, at first, somewhat taken aback. Some have never reconciled themselves to this "heretical" approach to justice. Others, however, have begun to appreciate that the ends of justice are inseparable from the means through which they are attained. This may seem like an elementary principle to political scientists and those trained in the law. It is less evident to practical men, convinced of their own honesty and integrity, who are constantly faced with practical problems demanding immediate solutions. The Public Review Board has helped to bring home to the UAW leadership the difference between "rule by men," no matter how honest and well-intentioned they may be, and "rule *by* law and *under* law" to use the Board's own words taken from its first annual report.

The impact of the Public Review Board is evident in a variety of ways. The international executive board exercises greater care in considering appeals, and appeals committees are more conscientious in their conduct of hearings and in the preparation of recommendations to the full board, than before the creation of the Public Review Board. A statistical comparison of cases decided by the executive board before and after the establishment of the Public Review Board is enlightening in this regard. According to the first annual report of the Public Review Board, the international executive board, during the period 1955–57, heard fifteen appeals from members convicted and penalized under local union trial machinery. Of these fifteen cases, the local union decision was affirmed in ten cases, reversed in three, and modified in two. In contrast to this record, the international executive board, in the year immediately following the establishment of the Public Review Board, affirmed the local union decision in only two of nine disciplinary appeals. Of the remaining seven cases, the local union was reversed in five and modified in two. While no definitive conclusion can be drawn from figures covering such a short period, it is not unlikely that the "before" and "after" contrast may be ascribed, at least partially, to a closer scrutiny of appeals by the union's executive board as a result of the existence of the Public Review Board.

Other effects of the Public Review Board can be seen in the increased attention paid to the drafting of amendments to the constitution and to the elimination of inconsistencies among constitutional provisions; the greater care given to the processing of cases through all phases of the appeals procedure; and the greater tolerance exhibited by union officials and staff in listening to complaints which, if permitted to go unheard and unsatisfied, might eventually result in Public Review Board cases. Thus it may be said that, apart from any actions it may take or decisions it may render, the mere existence of the Public Review Board has had a beneficial impact on the union.

Impartial review of internal union government has progressed beyond the experimental stage. Open and voluntary acknowledgment of a "public interest" in its affairs has neither threatened the position of the UAW leadership nor caused the union to surrender its right of self-government under its own constitution. Indeed, by having the courage to submit its decisions to review by a body of impartial and distinguished citizens, the UAW leadership has increased its stature in the eyes of the membership, thereby strengthening the union not only structurally but also as a political and collective bargaining organization.

7

Innovations in Collective Bargaining

Employer and union negotiators have spent much of their time in recent years discussing automation and other kinds of rapid technological change. Changing technology has been a prominent issue in bargaining, not because of its intrinsic interest to both labor and management, but because of the impact it frequently has on the nature of labor-management relations.

New or improved production methods may affect the complexity of jobs by either raising or lowering the skills required for successful performance. When this occurs, several bargaining questions arise: Who will get the new jobs? Will retraining be required? How will seniority units be affected? What will the new wage rate be?

Potential effects on the *numbers* of jobs raise even more pressing issues than those arising from modifications of the nature of jobs. The workers' fear of job reduction pressures union bargainers to seek agreements that will prevent worker displacement or, failing this, arrangements that will protect workers from income loss in the event of displacement. The union policies directing these efforts frequently conflict with the objectives of management—flexible manning arrangements and savings through reduction in labor costs. Jack Barbash, in the first article, points out that these circumstances seem to have produced a reversal of the usual bargaining tactics—from defensive to offensive for management and conversely for unions.

Bargaining over the effects of technology has produced some

novel collective agreements. Charles Killingsworth describes the arrangements agreed upon in West Coast longshoring when employers "bought
out" work rules that blocked technological improvements. In the Kaiser
Plan, described in the third selection, a cooperative arrangement was
worked out whereby both the company and workers stand to gain from
increases in productivity. But the kind of inventive arrangements
represented by the longshore and Kaiser plans do not meet the
adjustments required by technological changes in all industries. Thomas
Brooks describes the issues surrounding a difficult adjustment situation
for one of the oldest craft groups in the country—the printers.

Regardless of the type of adjustment agreed upon, bargaining
about technology has made it clear that the concept of job-property
rights is gaining acceptance. Management may not extend formal
recognition to the idea that workers' rights in jobs extend beyond their
paychecks, but its willingness to cushion the job impact of automation
implies tacit acceptance of the idea.

Reacting to the threat of automation, unions have sought a
variety of contract guarantees for worker job and income security. Early
retirement, "sabbatical" vacations, and area-wide seniority are examples.
These and other provisions are described in "The Union Agenda for
Security."

High unemployment in the 1960's has revitalized bargaining over
the shorter work week. If the hours worked by each employed person
were reduced, a larger total number would be employed to produce our
current output. The hours issue, however, does not concern this arithmetical truism but, rather, the size of the work-week reduction and the
question of who will pay for it. The National Association of Manufacturers presents the hours issue in terms of alternative choices—essentially
between income and leisure. Workers themselves must make that choice,
the NAM says. It is not entirely clear which the workers prefer, but the
little evidence available so far suggests that they usually choose income
over leisure (they will also accept both if given a chance). Sar Levitan
relates some of the information available about worker preferences on
this issue.

The AFL-CIO is on record in favor of reductions in the work
week; its case is presented in excerpts from a convention resolution on
that subject. However, unions as a whole have not bargained very hard
for shorter hours, possibly because of lack of worker enthusiasm. They
appear to be waiting for legislation to accomplish their stated purpose.

The final section on bargaining is devoted to developments in
strategy. General Electric's strategy, frequently called Boulwareism, is
not entirely new, but the challenge to its legality is. Extracts from the
Trial Examiner Report of the National Labor Relations Board describe

the strategy and the reasoning behind it. In its decision against G.E., the Board upheld the examiner's findings. Virgil Day, a G.E. executive, answers the report, telling why he thinks that decision seriously challenges management's responsibility. The legality of Boulwareism (the NLRB decision has been appealed to the courts) is an important issue in collective bargaining, for if it is lawful, the strategic policies open to management are considerably greater than if it is not.

One reason for the success of G.E.'s bargaining policy in the last ten years has been its ability to operate its production facilities during a strike—an ability not confined to G.E. Strike-proof operations are spreading to many firms as production methods become more automated. The future of the strike as an economic weapon has also been called into question by recent employer group bargaining and strike insurance and by larger union strike funds. Instead of brief, decisive work stoppages, we are now faced with the prospect of lengthy battles of financial endurance. Whether the public will tolerate the latter remains to be seen (this matter is considered further in the next chapter). James Stern, in the last selection, explains what he calls the "declining utility of the strike."

In assessing what has been happening in collective bargaining, we must praise the flexibility of that bilateral procedure in meeting the ever-changing needs of employers and workers—doing so has required much inventive adaptation. On the other hand, the limitations of collective bargaining are becoming all too evident. It does not help the unemployed or the unorganized, many of whom work in sectors of the economy where wages are low and job insecurity high (services, trade, agriculture). It frequently reduces the immediate job prospects of persons not yet in the labor force—by arranging job-reducing accommodations to automation. With a few exceptions, it has done little to increase the relative welfare of minority populations.

In spite of these obvious inadequacies, no responsible person would suggest that we do away with collective bargaining. Instead, we are beginning to accept its limitations and perceive it as a very useful, though limited, institution. To solve many of the labor problems of our day, we must turn to other institutions. It is partly because the practice of collective bargaining is so well established in this country that U.S. citizens have the time and energy to tackle their unsolved labor problems.

adjustments to automation

Jack Barbash
THE IMPACT OF TECHNOLOGY
ON LABOR-MANAGEMENT
RELATIONS

In the 1930's, the dominant note in the tone of industrial relations was union recognition; in the wartime period, wages; in the immediate postwar period, "fringe" benefits with special emphasis on health insurance and pensions. The leitmotiv of the contemporary industrial relations scene is expressed by one variation or another of technological change and its popular equivalent, automation.

Almost every major industrial relations problem that comes into public view seems to be interlaced with technological change. Just how insistently the theme of technological change keeps recurring in industrial relations is uniquely expressed by an issue of the *New York Times* (October 31, 1961) which caught my attention as I was preparing this chapter. Page 1 carried an Associated Press account of a "labor agreement guaranteeing a worker his job or equivalent wages during his lifetime . . . negotiated by the Southern Pacific Railroad and the Order of Railroad Telegraphers"; on page 18 a report of the remaining issues in the United Automobile Workers-Chrysler dispute, including "rules relating to production standards"; and on page 49, President Clarence Sayen of the Air Line Pilots Association said that the principal issues in a

"The Impact of Technology on Labor-Management Relations" by Jack Barbash, from *Adjusting to Technological Change*, edited by Gerald G. Sommers, *et al.*, pp. 44–53. Copyright © 1963 by Industrial Relations Research Association. Reprinted by permission of Harper & Row, Publishers.
Mr. Barbash is Professor of Economics, University of Wisconsin.

dispute with the TWA "are work rules and duty schedules. Since the introduction of jet-liners pilots have voiced increasing concern for limitations on flying hours, duty hours on the ground, and time away from home."

The main accent of this paper is on the "something new that has been added" to the contemporary union-management situation by technological change. The state of the facts does not permit, I believe, anything more than an agenda of the pertinent issues with some suggestions and impressions as to the possible directions which the answers seem to be taking. . . .

Technological change seems to have exerted the most immediate and powerful effect on the perceptions of the parties to industrial relations. Management's perception of technological change is producing an offensive strategy; the union's perception is in general producing a defensive strategy. Summarily stated at this point, automation from the union standpoint (to use the word most commonly used by union spokesmen) is an access link in a chain of economic consequences in which rapid technological change, recessions, plant abandonments, and relocation create reduced employment and earnings and, therefore, insecurity. For management the technological effect leads into another industrial relations chain reaction, including work practices (or more invidiously, "featherbedding") and "management's freedom to manage" or, symbolically, "management rights" and the "hard line."

On the eve of the 1961 bargaining sessions with American Motors, the United Automobile Workers' Vice-president, Norman Matthews, said, "Workers were more interested in job security than in 'pennies in their pay envelopes.'" Or, as a Chemical Workers local president put it, "we are not striking over money, we're trying to hold on to rights we've had for years." Recurring expressions by union spokesmen are "vast social and economic disruptions," "large-scale job displacement," "job security," "plight of the jobless," "the urgency of the job preservation problem," "reduced living standards," and "frenzied economic violence."

For management, technological change is taking on an urgent meaning in its industrial relations which it had not had before. Great transformations are taking place in American industry, transformations which management sees as requiring greater freedom and maneuverability in the organization of production and manpower. Management must take a stiffer position to prevent its industrial relations from falling too far behind its competitive needs in the national and international markets. These perceptions are leading to policies and action; and, accordingly, both union and management perceptions get reflected in collective bargaining demands and strategy and in the shapes of industrial conflict.

The unions' collective bargaining, broadly conceived, seems to be gearing to the pressures of technological change in three stages. Stage one is seen in provisions designed to maintain existing jobholders in their jobs at existing levels of earnings. The second line of defense represents a recognition on the union's part that jobs and earnings attrition can no longer be resisted *in toto* and that the union position must shift toward transitional measures "to cushion the shock of displacement." The third line of defense (perhaps coexisting with stage two) is the assertion of the claim that the loss of jobs and job prerequisites should be compensated for by a financial settlement in return for which the employer is permitted greater freedom for deployment of manpower. From the viewpoint of history it is notable that outright union obstruction to technological change is conspicuously absent in the contemporary situation.

During the first stage unions seek contractual provisions which prohibit layoffs of existing personnel, or prohibit reduction in wage rates for incumbents ("red-circling") or at least for senior employees, or freeze a specific manning schedule during the life of the agreement. The union demand for reduction in hours, which is being heard with renewed insistence everywhere except at the bargaining table (where it is not heard as frequently because the unions feel they lack the power to enforce it), is plainly not so much for more leisure but for the sharing of scarce jobs. Supplementary unemployment benefits are seen as providing the employer with an incentive for the stabilization of employment.

The renewed interest in earnings stabilization may represent the second half-stage (within stage one) after job protection. The operating railroad workers have been asking for a guaranteed annual wage, and the auto workers have been articulating the philosophy of "salaries for all workers." In order to maintain earnings, some unions have proposed a redesigning of wage payment and job classification systems in accordance with the radically altered work specifications of the automated job. Here, the union objective is, of course, to counteract the deterioration of earnings opportunities. To counter the management assertion that automated jobs are less demanding, unions stress the increased responsibility and human tension as work consequences of automation. Where automated jobs threaten to dilute traditional skill content some unions are insisting on the preservation of existing integrated skills. When management seeks to eliminate the incentive system in order to cut take-home pay, some of the unions are put in the position of supporting incentive systems rather than take cuts in take-home pay.

In stage two—which is where I think most of the unions are—the union strategy shifts from maintaining jobs and earnings (presumably because this strategy is no longer tenable) toward moderating the impact of displacement through contract clauses which seek to ease the period of transition. These transition-type clauses are both substantive and procedural in content. Substantively, unions seek to widen the seniority unit to take in interplant, intercompany, and interarea transfers as a matter of right for displaced workers. With increasing frequency unions are also asking in negotiations for relocation allowances and retraining. In respect to vocational training the historic "craft" unions in collaboration with their employers associations—notably plumbers, electricians (International Brotherhood of Electrical Workers), lithographers and printers (International Typographical Union)—assume the initiating and driving role in the training function as such. The "industrial" unions are more likely to leave the function to management.

On the procedural side unions are asking for the right to participate in some systematic fashion in the projection of technological change, plant shutdown, or relocation. The simpler forms of participation involve advance notice and advisory consultation. More elaborate are the joint consultation programs with research functions and with provisions for participation of public or private third parties.

The third stage—the most striking in terms of conception—turns on the explicit recognition of the principle that employees have vested rights in their jobs and that the loss of these jobs and job rights should be compensated by a financial settlement. This principle has been implicitly recognized in established collective bargaining provisions through severance pay, dismissal pay, or terminal payments (in the nature of liquidation of prorated rights in unused vacation and sick leave), and more recently in the augmenting of supplementary unemployment benefits by a separation-pay provision. The Pacific Coast longshore agreement is the most prominent recent example of the liquidation principles, and here even the measuring rod for determining liquidation of rights has undergone change. Instead of being based on a theory of sharing of savings it is now based on buying out union restrictions.

Woven in at all stages is the individual union's goal to preserve itself as an institution. This is achieved largely by provisions incorporating newly automated jobs within the existing bargaining unit and therefore within the incumbent union's jurisdiction.

If "job insecurity" characterizes the union's response to technology, the management capsule response is "management rights." Management rights have had a long history as management ideology, but its present thrust is derived from an assessment of the meaning of the new technology. The objective of management industrial relations policy and specifically of collective bargaining policy is seen as the recapture of initiative lost to the unions since the union upsurge of the thirties. In contrast to the union, which, we have seen, stresses the job scarcity consequences, management spokesmen at least in their public utterances tend to underplay automation as the cause of job scarcity. Managements stress stronger management rights clauses, with elimination of restrictive work rules, "soft" job standards, and limitations on subcontracting singled out as special targets.

The recapture of management rights is indeed a widespread management objective, but the methods employed to achieve this objective diverge. In approximate terms the methods can be designated as radical and conservative. By radical I mean the managements that seek to overturn the prevailing structure of work rules and "local practice" clauses in one concentrated attack. This conception of strategy is generally complemented by public relations programs and an employee communications program over the heads of union leaders which seeks to root the management program in a larger ideology of a free enterprise system and the avoidance of inflation. The most prominent practitioners of this approach have been the United States Steel Corporation and the railroad industry.

On the other end of the spectrum is the group of managements that I loosely term conservative. They are no less concerned with union obstacles in the way of productive efficiency, but they are reconciled to the strategy that progress in this area will have to be made gradually by acquiescence rather than by frontal attack, and that, moreover, strategy will have to be "sweetened" by collaborative mechanisms and by *quid pro quo's*. Representative of this "Fabian" element in management are perhaps the Pacific Coast longshore industry, Kaiser, Armour, and American Motors.

Technological change has induced an accented interest in legislative enactment. Union interest in legislation is nothing new, but the significant change that has taken place currently in the thinking of the labor movement is reflected in the central role which is now assigned to broad, economy-wide legislation. A composite union attitude could well take the following form: in dealing with the problem of job insecurity resulting from accelerated technological change, the best we can do in collective bargaining is to engage in a holding action to protect our people from being inundated and our unions from going under. Our main reliance in dealing with the problems of insecurity must be on public policy aimed at high level—if not full—employment. Only if we have a high level of production and employment will the economy have the necessary resiliency to absorb the people who are being displaced by automation and by the shift from the production of goods to the provision of services. The problems of distressed areas and retraining, which are more immediately related to technological change, are also proper subjects for legislation.

If the union spokesmen were to use the terminology of professional economists they would say that their collective bargaining efforts can have only a "micro" effect. The vexing problems of insecurity arising out of technology can be dealt with only through "macro" techniques. In our complex economy only the federal government has the necessary capacity to deal with these problems on a macro-economic basis.

The meaning of technological change for management's legislative objectives has taken the form of a proposal by the National Association of Manufacturers "to restore the function of managing a business to management where the responsibility rests and the function and authority belong." However, I do not believe that management circles believe that this kind of legislation has a serious chance of enactment, whereas the unions take a more optimistic view of their legislative chances.

Charles C. Killingsworth
THE WEST COAST
LONGSHORE PLAN

. . . As an industry, or a segment of one, West Coast longshoring is considerably less important (at least in terms of employment) than such national industries as autos, rubber, steel, and railroads. Nevertheless, West Coast longshoring merits attention because it is an example of a collective bargaining system in which the parties have almost completed the transition from one mode of accommodation between managerial flexibility and job security to a new and basically different mode of accommodation.

Few industries have ever developed a more comprehensive set of restrictive work rules than those which were in effect in West Coast longshoring up to 1961. Some rules required the performance of unnecessary work, such as the unloading of certain kinds of goods from a trucker's pallet to the floor of the dock and then reloading onto a longshoreman's pallet before they could be loaded on a ship. Other rules required excessive manning, to the extent that in many ports the men had

From "West Coast Longshoring" in *Cooperative Approaches to Problems of Technological Change*, by Charles C. Killingsworth. Copyright 1963 by Industrial Relations Research Association. Reprinted by permission of the author and the Association.

developed a "four on, four off" practice—four men would work while the other four would serve as "witnesses." Still other rules required the operation of equipment at much less than its capacity; for example, maximum sling loads of most commodities were prescribed at relatively low levels. Whatever may have been the origins of most of these rules, one of their principal purposes clearly had become that of making work for longshoremen. While the union might have objected to the use of such invidious terms as "make-work rules," its top officers were remarkably frank in their description of the situation at a union convention in 1957. "Our present policy," their report to that convention said, "can be described as one of intermittent guerrilla warfare directed against all changes which we anticipate will reduce the need for men. . . ." The employers had the contractual right to introduce new equipment, but generally the union resisted any concomitant reduction in manning—in fact, it sometimes sought increases in manning; consequently, the incentive for technological innovation was weakened.

This mode of accommodation had developed in a context of intense conflict between the waterfront employers' association and the International Longshoremen's and Warehousemen's Union (ILWU) during the thirties and forties. When the union won recognition in 1934 after a bloody, three-month strike, two of its principal objectives were control of hiring and control of the speed of work. The first was important to the union because of the casual nature of longshore work; the typical "job" lasts only for a day or two. To equalize work opportunities, hiring halls were established from which men were dispatched in rotation as jobs become available. The equalization of work opportunities had the effect (whether intended or not) of giving all of the men an equal interest in maximizing the employment available to the entire work force. The second union objective was a response to what the union called the brutal and inhuman work pace that the employers had enforced prior to 1934. Frequently, men had to run to keep up with the work, the union said; and the accident rate was extremely high.

The economic characteristics of the industry facilitated the efforts of a militant union to establish restrictive work rules. The casual nature of the employment relationship provided a rationale for the detailed contractual specification of such matters as minimum crews, work methods, and so on, to establish standardized conditions among a multitude of employers. Perhaps more basic is the fact that most of the direct employers of longshoremen (stevedores and terminal operators) work on a cost-plus basis, with ship-owners and shippers paying the bills. There is also an important time factor in longshore operations; port time is costly for the owners. A stoppage may impose substantial losses on the owners, but the longshoremen usually find that the work is still there after the stoppage, and it is often performed at overtime rates. Hence, longshoring provided an unusually favorable combination of means and motivations for the development of restrictive work rules.

The employers' association fought this development on several fronts—with publicity barrages, lockouts, appeals to government, and so on—but rather ineffectively. Then in 1948, after a ninety-five-day coast-wide strike, the employers fundamentally revised their policies. They designated new bargaining representatives who were committed to "getting along with the union." Thereafter, conflict decreased remarkably. The work rules remained substantially unchanged, however, and the employers viewed them as an increasingly serious competitive handicap as some cargoes were diverted to other coasts and to other forms of transportation. The union officers gradually became convinced, for their part, that the work-rules approach to job security should be reconsidered. Their rationale and recommendations were presented to a 1957 convention of the union. Despite the general technological backwardness of the longshore industry, and despite the union's policy of "guerrilla resistance," the officers said, innovations such as new bulk cargo-handling methods and containerization had begun to make inroads on employment opportunities. A continuation of existing policies in the face of prospective changes in technology might be no more than a delaying action, they said, which in the end would mean fewer jobs and no "share of the machine" for the workers. The officers recommended that the union offer the employers "a more flexible policy" in return for specific employee benefits and protection against speedup and unsafe operations. After lengthy debate, the union delegates accepted the recommendation.

More than three years of negotiations ensued between the Pacific Maritime Association (the employers' representative) and the ILWU. The details of the agreement were worked out in almost continuous sessions from April to October in 1960. What emerged was a fundamental revision of the mode of accommodation between managerial flexibility and job security in this industry. The union agreed to a complete overhauling of work rules for the explicit purpose of allowing the employers to "operate efficiently," "change methods of work," "utilize labor-saving devices," and "direct the work through Employer representatives while . . . avoiding speed up." The union further agreed "that the contract, working and dispatching rules shall not be construed so as to require the hiring of unnecessary men." To effectuate these principles, the agreement specifically eliminates some of the restrictive rules—for example, "there will be no multiple handling"—modifies some minimum crew sizes, and provides procedures for other changes, including appeal to the permanent arbitrator under the contract.

The *quid pro quo* for the union and its members was a benefit package, to be financed by employer contributions, totaling $29 million over the five and one-half years of the agreement. This fund will be used to finance two principal benefits for the "fully registered" longshoremen: vested early retirement rights and what amounts to an annual wage guarantee. The longshoreman who voluntarily retires at age sixty-two can collect $220 per month from the fund until the normal retirement age of sixty-five, after which he collects $115 per month from the industry and his regular federal social security benefit. Those who work until age sixty-five will receive a lump sum payment of $7,920. The parties may make retirement compulsory at sixty-two (in order to reduce the labor force), in which case the pension will be $320 per month until age sixty-five. The wage guarantee is intended to protect the eligible longshoremen against any shortage of work resulting from efficiency improvements (though not from a decline due to recession). The parties contemplate a guarantee of thirty-five hours per week for fully registered longshoremen, and there is apparently an understanding that the guarantee will not be vitiated by the "deregistration" of men. Hence, barring a severe recession in the industry, the eligible longshoreman has the double security of a no-layoff guarantee and a minimum income guarantee.

The employer representatives with whom I talked concerning this agreement believe that they made a good bargain. Their fund contributions are between 4 and 5 per cent of longshore payrolls. But their savings are considerably greater. During negotiations, an estimate was presented showing that the elimination of *only* the multiple handling rules, in Los Angeles *alone*, would save the employers more than their total fund contributions. The employers also gain from reduced port time for ships, and their incentive to adopt improved technology has increased. The union's officers also support the agreement enthusiastically. They believe that they have achieved unprecedented job security for their members and have done more than any other union to solve the problems of adjustment to technological change. Some local leaders of the union are much less enthusiastic, and some of the members are said to be startled to learn of the scope of the rules changes which the union has agreed to accept. This is perhaps one of the reasons why the implementation of the principles of the agreement is proceeding rather slowly. Nevertheless, top-level representatives of the union and the companies remain confident that the agreement will be fully carried out.

The impression has gained currency in some quarters that the West Coast longshore agreement is a response to the problems created by technological change. This is only partially true. From the standpoint of the ILWU, it was the anticipated effects of *future* technological change, rather than a currently serious displacement problem such as many industries have, which prompted the union to reconsider its policy. For the employers, the pressing problem did not grow directly out of changing technology in their own industry, but out of the heavy competitive handicap of restrictive work rules which had accumulated over two or three decades. The burden of the work rules on the employers undoubtedly facilitated the achievement of a new mode of accommodation once the union officers decided on a change in policy. The employers were able to offer a handsome price, in the form of a benefit package, and still realize substantial savings from the "modernization" of work rules. This modernization may facilitate future technological change, but up until now longshoring has been technologically backward compared with most other industries.

Gerald E. Balsley
THE KAISER STEEL PLAN

. . . In setting the stage to discuss our present situation it is difficult to know where to begin. Kaiser Steel has had a contractual relationship with the Steelworkers Union almost since our company first began production in 1943. On the whole, it has been a good relationship, subject to the ups and downs common to many collective bargaining situations. In addition, of course, the Steelworkers have contracts with Kaiser Aluminum, so Mr. Kaiser and Mr. McDonald have had many occasions for discussions over the years.

The start of our Sharing Plan, however, can be traced most directly to one dramatic event with which you are all familiar—the 1959 steel strike. The strike naturally had a catastrophic impact on both Kaiser Steel and our employees. Furthermore, it indicated that we had reached a point of complete impasse on many complex questions relating to work rules, benefit programs, and productivity.

Dr. George Taylor, as you probably remember, was appointed to head the Taft-Hartley Board of Inquiry established to review this

Abridged from an address to the Research Conference on Collective Bargaining, Institute of Industrial Relations, University of California, Los Angeles, 1964.

Mr. Balsley is Vice President of Industrial Relations, Kaiser Steel Corporation.

dispute. During the course of his investigations, Dr. Taylor expressed his growing conviction that there must be "a better way" to resolve the issues involved in situations of this sort. With this conviction, both Mr. McDonald and Mr. Kaiser were able to express wholehearted agreement.

As a result, when Kaiser Steel and the Steelworkers sat down to work out the details of a separate settlement, they were looking for a number of things to provide the "better way," including:

1. An organized and cooperative approach to the solution of mutual problems—such as work rules, to give but one example.

2. A long-range approach to economic issues in order to avoid "crisis bargaining," stalemates, and disastrous strikes.

3. The availability of outside counsel of their own choosing who could: (a) Develop an intimate and continuing relationship with the parties, understanding their problems and their aspirations. (b) Serve as advisors, counselors, and mediators. (c) Remove the need for outside pressures from mediators or other government representatives.

In keeping with this philosophy, when an agreement was finally reached on October 26, 1959, that agreement included a provision for the establishment of a tripartite committee which has since come to be known as our Long Range Committee. This committee was composed of nine men, consisting of three company, three union, and three public representatives, with one of the public members serving as chairman. . . .

The primary purpose for which the Long Range Committee was established was to provide a vehicle for the development of a long-range economic program. The stated objective at the time of the 1959 agreement was: "The establishment of a long range plan for equitable sharing between the stockholders, the employees and the public, of the company's future economic progress." This objective was further elaborated by the provision of more specific guidelines for any such plan. It was to:

1. Promote stability of employment.

2. Safeguard employees against increases in the cost of living.

3. Provide for equitable sharing of increased productivity.

4. Encourage the necessary expansion of the company.

This, then, provided the initial framework within which the committee began its operations. It should be noted that these guidelines covered more than just a "sharing of progress." In fact, they reflect a primary concern for economic and employment security, with any additional "sharing" as a secondary consideration. . . .

The Long Range Sharing Plan was completed, approved by the Long Range Committee, and accepted by the parties on December 16, 1962, subject only to ratification by the employees involved. In keeping with Dr. Taylor's[1] promise that the employees would be the first to know, the general outline of the plan was presented to mass meetings of employees and their families over the next two days. Following this, Marvin Miller of the Steelworkers undertook the task of explaining the plan, in detail, to small groups of employees on an around-the-clock schedule over a period of about two weeks. The plan was then ratified by a 3 to 1 vote of the employees on January 11, 1963, and was put into effect on March 1.

Turning now to the plan itself, I'm sure many of you are familiar with some or all aspects of it. If so, you are certainly aware that it is a complex program . . . I will try to give you a brief review of the three major sections of the plan and leave the technical aspects of how it is accomplished for you to garner from published sources. The three sections I would like to cover are those dealing with: (a) employment security, (b) sharing of cost-savings, (c) elimination of existing incentives.

Employment security: This portion of the plan attacks the major problem of employment security for those employees affected by changes in technology and work methods. Our plan offers three types of protection for such employees:

1. The first is an *employment guarantee* for those employees directly displaced or, on the basis of alternate formulas, those indirectly eliminated by technological or methods improvements. Such employees will not be laid off, but will be retained in an employment reserve and will be used in a variety of productive jobs in the plant, including vacation and absentee replacements, until they are reabsorbed on regular job assignments. These employees will be differentiated from those who may still be laid off because of a reduced level of production, and who will still be protected by our SUB program.

2. The second is a *displacement differential* for employees who would have been entitled to a higher rated job except for technological or methods changes, equal to the difference between the rate they would have received and the rate they actually receive. This differential is to be paid for up to 52 weekly payments over a maximum three-year period, unless the employee regains the higher rate or refuses an advancement in the interim.

3. The third is a *short week benefit* which provides for the payment of average earnings for up to 40 hours a week in those cases where technological improvements reduce scheduled hours below 40.

Sharing cost-savings: This provision, as the name implies, is the heart of our plan. As such, it is based on three simple principles, which are that:

[1] Chairman of the Long Range Committee (eds. note).

1. We can adequately measure cost-savings resulting from improved performance in our steel producing operations.

2. Employees should share in the savings in those areas where they exercise some degree of control, such as: (a) labor performance, (b) usage of materials and supplies, (c) improvements in yield, (d) utilization of technological improvements.

3. Employees should not be held responsible for conduct outside the sphere of collective bargaining in such areas as: (a) sales and investment policies, (b) selling, general, and administrative expenses, (c) depreciation, (d) sales of property and equipment, (c) interest, taxes, or profit.

Gains to be shared are determined by, first, establishing labor and material and supply cost standards for an actual base period, which in our case was the year 1961. The second step, then, is to measure cost performance each month against these standards to show the savings. Labor cost standards are adjusted monthly for changes in the Consumer Price Index, and material and supply standards are similarly adjusted for changes in the Wholesale Price Index of the appropriate categories of steel products.

Once the gross gain is calculated, the costs of any displacement differentials or short week payments are deducted. A deduction is also made for the cost of certain capital expenditures which improve productivity. The balance, or net gain, is the amount that is available for sharing.

Based on the historical fact that labor cost has averaged approximately 32.5 per cent of total manufacturing cost, the employees' share is 32.5 per cent of the net gain or cost-savings. The remainder is retained by the company, subject, of course, to the normal tax applications.

The employees' share is then distributed in two ways. First, a predetermined percentage is set aside in a Wage and Benefit Reserve, to cover the cost of future steel industry wage and benefit improvements. Let me re-emphasize this point: *All* future improvements in wages and benefits are chargeable to the employees' share of cost-savings under this plan through the mechanism of this reserve. The balance is distributed monthly as a cash payment on the basis of a formula which takes historical wage relationships in the industry and company into account.

Elimination of existing incentives: One of the objectives of our plan was to replace the existing incentive programs covering about 40 per cent of the employees. Since some of these plans pay substantial benefits, it was not possible to eliminate them overnight. Instead, provision was made for a series of options which will gradually permit employees to transfer over to the Sharing Plan.

To begin with, no new plans will be installed and no employees not now covered will participate in existing incentives. They will be covered by the Sharing Plan. For employees currently on other incentives, several options are possible. Any unit, for example, may elect to transfer voluntarily from incentives to sharing if they feel the latter will provide greater benefits. Under this provision, approximately 600 employees have made the transition from individual incentives to Sharing Plan coverage. In other cases, the company may offer, and the employees vote to accept, a lump-sum payment to eliminate an incentive plan and transfer to sharing. Again, about 170 employees have transferred on the basis of such offers. There are, of course, other provisions in this complex area, but these outline the intent, at least, to gradually eliminate other types of incentive plans without penalizing present participants.

Duration of the Plan

The Sharing Plan was intended to operate on a continuing basis and our agreement provides for this, subject to two provisions:
1. It is to be reviewed annually, and revised as necessary.
2. It may be cancelled during the fifth year or each fourth year thereafter.

We adopted this four-year period intentionally because we felt that it would take at least four years to provide a reasonable test period. We have not changed our minds, and we still feel that we don't have a solid basis for any final evaluation of its operation.

The fact remains that we are following the plan closely and have made some technical changes as we went along in a continuing effort to insure that the plan accomplishes, in practice, what the parties intended in principle. I mention this only to indicate that we sincerely regard this plan as an experimental program which is subject to change as operations indicate revisions are required—not as a sacred cow which we have developed to put on permanent public display.

Results during the First Ten Months[2]

Our plan has now been in effect for ten months, or at least I should say that we have now completed ten monthly calculations. We are constantly being asked, therefore, "How is it doing?" Those of you who have been associated with any such complex program can appreciate how tough it is to answer that question. You can all realize, I am sure,

---

[2] On January 1, 1966, the Kaiser Plan had been in operation for almost three years. The results for the longer period were similar to those described here for the first ten months, though the monthly cash payments to employees declined slightly after the first year (eds. note).

how short a time ten months can be in the life of such a program. Therefore, I believe you will appreciate what I can tell you and can't tell you about our plan at this stage.

Looking first of all at the cash payments, we started off at a level which I believe was higher than most of us had anticipated. We distributed 55 cents an hour for March, and this went up to 66 cents in April. On the other hand, with lower production in July and August, payments fell to 40 cents and 24 cents respectively. In September this rose again to 46 cents and held at about this level until December, when some year-end adjustments helped reduce it again to about 30 cents.

Cash payments, while significant, and certainly important to the recipients, don't tell the whole story. Because of our level of operations since the plan was installed, we have had no real drain on the plan from the employment security provisions. We have made no major technological changes and the people affected by minor ones have been readily absorbed. Neither have we moved too rapidly in the area of eliminating existing incentives. As I mentioned, a few incentive employees have transferred over voluntarily and we have made a major lump-sum payment to eliminate one system, but the total long-run effect of the incentive provision has not had a strong impact so far.

In addition, as we fully anticipated, progress under any program such as this is slow to show itself. Attitudes and habits don't change overnight, and we didn't expect supervisors or their employees to do an abrupt about-face because of the plan. Nevertheless, improvements in attitudes and cooperation are obvious. Employees *are* becoming more cost-conscious and are looking at their jobs from a new angle. There have already been many encouraging examples of how employees can contribute to improved performance if given the opportunity and incentive to do so. . . .

I would like to conclude my remarks at this point . . . Obviously, we are enthusiastic about the success of our committee and our sharing program thus far. It would also be unfair not to tell you we are highly optimistic that it will do what we expect of it. If I had to qualify this optimism, I would like to do it in terms of the role we expect it to play in our collective bargaining relationship. No plan or program is going to solve all of the complex problems facing us in the industrial relations field today. It doesn't replace union or management responsibilities, it doesn't replace our basic agreement, and it doesn't replace the continuation of a responsible relationship. At best, it can provide a framework within which we can succeed in our collective bargaining responsibilities *if* we want to and *if* we are prepared to work diligently to achieve this goal.

Thomas R. Brooks
DEATH OF A CRAFT?

Two years ago, the 114-day New York City newspaper strike ended on March 31. On the following day in the N.Y. *Times,* A. H. Raskin quoted a "top unionist" as saying, "This should be the strike to end all newspaper strikes." It was a widely shared view—then, about a strike with national implications. Today, no one is at all sure about the course of the current negotiations between the industry's ten craft unions, covering more than 17,000 employees, and the New York City Publishers' Association, representing the city's seven major newspapers. The ten contracts expire on March 30. The printers have already authorized a strike and, although Typographical Union No. 6 does not have a "no contract, no work" policy, "Big Six" President Bertram A. Powers indicated to me that the union negotiators felt that talks had gone on long enough to produce some results and that the union was not looking forward to prolonged negotiations beyond the contract deadline.

The unions, however, are not eager for a strike. Even allowing for late Easter advertising, April isn't exactly a crucial month as far as newspaper revenue is concerned. The publishers are in a better position to take a strike now than they were when the 114-day strike began on December 8, 1962, at the peak of the Christmas advertising season. Still, according to Powers, the publishers are not entirely over the effects of the last strike. Certainly, both sides approach the March 30 deadline with caution, leaving plenty of room for negotiations. . . .

The Association [has] offered a weekly raise of $3.50 each year for a total of $10.50 over a three-year contract period. The Printing Pressmen are asking $15 a week in a two-year agreement, $9 the first year and $6 the second. (The Printers are asking for $15 in a one-year agreement.) Several unions are reportedly close to an agreement. . . . With the money question on its way to resolution, automation becomes the central issue, with Big 6, the chief union, affected this time around.

From *Commonweal,* April 2, 1965. Reprinted by permission.
Mr. Brooks recently finished a history of labor, *Toil and Trouble.*

THE CRUCIAL ISSUE

What makes the problem particularly explosive is that every-body, except perhaps the printers, thought that the issue was settled the last time as a result of the long strike. And so it was, in principle. Originally, the publishers sought the right to have all their Stock Exchange and other financial tables set into type automatically through Teletypesetter tape supplied by the wire services. They also offered to guarantee that no existing employee would lose his job as a result. The union asked that a share of the savings made possible through tape be contributed to an automation fund to defray the costs of retraining, early retirement benefits and supplementary unemployment benefits.

In the settlement, the use of Teletypesetter tape was limited to the stock market transactions, about two-thirds of the material the publishers wanted handled by outside tape, and a joint committee was set up to study the savings made and to decide on the amount of payments into the fund. If the committee could not reach an agreement on the amount, the matter was to go to arbitration. Unhappily, the joint committee was unable to agree on the amount to be paid into the fund. The union wanted all the direct savings, leaving what it terms "substantial" indirect savings to the publishers. The publishers balked at this. The first arbitration hearings were scheduled for March 22, a delay that has had the effect of re-opening the issue altogether. Since the ratio of sharing the savings from the use of outside tape has not been decided, the possible precedent for a wider use of automation remains very much up in the air.

Meanwhile, automation has become more and more feasible. The *Daily News,* The New York *Times* and the New York *Post* have all bought computers for use in speeding up the printing process. "After they [the computer industry] are through with the banks," says Powers wryly, "they move in on us." Computerized typesetting systems, reports Joe Bailey, third vice president of the ITU, are in use on 77 newspapers, including the Kansas City *Star,* the Los Angeles *Herald-Examiner,* the Boston *Herald-Traveler,* the Baltimore *Sun,* Jersey City *Journal* and the Washington *Post,* and 33 more are on order. "The twin development of computer hardware and applications continues to progress at a faster rate than most realize," reports the trade journal, *Printing Production* in its recent edition on the newspaper industry. And, in the *ITU Review* of February 4, 1965, a headline reads: "Electronic Eye Would Eliminate Most All Newspaper Typesetters."

The typographer's craft has changed very little since the intro-duction of the Linotype machine in 1886. The Linotype itself was an early form of automation, replacing the old hand, character-by-character setting of type by the casting of a single line. The operator punches a keyboard, similar to that of a typewriter, releasing a matrix, or individual letter mold, which falls into an assembler. When a line has been assembled, the operator pulls a lever, sending the line into a molder for lead casting. After casting, the matrixes are redistributed automatically back to a magazine for re-use. While the machine sets type, the operator made two decisions requiring knowledge and training: He decided where to hyphenate words breaking the line and "justified" the line by spacing the words so each line ends squared off with the next. The computer completely automates typesetting by taking over these two decisions from the keyboard operator.

THE COMPUTER REVOLUTION

To program a computer for typesetting is simple enough. Each letter in a given font is given a numerical value describing its width. And, given the commuter's fabulous "memory," there is no limit on the number of type faces that can be employed and there is no problem in switching from one face, measure, or size to another.

All an operator has to do when perforating a tape is to indicate the first and last word of a paragraph. The computer does the rest. The tape is fed into the computer which reads the copy and relates each letter to its numerical value. It then adds all the numerical values for all the letters and all the spaces that are to go into a line and swiftly and automatically makes the correct decisions on word hyphenation and line endings. Having established the correct total needed to end the line, the computer produces a tape which tells the line caster or photo composer exactly what letters the line will have and where it will end.

A competent linotype operator is defined in the ITU contract as a man who can set 375 lines an hour; the electro-typesetter can produce up to 12,000 11-pica lines an hour if input tape is continuously available. A perforator operator can punch tape for the computer at about 600 lines an hour. According to Powers, a linotype operator can set 3 lines a minute, the tape system, 12–14 lines a minute. Moreover, anyone who can use a typewriter can operate a paper tape perforator to set type for either photo or hot-metal composition. A crack New York City typist can earn $2–$2.50 an hour; a linotype operator earns $4.00 an hour on the day shift.

What has saved the printers so far is the high cost of computers, roughly $250,000 to buy. Printing experts say that the savings from the use of computers for hyphenation and justification do not warrant the investment. Real savings, however, are to be had when the computer can be applied to corrections and assembly procedures. And, this is the next stage of automation in the industry and the one that ultimately threatens the printer's job. This threat is embodied in the combination of the electronic eye, the computer and the photo-printer. According to the *ITU Review*, the Electronic Retina Character Reader "gives promise of chasing all humans out of composing rooms." The Retina scans copy, character by character, and is capable of punching unjustified tape ready for the computer. Four such machines, reports the ITU publication, are now in use and a fifth is scheduled for use on April 1 "in the office of a notoriously anti-ITU newspaper."

"The ominous potential of the Retina," continues the *ITU Review*, "cannot be played down." It reads words just like the human eye, rather than intermittently like a movie camera. It does so at a speed of 2,400 characters a second, or 28,000 words a minute. It can sense black, white and an infinite number of shades of gray, giving it the capacity to recognize and correct imperfections of copy.

The Retina is flexible with available configurations ranging from a single-font reader to a system capable of recognizing six or more type fonts intermixed with numerals, upper and lower case alphabetical characters, and special symbols in each. It can activate almost any printing apparatus that can be operated by electronic impulse—computers, Photons, line-casting machines, Linofilms, and so on. The Retina is costly, leasing at $9,000 to $17,000 a month or it can be purchased outright for $500,000. To be economically feasible, concludes the *ITU Review*, the Retina would have to replace 25 tape punchers.

Corrections are costly in both newspaper publishing and in a job printing shop. In the near future, however, it will be possible for a computer to photo-print a justified-hyphenated text for proofreading while storing the text in its memory until corrected instead of immediately punching out tape for the line-casting machines. This would save on the recasting in lead corrected lines. Even proofreading, with the aid of the Retina, which can compare corrected copy with the original, will be automated at great savings. Type, at least in the job shop, need never be set until all corrections have been made.

USES OF ATTRITION

Manless composing rooms, however, are still a thing of the future. Present systems still have too many bugs for newspapers with their deadlines and changing editions to rely upon. But the protection of existing jobs, retraining, and all other automation related issues cannot be postponed much longer.

Attrition—the reduction of the workforce by deaths, resignations and retirements—is the publishers' answer to the problem of automation. On the surface, the publishers' promise that no one "regularly" employed at present will lose his job as a result of automation makes sense. But, as Powers is quick to point out, "it is only part of the answer to our problem."

Protection against job losses requires agreement on what jobs are to be protected. The union claims that under the present employer proposal as many as 25 percent of the printers in some shops would lose out, including some men with ten years' experience. The publishers, too, want not only unlimited freedom to introduce automated equipment but they also want to be free to hire outside typists for tape punching. The union wants its members retrained for that purpose. "In the long run," Powers told me, "we hope to gain with the publishers; meanwhile we want to survive as an organization."

"If we accept attrition," Powers explained, "with no other compensation for job losses, we will be unable to maintain our pensioners, present and future." He also said that the union wanted to accelerate the natural attrition rate by early retirement. To do so, said Powers, costs money. It takes six working printers now to carry one pensioner. If more printers are encouraged to retire, the ratio will increase.

Local 6 has 5,500 book and job members, 3,500 working for the newspaper publishers and 2,000 pensioners. There are 700 apprentices, or a six-year supply of new labor for the industry. The normal flow of workers is from the book and job side to the newspapers. If newspaper jobs dry up, the union fears that it will not have jobs enough for the newcomers. This, argues Powers, will require supplementary unemployment benefits.

When asked why the newspaper publishers should help to carry this financial burden (each division of the Local has its own welfare and pension system), Powers simply points out that the publishers have relied on book and job printing for a labor supply over the years and that it cannot simply turn its back on the printer frozen out of the job flow from one side of the printing industry to the other. The newspapers, with their greater capital resources, are in a better position to automate than job printers and their decision to do so affects all printers, Powers says.

Unlike the industrial unions, and many others, the ITU member pays for his pension benefits out of his dues, which are 6 percent of his weekly gross earnings. This breaks down as follows: 2.5 percent goes to an ITU pension fund, which pays pensioners, $22 a week; 1.5 percent goes to a Local 6 pension fund, which pays retired printers, $11 a week; and 1.5 percent is paid by the employers into a contract pension fund, which pays $40 a month, or close to $10 a week. Printers may retire at age 60 and work two days a week ($29 a day on day shift) without disturbing their pensions; at age 65, they can work a day a week without losing out on their pension payments. A retired printer, at age 60 and working two days a week, will have a little over $100 a week as against his full-time weekly rate for 37 hours of $145. It's not bad at all and printers are already what actuaries call a "low-age retirement group."

But it does place a financial strain on working printers that is bound to increase as their number declines. The local retirement fund is already running at a deficit. To end it will cost each member $1.40 a month. And this, the union fears, is only a beginning. Since these costs are likely to increase sharply as automation takes hold, the printers, not unreasonably it seems to me, are asking that the publishers set up an automation fund out of the savings brought on by automation. The industry, says Powers, faces a period of adjustment. "Our concern," he adds, "is that we have the wherewithal to make that adjustment."

At the close of the 114-day strike in 1963, the publishers agreed in principle to an automation fund. What they need to do now is act on it. If they should do so, and this seems likely, the printers will have a much needed cushion. And some, no doubt, will survive as computer punch operators or machinists servicing the new machines. Powers, essentially, is an optimist. He believes that after the period of adjustment, printing will be "a great industry. Costs will go down; more things will be printed." He obviously hopes that the union will survive. But the observer can't escape the feeling that he is watching a once great craft die.

[Eds. Note: *The automation issue described in this article was not settled by the agreement which was finally reached by the Publishers and the Typographical Union. This agreement, reached without a strike, calls for negotiations about the introduction of automated equipment between each publisher and Local 6 of the Typographical Union. The negotiations will be conducted while a two-year collective bargaining contract is in force.*]

worker security

Joel Seidman
THE UNION AGENDA FOR SECURITY

. . . The main varieties of union responses to worker insecurity are: (1) Programs to increase or preserve job opportunities and income security, (2) programs to allocate the remaining jobs equitably, and (3) programs to ease the burden on those displaced.

JOB AND INCOME PROTECTION

The labor movement learned long ago in this country as in others that it could not bar technological progress and that efforts to do so were sure to fail. Instead, unions have sought to control the rate of technological advance, to minimize its dislocating effects, to reduce the workweek, or to obtain for workers—both those displaced and those remaining in employment—a share of the proceeds. Some unions, as on the railroads, have fought a delaying action to preserve the largest possible number of jobs, while others, as in coal mining, have put no obstacles in the path of technological progress. Union manning requirements, along with resistance to new materials and output controls, have led to management charges of obstructionism, particularly in railroading, construction, printing, and entertainment. In some of the cases, however, safety or reasonable working speeds are objectives, along with the creation or preservation of job opportunities.

Excerpted from the *Monthly Labor Review*, June 1963.
Mr. Seidman is Professor of Industrial Relations, University of Chicago.

In a direct approach to job protection, the Railroad Telegraphers, hard hit by transference of work to other crafts, general force reductions, and the threatened closing of little used stations, won an agreement from the Southern Pacific Railroad in October 1961 that no more than 2 percent of a specified number of jobs could be abolished in any one year; the settlement guaranteed 40 hours' work or pay per week to men on the extra board, and provided severance benefits for laid-off employees. Similar issues led to a 30-day strike against the Chicago & North Western Railway in 1962, which was resolved by a similar agreement, except that the carrier won the right to abolish jobs, provided it gave 90 days' notice and severance pay according to length of service. The differences in the settlements may be due to the fact that the Southern Pacific had been expanding its operations in a rapidly growing section of the country, whereas the Chicago & North Western had been retrenching.

A somewhat less rigid approach has been taken by the Transit Authority of the City of New York, which has agreed with the Transport Workers that permanent employees will not be laid off because of automation or other improvements in efficiency of operation but will be assigned to other duties without reduction in pay. Similarly, the recent New York City newspaper strike settlement permitted the publishers to set stock exchange tables with the use of outside teletypesetter tape, provided no employees would be laid off as a result; publishers will make savings by reducing the force as printers leave their service.

In the basic steel industry, the clause denying companies the right to change local working conditions even in the absence of technological innovation was retained after figuring prominently in the 1959 strike, though not all companies had the clause or found it a burden. Nevertheless, some job losses not related to technological change have occurred in particular operations in the recent years of low plant capacity use in instances when management traded increased production at a plant for the size of crew it thought appropriate. . . .

Following a different approach, the Musicians established Music Performance Trust Funds in 1948, placing a tax upon mechanical devices to support personal performances by instrumental musicians. Under the current agreement, recording companies pay to a trustee from 1.2 to 2.9 percent of their manufacturer's suggested retail price, for free performances at educational, charitable, or civic activities.

Much of the union effort to increase the number of job opportunities has taken the form of reduction in the hours of work without a cut in take-home pay. . . . In the controversy over shorter hours, it is sometimes forgotten that the 40-hour workweek is no longer standard, shorter hours having already been achieved in a number of industries. Akron rubber companies, for example, led by Goodyear, instituted the 6-hour day and 6-day week in 1930 in an effort to share the work. The International Ladies' Garment Workers' Union won its first 35-hour, 5-day agreement in 1933. In the printing industry, the prevalent workweek has long been shorter than 40 hours.

New York City construction electricians, who had enjoyed a basic 30-hour workweek since 1934, won a basic 25-hour week in January 1962; under both agreements, 5 hours of overtime were guaranteed weekly at time and a half. In the fall of 1962, construction electricians in Chicago won the 7-hour workday, and in a number of other industries the 37½- or 35-hour workweek has already been achieved.

Another way of reducing hours of work, thereby opening up job opportunities for the unemployed and for new entrants to the labor force, has been lengthening paid vacation periods. Once limited primarily to salaried, white-collar workers, paid vacations for manufacturing workers expanded in the late 1930's, with an employer-financed, pooled vacation fund established in the ladies' garment industry in 1937. The freeze on direct wage increases during World War II gave a strong impetus to the spread of paid vacations.

The principle of paid vacations is now generally accepted for blue-collar workers, except in industries where job changes are frequent and seasonal layoffs common. Whereas the 2-week paid vacation was most common a decade ago, by the late 1950's the 3- or 3½-week vacation maximum was most widely in use, and at the present time, the maximum is 4 weeks in a large and growing number of graduated vacation plans, with the 5-week maximum found in some instances.

In 1962, the United Steelworkers negotiated an unusual vacation clause with the Continental Can and American Can Companies, providing a 13-week vacation every 5 years for employees with 15 or more years of service. Teamster local unions in the New York City brewing industry, which had already achieved a 35-hour workweek with 4 weeks' vacation after 5 years' employment, recently negotiated a "vacation security" clause under which vacation time has been increased to a maximum of 7 weeks for those with service over 25 years. For the first 2 years, the additional weeks can be taken only as needed, under joint union-management decision, to prevent layoff; at the end of that time, the unused time may be taken by the employee at his own option. . . .

While overtime, with its premium rate of pay, is welcome to large numbers of workers, the UAW has criticized some managements for scheduling overtime rather than increasing the number of workers on their payrolls. To discourage this practice, for which it says penalty pay of time and a half is not a sufficient deterrent, the UAW proposes double pay for overtime, with triple pay for work above 10 hours a day or on Sunday.

Whereas the movement toward shorter hours of work has as a major objective the creation of additional job opportunities, the effort to obtain work or wage guarantees seeks greater income security for those already on the payroll. Beginning in the latter years of the last century, various types of wage and work guarantees were extended by management, usually in relatively stable consumer goods industries. Following World War II, labor efforts to obtain comparable guarantees in such industries as automobiles and steel manufacturing led to the extension of supplemental unemployment benefits, beginning with the Ford-UAW agreement of 1955.

Work or wage guarantees have been developed extensively in the meatpacking industry. Even under the recent downward modification, the Hormel plan, one of the oldest and best known in American industry, still guarantees annually, to every worker who establishes seniority, 1,872 work hours or the equivalent pay, with provision that no one can be laid off without 52 weeks' notice. In the sugar refining industry, the Packinghouse Workers has attained a work guarantee of 52 weeks of 40 hours each year. In its contracts throughout the packing industry, the same union has a provision, first obtained in 1945, that a worker who is not laid off by the end of a working week enjoys a guarantee of 36 working hours for the week that follows.

A number of other unions have negotiated some sort of guarantee. Such guarantees are found in the organized retail industry, where the contracts of the Retail, Wholesale and Department Store Union generally provide for 52 weeks' pay yearly for all full-time employees.

The Teamsters Union has obtained a number of guaranteed wage plans, especially in the St. Louis area, with a guarantee of 2,000 hours of work a year applying to a varying percentage of the work force in different plants. Laundry workers in New York City, represented by an affiliate of the Amalgamated Clothing Workers, are guaranteed either 40 hours of work a week or a weekly wage. A UAW contract with the Buffalo Machinery Co. provides an annual salary for shop workers, to be paid despite sickness, absence for urgent personal reasons, or production difficulties. This represents the achievement, on behalf of production employees of a small company, of the kind of income security enjoyed by white-collar workers—a bargaining objective that the UAW is asking to obtain throughout its industry. The UAW contract with the Air Reduction Sales Co. of Lima, Ohio, stipulates that any employee who works at any time during a workweek is guaranteed 40 hours of working opportunity during that week or its equivalent in pay. . . .

A few unions, particularly those in the needle trades, have sought to increase job opportunities for their members by promotion of their industry's products. Union label campaigns are another device to promote the sales of unionized segments of industry.

The Millinery Workers has engaged in other unusual efforts to conserve jobs. In 1961, when the Merrimac Hat Co. of Amesbury, Mass., found itself in a precarious financial position, the union raised half a milion dollars of capital funds to become majority stockholder, thus preserving the jobs of its 325 members in the company's employ. In 1954, when the Kartiganer Hat Corp. was in financial difficulty, the union lent $50,000 to the company and encouraged the unionized employees to lend an additional $200 each, increasing the rescue fund to $180,000. The latter firm, which is in a healthy position today, has repaid the loan in full. The union has also purchased one loft building and lent mortgage money on a second, in order to preserve buildings in which women's hats were manufactured and sold. The Amalgamated Clothing Workers, which for many years has operated its own banks in New York City and Chicago, has also extended credit to employers in order to save jobs. In other cases, as in the hosiery industry and in meatpacking, union members have taken substantial cuts in pay to dissuade employers from closing their plants or from moving to lower wage areas. . . .

PROTECTION OF THE DISPLACED

A number of programs ease the burden on those who are displaced by technological advance or who lose their jobs for other reasons beyond their control. Of particular importance are severance pay, supplementary unemployment benefits, liberalized pensions and early retirement provisions, and retraining programs. In addition, there have been several joint union-management efforts, of which the Armour Automation Fund is perhaps the best known, to study the human problems caused by technological displacements.

SEVERANCE PAY. Recently, there has been increasingly wide acceptance of the principle of severance pay, the amount of which is usually linked to the employee's length of service. Some unions, such as the Newspaper Guild, have long negotiated a model contract clause providing that the employee, upon termination of his employment, is to receive a lump sum equal to 3 weeks' pay for each year of service. Some unions negotiate a graduated scale, with workers receiving more severance pay per year for service after perhaps 10 or 20 years. The ILGWU negotiated an industrywide plan in 1960, covering 450,000 garment workers, providing for weekly payments of $12.50 to $25 to be paid for as long as 48 weeks. Each eligible worker also receives one-fourth of his total benefits in a lump sum. The fund, planned to reach a total of $10 million, is financed by employers' contributions of 0.5 percent of payrolls.

One of the highest benefit severance pay plans was negotiated in 1962 by Trans World Airlines in resolving the stubborn dispute involving the Air Line Pilots Association and the Flight Engineers incident to the reduction of jet cockpit crews from four men to three. Incumbent engineers were given priority to fill the third cockpit seat, providing they qualified as pilots. For those who decided against taking pilot training, or who failed the course, severance pay ranging from $10,000 to $39,400 was provided. In Hawaii, displaced longshoremen receive severance allowances under ILWU contracts that sometimes exceed $10,000, with the unusual provision that men wishing to return to their country of origin— usually the Philippines or Japan—may receive free transportation.

SUPPLEMENTARY UNEMPLOYMENT BENEFITS.   Supplementary unemployment benefits, earlier referred to, have spread widely since their adoption in the automobile industry in 1955. Since then, there have been constant efforts by unions to increase the sums paid under the plans and to lengthen the period of benefits. The 1961 General Motors agreement, for example, raised the combined payments under unemployment compensation and supplementary unemployment benefits from 65 to nearly 75 percent of take-home pay, and increased the benefit period from 26 (temporarily 39) weeks to 52.

PENSIONS AND EARLY RETIREMENT.   Recognizing the difficulties confronting older workers who are displaced, a large number of unions have sought to ease the burden on them through pensions that supplement social security benefits or that provide for their wants until they are eligible for such benefits. In some cases, early and liberalized benefits are provided under union-management pension funds in order to persuade senior employees to retire, thus securing job opportunities for younger workers or preventing their displacement. Though early retirement can be very costly, it protects the group that would have greatest difficulty finding other jobs. By late 1960, over 11 million workers, or 60 percent of those under union contracts, were covered by collectively bargained pension plans. Nearly nine-tenths of 300 plans analyzed by the BLS in the fall of 1959 permitted retirement under early or disability retirement provisions. Three-fifths of them provided for compulsory or automatic retirement, or some combination of these involuntary provisions.

One of the early union-management pension plans was set up in the bituminous coal mining industry as part of a general welfare program financed by a royalty on tonnage mined. Under this program, which also provided sickness, disability, and death benefits, miners who had worked

20 years in the industry were eligible for pensions of $100 a month when they reached the age of 62. More recently, however, as the fund has encountered financial difficulties, pension and welfare benefits payable under its provisions have had to be reduced. Such difficulties, to be expected in a declining industry with large numbers of aged former employees, illustrate the problems that may be encountered in a nonvested, privately negotiated plan, dependent upon revenue from a single industry, as against a broadly based Government program supported by taxes.

Where small employing units predominate, unions have negotiated industrywide pension plans, permitting labor mobility without loss of benefits while easing the financial burden on each employer. The ILGWU set up an employer-financed pooled retirement fund in 1943, and the Amalgamated Clothing Workers has arranged, through reciprocity among areas and branches of its industry, for members who change jobs or move to retain their rights to retirement benefits, prorating the costs among the various funds involved. Workers represented by the UAW at General Motors and Ford since 1955 have had vested pension rights. While some unions urge pension plans with vesting, other do not, permitting the loss of accumulated pension rights for workers who leave the industry and the union. The Retail Clerks in California has developed areawide pension programs, under which employees may shift from company to company without loss of rights.

Several other union-negotiated or union-sponsored pension provisions will illustrate the wide variety of practices found in this field. . . . The Central States, Southeast, and Southwest areas pension fund of the Teamsters has recently reduced the normal retirement age of covered workers from 60 to 57. The retirement plans of the Packinghouse Workers, amended in 1961, now call for payment of $2.50 a month for each year of service. An employee of 55 with 20 years of service who is displaced because of technological advance or plant shutdown, draws his full pension plus 50 percent until he is eligible for his social security pension, at which time his payment from the industry will be reduced to its normal amount. Retirement is compulsory at age 65. The UAW has negotiated comparable provisions in the automobile and farm equipment industries. Under agreements of the Street and Electric Railway Employes in Washington, D.C., and in St. Louis, employees who cannot qualify for positions as a result of changeovers from streetcar to bus operations are entitled to pensions. The Typographical Union, whose members' pensions are paid from union dues, is now seeking additional pension benefits through collective bargaining.

In an unusual experiment, contracts of New York District 65 of the Retail, Wholesale and Department Store Union provide for trial retirement for workers age 60 or older, who may retire for as long as 6 months and then return to work without loss of seniority or other benefits. The union, which is opposed to compulsory retirement, found that many members failed to take advantage of voluntary retirement programs because they feared that the reduced income would be insufficient for their needs, or because they were fearful in other ways of their future in retirement. Most of the two dozen members who have taken advantage of trial retirement have chosen to remain retired, the others returning to work for short periods of time or on a part-time basis.

RETRAINING PROGRAMS.   Unions have also sponsored, sometimes alone and sometimes with industry, government agencies, or both, a variety of programs to help prepare those currently employed for more demanding jobs or to retrain workers displaced by technological advance for skills more in demand in American industry. Under the rulings in some States, however, unemployed workers who attend retraining programs lose their right to unemployment insurance, since they are considered unavailable for work. A great many craft unions have supplemented apprenticeship programs with efforts to develop journeyman job skills or keep members abreast of changing technology. Perhaps the most elaborate such effort sponsored solely by a labor organization is that conducted by the Typographical Union, which operates a $2,500,000 training center in Colorado Springs, Colo., which has trained some 2,000 members in various new printing processes since it opened several years ago. The International Brotherhood of Electrical Workers, which among other educational projects has developed a 2-year industrial electronics course, estimated in the fall of 1962 that 50,000 journeymen members of the union were then engaged in or had completed one or more courses designed to improve their job skills.

A number of unions have agreements with employers which provide for retraining displaced workers or create a fund to finance such training programs. One of the most ambitious of these, established in 1959 by Armour and Co. in cooperation with the Packinghouse Workers and the Amalgamated Meat Cutters, has sought to train displaced workers for whatever skills seemed to be in demand for which they had the necessary basic qualifications. Several hundred workers have thus far participated in retraining programs, with inconclusive results. Nevertheless, such efforts contribute to an understanding of the problems involved in technological displacement and retraining.

Another union-management venture, similar in many ways to the Armour effort, was developed in February 1962 by U.S. Industries, Inc., and the Machinists, which have set up a Foundation on Automation and

Employment, financed by contributions scaled to the sale or lease price of the company's automated machines, to study the problems of workers affected by technological change.

In 1961, International Good Music, in cooperation with the IBEW, set up a trust fund, financed by 5 percent of its receipts from the sales of automated equipment and program service, for retraining radio or television employees displaced as a result of such sales. In other situations, workers are retrained for jobs with the same employer, as when local transportation companies change from streetcars to buses. The UAW has proposed a program of aptitude tests, training opportunities, and job preference, to facilitate transfer of production workers to white-collar vacancies with the same company. A local of the Communications Workers of America has itself subsidized testing of operators who might be displaced by automatic equipment, to see whether they have the aptitudes necessary for clerical jobs with the company. Several operators whose tests showed high aptitude were then tested by the company and transferred to clerical work.

CONCLUSIONS

This review of union efforts to alleviate insecurity illustrates the wide diversity of programs that have been undertaken, particularly in recent years. Relying primarily upon collective bargaining, but also seeking to influence governmental action where appropriate, unions have sought to preserve or increase the number of jobs, to allocate declining job opportunities equitably through the operation of seniority, and to provide severance pay, retirement benefits, or retraining to ease the lot of displaced workers. Though most such measures find unions arrayed against managements, in some instances labor and management in the same industry have joint interests against rival industries. Still other issues, such as the "bumping" rights of displaced workers or the carrying of seniority to other plants of multiplant companies, reveal differences of interest within union ranks, while measures such as the raising of the statutory minimum wage may split management groups. Struggles over jurisdictional rights, on the other hand, find different national or local unions in conflict with each other.

As a chronic problem of insecurity developed in the postwar period, a wide variety of devices in various industries and over a period of years have been employed in efforts to solve the problems of job and income insecurity. Devices developed to deal with one problem have sometimes been adapted to serve another purpose as well, as with the use of bargained pension plans, originally devised to supplement social security benefits, to promote early retirement.

Faced with a general problem of job and income insecurity, the leaders of each union have sought to develop protection for their members in the light of the particular situation. How successful they are in this, as in other bargaining demands, has depended upon many factors. Once a particular measure has been achieved in a key union-management bargain in a leading industry, a pattern-following process is set in motion in that industry, along with a widespread tendency for the device to be copied by or adapted to a number of other industries.

Sometimes a farsighted management with a sense of social responsibility has taken the initiative in solving some of the problems of insecurity that industrial developments have brought in their wake. In other cases, the problems have been beyond the ability of particular companies and unions—or even of industries—to solve, and have depended on governmental action. Union-management programs in some cases have been able to provide job security to those already employed, although at the price of providing less opportunity to the unemployed or to new entrants to the labor force. Efforts to provide improved benefits to the unemployed or to those past retirement age depend primarily on legislative enactments, just as the development of a full employment economy is a task for which Government must take final responsibility. With the failure of our economy to expand sufficiently rapidly in recent years, unions have placed more emphasis on Government programs to provide job protection and encourage economic growth.

Even the achievement of a full employment economy, however, would not solve all the problems of worker insecurity. Shifts would still occur in the occupational structure of the country, particular companies or industries would decline as others expanded, and particular areas of the country would experience a relative loss of job opportunities. Unions would still seek as best they could to provide income and job security for their members. With greater security in the economy as a whole, however, unions and management would be more likely to cooperate for productive efficiency, with higher living standards the reward for all.

hours of work

*National Association
of Manufacturers*

THE ISSUE
OF THE SHORTER WORK WEEK

The discussion of the "shorter work week issue" which follows is intended solely as a contribution to public understanding of the subject. It is no part of the purpose of this document to present any point of view as to how long the work week ought to be. In a free society the choice between leisure and productive work is one to be made by the people. Industry has neither the power nor the desire to make that choice for them. . . .

It is pointless to argue that, in some absolute sense, we cannot "afford" a shorter work week. We can always afford it if we are willing to pay the price. It has been estimated, for example, that if the American people were willing to live at the standard of living prevalent a century ago they could produce enough goods and services for that purpose by working only 12 hours a week. It is not likely that modern man would be content with the same standard of living as his great-grandfather, but the choice is at least theoretically open to him.

DOES MORE LEISURE HAVE A PRICE?

More realistically, the chief current danger comes from another kind of misunderstanding—the notion that somehow we can have a

Abridged by permission from *What Is at Stake in a Shorter Work Week?* Industrial Relations Division, National Association of Manufacturers, undated.

shorter work week without giving up anything in return for it. The thought is seldom stated so directly, but it is clearly implied by some current arguments. Thus the slogan "40 hours pay for 32 hours work," seems designed to create the impression that there is some magic in wage policy which would allow us to get around the fact that what we have to consume is only what we produce, and we can always produce more in 40 hours than in 32.

In the past, the American economy has had a gradual increase in its productivity, although this has not occurred uniformly in all sectors of the economy or in every year of our history. The growth of productivity has been the result of improvements in technology and increased investment in productive facilities. Output per man hour has increased at a long-term average rate of about two and one half per cent a year—perhaps not a very impressive figure on a year-to-year basis but one which accumulates to impressive totals over the decades.

Historically, American workers have taken the benefit of that increased productivity partly in the form of increased leisure and partly in the form of increased "real wages." They have had both a reduction in the average work week and an improvement in their standard of living, as measured in terms of their per capita consumption of goods and services.

There is no reason why this process should not continue into the future, if that is what people want. The point is that if we are to have a simultaneous increase in leisure and in standards of living, the two together cannot exceed the gain in productivity, which in the past has been at an average rate of about two and one half per cent a year. If we are to have both, both must occur at a very gradual pace. Thus it would appear that any abrupt, drastic, and widespread reduction of the work week is ruled out.

It is well to remember that even a gradual and a moderate reduction in the work week has its price. Such a process means that living standards cannot rise as fast as they would if the benefits of rising productivity were wholly allocated to increased output.

But there is a larger question to be asked. Do people really want more leisure? Or, if given a free choice, would they prefer to take *all* the gain from rising productivity in the form of more goods and services?

There is a certain amount of evidence to indicate that at present the desire for more goods or services is stronger among American consumers generally than is the desire for more leisure. The question may be left open, but in any case a choice in favor of maintaining the present work week would certainly be legitimate and understandable. . . .

SOME FACTS ABOUT THE WORK WEEK

A few elementary facts about the length of the working week may help to put the issue in broader perspective.

First, although the 40 hour week is generally regarded as "standard," the working time of American employees actually varies over a considerable range. To illustrate, the table which follows shows the distribution of the total average number of people at work in 1963, classified according to the number of hours they worked per week:

	NUMBER OF PERSONS (MONTHLY AVERAGE, 1963)
Worked 1 to 14 hours	4,245,000
Worked 15 to 21 hours	3,265,000
Worked 22 to 29 hours	2,678,000
Worked 30 to 34 hours	3,200,000
Worked 35 to 39 hours	4,114,000
Worked 40 hours	26,058,000
Worked 41 to 47 hours	5,159,000
Worked 48 hours	4,245,000
Worked 49 to 59 hours	6,009,000
Worked 60 hours or more	6,400,000
Total persons at work	65,308,000
Average working week	40.4

Of the over 65 million persons at work only 39.8 per cent were reported as working exactly 40 hours. Over 17 million persons worked less—some of them substantially less—than 40 hours. About 22 million worked more than 40 hours, including almost 6½ million who worked more than 60 hours.

This variation in the length of the working week reflects on the one side the varying requirements of different businesses and on the other the varying employment needs and desires of the labor force.

Several points may be drawn from these statistics. First, the American economy provides a variety of "working weeks" in different situations, and this gives people a measure of choice as to the hours they will work. Second, it is rather pointless to speak of the working week, or to discuss the issue as though a monolithic decision could be made as to how long *the* working week ought to be in the future.

Another set of facts with an important bearing on the issue is the record of past changes in the length of the average work week. The past record is as follows:

	AVERAGE NUMBER OF HOURS WORKED PER WEEK (EXCLUDING FARM WORKERS)
1890	60.4
1900	58.7
1910	55.6
1920	50.9
1930	47.8
1935	42.6
1940	43.3
1945	45.3
1950	41.8
1960	40.4
1963	40.1
1964 (10 month average)	39.7

This record is interesting in several respects. Aside from the fluctuations due to the depression in the 1930's and World War II, there has been a fairly steady downward trend in the length of the average work week. There is no evidence of any recent acceleration in the rate of change. In the thirty-four years between 1930 and 1964, the average work week was reduced by 8 hours, and in the preceding 30 years it was reduced by almost 11 hours.

There is no clear indication in these figures that the Fair Labor Standards Act passed in the late 1930's, or the other social legislation of that period, or the growth in labor union strength resulting from the Wagner Act, had any substantial effect in reducing the length of the work week. What has occurred during the past three decades seems to be a continuation of previously established trends.

WHAT DETERMINES THE LENGTH OF THE WORK WEEK?

It is clear that we can speak of *the* work week only as an average of widely-varying individual experiences.

There are some few individuals who work on a free-lance basis and can make their own choice, practically on a day-to-day basis, as between income and leisure. Most of us, however, prefer a steady job and thus must fit our own desires in with the needs and customary procedures of the organization. It is simply not practical to allow employees to decide for themselves each day whether they will report for work, or whether they will forego income in favor of leisure for that day. In addition, employees must in many cases adapt themselves to changes in the working week necessitated by short-term changes in the level of business. Management has, and must have, a considerable area for discretion in scheduling the work week.

Does this mean that employees have no choice as to how their lives are to be divided between work and leisure—that management makes the choice for them? Such a conclusion is only partly true in the short run, and it is not true at all in the long run.

In the short run problem of scheduling working time week-by-week, management discretion is limited in many ways. Firms in interstate commerce have to face the fact that working time beyond 40 hours a week must be paid for at premium rates. In many cases labor agreements prescribe additional limitations on management's freedom to schedule work. Even in the absence of such agreements, custom in the industry and the locality often limits the employer's freedom in this respect. Finally, even in the short run, no firm can ignore the desires of its employees as to working time without risking increased labor turnover, damage to employee morale and hence increased cost by a reduction in productivity.

In the long run, management has to face the problem of attracting and keeping the number and quality of employees it needs. It will not be successful unless it can offer arrangements as to working time which, in broad outline at least, are satisfactory to prospective employees. In the practical workings of business, employers cannot gratify every whim of every individual who works for them. But neither can they completely flout the wishes of their employees who, after all, are free to stay or to go.

In answer to the question "What determines the length of the work week?" the most that can be said is that it represents a meeting of the minds between employers and employees. Neither side can ever be completely satisfied; that would be too much to expect. But both sides must find the situation satisfactory in a broad-gauge sense or, being free individuals, they would not consent to it.

This meeting-of-the-minds process has resulted in a reduction of the average work week from almost 60 hours at the turn of the century to about 40 hours at present. As already stated, it does not appear that the Fair Labor Standards Act resulted in a reduction in working hours any more rapid than occurred prior to that legislation. Thus the conclusion is that the trend in the work week has been in conformity with the free choice of working people as to how they wanted to divide the fruits of technological progress between more leisure and more goods.

Would we be better off if we substituted some form of arbitrary intervention for the "meeting-of-the-minds," in the determination of the length of the work week in the future? Such a development would not affect the fact that all we have to divide is the gains from rising productivity. Arbitrary intervention would simply mean that the outcome is less likely to be in accord with actual gains in productivity or with people's desires. . . .

There has been much discussion recently of our "new" age of technology, and some people have concluded that productivity is now growing at a much faster rate than was historically the case. Yet there is no evidence for this conclusion. The growth of productivity since World War II has been well within the range of previous experience. In examining the possibility for decreasing the work week in the future the safest assumption is that productivity growth will continue at a rate of about two and a half per cent per year.

As an illustration of the amount of leeway this gives, it may be pointed out that a reduction in the average work week from 40 hours to 32 hours would require an offsetting increase in productivity of 25 per cent. At two and a half per cent a year it would take a decade to achieve this. But it would be a decade—the first in our history—in which real wages did not increase at all. If productivity growth is allocated wholly to providing more leisure there is nothing left over for raising the standard of living.

If the American people chose to use their productivity increase in increased leisure time, there remains the question as to what form this increased leisure would take. They would have the option between more individual holidays, longer vacations, extended weekends, a shorter day, earlier retirement, longer schooling prior to entering the work force and other forms of time off from working.

The intention in citing these illustrations is not to dismiss the shorter work week as completely impractical. It is practical, but only within limitations that are narrower than is generally realized, and only at a price that is not always taken into account.

The shorter work week proposal sometimes takes the form of the recommendation that, either through legislation or collective bargaining, the point at which premium over-time rates start should be lowered. Thus time-and-a-half might be paid for working time in excess of 32 hours a week, instead of for working time in excess of 40 hours a week. People are led to believe that they would continue to work the same number of weekly hours, but that a greater number of their hours would be paid for at the attractive over-time rates.

To the extent that actual working time *is* maintained, such a measure would be merely a disguised form of wage increase. It would have exactly the same inflationary effects as any other kind of wage increase which is in excess of the productivity increase.

But, whatever might be the intention, there is no guarantee that a proposal of this type would not eventually result in a cut in actual working hours. Certainly under such an arrangement employers would have a strong incentive to reduce working hours by hiring more people or by changing their production methods. Employees who had hoped to earn more premium pay might find that instead they were sharing their old weekly pay-check with newcomers. . . .

It is a misunderstanding of the problem to say that, in order to preserve their jobs, workers *must* take the benefit of automation or other improvements in technology in the form of shorter hours—whether they want to take it that way or not. The question of the length of the work week should rather be viewed as an option: what is the relative value to workers of more leisure as compared with more income?

The American productive system has performed great things in the past in providing both more leisure and more goods for the American people. There is every reason to believe that it can continue to do so provided that decisions with respect to economic issues, such as this one, take into account the considerations outlined above as they apply to individual enterprises.

AFL–CIO
RESOLUTION ON REDUCTION OF HOURS

. . . One important way of increasing job opportunities, a way not given adequate attention in recent years, is to reduce work time without loss of pay. Organized labor does not argue that reduction of hours will itself solve all employment problems. We will continue to press with all our might for the variety of national policies and programs necessary to provide full employment. But in this economy, in which the choice is often cutting employment or cutting hours, reduction of hours without loss of pay must be an ingredient of our attack on unemployment.

We continue to hold an open mind on the pace, method, and form of hours reduction. But we cannot close our eyes to the evidence of new technology's impact, the coming expanded flow of youngsters into the labor market, and the inability of existing national economic policies to achieve full employment. We believe active attention must be directed now to obtaining substantial reduction of standard working hours in the 1960s.

Adopted by 4th AFL–CIO Convention, December 1961. Reprinted by permission from *Shorter Hours: Tool to Combat Unemployment*, AFL–CIO Department of Research, undated, pp. 49–53.

The speed of hours reduction must depend on the rate of national economic growth and the practical situation in the labor market. If economic growth proceeds so slowly that unemployment remains at high levels and threatens to mount further, standard working hours should be cut at a rapid rate, with no loss in take-home pay, in order to spread employment opportunities. If economic growth picks up so rapidly that it succeeds in reducing unemployment substantially below the level of recent years, then the pace of standard hours reduction could be slowed.

Collective bargaining is a fundamental method through which standard working hours can be cut, but public action, principally through legislation, must also be undertaken to provide the most widespread reduction.

Labor and management should through their collective bargaining move to find and make effective various means of reducing hours. Lowering the hours in the standard workweek through reduction in the number of hours per day or days per week is the most common approach, but consideration should be given as well to other means:

Substantial extension of paid vacations and paid holidays can reduce the number of hours worked per year. (An additional 4 weeks' annual paid vacation for each worker would reduce typical worktime by 160 hours a year or, in effect, by only about 3 hours a week.)

Earlier retirement, with benefits sufficient to make it a reward rather than a punishment for age, would reduce years of work.

Phasing retirement, so that the potential retirees' work time is gradually reduced as they approach retirement age, could helpfully reduce hours and serve retirement-preparation needs.

The paid sabbatical leave approach, as observed in the teaching profession, would provide hours reduction and enable workers to pursue avocations for which leisure time is now inadequate.

A control of overtime work during periods of unemployment would help assure that such hours of work are not simply for the convenience of management but are economically just.

Collective bargaining measures, though extremely vital, proceed essentially on an individual company or industry basis and therefore can at best affect only limited sectors of the economy in any period. It cannot be relied on to .achieve hours reductions as rapidly and widely as required by the economy as a whole.

The federal government can helpfully facilitate bargaining progress in this field by encouraging management and labor to reduce hours according to the practical conditions in each industry and labor market. But broader government action, through legislation, is required in order to have hours reduced on the scale needed to meet the overall national problem. . . .

Although the principal value of hours reduction is its contribution to solution of the unemployment problem, shorter hours of work are of course desirable for noneconomic reasons as well. It is appropriate socially and morally that part of our technological progress be translated into a reduction of the hours workers are required to labor. Reduction of hours of work will open paths to new and expanded social, cultural, recreational, and educational activities for the working population. And for many it is needed to help offset the increasing travel time to and from work required by urban traffic congestion and lengthening of commuting distances. . . .

Now therefore, be it resolved:

> Reduction in standard hours of work with no loss of pay should be sought as a vital part of our total program to solve the problem of unemployment, to convert our rapid technological progress into a boon rather than a burden, and to bolster the long-term economic and social health of our society. We shall seek urgent exploration of the various approaches and obstacles to such beneficial reduction of hours.
>
> We call upon all affiliated unions to give the highest priority to the search for and negotiation of ways to reduce hours of work to assure adequate job opportunities now and in the future.
>
> We urge the Congress to devote immediate attention to the legislation necessary to provide adjustments in the standard workweek without loss of pay consistent with the economic needs of the nation and the national objective of a full-employment economy.
>
> We urge favorable consideration of the proposal for flexible adjustment of the standard workweek based upon levels of unemployment and utilization of the labor force.
>
> We urge the International Labor Organization to adopt the international recommendation it is considering for a shorter workweek to help aid the improvement of hours standards around the world.

Sar A. Levitan
REDUCTION OF HOURS:
WORKERS' ATTITUDES

It is difficult to generalize about workers' preference between extra leisure and added income. Evidence seems to indicate that younger and older workers and females, particularly married women with household responsibilities, prefer shorter hours to additional income. The bulk of the 13 million who worked part time and averaged 22 hours per week in 1963 belonged in these groups and did not desire full-time work. A significant proportion of these might not have worked at all if they had been required to work regular hours. On the other hand, males of the prime labor force participation age seem to prefer to maximize income instead of leisure. The available data on moonlighting supports this generalization. While women constituted more than a third of the total labor force in 1963, they accounted for only a seventh of the total moonlighters. Nearly half of the multiple jobholders were males aged 25 to 44, though they comprised only two-sevenths of all those employed.

A study of grievances arising under collective bargaining agreements suggests that workers seem to place a high premium on overtime work. According to an American Arbitration Association study, claims by employees that they were not given their rightful share of overtime work ranked fourth as a cause of grievance. Frictions arising out of matters pertaining to discipline, seniority, and job-content changes were the only causes of grievance cited more frequently.

Public opinion polls would seem to indicate strong oppositon to shortening the hours of work, even among union members. In response to a Gallup Poll question on whether weekly hours should be reduced from 40 to 35 hours, 42 percent of union members responded affirmatively, 52 percent opposed the reduction in hours, and 6 percent offered no opinion. The poll inquired whether "the workweek in most industries should or should not be reduced from 40 to 35 hours," but gave no reason for the need to reduce hours. The AFL-CIO has justifiably questioned

From Sar A. Levitan, *Reducing Worktime as a Means to Combat Unemployment,* The W. E. Upjohn Institute for Employment Research, 1964, pp. 10–11.

the objectivity of the Gallup Poll. For example, an International Association of Machinists local in San Diego polled its members on the same point as the Gallup Poll, but pointedly questioned the members whether they would favor a reduction in hours "in view of the prospect of more layoffs. . . ." Ninety-six percent of the respondents in this case favored the reduction in hours. They were not asked whether they would be willing to reduce their hours and earnings in order to share the work with the laid-off workers. It is questionable whether the union members would have been as enthusiastic about a reduction in hours if it had involved a reduction in their earnings.

The experience of the Teamsters Union suggests the preference of workers to maximize earnings at the cost of excessively long hours of work. Over-the-road truckers are not covered by the Fair Labor Standards Act and do not receive premium overtime pay after 40 hours of work per week. Long hours of work up to the legal limit of 60 hours per week are common in the industry. When a bill was proposed in Congress to extend coverage of the FLSA to over-the-road truckers and thus to require the payment of time and a half after 40 hours of work per week, the union opposed the provision because it would encourage employers to reduce hours of work and thus cut the earnings of the members. Formally, the union's opposition to applying FLSA overtime provisions to over-the-road trucking was based on the argument that the railroad industry, the major competitor to trucking, is not subject to FLSA provisions, and that if FLSA coverage were to be extended, it should apply equally to both industries.

The early experience under the "sabbatical" plan of the steel industry would also support the contention that workers normally prefer added income to increased leisure. According to the *Wall Street Journal* survey, mentioned earlier, the majority of non-union employees who were granted the same vacation plan won by the union preferred the extra pay instead of the 13-week vacation. The contract specifically prohibits production workers covered by the contract from accepting extra pay in lieu of the extended vacation, but nonexecutive salaried workers who are not covered by the contract were given that choice by some companies. One company gave its clerical workers a choice of two weeks' extra vacation or two weeks' extra pay each year; 45 percent of the workers chose the additional earnings.

The evidence seems to be clear that union championing of reduced hours is based on the desire to reduce unemployment rather than to increase leisure time. . . .

strategy

Arthur Neff
BOULWAREISM
AND THE DUTY TO BARGAIN

. . . General Electric's present approach to employee and union relations was first conceived in 1947 and developed largely under the guidance of Lemuel R. Boulware, then and for many years later GE's Vice-President-Relations-Service. The approach has often been referred to as "Boulwareism," although GE itself abjures use of that term, claiming it has been misconstrued by outsiders to reflect a concept not actually GE's. It came into being as an aftermath of a lengthy company-wide strike which the UE had conducted against GE in 1946. That strike was settled only after GE raised its wage offer from a prestrike 10 cents an hour to a poststrike 18½ cents an hour. As appears from one Company report, GE's management regarded UE's "highly successful strike" as "little short of a debacle." Management had theretofore had a "feeling" of "security in the knowledge that the Company had been a good employer [which] had treated employees fairly, and had pioneered in the voluntary installation of many employee benefit programs." Nevertheless, the strike had been "broadly supported" by employees. The realization that

Excerpted from the Report of the Trial Examiner (Arthur Neff) to the National Labor Relations Board in the case of General Electric Corporation and the International Union of Electrical, Radio and Machine Workers, 1963. The Report found that GE had not fulfilled its "duty to bargain" legal obligation. This decision was upheld by the NLRB and was subsequently appealed to the Federal courts by GE, where it is now pending.

its earlier feeling of security had been a false one was a "somber event" for GE management.

The jolt of the 1946 strike led GE management to take a new look. GE sought to determine why it had failed (as it saw it) to achieve the same high degree of success and effectiveness in its employee relations as it had in other areas of its operations, such as, for example, in product development and marketing. Management concluded that to gain employee job satisfaction, loyalty and support, it was not enough that the Company be a good employer. It was equally if not more important that the Company be *known* to its employees as a good employer. With regard to employee pay, benefits and other terms and conditions of employment, as well as other elements entering into employee job satisfaction, the employees must be made to understand that it was the Company's aim "to do right voluntarily" and to allow its employees all that was fairly warranted, bearing in mind the "balanced best interests" of employees and all others having a stake in the Company's enterprise. Moreover, the employees must also be made to understand that, just as there was no need to drag reluctantly from the Company all that was fairly coming to them, so, too, there could be no profit in a show of force by a labor organization designed to extract more for the employees than the facts—as management evaluated them—justly warranted. This involved essentially a selling problem, or, as the Company termed it, one of "job marketing." If the Company was to achieve ultimately the same success in job marketing that it had accomplished in its highly successful product marketing, it must assimilate to the latter what it had learned in the former about sound product planning and research, market development and merchandising.

Application of this program necessitated a revision of the Company's approach to collective bargaining. The Company had theretofore engaged in the traditional type of bargaining, under which a union initially asks more than it expects to get and an employer offers less than it expects to give, and, through the process of compromise and give-and-take, both sides, if bargaining is successful, eventually arrive at a mutually acceptable middle ground. But that type of bargaining had to go if the Company was to establish its credibility with employees that it was putting into effect *voluntarily* and without need of outside pressures all that was warranted in the way of wage and benefit improvements.

Under GE's present approach to bargaining, as GE states it, the Company itself seeks through extensive year-round research into all pertinent facts to determine what is "right" for employees. Its research includes not only a study of business conditions, competitive factors, economic trends and the like, but the gathering of its own information as to employee needs and desires through independent employee attitude surveys, comments made by employees at informative meetings, direct discussions by supervisors with employees and statements in union publications. When bargaining begins, the Company, as part of its overall research, listens to the presentations made by all the unions with which it deals, and evaluates the unions' demands with the help of all the facts it has on hand, including those supplied by the unions.

On the basis of its study so made, GE makes its own determination of what is "right." GE then makes an offer which—as it declares to the unions and to its employees—includes *everything* it has found to be warranted, without anything held back for later trading or compromising. GE makes precisely the same basic offer to substantially all unions with which it is engaged in negotiations. Contrary to the assertion of the General Counsel, GE does not initially present its offer on an avowed "take-it-or-leave-it" basis. It professes a willingness to make prompt adjustments in its offer whenever (but only when) new information from any source or a significant change in facts indicates that its initial offer fell short of being right. But GE believes—or at least so declares—that if it has done its preliminary research into the facts accurately, no substantial reason for changing its offer should ever exist, save in the event of some new unforeseen development having an impact on the economy as a whole. And GE repeatedly emphasizes, especially to employees, that as a matter of policy it will not make any change it believes to be incorrect because of a strike or threat of strike and that it will "take" a strike of any duration to resist doing what it considers to be "wrong."

The Respondent [GE] extols its "fair and firm offer" approach as a straightforward one that removes doubt from employees' minds as to precisely where it stands. It disparagingly refers to the "ask-and-bid" or "auction" form of bargaining as a "flea bitten eastern type of cunning and dishonest, but pointless, haggling." Such bargaining, according to the Respondent's articulation, allows a union to *appear* to get more than an employer is willing to give, though that is often not the case, and this only serves, it says, to mislead employees into believing that union officials are useful in ways they are not, thus falsely enhancing the union's prestige while diminishing that of the employer and encouraging employee support of union shows of strength. The Respondent's approach on the other hand, it says, makes it obvious to employees that the Company "is not being forced to be fair by the belligerent action of a labor union."

All that has been said above is tied to what clearly appears to be the keystone of Respondent's bargaining philosophy—the marketing of management positions directly to employees so that the employees in turn may influence union acceptance. It is a stated policy of the

Company to achieve maximum involvement and participation of employees in decisions affecting its business, including specifically though not limited to decisions relating to collective bargaining; to minimize opposition to steps management takes; and to build active employee support for management's goals and objectives. Toward that end, GE has fashioned an elaborate employee communications system, making use of plant newspapers, daily news digests, employee bulletins, letters to employees' homes, television and radio broadcasts and other media of mass communication, as well as personal contacts. Supervisors are instructed as to GE's views on controversial subjects and are expected to speak out to employees on such subjects and seek to gain employee confidence in the correctness of company decisions. The direct employee communications—if 1960 may be considered as representative—are utilized on a most extensive scale both before and during negotiations to influence employee attitudes to a favorable reception of the Company's views and rejection of the union's conflicting positions. After the Company's offer is presented to the unions, the flow of communications, directed toward that end, reaches flood proportions. At that time, the Company also discusses the terms of its offer at plant meetings; invites employees to take up individually with their supervisors or managerial officials any questions they may have about the offer; and seeks through direct contact of its supervisors with employees to sound out for its own guidance employee reactions to its offer. The avowed purpose of the communications program is to equip employees to render their own independent judgment on matters commonly affecting their own interests and those of the Company. But, as related to bargaining issues, the record in this case, as will be seen, leaves no doubt that GE's more basic purpose is to compete with the bargaining representative for the allegiance and support of employees. . . .

The Respondent's negotiating frame of mind during the negotiations which formally began on July 13, 1960, must be assessed against the backdrop of its bargaining philosophy, outlined . . . above. Analysis of the record shows that the Respondent substantially adhered to that philosophy during its 1960 contract negotiations with the IUE.

Some 6 weeks of meetings (18 sessions) preceded the presentation of the Respondent's offer. During that time the Union was afforded an opportunity formally to present and argue its contract demands. It is quite clear, however, that the Respondent regarded the pre-offer meetings primarily as "listening" sessions, forming but one element of the "research" in which it engages before making its unilateral determination of "everything it believes to be right" for incorporation in its "fair, firm offer." . . .

During the 2 weeks devoted to the presentation of the Union's general demands, other than employment security, the Respondent continued to take the position that it was primarily interested in "fact finding," thus following the script of its approach to collective bargaining as set out . . . above. Though the Respondent discussed with the Union the latter's specific demands and in many instances expressed positions on such demands, where its position was one of rejection, it declined to declare any affirmative views on the key subjects of wage increases, pensions, insurance and other economic benefits, except to make clear that it intended to eliminate the escalator clause. Standing alone, no inference of bad faith may be drawn from the Respondent's failure to declare itself affirmatively at this time. Whether an employer declares his affirmative thinking on each item of a union's proposal before passing on to the next, or elects instead to hear out the union on all its demands before making any counter-proposals, is normally a matter of bargaining technique that lies outside the scrutiny of the Board. Listening to a union's demands is part of the process of collective bargaining, though not the fulfillment thereof. In this case, as in others, however, the Respondent's conduct must be examined in the light of whether it was prepared in truth, not merely in form, to complete the process of bargaining later. To suggest, as the Respondent's declared bargaining approach appears to do, that an employer need only listen to a union's demands and supporting arguments as part of a broader research program, frame an offer on the basis of his own overall research, and then consider only such *new* information as might reveal a factual error in the offer, is to place a union in the role of an advisor rather than a participant in the determination of employment terms through the process of collective bargaining; it is to deny the Union the status to which the Act entitles it. At any rate, the fact remains that until the Respondent gave specific indication of its own line of thinking on key issues, there could be no full or meaningful bargaining, for, without issue joined, discussions could take place only in a vacuum, precluding any possibility of give-and-take that might be necessary to forge agreement.

Thus, if any genuine bargaining were to occur, it had to begin at the time the Respondent's offer was made.

When the Respondent formally presented its offer on August 30, it was responsive to the Union's demands only in small part. It contained features relating to benefits, employment security and even contract language that were entirely different from those that had been requested by the Union. During the earlier negotiations there had been neither mention nor discussion of them as contemplated alternatives to the Union's proposals. The Respondent explained to the Union, as it did later to the employees, that it had made its offer responsive to "employee desires" as determined by its own extensive research and surveys. The

Respondent thus made it plain that it assigned the Union a subordinate or at most only a contributing role as the spokesman for employees.

The Union declared the same day that the offer was unacceptable, and that the proposals of both parties should form the basis of collective bargaining. It requested that negotiations continue for 3 days without the pressures and glare of publicity. The Respondent, however, rejected the Union's request, giving as its reason that employees should know at once what was on the table. And the following morning, it proceeded to publicize its offer, release it to other unions, and present it directly to employees at plant meetings as well as through employee communication channels, disregarding the Union's vigorous objection that to do so would prematurely "freeze" its position and thereby interfere with good-faith negotiations.

In the particular circumstances of this case, I find that the Respondent's haste to publicize its offer reflected the want of an earnest effort on its part to seek through the processes of collective bargaining a possible basis for mutual agreement, and constituted clear evidence of bad faith. . . .

The course taken by the Respondent in the negotiations is not alone enough to establish, but neither is it such as to rebut, if found established by other circumstances, an inference that the Respondent negotiated with a fixed predetermination not to deviate materially from its bargaining policies. During the approximately 25 meetings that took place between August 30, when the Respondent presented its offer, and October 19, when the Respondent declared an impasse, the Respondent made only two changes in its offer that it considered of sufficient consequence to mention in its employee communications. One was the "early signing bonus" change, not requested by the Union, which was announced just before the IUE convention recess and was thereafter capitalized upon in the Respondent's communication program aimed at weakening employee support of the Union. The other was the holiday-vacation option which was offered in the face of the Union's theretofore declared opposition thereto and was represented to employees as being a voluntary rearrangement of its offer in response to employee desires. Far from showing good faith, or a departure from the Respondent's declared bargaining policies . . . it is found, precisely the opposite.

The factual findings earlier made leave little doubt of the Respondent's determination to rely primarily on its employee communications program rather than on negotiations as the means of gaining acceptance of its offer. Thus, Moore[1] in his swing around the GE chain in early 1960 made clear to management personnel that the solution of the

---

[1] Manager of union relations for GE.

1960 negotiating problems would depend on the Company establishing through its written and oral communications its "credibility" on which it might draw "this fall when the votes are cast whether the folks believe you or believe the opposition." Long before negotiations began, the Respondent laid out, and thereafter followed, a carefully designed program to condition employee attitudes and opinions for the favorable reception of the Respondent's offer and rejection of the Union's competing demands. The paramount importance the Respondent assigned to direct employee persuasion over negotiations is clearly illustrated by its insistent haste in publicizing its offer so that it might get underway the elaborate communications program it had in readiness, despite the Union's reasonable request that such publication be withheld so as not to interfere with bargaining. After presentation of its offer, the Respondent's communications program relating to the negotiations reached massive proportions, thereafter maintained until the end of the strike. The offer, along with the Respondent's justifications for it, was orally presented to employees at plant meetings in a manner calculated to minimize the influence of collective bargaining, to impress upon employees that the Respondent had gone as far as it could without endangering the future of its business and the security of employee jobs, and to make it appear that the only alternative to acceptance was a "long pay-losing strike." At about the same time, the Respondent began, and thereafter continued, to deluge employees with communications, numbering at some plants at least one and sometimes as many as three or four a day, in the form of plant newspapers, daily bulletins, letters to homes, newspaper ads, radio and television messages, etc., extolling the merits of its offer and advancing the Respondent's positions on other issues as they arose, while continuing in the meantime to provide employees with reports, highly slanted in its favor, on the daily course of the negotiations. The Respondent also instructed its supervisors not only to impress upon employees the merits of the Respondent's bargaining position, but also to sound out employee reactions thereto. In addition, the Respondent invited and encouraged employees to discuss directly with plant management questions they might have about the offer, and at one large plant held a series of roundtable meetings for that purpose. The Board has held it to be a form of bypassing, and hence evidence of bad faith, for an employer to invite employees to talk directly to management about bargaining matters, or to seek to learn directly from employees their reactions to his bargaining position. It is accordingly so found in this case.

The very massiveness of the communications program is itself a measure of the Respondent's determination to deal essentially, not with the employees through the Union, but with the Union through the employees, evidencing, I find, a purpose to undercut not only the Union's bargaining position, but its authority as bargaining agent as well. The Respondent, to be sure, was not seeking to undermine the Union in the sense of displacing it as the employee representative whose ultimate consent would be required for a contract. But the question here is not whether the Respondent's conduct was illegal *per se*—I have already found it was not. Rather, it is whether such conduct tends to support at least a tentative inference of a frame of mind antithetical to simultaneous good-faith bargaining in the conference room. I think clearly it does. . . .

The Respondent, in furtherance of its campaign to induce employees to vote for acceptance of its offer, took steps to announce to employees, *even before it announced to the Union*, that its *full* offer was now on the table and that as a matter of company policy the Respondent would not "up" its offer because of a strike or threat of strike ". . . it never has in the past, and it won't now."

To give support to the declarations already being made to employees, the Respondent hastened to announce to the Union, almost as the first order of business when negotiations were resumed on September 20, that its offer was now "final" and would not thereafter be altered, a declaration of position which it thereafter continually reiterated during the negotiations and duly reported to employees. To impress further on employees the credibility of its assertions as to the finality of its bargaining stand, the Respondent on the same day authorized its operating managers to make effective for nonrepresented employees, as of September 12, the wage increases provided for in the Respondent's basic offer to all unions, and to announce the establishment of other benefits that were to become operative on October 2. . . .

There can be little doubt from the totality of its conduct that the Respondent was determined—certainly after the resumption of meetings on September 20—merely to go through the motions of bargaining in the conference room and to rely entirely on the effectiveness of its direct "sales" approach to employees to resolve the bargaining issues in its favor. . . .

Virgil B. Day
BAD FAITH BARGAINING?

The challenge of industrial relations, or, more broadly, of manpower utilization, is not just business' problem. It is the central economic challenge before the nation today, and underlies most of its political issues as well.

However, what I am going to suggest is that now, at a time when the challenges before industrial relations demand vigorous and innovative work from management, some recent policy trends of the National Labor Relations Board have raised serious obstacles in the path of progress.

These trends have prompted one experienced labor relations lawyer to question whether true collective bargaining can survive what he calls "the suffocating blanket . . . the Board is throwing over the effective carrying out of managerial responsibility."

I would not presume to cover the whole range of issues which the Board's decisions have raised in recent years, but there might be some interest in my comments on the case involving General Electric.

First, let me sketch briefly how General Electric approaches the process of collective bargaining.

General Electric exhaustively researches and studies on a continuing basis all the available facts of the issues involved. We try to listen, year-around, to union officials and to our employes. We pay careful attention to all the demands brought in by the union representatives with whom we bargain and solicit their help in getting all the pertinent information that bears on our situation.

Finally, after weeks of discussion across the bargaining table, obtaining all of the thoughts we can from union representatives, and carefully considering their proposals, we make a fair and firm offer.

This lengthy procedure, incidentally, is in sharp contrast to the common misrepresentation which portrays us as starting negotiations with a proposal, which we then allegedly refuse to alter. We do modify

From an address to the Industrial Relations Conference of the Electronic Industries Association, April 1965, by permission of Virgil B. Day.

Mr. Day is Vice President, General Electric Company.

and have made various concessions on our offers or have recast our offers in the light of discussion with the union or new information a union may provide—but not just to "prove" that we are bargaining.

In 1963 negotiations, a constructive adaptation of our approach was the advance use of specialized committees of management and union negotiators to examine, in depth, particular aspects of the contract.

Throughout negotiations, we also engage in full and open effort to keep employes truthfully informed. We believe that employes have the right to know where the company stands on controversial issues between their management and their union—and that they have the right to hear it from their company as well as from their union.

THE BOARD'S FINDING

The National Labor Relations Board's split decision late last year in the General Electric case grew out of our 1960 negotiations. The Board majority's finding against General Electric's approach raised two issues which I think may be of some general interest:

First, whether General Electric's presentation of a "fair and firm offer" and its associated techniques constitute a failure to bargain in good faith.

Second, whether conscientious communication of a company viewpoint during negotiations also contributes to a failure to bargain in good faith.

On the first issue, the Board majority claims General Electric's bargaining approach "devitalizes negotiations and collective bargaining and robs them of their commonly accepted meaning." The Board has much to say about this approach and concludes that what we call a "fair and firm offer" was in fact an "intransigent" position.

Several points must be made here.

As I have emphasized, we do not enter negotiations with a firm and inflexible proposal which we then hold unyieldingly. The dissenting Board member, Boyd Leedom, noted: "The respondent's initial attitude with respect to its offer does not appear to have been appreciably, if any, more intransigent than that of a union representative presenting its proposed changes. It is clear that as negotiations proceeded the union backed down considerably and the company acquiesced in a number of changes from its original proposals."

So one point is that we are not as inflexible or intransigent as the Board majority implies.

But another point, and one with far wider significance, relates to the fact that, while we do modify proposals, we do so only if we are honestly persuaded that the facts merit such modifications.

This point is significant because the Board's majority seems to be questioning the right of an employer to put into its own offer everything which it believes should be there and which may in fact end up in the final agreement.

The Board does not say expressly that the employer should deliberately hold something back; or that he should modify an offer even if he is not convinced that such modification is merited. To state these explicitly as legal requirements of "good faith" bargaining would be absurd.

But clearly the Board is uncomfortable with an employer initiative of the type General Electric showed and believes that we should have given the union a somehow larger role in shaping and changing our proposal. But how much larger a role? And how "assign" it?

The Supreme Court, in a recent decision, as it has before, warned the NLRB against injecting itself into the detailed evaluation of the relative strength of bargaining parties.

The Court's exact language goes as follows: ". . . we think that the Board construes its functions too expansively when it claims general authority to define national labor policy by balancing the competing interests of labor and management . . .

(The law's provisions) "do not give the Board a general authority to assess the relative economic power of the adversaries in the bargaining process and to deny weapons to one party or the other because of its assessment of that party's bargaining power."

After all, what is the objective here—to make one or the other party look good politically? Or to achieve good, sound contracts, beneficial to employes?

I submit that in the context of today's competitive realities, collective bargaining is too important to be conducted on a "haggling for haggling's sake" basis.

THE RIGHT TO SPEAK

The second issue of broad significance in this NLRB ruling concerns the fundamental question of an employer's right and responsibility to communicate fully and frankly to all employes, including union members.

Maybe the best way to reexamine this question is to go to the language of the decision itself. A key passage reads as follows: "It is inconsistent with this obligation (of good faith bargaining) for an employer to mount a campaign, as Respondent did, both before and during negotiations, for the purpose of disparaging and discrediting the statutory representative in the eyes of its employe constituents, to seek to persuade the employes to exert pressure on the representative to submit to the will of the employer and to create the impression that the employer rather than the union is the true protector of the employes' interests."

It is true that this language does not prohibit an employer from speaking at all. It does not because it cannot. Outright prohibition of free speech by an employer would, of course, fly directly in the face of the law and of everyone's sense of fairness.

What this ruling does is to censor rather than prohibit. In plain English, this language censors employer communications which criticize union officials; or which persuade employes of the validity of company positions on bargaining issues; or which seek to create a favorable image of the employer in the eyes of his own employes.

The one-sided impact of these ground-rules is clear. While the Board would censor employer communication which it construes as "disparaging or discrediting" the union, this union's communication during 1960 and all prior negotiations repeatedly characterized management as "greedy," "monolithic," "arrogant," "ruthless."

In our communications concerning negotiations, we reported the intemperate views of the top union official. NLRB did not find that General Electric falsely described his views or conduct. The meaning of the Board's ruling that a union must be protected against "disparagement," therefore, is that if a union official acts badly or intemperately or unwisely, the company must keep silent on this subject.

Although the employer may not seek to persuade employes as to the merits of his counterproposals, the union continuously trumpeted to employes the merits of its proposals.

As to the vague interdiction against seeking to create the impression that the employer, rather than the union, is the "true protector of employe interests," little can or need be said. Every employer worth his salt thinks he is, and every sincere union thinks it is, sincerely and effectively attempting to promote the employes' interests. The debate is inevitable and proper—and inevitably and properly two-sided.

These then are the two main points about this NLRB ruling which have serious implications for all of us: An employer's right to make a fair and firm offer and bargain on that basis; and an employer's right to communicate fully to employes concerning bargaining matters.

Underlying the question of employer communication is the basic issue of whether management's relationship to its employees should be carried on exclusively through the union; or whether management has an additional responsibility to present its views directly to employes, once presented to the union. This is no straw man—there is a viewpoint current that the union should handle everything for employes.

THE IUE'S POSITION

During the trial of this case, the IUE's general counsel stated: "The company was saying to employes . . . after all, who is the union, your master or your servant? They are not saying . . . your union is your master. That's the trouble!"

Let me cite also the NLRB General Counsel's words: "It takes merely a moment of analysis and reflection to realize that the average employe cannot be informed enough concerning economics, the prevailing wage and working hours in the electrical industry, and related industries, and on a multitude of other matters which a negotiator must consider in taking and changing positions during negotiations."

That viewpoint poses a fundamental question. In all democratic processes, these "average" employes are depended on to vote wisely after hearing facts and analysis on complex questions.

Three hundred years ago, in his classic defense of free speech, the Areopagitica, John Milton rested his case ultimately on the basic intelligence and independent judgment of the people. His language may be out-of-date, but his thought, I submit, is more in tune with the times than the position of the modern-day censors, when he cries: "Lords and Commons of England, consider what Nation it is whereof you are, and whereof you are the governours: a Nation not slow and dull, but of a quick, ingenious, and piercing spirit, . . . not beneath the reach of any point the highest that human capacity can soar to."

It is this faith in the capacity of free men to exercise sound judgment . . . this "decent respect to the opinions of mankind" . . . this commitment to the "consent of the governed". . . which underlies not only our political system (with which we normally associate the phrase) but forms the basis of all free institutions in a democratic society.

We cannot permit these basic concepts to stand as meaningless generalizations or assume that they are satisfied merely by holding free public elections every year, or two, or four. The "competition of ideas" must be allowed to enrich all free institutions, as in fact it can and does in the field of free collective bargaining when not suppressed by the kind of "suffocating blanket" which I have discussed.

James L. Stern
DECLINING UTILITY
OF THE STRIKE

IMPROVED STRIKE PREPARATIONS

. . . Since the end of World War II, the ingenuity of management, and to some extent that of labor, has been turned increasingly to the development of better ways to survive a strike. More attention has been directed toward the development of plans to protect the parties in case of a strike than to formulating plans on how to avoid it.

The equivalent of the military's early warning system was introduced into collective bargaining by the 1947 amendments to the National Labor Relations Act, requiring sixty-days' notice of contract termination and thirty-days' notice to the government before strike action could be undertaken. In theory, the notice system eliminated the impulsively called strike by giving the parties time to reflect on the problem.

After the time interval specified by the notice requirements has elapsed, however, action can then be taken abruptly. The notice system is of obvious benefit to management in that it provides time for preparation. Production schedules can be increased prior to the deadline. Inventory can be shipped from the factory to warehouses or yards around the country. Customers can be informed of the advisability of increasing purchases in anticipation of and to avoid shortages arising from a strike. Price policies can be formulated to protect cooperating customers from loss if the strike is averted.

The time prior to the expiration of the notice period is also beneficial to unions who use it for the development of programs that will provide increased protection to members during a strike—if it occurs. A community services program is established or revitalized so that community resources can be mobilized to mitigate the financial problems of the workers that will arise during a strike. Strike funds are strengthened. Many union members postpone major purchases and reduce expendi-

From the *Industrial and Labor Relations Review*, October 1964. Reprinted by permission of the publisher and author.
Mr. Stern is Professor of Economics, University of Wisconsin.

tures in order to provide a cushion against the days when there will be no pay checks.

Strategies controlling timing of strikes have become more sophisticated. Management no longer customarily allows the union to select the crisis date. It may actually terminate the agreement, as did the automobile companies in 1958. Unions, in turn, have forsaken some of their venerable traditions. The "no contract, no work" position has been relegated to the category of folklore. In 1958, the automobile workers worked several months without a contract before serving strike notice. The strategy of the parties and the pertinent sections of the National Labor Relations Act tend to delay the crisis date until a time when the parties are fully prepared to do battle.

INCREASED DURATION AND EXTENT OF STRIKES

In the situation where no attempt is made to operate a struck plant, economic pressure on both sides to settle mounts steadily, and the parties are often forced in time to accept a compromise which might have been unacceptable just prior to the strike. In some instances, a strike may cause the capitulation of one side so that it must accept the pre-strike terms of the other. Several financial mechanisms have been developed, however, which enable the parties to withstand economic pressures more effectively than formerly. These mechanisms, by strengthening the contestants, have tended to increase the duration of strikes. BLS statistics show a one-third increase in the average length of strikes in the past seven years. Duration has again approached the level of the turbulent 1930's, although the number of strikes in 1962 was relatively low.

Companies have banded together to establish strike insurance funds. In the airlines industry, for example, the airlines that continue to operate during a strike pay a portion of their revenues to the individual line that has been closed down by the union. This increases the ability of an individual company to withstand a strike and, in turn, leads the union to consider striking simultaneously all of the parties to the strike insurance agreement.

Unions also have increased their ability to withstand long strikes. Strike funds have been expanded, and union constitutions and procedures have been liberalized to provide specific levels of strike benefits so that striking members of many unions can expect to receive income as a matter of right, regardless of need. Various international unions have donated large sums to other unions engaged in major strikes. Public welfare programs for persons in need have given greater assistance to strikers because of the operation of the union community services program. As a result, it is clear that strikers while, in no sense affluent, can count on financial support that will enable them to continue a strike for a longer period than in the past.

Other factors besides these arrangements developed by the contestants tend to reduce company strike losses and thereby allow companies to withstand long strikes. Technological advances enable management to make up production lost by strikes more rapidly than in the past. Trends in the steel industry show that, within six months after the extended 1959 strike, market needs had been met and employment was reduced. Excess capacity is more characteristic of industry today than previously. Economic growth has lagged behind technological improvements, and there is increased slack even in good times between actual output and maximum potential output.

This standby capacity allows management to increase production before and after a strike. In the dock strike, for example, statistics of the New Jersey-New York Waterfront Commission indicate that the twenty-five days lost in January were made up partially by increased activity in the month prior to the strike and by greatly increased activity in the months following the strike. Daily hirings in February 1963 of 466,000 were over a hundred thousand higher than the 357,000 daily hirings recorded in February 1962. It was anticipated that the total of daily hiring from December 1962 through April 1963 would equal that of the previous years for the same period despite the twenty-five days lost to strike activity.

Workers also benefit from the increased activity before and after strikes through the increased overtime worked. The additional income generated by working overtime before a strike provides a small cushion which enables the worker to strike longer. The expectation of overtime after the conclusion of a strike tends to reduce the anxiety associated with the depletion of personal savings during the strike.

Although it is difficult to estimate how much output is lost as against how much is produced in advance or made up by extra output after the strike, a convincing case can be made that a strike mainly *changes the timing* of the loss of output rather than causes it. Wages and profits are similarly affected, so that it is difficult to assess the net strike loss to labor and management. It is clear, however, that the ability to offset strike losses increases the potential duration of strikes which the parties can take.

The scope of a strike, that is, the number of employees and companies involved in any one strike, is also widening. Company cooperation in financial protective arrangements is replaced in some instances by agreements to lockout all employees in the industry or area when one company is struck. The New York City newspaper strike, where more papers were closed by lockouts than by strikes, illustrates how the extent of a strike may be increased by this tactic. International unions also have developed closer cooperation which tends to extend the boundaries of a strike. In the aerospace industry, where the two unions involved had a long history of rivalry and separate bargaining, coordinated bargaining efforts in 1962 resulted in the setting of a common strike date covering a large portion of the industry.

While the parties have increased the duration and extent of strikes that can be withstood, the public toleration of such disputes may have declined. Again we have no reliable measure of how quickly public clamor for the termination of a dispute will arise. For several reasons there appears to be less sympathy and less toleration for strikes that inconvenience the public than there was earlier. . . .

OPERATING THE STRUCK PLANT

The nature of the automated production process makes it easier for management to operate a plant despite a strike of the bargaining unit. There is no longer the need to recruit a substitute labor force. Skeleton supervisory crews can man the minimum number of positions needed to continue production. Maintenance is postponed. Inspection activities are reduced. Automatic machinery does the work with the aid of technicians and supervisors who serve as controllers of the automatic process. Changes in the labor force associated with the introduction of automation have meant a marked increase in the ratio of supervisors and of technicians to employees in the conventional bargaining unit. In industry generally, this ratio has reached one to three, and in technologically advanced industries, such as aerospace and petroleum refining, it is approaching one to one. When the union men walk out, they know that they leave behind in the plant this increased number of potential out-of-unit replacements. In automated industries, the strike will be used less often in the future because the unions will recognize that the odds are increasingly against their being able to conduct an effective strike.

Similar to the unfavorable balance of power facing unions in technologically advanced industries is the unfavorable situation facing some employers in the construction, service, and transportation sectors of the economy. The odds against a small employer single-handedly triumphing in economic conflict over a large union have been recited frequently by businessmen in support of demands to break up powerful unions. Where an individual management falls into this category, the strike theoretically serves no useful purpose because each individual management acquiesces to the union demand, secure in the knowledge that the union will force its competitors to do so also.

If resistance is contemplated, it rarely is undertaken by a single management. Instead, employers have formed area-wide associations for bargaining purposes. Where these associations have strengthened management's position sufficiently to permit it to engage in an area-wide conflict, the duration and the extent of the combined strike and lockout which the contestants can endure exceed that which the public will tolerate. The New York City newspaper strike mentioned previously illustrates this point.

It would appear then that technological changes and institutional forces are generating trends which reduce the role of the strike in labor-management relations. Where technology makes it possible for management to operate despite a strike, the imbalance of power makes economic conflict less likely and less useful as a means of remedying abuses of power. The same is true, in reverse, in the local product markets where individual employers find resistance irrational. When employer associations and unions engage in an expanded conflict in a geographic area, or when large national unions and major corporations covering an entire industry are involved in a strike, the ability of the participants to continue the dispute exceeds the willingness of the public to allow it to continue. The weapons are found to be too powerful for the battle, particularly so in the eyes of the public when the issues are complicated, technical, and without readily apparent solutions. . . .

8
The Role of Government in
Industrial Relations

The appropriate role of government in American society is still in the process of being defined. This is as true in the area of industrial relations as elsewhere. Thirty years ago our society decided that, in the interests of economic justice and industrial peace, the rights of workers to organize and to bargain collectively with employers should be governmentally supported and protected. Collective bargaining has come a long way since then, and today it is performed by powerful organizations— trade unions and employers. Some of these institutions have the potential, through the results of their bargaining, to affect the welfare of the whole nation (at least temporarily) as well as the particular livelihoods of many of its citizens. When so much is at stake, governmental concern with the behavior of these institutions is inevitable. W. Willard Wirtz, in the first selection, describes this concern in terms of the very ambiguous concept of the "public interest."

Elected officials must be concerned with the public interest, but that, by itself, does not imply any specific role for the government in industrial relations. It is possible that the private parties—labor and employers—could recognize the consequences of their actions and discipline their behavior so that the need for government intervention would never arise. All Presidential administrations since the end of World War II have encouraged such self-discipline; but their efforts have not always been successful.

On the other hand, some argue, as Milton Friedman does in the second selection, that acceptance by business and labor of this kind of social responsibility would be undesirable—chiefly because their responsibilities could be defined in a way that would conflict with some of the best interests of the populace. Friedman would establish a framework of laws that would allow employers and labor to pursue their own self-interests while taking from them the power to injure the public. Those who favor this approach rarely propose specific laws to accomplish their purpose. Whatever the legal specifics might be, it is probable that they would increase, not reduce, the role of government in industrial relations.

It is clear that private self-regulation has not always protected the public interest in collective bargaining, as a result, recent Presidential administrations have defined this interest more precisely and defended it more vigorously than in the past. They have shown special concern about decisions on wages and prices. A selection from the *Report of the Council of Economic Advisers* presents the Presidential "guidelines" for these decisions. Arthur Ross's critique on the report follows.

As Ross explains, the adverse balance-of-payments position of the United States in recent years is primarily responsible for the present governmental emphasis on wages and prices. Similarly, the demands of the international cold war and the hot war in Vietnam have been used to justify increased governmental intervention in collective bargaining disputes that result, or threaten to result, in strikes.

International conflict may be a valid reason for government action when production is disrupted in one of the few key industries, but it can hardly justify rushing governmental "assistance" to bargaining situations to avoid strikes that would have a negligible impact on the national economy and only slightly more on local business. Why the government has intervened with some frequency in the latter instances during the past several years is not clear. The explanation cannot be in the number of strikes—there are fewer now than there used to be. Perhaps we, the people, are to blame in that we are becoming unwilling to be inconvenienced by a strike.

George Shultz suggests that strikes are a part of collective bargaining, not symptoms of national neuroses, and, thus, we should learn to live with them. If we really wish private collective bargaining to continue, the citizenry and our government will have to accept these suggestions. Many observers believe that when even the possibility of government intervention exists, bargaining tends to be carried out ineffectively—that is, without a timely agreement being reached. The intrusion of government could change the power relationship—a welcome prospect for the weaker party, whether it be labor or management.

Experience with students has taught us that some clarification is needed at this point. Contrary to what many seem to believe, there is almost no compulsory arbitration of the terms of collective bargaining agreements in the United States—thus, the special legislation authorizing arbitration of the intractable dispute involving railroad firemen in 1963 stood out as a strikingly unusual procedure. The role of government when it enters collective bargaining disputes, usually through the Federal Mediation and Conciliation Service, is mediation—that is, searching for terms acceptable to both parties. The government mediators are not authorized by law to recommend terms of agreement. If they make such recommendations privately, the union and employer are free to ignore them, though there can be no doubt that terms recommended by a representative of the President carry more weight than those of an ordinary citizen.

There is little support among economists or among business and labor leaders for the view that the government ought to decide the terms of the union-management employment contract (there is support for this view among the general public, however, as shown by a 1965 Gallup Poll, which found a majority willing to support compulsory arbitration of contract disputes). There is a subtle issue at stake in this question. It involves the effects of increasing governmental participation on the institution of private collective bargaining—whether that participation takes the form of dispute mediation, private recommendation of settlement terms, or speeches by governmental officials designed to influence public opinion. If the government intervenes widely in actual or threatened strikes, will collective bargaining become a mere ritualistic process up to the point that the sentiments of the third party—government—are made clear?

Another issue is government procedure in "emergency" disputes. There are occasions when strikes cannot be tolerated, though these occasions are far fewer than is generally thought. The national-emergency dispute provisions of our federal labor law are designed to deal with strikes that would place an intolerable burden on the national welfare. The last selection, from the report of a respected study group, suggests a number of modifications in these provisions, designed to provide the public with greater protection from labor disputes that truly threaten its welfare.

the public interest

W. Willard Wirtz
THE FUTURE
OF COLLECTIVE BARGAINING

When a company representative says, at the bargaining table, "I won't discuss what happens to the people we have to lay off when we bring in new equipment; we're in business to make a profit, not to run a charity ward"—he is in effect asking the Government to take over a responsibility, the discharge of which he will then later condemn, probably as "socialism."

When a union representative meets that same problem by insisting that permanent sinecures be arranged for men who are no longer actually needed in the plant, he weakens collective bargaining by using it to produce a wrong answer, which won't stand up—for an economy that must achieve its full growth to survive cannot afford a manpower waste.

When a company and a union agree on a wage increase which will require a price increase making the product non-competitive as against foreign goods, and then put "Buy American" stickers on their automobiles and go to Washington to demand higher tariffs or import quotas, they are using collective bargaining to sap the national economy of its strength. For we are going to depend more and more on *exports* for our necessary national income and for jobs. If we refuse to take other

From an address at the Labor-Management Day luncheon, International Trade Fair, Chicago, August 3, 1961.
Mr. Wirtz is Secretary of Labor.

countries' exports, they will refuse to take ours. If we insist on "buying American" they will see to it that we sell American, too. Protectionism does not mean more jobs for Americans. It means fewer jobs.

The question of what collective bargaining can do to meet these problems remains to be answered. But these are illustrative of the key problems today in labor relations. Unless collective bargaining does have room to accommodate them, and answers to offer, it will be relegated in the future to matters of house-keeping in the plant, to administering procedures for handling discharge cases, establishing safety programs, devising seniority systems that don't cover the crucial cases, dividing up pies whose size is determined someplace else.

I assert, therefore, this first proposition: that in a world that has shrunk overnight and a national economy in which each part now depends on every other part and on the health of the whole the continuation of private collective bargaining as the important force in the future it has been in the past depends on the decision of the bargainors to exercise, or not to exercise, responsibility for the concerns that affect the whole economy.

These concerns are not easily defined. Those who talk most easily in this area about the "public interest" are most apt to use the phrase as a wrapping for their own private interests. Yet it has some identifiable elements.

It includes the achievement of an equitable sharing of the costs and the fruits of production or service—finding the meaning of "equitable" more in experience than in logic.

It includes the maintenance of economic stability—the avoidance of spiralling inflation.

The "public interest" includes, perhaps most significantly today, the achievement of the nation's full capacity for economic growth. We have paid more attention in the past to stability than to growth, reflecting a characteristically larger concern about fears than opportunities. Yet stability without growth is as inadequate a goal as growth without stability. And growth today is not just an opportunity; it is a necessity.

These are vaguely stated principles: equity, stability, growth. Yet to have worked with collective bargaining is to realize that it proceeds necessarily from very broad guiding principles, and that central importance attaches to whether bargaining is conducted under such conditions and in such a way as will permit the effective application of those principles to particular cases.

So I suggest, as a second proposition, that the future of collective bargaining depends on whether its motive power and its procedures can be adjusted and revised to permit a larger recognition and reflection of the common national interests, particularly those in the achievement of stability and growth.

I think there is already evidence of significant and encouraging developments on this score.

One of these has to do with the role of economic force.

Collective bargaining has grown up on the theory that its essential motive power is the right of either side to say "no," regardless of justification or lack of it, and to back this up by shutting down the operation. To believe deeply in the efficacy of collective bargaining and to recognize fully that it has contributed immeasurably to economic and social welfare, is not to be blinded to the fact that it has been much more an interplay of economic power than an exercise of pure reason.

Yet there is reason to suspect that the same thing may be happening to the concept of force in the labor relations field as in the international arena, that the destructive power of the available force has become too great for it to be used freely and fully. The strike and the lockout, like the force of arms in international relations, may continue to be regarded as effective in comparatively small, limited disputes. But the big strike, the big lockout, covering a whole, vital industry, may well be moving into much the same position as the atom bomb.

It is not that there is any prospect that the right to strike or to lockout will be taken away. It won't be. It is simply that there is now such general recognition of the lethal effects of closing down an essential industry, such realization that the public will not tolerate this, that private statesmen—the administrators of the collective bargaining process who are also its architects—are working purposefully to find substitutes.

One kind of substitute is illustrated, without trying to characterize it, by what has happened in the coal industry. Fifteen years ago the coal fields were battlegrounds of belligerence bordering so close to apparent anarchy that the President spoke seriously of drafting the miners into the army. Today the bituminous coal operators, the United Mine Workers, the utilities which are the principal users of coal, as well as the railroads which carry it, are all members of The National Coal Policy Conference—whose jurisdiction, as its most famous architect describes it, is "anything we can agree on." There hasn't been a major coal strike for nine years, and such unity prevails that the problems of the industry are now more with the Anti-Trust Division than the National Labor Relations Board.

The National Coat and Suit Industry Recovery Board is another example of much the same thing. By broadening out the area of recognized mutual interests of the industry and the union, some basis is found for moving away from trial by combat and toward an at least more peaceful form of decision-making.

Such developments may, or may not, present other "public interest" questions, but so far as the public's preoccupation with labor peace is concerned, that interest has in these cases been satisfied.

A perhaps more widespread development involves the increasing use of neutrals, independent third parties, "public members," as integral agencies of the collective bargaining process; not just as arbitrators called in after the parties are set on a collision course, but as participants in the negotiation process itself, or even in the pre-negotiation phases of the private deliberations. . . .

If these neutrals serve only as agreement brokers, bringing the private parties perhaps more painlessly to the same conclusions their own devices would lead them to, these are not significant developments. The accumulating evidence suggests, however, something quite different. It is that these procedures are resulting in the development of factual data from which more rational bargaining can proceed; that points of view are being presented to the parties which are based not just on compromise, but on more responsible reason; that the parties are being given in advance a clearer picture of what they may expect in terms of public reaction to their positions, which will ultimately be so influential on any disputed settlement.

There is substantial indication here, I think, of an evolving pattern of resort in one form or another to that arbitrament of reason, rather than of economic force which may well be essential to the continued vitality and effectiveness of significant private collective bargaining.

Yet the question remains of how, and even whether, collective bargaining covering a particular employment relationship can, at its best, provide an adequate national response to such problems as technological displacement, or the reconciliation of high standards of living and free trade as coordinate national objectives.

The answer seems to me to be that it can do so only in part, and that the more complete response to these new demands will necessarily involve new forms of activity by the agencies of government. But this does not, in my view of it, mean more government as opposed to private administration. It means rather—and I would suggest as a third and final proposition—that the effectiveness of collective bargaining in the future depends upon the working out of significantly new forms of coordinated private and public administrative processes.

It is at least relevant that this pattern of convergent private and public decision-making has already emerged in virtually all of the other democratic nations, most notably in the Scandinavian countries.

What this means is most readily illustrated by reference to this matter of technological displacement.

A private collective bargaining agreement can include severance pay provisions. The joint study group set up by Armour, the United Packinghouse Workers, and the Amalgamated Meat Cutters, has also been exploring the possibilities of private arrangements for doing some retraining of displaced employees and even for moving them—where circumstances permit—to other plants of the same company. It is conceivable, although perhaps unlikely, that private procedures can be worked out to satisfy the equity of a displaced employee and permit him to carry to the new employer the pension, perhaps even the seniority, credits built up in his previous employment.

There is also a job for collective bargaining, as we move into this age of automation, of seeing to it that there are eliminated from the private employment rules and practices of the nation any anachronisms which restrict unduly men's performance of available work.

Yet these are only some of the problems "automation" poses. After thorough study of this situation, the Armour committee reached the conclusion that: "Only through a coordinated approach in which public policy and private action mutually reinforce one another can the employment problems of technological change be met. Collective bargaining by itself cannot fully solve these problems."

It is clear that the brunt of the retraining job must fall upon the Government. President Kennedy has asked the Congress for the authority and the appropriations to assume this responsibility; and the Committees in both houses have now reported out favorably the Manpower Development and Training Act of 1961.

The President has also been urging modifications of the State unemployment compensation laws to correct the present situation which is that many of these laws result in an unemployed man losing his unemployment benefits if he is taking a retraining course.

Secretary Goldberg has also instituted a complete retooling of the U.S. Employment Service to meet the demands of this new type of unemployment situation. It will not be effective, however, without a greatly enlarged degree of cooperation from private industry. In Sweden, there has developed a virtually uniform practice of employers' advising the Labor Market Board whenever they face the prospect of displacing any significant number of employees—so that retraining and re-assignment procedures can immediately be instituted; which is at least part of the reason the unemployment rate in Sweden is down around one percent (although they record unemployment differently from the way we do).

The heart of this whole problem, furthermore, is that there must be more jobs to be filled—which is obviously beyond the competence of any particular team of collective bargainors. There has been no better statement of this than that which came recently from the National Association of Manufacturers:

"The most pressing domestic problem facing the nation today is the creation of more opportunities for the productive and efficient employment of the energies and abilities of our people . . . According to reliable estimates, about 2,000,000 new jobs will be required each year to provide opportunities for everyone seeking work. Unless these jobs are created, every one of our national aspirations will be in trouble."

It is important to be clear that the problem is neither technological development nor technological displacement. Such development is essential to the economy's growth, and the displacement follows inevitably. The problem is that there are not today enough other jobs for the displaced employees. These are growing pains we are suffering, not economic arthritis. This doesn't make it any less serious, but it does suggest the need for national rather than localized therapy.

So only part of this task can be performed by the private agencies of collective bargaining. Part of it requires broader attention. But the two approaches must be closely integrated, or at least coordinated.

Similarly of the imports problem. Surely part of this problem can be, and must be, met privately. This is not only a matter of recognizing, at the bargaining table, that foreign competition may properly be a factor in determining what wages can be paid. There are, beyond this, infinitely various approaches—many of them lending themselves to union and company cooperation—to the possibilities of improved productive efficiency. . . .

There are other recent and significant illustrations of new forms of coordinated public and private action in meeting developing labor relations problems.

Labor disputes at the missile sites have been placed in the hands of a Commission whose authority stems directly from a Presidential Executive order but is based on private no-strike, no-lockout pledges; and the membership of the Commission includes both government officials and the representatives of the companies and unions which are affected.

The Government's Equal Employment Opportunity program depends for its effectiveness on the participation of a broadly based Committee of private citizens.

On Friday of this week, Secretary Goldberg will meet with a panel of some twenty public, management and labor representatives to work out recommendations for proposed changes in the emergency dispute provisions of the Taft-Hartley Act.

On the second Monday of every month, fourteen leaders of American labor and management meet at the White House with the Secretary of Labor, the Secretary of Commerce, and five public representatives to discuss key problems of labor-management relations and wage and price policies, and to prepare recommendations regarding these matters for the President.

I think it is the general conclusion of those who are participating in these programs that they represent not Government intrusions upon private precincts, but rather a strengthening of private processes by the close working cooperation of the Government where the problems go beyond what private powers and resources can meet.

I conclude then with this picture of the future of collective bargaining: that it will necessarily, if it is to preserve its meaningfulness, take a larger account of the responsibilities which the new forces loose in the world have thrust upon the nation; that the procedures of collective bargaining are already developing along new lines which make it a more reasoned sort of process, and that an essential part of this development will be a converging and a coordination of public and private decision-making in the whole area of labor relations.

I see, in short, a prospect of more reliance in collective bargaining on the principles of government, more use in government of the resources and procedures of collective bargaining, and that coordination of the two processes which will enhance the effectiveness of both.

Nothing I have spoken of here is suggested as dogma. It is plainly not the product of any divine revelation, but is subject rather to the futility of trying to see ahead, a privilege which is—unfortunately—denied to men. I urge only the imperative of recognizing the new demands today's ferment of progress and change places on the administrators and architects of American labor relations—the crucial need that Man's administrative invention keep up with his scientific genius. . . .

Milton Friedman
SOCIAL RESPONSIBILITY
OF BUSINESS AND LABOR

The view has been gaining widespread acceptance that corporate officials and labor leaders have a "social responsibility" that goes beyond serving the interest of their stockholders or their members. This view shows a fundamental misconception of the character and nature of a free economy. In such an economy, there is one and only one social responsibility of business—to use its resources and engage in activities designed to increase its profits so long as it stays within the rules of the game, which is to say, engages in open and free competition, without deception or fraud. Similarly, the "social responsibility" of labor leaders is to serve the interests of the members of their unions. It is the responsibility of the rest of us to establish a framework of law such that an individual in pursuing his own interest is, to quote Adam Smith, "led by an invisible hand to promote an end which was no part of his intention. Nor is it always the worse for the society that it was no part of it. By pursuing his own interest, he frequently promotes that of the society more effectually than when he really intends to promote it. I have never known much good done by those who affected to trade for the public good."[1]

Few trends could so thoroughly undermine the very foundations of our free society as the acceptance by corporate officials of a social responsibility other than to make as much money for their stockholders as possible. This is a fundamentally subversive doctrine. If businessmen do have a social responsibility other than making maximum profits for stockholders, how are they to know what it is? Can self-selected private individuals decide what the social interest is? Can they decide how great a burden they are justified in placing on themselves or their stockholders

Reprinted from *Capitalism and Freedom* by Milton Friedman by permission of The University of Chicago Press, pp. 133–135. Copyright 1963 by the University of Chicago.

Mr. Friedman is Professor of Economics, University of Chicago.

[1] *The Wealth of Nations* (1776), Book IV, Chapter ii (Cannan ed. London, 1930), p. 421.

to serve that social interest? Is it tolerable that these public functions of taxation, expenditure, and control be exercised by the people who happen at the moment to be in charge of particular enterprises, chosen for those posts by strictly private groups? If businessmen are civil servants rather than the employees of their stockholders then in a democracy they will, sooner or later, be chosen by the public techniques of election and appointment.

And long before this occurs, their decision-making power will have been taken away from them. A dramatic illustration was the cancellation of a steel price increase by U.S. Steel in April 1962 through the medium of a public display of anger by President Kennedy and threats of reprisals on levels ranging from anti-trust suits to examination of the tax reports of steel executives. This was a striking episode because of the public display of the vast powers concentrated in Washington. We were all made aware of how much of the power needed for a police state was already available. It illustrates the present point as well. If the price of steel is a public decision, as the doctrine of social responsibility declares, then it cannot be permitted to be made privately.

The particular aspect of the doctrine which this example illustrates, and which has been most prominent recently, is an alleged social responsibility of business and labor to keep prices and wage rates down in order to avoid price inflation. Suppose that at a time when there was upward pressure on prices—ultimately of course reflecting an increase in the stock of money—every businessman and labor leader were to accept this responsibility and suppose all could succeed in keeping any price from rising, so we had voluntary price and wage control without open inflation. What would be the result? Clearly product shortages, labor shortages, gray markets, black markets. If prices are not allowed to ration goods and workers, there must be some other means to do so. Can the alternative rationing schemes be private? Perhaps for a time in a small and unimportant area. But if the goods involved are many and important, there will necessarily be pressure, and probably irresistible pressure, for governmental rationing of goods, a governmental wage policy, and governmental measures for allocating and distributing labor.

Price controls, whether legal or voluntary, if effectively enforced would eventually lead to the destruction of the free-enterprise system and its replacement by a centrally controlled system. And it would not even be effective in preventing inflation. History offers ample evidence that what determines the average level of prices and wages is the amount of money in the economy and not the greediness of businessmen or of workers. Governments ask for the self-restraint of business and labor because of their inability to manage their own affairs—which includes the control of money—and the natural human tendency to pass the buck.

wage-price policy

Council of Economic Advisers
GUIDELINES
FOR WAGES AND PRICES

Maintaining essential price stability in 1965 must be a national objective of high priority. The record of price stability in recent years has made possible a substantial improvement in our ability to compete in world markets. This record has also contributed to a balanced advance and has kept fiscal and monetary policies free to be expansionary. Furthermore, price stability has promoted equity by preserving the purchasing power of people with fixed incomes and liquid assets.

We have not yet succeeded in reaching our employment goals in this environment of stable prices. The ability to reconcile full employment and price stability will have a major influence on our long-term ability to grow, to maintain a leading position in the world, and to build a better life for all Americans. Now, with improved prosperity and reduced margins of idleness, our institutional arrangements for setting prices and wages face a stiffer test in avoiding tendencies toward inflation.

Our institutions are adapted to modern technology, which, in many industries, requires an enormous scale of operation and huge investment in productive facilities and distribution systems. The resulting large firms necessarily possess substantial market power, and may be in a

From the *Annual Report of the Council of Economic Advisers*, in the *Economic Report of the President*, 1965, pp. 107–110.

position to raise prices even when demand does not exceed supply. Still, the discipline of competition is always at hand. Competition from abroad often challenges industries with heavy domestic concentration. Competition between industries selling substitutable products reinforces competition within industries. An antitrust enforcement helps to promote competitive behavior. Thus, the pricing process reflects both the exercise of discretionary market power and the influence of impersonal market forces.

In labor markets, unions have been formed to allow workers to bargain on equal terms with these large firms. Many unions have become powerful, and they are in a position to hold their own in the periodic collective bargaining process. Although they are constrained by market forces, powerful unions can, and sometimes do, obtain wage increases that outrun productivity even when labor supply is relatively abundant.

Because flexible and competitive market forces are not alone in affecting prices and wages, a modern economy needs new policies to reconcile the objectives of full employment and stable prices.

In one way or another virtually every advanced country has devised policies aimed at this reconciliation. Several nations have pursued such policies for many years. In December 1964, the United Kingdom launched a major new venture aimed at the cost problems which have contributed so much to her economic difficulties: leaders of business and labor signed a declaration of intent to pursue price, wage, production, and employment policies that will result in over-all price stability and an improved competitive position.

Because of differences among nations in political and economic systems, each country must find a solution appropriate to its own institutions. The U.S. economy is larger than the others and, as a result, many of our industries, including heavy industries requiring large scales of operation, are more competitive than in Western Europe or Japan. Major discretionary market power is found less frequently here, but it is found in important industries which have a wide and pervasive influence on prices and wages elsewhere through emulation and direct cost-push.

To deal with the problem of reconciliation—achieving noninflationary price and wage behavior under prosperous conditions—the Council's Annual Report in 1962 advanced the guideposts which were endorsed by President Kennedy and have been firmly restated by President Johnson.

The basic guideposts are simple and straightforward and contain an inescapable economic logic.

1. The general guide for wages is that the percentage increase in total employee compensation per man-hour be equal to the national trend rate of increase in output per man-hour.

If each industry follows this guidepost, unit labor costs in the over-all economy will maintain a constant average.

2. The general guide for prices calls for stable prices in industries enjoying the same productivity growth as the average for the economy; rising prices in industries with smaller than average productivity gains; and declining prices in industries with greater than average productivity gains.

If each industry follows this guidepost, prices in the economy will maintain a constant average.

Some exceptions to these guideposts are necessary to promote an efficient allocation of resources and a high rate of growth, and to redress inequities which have kept certain workers at the bottom of the wage scale. Wage increases above the guidepost level may be necessary where an industry is unable to attract sufficient labor to meet the demands for its products, where wages are particularly low, and where changes in work rules create large gains in productivity and substantial human costs requiring special adjustment of compensation. Because the industries in which market power is concentrated are largely high-wage industries with a relatively low long-term rate of increase of employment, the first two of these exceptions are rarely applicable.

On the price side, increases in price above the guidepost may be necessary to allow for increases in nonlabor costs or to correct an inability to attract needed capital.

Each of these exceptions has a symmetrical counterpart calling for downward departures from the guideposts. Wages should rise less than the guidepost rate where an industry suffers from above-average unemployment and where wages are exceptionally high for the type of work. Price increases should be smaller—or price decreases larger— where unit nonlabor costs fall, where capacity is too large, and where profits are based on excessive market power.

The guideposts are not meant to preclude the possibility of a change in distribution of income between labor and capital in industry. Where one side or the other is able to increase its share of industry income, but not at the expense of the public, the national interest need not be involved. However, it should be kept in mind that in most concentrated industries the division of income between labor and capital remained essentially unchanged all through the wage-price spirals of the 1950's. The repeated attempts to alter income shares proved self-defeating: neither side gained, and both lost through higher prices, weaker markets, reduced profits, and lower employment.

Table 1 illustrates the postwar experience with prices, wages, and productivity in the United States. Recent changes in employee compensation have conformed to productivity gains much more closely than in the 1950's, and price increases have been much more modest.

The guideposts offer a standard for responsible business, labor, and Government leadership in an environment of informed public opinion. They are an attempt to operate our economy as it is—without

TABLE 1. *Changes in productivity, wages, and prices in the private economy since 1947*

YEAR	PRODUC-TIVITY[1]	TREND PRODUC-TIVITY[2]	TOTAL COMPENSA-TION PER MAN-HOUR	PRICES		
				IMPLICIT GNP DEFLATOR	WHOLESALE	CONSUMER
			PERCENTAGE CHANGE[3]			
1948	3.6	—	8.6	6.8	8.3	7.7
1949	2.8	—	2.5	−.8	−5.0	−1.0
1950	7.1	—	5.7	1.2	4.0	1.0
1951	2.5	—	9.3	7.9	11.4	8.0
1952	2.2	3.7	5.9	1.6	−2.8	2.2
1953	4.0	3.7	5.8	.6	−1.4	.8
1954	1.8	3.5	3.3	.8	.2	.4
1955	4.4	3.0	2.9	.9	.3	−.3
1956	.2	2.5	6.1	3.1	3.2	1.5
1957	3.5	2.8	5.9	3.5	2.9	3.5
1958	2.4	2.5	3.6	1.7	1.4	2.8
1959	3.6	2.8	4.6	1.6	.2	.8
1960	2.0	2.3	3.6	1.2	.1	1.6
1961	3.4	3.0	3.6	1.0	−.4	1.1
1962	4.5	3.2	4.0	.7	.3	1.2
1963	2.9	3.3	3.1	1.2	−.3	1.2
1964	3.1	3.2	3.8	1.4	.2	1.3

[1] Output per man-hour for all persons; labor input based primarily on establishment data.
[2] Average annual percentage change in output per man-hour during latest five years.
[4] Percentage change from previous year, except trend productivity.
Sources: Department of Commerce, Department of Labor, and Council of Economic Advisers.

controls, without wholesale fragmentation of our large, successful enterprises—and to maintain stable prices while using our resources, our capital, and our labor to their full potential. They are in the tradition of America, asking those to whom the society has entrusted economic power to exercise it in ways consistent with the national interest.

Large corporations and labor unions can—and generally do—use their power to play a constructive role in our economy. At the same time they must be accountable for their actions to public opinion, and must recognize that the public will ask "Why?"

—when a union insists on a wage settlement that, if universally applied, would mar the price record of the economy;

—when a firm or industry agrees willingly to a wage settlement above the guideposts which it then translates into higher prices for its products;

—when a firm or industry with extraordinary productivity gains fails to share the benefits with consumers in the form of lower prices;

—when a firm or industry with average productivity gains chooses to raise its prices.

Arthur M. Ross
WAGE RESTRAINTS IN PEACETIME

The celebrated "Guideposts for Noninflationary Wage and Price Behavior" have occasioned more comment and criticism than any previous pronouncements by the Council of Economic Advisers since that body was established in 1946.

Promulgation of the Guideposts was preceded and succeeded by numerous statements from high government officials—including the President, Secretary Goldberg and Chairman Heller—to the effect that important wage and price decisions were no longer a purely private matter but now partook of the public interest. The government would henceforth concern itself with the content of collective bargaining agreements and not merely with procedures for peaceful negotiation. After five years of slackness in the economy, the Administration was determined to restore full employment (although the concept of full employment had been loosened somewhat). It was feared that as full employment was more closely approached, price inflation would set in, by virtue of collective bargaining and administered pricing, even though economic resources were still in ample supply. Inflation would make it more difficult to increase the favorable balance of commodity trade, which approximated $5,000,000,000 in 1961. But unless the balance of

From *Proceedings of the Western Economic Association*, 1962. Reprinted by permission.

Mr. Ross became Commissioner of the United States Bureau of Labor Statistics in 1965. He was formerly Professor of Industrial Relations, University of California, Berkeley.

trade could be improved, the country could not meet its military and economic responsibilities around the world without encountering an intolerable gold loss.

Economists had been wrestling for some years with the question of whether full employment and price stability could both be achieved with existing price- and wage-determining institutions. In the 1950's there was a widespread conviction we could not have the best of both worlds, and that creeping inflation was preferable to creeping stagnation if a choice had to be made. This earlier debate was conducted primarily in a domestic context, however. Emergence of the foreign exchange problem gave another twist to the screw and inspired renewed efforts to find ways and means of reconciling our principal economic objectives.

Before turning to the Guideposts themselves, we may observe that the United States is not the only country currently endeavoring to restrain wage increases, in order to prevent inflation, without implementing full-blown wage and price controls. Since 1955 the Conservative government in Great Britain has experimented with various techniques. Most recently the Chancellor of the Exchequer, Mr. Selwyn Lloyd, instituted a "wage pause" in the Civil Service, the nationalized industries, and other activities subject to direct control of the government. It was hoped that this policy would set a good example for the private sector. It is not at all clear that this hope was realized, but it is amply clear that the "wage pause" contributed to the sagging popularity of the Tories and to Mr. Lloyd's replacement as a Cabinet member in July of this year.

Similarly, Chancellor Adenauer and the President of the Reichsbank have been sounding warnings against wage increases in excess of four percent, which is stated to be the average annual increase in man-hour productivity in West Germany. These warnings have been enthusiastically seconded by BDA, the central confederation of German employers. The individual employers have ignored them almost completely, however, and have been granting wage increases which would seem astronomical even in the California construction industry.

In France, as in Britain, an austerity wage policy has been pursued in the public services and nationalized industries. Great unrest has resulted, particularly among transportation workers. When Prime Minister Debre addressed a letter to the employers' confederation urging restraint in wage bargaining, the union groups reacted angrily against this one-sided intervention.

Here in the United States, the Council of Economic Advisers has made repeated observations on wage policy during the past decade. In January 1952, President Truman's outgoing Council urged that wage increases be held to the level of productivity gains, about two or three percent annually. President Eisenhower's Council more than once endorsed the same proposition in rather general terms. In the 1959 steel dispute, Administration pressure probably held down the size of the wage package, but also encouraged the employers' intransigent bargaining posture and the long strike over local working practices.

Thus the Guideposts are not new in principle. What is new is the more detailed exposition of these principles by the Council and the ardor with which the Administration has embraced them.

The Council's central proposition is that "if all prices remain stable, all hourly labor costs may increase as fast as economy-wide productivity without, for that reason alone, changing the relative share of labor and nonlabor incomes in total output." This is the Delphic pronouncement which was widely interpreted as establishing a "three percent productivity limit." Actually no percentage figure is stated, but a table is supplied showing average rates of growth of output per man-hour in various parts of the economy during various time periods. Three percent is the average annual increase in the total private economy between 1947 and 1960.

The Council then modestly observes that productivity is a guide rather than a rule for appraising price and wage behavior. There are problems in measuring productivity change; the existing distribution of income between labor and capital is not necessarily immutable; and "the pattern of wages and prices among industries is and should be responsive to forces other than changes in productivity. . . ."

At first blush the Guideposts seem simple enough but on further analysis, numerous problems of interpretation and application arise.

Are the Guideposts only a means of assisting the general public in appraising the wisdom of private wage and price decisions, or are they mandatory and subject to enforcement through the exercise of executive power? The Council's Report insists that the Guideposts are intended as a contribution to "public discussion and clarification of the issues." But the President and Secretary Goldberg have stated on more than one occasion that the government cannot stand idly by when the public interest needs protecting.

How are the Guideposts to be interpreted? Three possibilities suggest themselves. The first is that increases should not exceed 3.0 or 3.5 percent. Although the Council strove to obviate such an interpretation, the Administration has contributed to it by publicly praising significant wage settlements "within the limits set by productivity," and remaining silent on those exceeding 3.0 or 3.5 percent.

The second possible interpretation is the one which the Council urges: that average wage increases should not exceed average productivity gains, but that specific adjustments may deviate upward or downward in accordance with the Council's suggested criteria. The criteria themselves have some startling implications, such as the notion that wage increases under free collective bargaining can and should be inversely proportional to the workers' bargaining power. The Report betrays a curious innocence of the pressures and energies at work in real collective bargaining situations. But there is an even more fundamental problem: how can a desired *ex post* statistical result be converted into thousands of *ex ante* wage decisions? Has the Council really given us policy guides or merely tools of economic analysis? Moreover, do not the criteria easily lend themselves to opportunistic re-labelling of wage demands and adjustments? The United Automobile Workers, ingenious as ever, led the way by asserting that increases in excess of average productivity gains should be negotiated in the aerospace industry in order to "catch up" previous deficiencies. Also, has the Administration now established an inflationary "bargaining floor" of three percent, as many employers complain?

A third possible interpretation of the Guideposts is that they provide a serviceable tool which the Administration may use as the basis for exerting pressure in a few key situations such as steel. This is probably the most practical and realistic view, but here also there are some sticky questions to be answered. Aside from the basic steel industry, where are these key situations? As Solicitor General Archibald Cox recently confessed, "steel is almost unique." He said that "the trick may be to pick out those few key situations which have the same potential as steel for setting off a chain reaction." Automobiles, aluminum, petroleum and aircraft were mentioned as possibilities, but of these only the first really has the power to set off a chain reaction in other industries.

All four of Mr. Cox's candidates, like basic steel, are industries with a few big corporations which negotiate company-wide agreements with industrial unions. As many observers have noted, the Administration has not found any practical method of putting its finger on the construction industry with its highly decentralized bargaining structure. Is it equitable to concentrate on a few industries and unions which are exposed politically by virtue of size and concentration? Moreover, is it practical, or will the so-called "responsible" unions find the price too great? . . .

Regardless of how the Guideposts are interpreted, there are some additional problems to be noted. When the government endeavors to influence the results of a decentralized bargaining system while preserving the right to strike, we really have a dual basis of wage determination. The weak unions will expect the government to assist them in securing "the productivity formula," while the strong unions will exert their bargaining power. As we learned from the experience of the Wage Stabilization Board during the Korean War, the net result is likely to be stimulation rather than restraint of wage increases.

Subjecting the wage-setting process to a formula would sterilize the central function of trade unions at a time when the labor movement is already in deep distress. Can organized labor accept voluntary sterilization? The case might be different if something were offered in return, as the War Labor Board offered union security in return for wage control during World War II. But nothing is provided to help the unions solve their institutional problems. Under these conditions it is certainly doubtful that the Administration could implement the Guidelines in a serious way without sacrificing labor support.

Finally, we must ask whether active emphasis on wage restraint is appropriate when economic recovery has fallen so far short of full employment. So long as the rate of unemployment hovers between five and seven percent of the labor force, inflation is not a serious threat. . . .

I have no desire to deprecate the problem to which the Guideposts are directed. Standards of economic performance have become more exacting; creeping inflation is no longer as acceptable as it seemed a few years ago. There is little reason to doubt that the price level would begin to climb once more if we should come close to full employment, that a cost push originating in administered-price industries would contribute to the trend. Most of the economically advanced countries are struggling to find ways and means of encouraging noninflationary wage settlements without sacrificing the institutions of free collective bargaining. The fact that they have not yet been successful does not mean that the search should be abandoned.

The next step for us in the United States, I believe, is to understand more fully the requirements of successful wage restraint in peacetime and to appraise our situation realistically in the light of these requirements.

1. The first requirement is public acceptance of an overriding national need justifying restraints on private behavior. There was public acceptance of the need during World War II, of course. Some European countries have experimented successfully with wage restraint during the postwar period; in these countries foreign trade is such an important part of the economy that the exchange problem is clear to all concerned. On the other hand, American labor and management have certainly not been persuaded that these traditionally private areas of decision have now entered the public domain.

2. Second, decision makers and opinion leaders must have at least a general understanding of the economic relationships involving wages, prices and productivity. In the United States labor and manage-

ment each employ their own distorted caricature of economics, as contrasted with a country like Sweden where one finds a basic consensus on these matters. The relatively low level of economic understanding in the United States has several explanations, in my opinion; foreign trade has been only a minor component of total business activity; economic constraints in general have not been as taxing as in Europe; professional economists have too often shied away from public affairs, preferring to sharpen their analytical tools rather than use them.

3. Next, a successful national wage policy must have positive as well as negative elements so that all the pressure will not appear to be directed against the workers. In this connection it is interesting that some European countries combined wage restraint with a policy of "wage solidarity," an explicit commitment to improve the relative position of those at the bottom of the income pyramid. One of the difficult elements in the Administration's approach is that all the praise is reserved for the low settlements. The federal minimum wage has been increased, it is true, but legal enactments do not contribute directly toward balancing out the performance of the collective bargaining mechanism.

4. Wage restraint must be sought in an appropriate context of economic policies designed to implement a full-employment commitment. Until very recently, the Administration seems to have been unduly preoccupied with fears of inflation and insufficiently concerned with restoring full employment. At times we have been given the impression that wage restraint is vitally needed in its own right even with a five or six percent unemployment ratio. Surely this is not correct. Concededly the Administration has a difficult row to hoe in persuading most Americans to accept the economic policies necessary to maintain full employment. Resistance to planning and controls, the tradition of corporate autonomy and the strength of business unionism are powerful barriers. . . .

5. History shows that effective wage restraint cannot be imposed on the parties from the outside. On the contrary, it must be developed through consultation between labor, industry and the government. For this purpose there must be a potent, competent consultative mechanism capable of producing an authoritative consensus. In the President's Labor-Management Committee we have an interesting experiment in top-level consultation, but the effectiveness of the Committee in controversial areas is not yet demonstrated. The central problem seems to be that of interest-group leadership. Who speaks for American employers? If N.A.M. and Chamber of Commerce officials are selected, they will adhere to rigid organizational positions. If prominent industrialists are chosen, their individual views will not necessarily be binding on industry as a whole. In selecting labor representatives, the Administration neces-

sarily turns to the heads of the AFL-CIO and of major unions; but here again it has not yet been shown that these representatives will deviate publicly from their institutional doctrines. . . .

6. Finally, any influential national wage policy must be impregnated into the collective bargaining apparatus. Otherwise it will merely serve as a target or beacon for the weak unions without restraining the strong. There are several possible ways in which a wage policy might be incorporated into the collective bargaining system. (a) There might be a highly centralized bargaining structure, with leadership and coordination supplied by powerful labor and employer federations. This is the situation in Norway and the Netherlands, which are regarded as the most successful practitioners of conscious wage restraint in peacetime. (b) There might be a tripartite government board with mandatory power, such as the National War Labor Board of World War II. (c) The collective bargaining scene might be dominated by a few unions with centralized bargaining policies. If sufficiently secure from factionalism, rival unionism, and internal unrest, these unions might be amenable to government pressure. (d) Conceivably, the public sector of the economy might be so large that the wage policies of government, acting as an employer, would set the pattern for the private sector as well.

To list these possibilities is enough to show how remote they are at the present moment. The American bargaining structure is among the most decentralized in the world, and the federations of industry and labor are very weak. Certainly the nation is not now prepared to accept the equivalent of compulsory arbitration and direct wage-price controls in peacetime. Union members are divided among scores of organizations; and many of these—such as the construction unions—practice decentralized bargaining. And certainly the public sector is not a pattern setter, nor likely to be one in the foreseeable future.

Thus a realistic appraisal of the situation gives no grounds for easy optimism over the prospects of wage restraint in peacetime. Yet the underlying problem is still with us if we continue to believe that a five percent unemployment rate is too high, a three percent growth rate is too low, and a two or three percent rate of creeping inflation is too much. All this means that we will have to develop a more sophisticated consensus on economic facts and relationships. We will need greater acceptance of overriding national goals and a proper "policy mix" in which wage and price restraint have their necessary place in a full employment strategy. We will find it necessary to develop some new institutions and adapt existing institutions. These things will take considerable time unless we should enter a period of crisis. . . .

strikes

George P. Shultz

STRIKES: THE PRIVATE STAKE
AND THE PUBLIC INTEREST

It has been widely observed that Congressional approval of compulsory arbitration in the railroad industry marks a breakdown of private bargaining, and may well lead to compulsory arbitration for a wide range of vital industries.

This is a tragic half-truth.

The misunderstanding of what has taken place on the railroads and in other cases of intense government intervention may well lead to a drastic and, I believe, undesirable shift toward compulsion in our system of industrial relations. But this will not reflect a breakdown of private bargaining.

There has been no real private bargaining on the railroads for decades. What has failed is government-dominated bargaining. Ironically, when this much-government system finally failed completely, the answer was more government—in the form of compulsory arbitration— rather than less. And the irony is the more striking since free and more-nearly-private bargaining is, by and large, working well.

My purpose here is to convince you that a free and private system of industrial relations is far superior to a government-dominated one; and that this alternative is really available, despite the many and

Selected Paper No. 8, Graduate School of Business, University of Chicago, 1963. Reprinted by permission of the publisher and author.

Mr. Shultz is Dean of the Graduate School of Business, University of Chicago.

serious steps taken in the other direction during the past few years. To do so, I know, I must face up directly to the questions raised for the community by strikes, especially strikes involving large numbers of people or strategically placed workers. I must present a way of dealing with major labor disputes that you judge to be a workable, practical way. No doubt government has important responsibilities which will tax its capacities in this area, but its role must not be the dominant one toward which it now seems headed.

My theme will be developed through discussion of the following points: (1) Some general comments about labor policy and current labor relations problems. (2) Examination of the role of conflict in labor relations and of objectives, private and public, other than simply labor peace. (3) Analysis of why the present course of developments is wrong. (4) Advocacy of a different course—one more consistent, I think, with the values of free institutions operating in a market economy.

GENERAL COMMENTS

Possible approaches to labor policy can be classified broadly into two types. The first, and most tempting to many people, is direct and solution-oriented. Its apparent simplicity is attractive. If we do not like strikes, outlaw them. If we don't like featherbedding, prohibit it. If we think wage rates are too low, raise them by action of the government; or if they are rising too fast, establish guides to control the rise. The emphasis here is always on meeting a pressing problem with a direct solution—or at least what may appear to be a solution. This approach can be summarized by the old saying, "There ought to be a law."

The other approach looks at the structure and processes from which solutions emerge, rather than at any individual result. When results in general are unsatisfactory, it asks what kind of process is producing them; and it leads to suggestions for changing the process, thus affecting results—but indirectly. I find it hard, by way of a process-oriented example, to accept an arrangement that involves the payment of unemployment compensation to strikers, as in New York or on the railroads.

On the whole, an approach that emphasizes processes seems to me preferable to one that goes directly to a particular result. This in part is a practical judgment about what is most likely to work. But it also is a statement of ideological preference—a preference for arrangements that allow freedom of action for companies, unions, and collective bargaining arrangements, and is in tune with the objectives of a society with at least major emphasis on individual and organizational liberty.

My second general comment is made in the interests of realism. In the field of labor relations policy, as in many others, there is hardly ever a course of action that is all gain. We are constantly engaged in weighing and balancing costs *versus* gains. We are always saying, "Yes, it would be nice to have a little more of this; but if we have more of this, we must be reconciled to a little less of something else which is also desirable, or which someone else may want."

By way of example: Both labor and management people could doubtless agree that you can find some uneconomic work practices, in some industries, if you look hard enough. I think it is very unlikely, however, if you want to get rid of some of these practices, that it will be done unless companies—and in some cases the public—are willing to pay the price in terms of a little conflict. There may be a gain; but there is also a cost. If you are not willing to put up with any conflict, you are not going to get many of these gains.

Or, in a completely different type of example: the National Labor Relations Board has recently been struggling with the problem of how long a contract should bar an election to determine the representation wishes of workers. I believe they have now settled on three years; but at any rate, it is quite apparent that the longer the period you allow, the more you are putting emphasis on the goal of stability in labor-management relations. You are saying, "Let a situation settle down a bit; let people work together and give them time to see what they can do."

At the same time, you are paying a price. The price is that there will be some workers who are dissatisfied with the labor-management relationship, and they are not able to change it. You are telling them they can't do it. In that sense you are paying a price in terms of some loss of individual liberties.

So the point here is that we frustrate and delude ourselves in this field if we seek something that is perfect in the sense of being a costless solution. There are no costless solutions. . . .

THE ROLE OF CONFLICT

It has been said that "job-security" now outweighs "wages" in importance as an issue for collective bargaining. Certainly, all the well-publicized recent disputes—railroad, newspaper, longshore—revolve around the issue of jobs; or perhaps more accurately, around the jobs that used to be there but may now be on the way out. So like it or not, we will have to struggle in labor relations with all the stresses and strains that inevitably accompany important changes in the structure of jobs. No one should be surprised if these stresses occasionally break into the open.

So much emphasis has been placed in recent years on the public interest in labor peace that other important goals in labor relations—goals in which there is also a private stake and a public interest—have been almost totally obscured. Let us take a look at the role of conflict in attaining these goals. In doing so, we need not get in the position of advocating strikes, of condoning the purely destructive conflict that you see occasionally, or of denigrating in any way the importance of knowing how to resolve differences without strikes. Much has been learned in this area over the past three decades and many interesting and novel experiments are now under way. All these are to be applauded and encouraged, but not to the point where we become Pollyannaish about labor relationships.

First of all, we must acknowledge that conflict, of which the strike is but one example, is a widely used method for producing generally desirable results for our society. We use it in the academic community, where much is made of the idea that a clash of views, a back-and-forth exchange, will yield illumination on the subject at hand. We have organized our economy on the basis of freedom to enter new businesses, to innovate, to engage in competition for markets. Let there be many companies in the field and let them fight with each other so that the consumer gets better products and lower prices. Some people get hurt by these processes; . . . they can on occasion be rough. But, by and large, they are productive.

By the same token, in the field of industrial relations the possibility of challenge and response, from a base of some power on both sides, can be constructive. It provides an opportunity for people who have different backgrounds and orientations to bring out and represent their interests forcefully. Such representation can be productive, but it cannot take place if we do not allow for the possibility of a clash in views and the likelihood of an occasional explosion.

Second, we must all realize, whether as members of "the public" or in our private capacities, that we have a tremendous stake and a great interest in the vitality of private parties and private processes. If you have a management that is moribund and is not doing anything, or if you have a union that is lazy and is not representing its workers adequately, you really do not have a healthy situation at all. We want, instead, companies and unions who are alert, energetic, driving—who are analyzing their interests and representing them vigorously. So we have a great stake, as the public, in having private parties who are vital in this sense. And if, because of our abhorrence of strikes, we take action that in effect takes the play away from private parties, we will sap their vitality, and wind up with a peaceful, stagnant inefficiency on both sides.

A good case in point is the railroads, where the government-dominated system of collective bargaining, at least until very recently, has fairly well sapped the vitality of the processes involved and has left the situation much worse than it otherwise might be. When it takes six years to settle a simple grievance, you surely have a bad situation.

LET PARTIES BE RESPONSIBLE

Third, in this effort to suggest that the public has a stake in strikes other than only to get them settled, I offer you the great importance of having private parties *be* responsible, *feel* responsible and *take responsibility* for the results of their efforts. Whatever settlement is reached—good, bad, or indifferent—somehow it must be their own settlement. It is the settlement of the people who have worked it out, not somebody else's doing. "If we're responsible for it, we've got to make it work; it's our baby." It seems to me that the public has a great interest in seeing this kind of attitude develop.

Finally, we must recognize that some strikes are simply part of the price we pay for free collective bargaining. If you tell people they are not allowed to strike or, in the case of management, take a strike, then they are simply not free to pursue their interests as they see those interests. It is just one of the costs that goes with the gain of having a free system. This is a very simple—sometimes a very harsh—but surely a most important point.

Now, I am not saying that the public does not have a stake in damping conflict as much as possible; in making it orderly; in seeing it channeled to some degree; in doing all kinds of things to pound a little sense into the people concerned and make them see just what is coming before they get involved in overt conflict.

But on the other hand, there are these other private stakes and public interests which are important but which hardly ever are mentioned. They get completely obscured by this great emphasis upon peace and tranquility on the labor scene.

Of course, the greater the costs of labor-management conflict, the less happy we are to pay them. This point, then, is of great importance: The price we are paying for free bargaining in this country is an exceedingly small one, and we should not be reluctant to pay it.

We are all familiar with the statistics; by this time perhaps we all tend to dismiss them. But you just cannot get away from the fact that the volume of strike activity, of overt conflict, is very, very small. It runs in the neighborhood of less than one-fifth of one per cent of man days worked lost through strikes each year. It is down at that low level right along. So we are not dealing these days with a situation in which somehow conflict has gotten all out of bounds and is all around us. It isn't. It may seem to be, but on a statistical basis, it isn't.

Moreover, I will assert that there are very seldom times when strikes pose genuine threats to the health or safety of the community, or even to the operation of the economy. The resiliency of the economy, its ability to adapt and insulate itself from these things, is really very remarkable and should not be underrated. According to elaborate reports of people who have studied big strikes, the supposed dire effects from the impact of a strike are very hard to find.

THE LONGSHORE CASE

Now, perhaps you will say that the recent longshore strike, in which a Taft-Hartley injunction was used, is a case against me. That may be, but I think it is worth noting that the President sought and got an injunction against such a strike on the grounds that, if the strike were permitted to occur, it would create a national emergency. But after the injunction expired, a strike did run for over one month and what did people talk about? All I read about in the *Wall Street Journal* was the bananas; you are not going to get bananas, they are doubling in price. My, oh my, should we throw away our freedoms for a hand of bananas? Just for fun, one morning in New York after the strike had been on some weeks, I ordered bananas with my shredded wheat to see if they would come. The waiter didn't even give me an argument, he brought the bananas. Or *a* banana, I should say. Maybe he only had one. This is not to deny the genuine economic hardship and public inconvenience that can be caused by a prolonged strike on the docks or in some other industries. But the allegations of hardship need the closest scrutiny, and the true costs must be balanced against the price of intervention.

It should be further noted that, in the face of this crisis, the Senator Morse Board was appointed and was able to bring about a settlement under threat of Congressional involvement. The wage package was certainly steep and the settlement made little contribution to resolution of the basic issues of efficiency of operation and job security. I would rather have seen the parties fight it out.

So, in summary, my point is that the public has vital interests in allowing people freedom to strike—or take a strike—if they want to, and if these interests are disregarded, the system of industrial relations is going to change very drastically.

Furthermore, in taking this position, at least in this day and age, we are really not taking such a terrible risk, because the volume and the impact of strikes are not nearly so great as alleged. Most goods and services turn out to have fairly close substitutes, which, indeed, is one reason for prompt settlement of most disputes. Or, alternatively, inventories may provide a considerable hedge against the impact of a strike.

There are problems, of course, but they are far overrated, and the health and safety aspects are usually not present.

A DANGEROUS COURSE

The present course of national policy has seemed, at least until very recently, to be: Intervene early; intervene with preconceptions of what the right answer is; and intervene frequently, over a wide scale, with high officials. And now the picture is further complicated by the fact that Congress, albeit reluctantly, is in the act.

I do not think that is a considered policy, but is just what has happened. That is in a sense the effective policy we have, and it has been born out of all sorts of frustrations, out of all sorts of problems arising from the structure and issues of collective bargaining.

Let us make the following points about this course:

This is an instance, to use the economists' terminology, where supply creates its own demand. As my colleague, Robert Livernash, put it: "If the President hangs out his shingle, he'll get all the business." People will come to a high official if he is willing to have them. So what we see as a result is a lot of pressure for intervention, from whichever party thinks it has more to gain. And there is also a lot of pressure for high-level attention. Who can be satisfied with just a plain old Federal mediator? Who's he? Or even the director of the Federal Mediation and Conciliation Service. It is getting to the point where you are not a big boy any more unless you have the Secretary of Labor involved. One thing leads to another in a cumulative process that is difficult to reverse.

Furthermore, when these high-level procedures are used with great frequency (and no doubt you have to use them sometimes), they completely lose their impact. Somebody who is very high up should be saved. He should not be running around, doing this, that, and the other thing with all kinds of disputes that everybody and his brother get into. Regardless of how much and how genuinely he wants to be helpful, he just cannot, because it depreciates the currency, so to speak.

POTENTIAL FOR FAILURE

This process also demands solutions, as in the case of the Morse Board. If you are going to take the intervention route, then you have to provide the answer. If parties feel they are not getting what they want through bargaining, they are certainly going to find out what the government's answer is and try to use that leverage as much as possible. We are all familiar with this process. And it can ruin private bargaining because it forces each party to hold back any concessions that might normally be made. Anything you concede will be held against you in the next higher round of discussions. This is precisely what has happened on the railroads, where the one thing everyone agrees on is that there has been little real bargaining until recently.

Finally, this course has in it a very, very great potential for failure. We are going to run into situations, right along the line, where all these procedures are going to be indulged in, and where one party or the other—management in some cases, union in others—will say: "With all due respect to you, Mr. President, or to your Board, I just don't agree with you, and I'm standing on my position."

When that happens—and it already has on at least one occasion —the gauntlet is down. That is a terrible situation for the President to be in. As President Kennedy said, in effect, in a television interview last Spring, commenting on the steel price conflict, "Well, what could I do, after all this had happened, there I was and I had been defied? I had to pull out all the stops."

The question one needs to ask is: Was it wise to get in that position in the first place? I ask this with respect not only to steel but to a whole range of cases. The potential for failure not only is great, it is absolutely certain that the high authority is going to be defied by the strong-minded groups we have in this country. And the results of failure of this kind of an approach drive you inevitably further into all sorts of relatively drastic types of solution that are not process-oriented but result-oriented. The big one that is always mentioned—everybody falls for it, I think—is compulsory arbitration. And now, as a friend of mine put it in discussing the railroads, "Here we is, damned if we ain't."

WHAT SHOULD BE DONE?

The implications of the present course are serious. We have gone quite a long way, and we ought to ask ourselves: Isn't it time for a fresh look? There are, of course, all sorts of places where blame can be put. But our problem, at least as I see it, is to say: "Where do we go from here? How do we rearrange things so that we can have a reasonable process of bargaining, and so that we don't get our high public officials involved in these impossible situations?"

Let me throw out a few ideas in the full realization that it is much easier to be critical than to be constructive.

First of all, as an administrative proposition, it seems very important somehow for the government to change its stance, to make a more considered assessment of the possible impact of strikes, and to help the public make such an assessment. The government seems now in the position of always playing up the possible damaging impact of a strike. I would like to see a shift to a stance in line with what the facts are, with the public being told, "All right, so there's a strike; there are still plenty of bananas. Relax, it isn't a crisis after all." Now, of course, a serious situation must be labelled as such; but it seems to me that the cry of an impending crisis comes all too quickly. And in this the press seems all too ready to cooperate. So my first point is to educate the public about what is really going on.

REFUSE TO GET INVOLVED

Second, it is very important for the high-level people to virtually refuse to get involved, and to say, "I've had it and I'm just not going to spend so much time on labor disputes any more." Let the top officials disengage themselves and try to get the problem pushed into an area where there are professional people who are supposed to spend all of their time doing this kind of thing. The mediation resources of the community are vast; and with leadership from a Mediation Service that is given a real chance, these resources can do a great deal.

My third point rests on a common analysis of the impact of major strikes. One almost always finds that the public health and safety aspect or defense aspect of the strike, when present, is a very small component of the total picture—involving the transportation of food from the Mainland to Hawaii, for instance, or the production of certain special types of defense steel.

So perhaps we can use an approach that has not been tried much but which would seem to offer real potential for protecting the public interest. We could have limited, continued operation, but still let most of the strike go on—an approach built on the possibility of partial operation of struck facilities. To be sure, there are all sorts of political difficulties, but the difficulties are worth facing up to.

Now some may say, "Partial operation—that's just strike breaking," or "This is just giving the employer a chance to divide the union against itself," or "giving the union a chance to divide the employers," by picking a little piece out of the total situation. After all, the industry wanted industry-wide bargaining for the sake of strength. The union wanted to have the industry sewed up for the sake of strength. So, some might argue, partial operation is simply a way of favoring somebody in their strategy.

I do not agree. Of course, if you let the union or the company call its shots on partial operation and have it done exactly the way either one wants, then partial operation could be manipulated in this way. But if you have your partial operations directed by a public official whose objective and legal responsibilities are purely and simply to get certain goods transported, or produced, in certain small quantities, then it seems to me the bargaining strategy argument really ought to fall by the wayside.

Finally, just to show you that I haven't lost my mind completely, let me assure you that I believe it is very important to encourage a wide variety of mediation approaches, private approaches. Private approaches have been producing and will produce good results. I hesitate to mention third parties, because that always seems to come with little grace from someone who acts occasionally in that capacity. But I'll mention it in part to say that, at least in my observation, some of the most effective third parties are drawn from unions or companies into some particular dispute. So it isn't always a so-called neutral. It may be that procedures which involve people with some standing from a company or from a union, in a private way and without commitment of all the superstructure of government, can produce a good result.

Together some of these things can help any administration give the public assurance that the government *is* doing something. It is trying to help get things settled; it is protecting the public interest in at least partial operation. Perhaps, if accompanied by sane and careful statements about the impact of a strike, these measures will diminish the pressure from the public somewhat and allow some of these less spectacular procedures to operate.

In any case, you can see that the cornerstones of my position are an assessment that the strike situation in this country does not present us with a crisis, that private processes can work well, but that private processes are doomed unless we develop more tolerance for at least a minimum level of conflict.

To be sure, there are costs as well as gains. But for my part, freedom and the vitality of private parties and private processes are worth the cost.

Independent
Labor Study Group
THE PROBLEM
OF EMERGENCY DISPUTES

. . . Agreement by the parties is our basic method for reaching fundamental settlements to labor disputes. Even in cases involving large numbers of workers or the threat of an emergency, in our view, the

Reprinted by permission from *The Public Interest in National Labor Policy* by an Independent Labor Study Group, Committee for Economic Development, New York, 1961, pp. 95–104.

principle of ultimate private agreement must guide the design and use of government procedures for dispute settlement. Nevertheless, we must recognize that the use of economic force by the parties in certain vital industries or at certain critical times can inflict serious harm on the public interest. Some protective instruments must be placed in the hands of the government. Since such instruments interfere with the freedom of the parties, they must be employed with great discretion and should be entrusted only to the President.

In considering the questions of what procedures to establish and of how these procedures should be used, we are now able to draw on extensive experience at both the state and federal level. Certain aspects of this experience deserve special comment.

1. True emergencies have been rare. Since 1947 when the Taft-Hartley machinery for handling emergency disputes became effective, this machinery has been used only nineteen times and in several of these cases the existence of a genuine emergency was at least doubtful. State legislation on emergency disputes is largely inactive today but there is no evidence that communities are plagued with this problem. Study after study has shown that the emergency potential of a given labor dispute is always grossly exaggerated at the moment it occurs. Dire conjectures about "what would happen if" seldom become reality. The parties have the capacity for behavior that takes account of essential public needs. In addition, the resiliency and flexibility of a free economy are impressive. All this suggests that any special procedures should be used with utmost caution and reluctance.

2. The President is always subjected to heavy political pressures to move into an important labor dispute. These pressures he must resist, though to do so often calls for great political skill and courage. To do otherwise invites frequent use of whatever procedures are devised; and, in turn, frequent use undermines the process of bargaining that must ultimately produce the settlement. We note subsequently how this very pattern of too frequent use has emerged in the railroad industry. It is better to rely on intelligent behavior by the parties as the principal method for resolving disputes, while seeing that the most essential needs of the community are protected.

3. It has been frequently observed that partial operation of a struck industry or facility may be all that is necessary to protect the public interest in continued availability of the good or service involved. Thus, a study completed in January 1961, for the outgoing Secretary of Labor suggests that partial operation of the steel industry might well have been a feasible method for taking care of defense needs. It may be noted in addition, that the speed with which steel inventories were rebuilt after a strike lasting 116 days and the high level of inventories

accumulated before the strike suggest that the impact on the steel industry's customers was less than assumed at the time Taft-Hartley procedures were invoked. At any rate, the possibility of partial operation offers hope in many industries, including those providing transportation services, of protecting public interests while allowing private pressures on private parties to bring about a voluntary settlement.

The President is entitled to have this possibility explicitly recognized in the law and he should explore the feasibility of partial operation before he seeks a broader remedy in any individual case.

4. Disputes vary in their scope, their history, their points of impasse, and in many other ways. Each one is unique. It is therefore sensible to equip the President with a variety of possible courses of action. This would enable him to adapt his efforts to the circumstances. Further, it has the advantage of making his actions somewhat less predictable to the parties than is the case in the clearly prescribed procedures now found in the Taft-Hartley and Railway Labor Acts. An uncertain procedure is difficult for the parties to anticipate in their own bargaining strategy. It may therefore have the effect of encouraging them to avoid the procedure by settling disputes for themselves.

A distinction must be drawn between two essentially different kinds of government intervention: (a) that designed to prevent a national crisis or emergency from developing, and (b) that to be used in the rare instance when we have such a national crisis or emergency.

In the first category would fall a variety of means aimed at imparting greater vigor to the mediation process, which in turn has as its purpose stimulation of and assistance to the parties in working out agreements. Some of the ways of developing greater effectiveness in mediation are discussed in the preceding section. Here, however, we suggest additional measures for disputes in industries which are potentially the source of national emergencies.

Too much is sometimes left for settlement during the stress of negotiations on the eve of the termination of agreements. There are many problems of more or less complexity which could get far more rational and objective treatment at more placid times, but for some reason consideration is postponed until no further temporizing is possible. Our suggestion is that the Federal Mediation and Conciliation Service, or the National Mediation Board, depending on the industry, encourage the principals to address themselves to such anticipated problems throughout the term of their current agreement, possibly with the help of a competent and acceptable neutral familiar with their industry. This could well be an experienced mediator affiliated with these agencies, preferably designated by the parties; or it could be someone not in government service on whom they would agree. The arrangements suggested earlier for the Mediation Service should help make this step possible and workable.

Another constructive step toward development of preventive mediation would be a more useful employment of facts and the fact-finding process. We recognize, of course, that "facts" by themselves will not settle all disputes. Yet there are sometimes harsh and protracted arguments over facts, arguments which serve no purpose but to delay the parties in grappling with the real issues. This is both needless and irritating. Many of these facts could be ascertained in advance and others during the course of negotiations, as questions arise over the impact of particular proposals. The parties should be encouraged to set up fact-finding teams, possibly from their own ranks, possibly including or limited to skilled third parties. Such a team could respond to requests for whatever array of facts was designated as most relevant by the parties and could draw on the resources of statistical agencies of the government as well as on private records. As much of such information as possible should be made available at least 60 days before the expiration of the contract. In the hands of competent negotiators and mediators, this information could help avoid the kind of sentiment which leads to wasteful economic turmoil.

The inevitable question still persists, however: what if all this fails? We must never overlook the essential proposition on which everybody agrees, that the most desirable course is to have the parties work out their own agreements. We must therefore be exceedingly careful not to introduce procedures in our eagerness to provide protection for the public welfare, which will in themselves interfere with the parties' ability to arrive at voluntary agreement. Experience has shown that, at both the state and federal levels, the very existence of legal procedures that can be invoked when the parties fail to agree in collective bargaining tends to promote such failures.

It is for this reason that we recommend the stepping up of informational and mediatory functions, rather than the prescription of definite and calculable steps to be taken by government when, in a major or basic industry, the parties are unsuccessful in resolving their disputes.

We have here a dilemma. If we favor voluntary agreement and subscribe to the view that that is the truly desirable end, we cannot at the same time set up a course for government to follow which will provide perfect protection for the public if voluntary agreement is not reached. It would be almost self-defeating to do so. Agreement is two-sided. Either party can readily prevent it, and a stipulated or definite series of governmental procedures will tend to cause at least one of the parties to measure the cost or the terms of the possible voluntary agreement against what is likely to be attained through disagreement followed by the steps government will thereafter take. Hence there must be no assurance in any dispute that the President will make any moves except such as will help to induce the parties as quickly as possible to come to their own agreement.

The President, on the advice of the Director of the Mediation Service, may wish to step up still further the mediation efforts already in operation. As a means of doing so, he should be able to designate at least 10 days before the strike deadline a Board of Experts, thus establishing a group at the Presidential level, able to engage in further mediation and to provide the President with information that will help determine his own course in the future.

This Board would normally be composed of neutrals, but it might be desirable in some cases to have individual members with industry or labor backgrounds, on the theory that in the stepped-up mediation efforts such people could be more influential with the respective parties. During war periods and at other times of crisis, government agencies have found such people to be invaluable in helping avoid or shorten strikes. Such a Board would complement the mediation work being carried on by the mediation agencies of the government. It could find facts, narrow the issues, suggest procedural techniques for resolving issues, and report to the President its views on all other matters which he deems to be of relevance. These various possibilities could be most helpful to them in their capacity as a mediation body.

The steps suggested thus far, including the early availability of pertinent data, the preventive or anticipatory work carried on by the parties in advance of negotiations, and the active cooperation of the mediation agencies, could avoid or shorten many serious strikes.

We must assume, however, that there will be some obstinate disputes in critical situations. This possibility leads us to the view that some further steps should be made available to the President. Since such steps inevitably involve a greater degree of compulsion than any suggested thus far, they should be undertaken only if the President is convinced that there is no alternative in the public interest, remembering that there is a strong public interest in having management and labor work out their own differences.

We have already suggested that, among other possibilities, the President be empowered to require partial operation of struck facilities. Whether he requires partial or full operation, he should first convene a Board of expert public representatives or, if he wishes to do so, to make this a tripartite Board, with management and labor representatives selected in consultation with the parties. He should be authorized by law to ask the Board for its recommendations, including its views on an appropriate effective date for any changes in compensation, and to have discretion over whether and when to release these recommendations. The parties should not be permitted to strike or lock-out under these procedures for a period of 80 days nor to make unilateral changes in prevailing conditions of work, as is now the case in the Taft-Hartley procedures.

During this period both the President's Board and the Mediation Service would be under instructions to join forces in working actively with the parties in an endeavor to reach an agreement. Moreover, throughout this period, or at any other point, the President would of course, be free to address a message to the Congress recommending some additional legislative remedy or protective device, if he considers this necessary. In any event, shortly before the end of the 80-day period the Board would report to the President, if agreement has not yet been achieved, indicating the remaining areas of difference and the likelihood of settlement within a reasonable time. The President would thereupon determine whether to recommend any action by the Congress. The importance of the possibility of recommending legislative action must not be discounted. In the past decade or so this possibility played a great part in inducing parties to work out an agreement in so-called emergency disputes.

None of the foregoing moves by the President would be mandatory. He would have discretion to take none of the steps, or if he has taken one, there would be no requirement that he take the next. It would be a process of constant assessment and appraisal in the light of conditions and of the developments in the negotiations of the parties. There would be a strong sense of uncertainty as to whether and how he would act throughout.

The differences between the procedures recommended and those stipulated as emergency disputes procedures under the Taft-Hartley Act are substantial. The President's Boards would have far more discretion and flexibility than is now entrusted to the Boards of inquiry. They would be actively engaged in trying to assist the parties in arriving at agreement. They would inquire into all the pertinent facts. They could recommend alternative procedural means of resolving specific issues. They would act as mediators. They could request authority to recommend the type of settlement indicated by the facts and equities. They could intelligently advise the President as to the action he should take if the dispute persists. They could be called into the dispute before the strike starts and hence before the respective positions have become too frozen, and they would have the benefit of a wider array of facts and data. . . .

We believe the procedures we have recommended would foster

the kind of behavior on the part of unions and managements called for in these times and that the procedures would therefore be seldom employed. And we believe that together they contain enough variety and enough uncertainty to assure that the procedure used could be suited to the circumstances of each case. In addition, the parties would find it difficult to predict in advance what course of action the President would pursue, thereby making it difficult for them to include the procedures in their own bargaining strategy.

Opinions as to how emergency labor disputes should be handled have been changing in recent years. Time and changed conditions have influenced these views. It is now clear that the state of world affairs, political as well as economic, calls for reassurance to the American people that irresponsibility in the conduct of labor-management affairs in vital industries or at unusually hazardous times will find our government able to defend the public interest.

9
Labor and Politics

Three themes have dominated discussion of the political activities of American labor. The first is the question of whether labor should or can promote, or even wants to promote, the development of an independent political party. The second theme is the relationship between organized labor and the established political party structure and legislative process. A third major theme (reinforced by the advent of the pollsters) concerns the political attitudes and behavior of rank-and-file workers. The selections in this chapter explore these themes along with some other issues that we believe will become of increasing importance in the future.

In the lead article, John Hutchinson sees recent generations of labor as less suspicious of government and more adept at directly affecting the outcome of elections; also, labor has solidified its ties with the Democratic party without dominating it or being dominated by it. In this view, the relationship between labor and the Democratic Party may be considered a marriage of convenience—maintained by mutual dependence and a paucity of alternative partners.

Those who advocate a "class party," led by organized labor and directed toward socialism, say that a labor party is required by the nature of the American economic system, its working class, and its existing political parties. Gus Tyler agrees that the role of organized labor must be examined in light of these basic features of the American system. However, he maintains that the proponents of a political party led by labor have taken too superficial a look at the American system. In Tyler's opinion, the challenge for labor is not to become a political party, but to become an effective political force by entering into coalitions with progressive elements wherever they may be found.

The tradition of "reward your friends and defeat your enemies" is still in force in labor politics. And labor finds most of its friends in the Democratic party. An occasional top labor leader will endorse Republican candidates and many rank-and-filers vote for Republicans. But both are usually minority actions. Labor generally supports Democrats because their candidates agree with labor's position more frequently than do Republican candidates. Nevertheless, labor often expresses disappointment with Democratic candidates it has supported because of what it considers their timidity and conservatism on important issues. Organized labor likes to emphasize that the programs and policies it is concerned with are not narrow, partisan, group-interest issues. It sees itself as a progressive force promoting issues that help all Americans. Of interest in this regard is labor's generally conservative posture on matters involving American foreign interests. It has not been noted for encouraging progressive forces in other countries.

Labor's activities are not confined to broad political issues. Kirk Petshek discusses labor's participation in the local community. Although the personal participation of union leaders is important, the feeling persists that this participation stems from motives associated more with the narrow interests of labor than with a broad concern with the community and its problems. Sometimes this suspicion of labor's intentions is justified, sometimes not. The business community and other established power blocs have resisted labor's efforts to contribute. At the same time, Petshek makes clear, many labor leaders consider representation on community boards and other agencies as a form of status that is reward enough.

Experience has demonstrated that unions' organizational objectives must hew pretty closely to what rank-and-file members are willing to support through participation, or at least tacit agreement. One reason unions have not pursued an independent political course is that their members have shown little zest for the implications of the task. By the same token, union endorsement of a political candidate does not guarantee "delivery" of member votes to that candidate. Chamberlain suggests that the closest we come to a "labor vote" is when basic economic issues dominate the workers' thinking.

The study by Kornhauser, Mayer, and Sheppard suggests that, at least among automobile workers in the Detroit area, there is much more agreement than disagreement between the union and its members. The union exerts a strong influence on the political attitudes of its members, and even "middle-class" affluence is unlikely to disrupt this relationship. The dynamics of American society are such that workers will continue to need a strong voice to speak for them on political matters, and unions provide this voice.

John Hutchinson

TRENDS IN UNION
POLITICAL ACTIVITY

"And now where is the challenge?" asked AFL-CIO President George Meany in 1955. "The challenge is in the legislative halls, and our answer is political education, and political activity."

The political activities of American labor have undergone three important changes in the last generation. The first has been a broadening of legislative objectives. Before the 1930s American trade unionism was primarily an economic movement, suspicious of government, concerned with politics essentially for the protection of its power at the bargaining table. The tradition changed with the great depression. Then the clear need for legislative intervention in a faltering economy, the increased interest of the state in labor-management relations, the rise of a socially conscious and politically aggressive labor movement in the Congress of Industrial Organizations, a growing appreciation of the range of issues with which organized labor had a duty to be concerned, and, in time, the onset of restrictive labor legislation, all contributed to an enlargement of the political ambitions of American labor. The trend was progressive. From natural resources to social security, from civil rights to national defense, from local ordinances to world peace, there is today literally no political issue of importance on which the labor movement is not a committed partisan.

The second change has been in political method. For most of its life the American Federation of Labor was a lobbying organization, dependent largely on persuasion and good will, with no field organization to buttress the claims it made on the legislatures. The CIO was more

From *The Political Quarterly*, April–June 1962, Thomas Nelson & Sons Ltd., Publishers, London. Reprinted by permission of the author and publisher.

Mr. Hutchinson is Associate Professor of Industrial Relations, University of California, Los Angeles.

ambitious, and through Labor's Non-Partisan League engaged modestly in machine-building. Adversity accelerated the pace. The passage in 1943 of the federal Smith-Connally Act, which controlled strike activities, as well as various other attempts to enact restrictive labor legislation, prompted the creation of the CIO's Political Action Committee—perhaps the first attempt by American labor to establish a nation-wide electoral organization capable of garnering votes as well as soliciting concessions. The Taft-Hartley Act of 1947, which prohibited union contributions to federal election campaigns and imposed new limitations on the economic functions of unions, moved the AFL to form Labor's League for Political Education—LLPE—an organization similar in purpose to the CIO-PAC. A new tradition was established. The merger of the AFL and CIO in 1955 was accompanied by the formation of the AFL-CIO's Committee on Political Education (COPE) which, supported mainly by voluntary contributions, conducts or coordinates trade union political activity at every level of government in the vast majority of electoral districts throughout the country. A further impetus to labor political action was provided by the Landrum-Griffin Act of 1959; arising out of the McClellan Committee investigations into corruption in labor-management relations, the new law added to the economic restrictions of the Taft-Hartley Act and regulated in detail the internal operations of trade unions. Its unwelcome features, notably its prohibitions on economic activities essentially irrelevant to corruption, helped to account for the fact that trade union participation in the 1960 elections was probably the most intensive in American labor history.

The third change has been the decline, in practice if not in theory, of the principle of non-partisanship. The AFL was a genuinely nonpartisan organization, seldom made political endorsements, carefully sought accommodations with both major parties, and rarely—until 1947 —became organizationally involved in election campaigns. The CIO, while officially non-partisan, gravitated rapidly toward the more receptive Democrats and began the custom of close association between party and movement. The LLPE was more sedulously uncommitted than the CIO; but in practice it endorsed almost as many Democrats, and many AFL as well as CIO officials became prominently identified with the Democrats. The AFL-CIO has retained the doctrine of non-partisanship, but there is little consorting with Republicans. "It is a simple fact," the federation has said, "that many more Democrats than Republicans qualify for COPE support." The superior acceptability of the Democrats is not entirely a matter for compassion on their part.

The alliance is reflected, in many states, in the involvement of union officials in state and local Democratic party machinery, in their appointment to government jobs by incumbent Democrats, and in their selection in progressively greater numbers as delegates to Democratic political conventions. It is also shown in the reception given to labor proposals concerning the party platforms—attentive and frequently adoptive in the case of the Democrats, formal and usually declinatory on the part of the Republicans. It is strongest of all in Michigan where, if the United Automobile Workers and other unions do not control the state party, they at least exercise a contingent veto over its decisions. It is official in Minnesota, where the Democratic-Farmer-Labour Party has been a major political force for over a decade. It is a factor of varying but substantial importance in California, Colorado, Connecticut, Illinois, Massachusetts, Montana, New Jersey, Ohio, Oregon, Pennsylvania, Washington, West Virginia, and Wisconsin. It exists in some form in the farm and border states. It is weakest of all in the South; but if trade union influence in Southern Democratic politics is generally slight, the labor movement shows no sign that it might prefer the embrace of the awakening Southern Republicans to that of the Democrats. It would be wrong to infer that labor either dominates or is dominated by the Democratic Party; or that the relationship is effectively exclusive, always smooth or wholly welcome on either side. But the alliance is national, enduring, and close, a major political fact, more important than the ceremonies which might appear to deny it.

The American labor movement is thus committed to a wide range of political interests, organized in considerable part for electoral as well as pressure politics, and engaged in a close if not organic alliance with the Democratic Party. It has rejected, conspicuously and no doubt permanently, the political philosophy and method of its forbears. It now believes—or at least many of its leaders believe—that strength in politics is comparable in importance to strength in collective bargaining; and it has, in recent years, made great investments of time, energy, and money towards creating the apparatus for success. . . .

In politics, also, American labor suffers from a number of important disadvantages. A strong majority of Americans, if properly asked, will concede the fundamental utility of trade unionism and express sympathy with at least some of its economic and legislative aims; but the endorsement is too seldom enthusiastic, and does not preclude a highly critical attitude towards some modern aspects of the institution. Even some Northern Democrats, ostensibly friends of labor, are embarrassed by its embrace, welcome its support only at election time, resist its participation in party affairs, and are happy to play the Pharisee when occasion permits. In general, there are majorities or near-majorities among the general public for further restrictive labor legislation in a number of fields; in particular, there appears to be strong and perhaps majority support among union members for such legislation at least on the issues of labor monopoly and corruption. It is possible, of course, as one study of the United Automobile Workers in Detroit has shown, for a union to influence favorably the political opinions of a comfortable majority of its members; but few unions enjoy the energy of leadership and thoroughness of educational activity of the UAW. In appeal, the labor movement suffers from the widely conceived bilateral responsibility of employers and unions for the secular spiral in wages and prices; from the contrast between its advocacy of racial equality and the discriminatory practices of some individual unions; and, despite its unprecedented disciplinary actions against the corrupt, from the enduring stigma of the McClellan Committee hearings. It is, finally, weaker in state politics than in federal because of rural over-representation in the state legislatures; and in the absence of national political leadership prepared to exercise the pre-emptive powers of the federal government is susceptible to state open shop and other unfavorable legislation. The labor movement suffers from both determined enemies and uncertain allies.

It is a matter of perception, policy, and organization. The need for political strength is not equally appreciated among American trade union leaders. Not all of them take the broader view. For a few the creed of business unionism is still holy writ. For some the idea of a labor movement primed for public responsibility is the heresy of the interfering intellectual. The parochialism of some union leaders sometimes leads—as it did during the Congressional debate on the Landrum-Griffin Bill—to a search for concessions in their own interest at the possible expense of their fellows. In other cases—not at all peculiar to the labor movement—it produces the defeat of policy proposals or legislative measures, conceived in the public or general trade union interest, which might adversely affect a small, if improperly protected, minority. In general, it presents the problem of a lack of preparation in ideas which, when the legislative claims of labor are judged by a more critical audience than at present, might pose special dangers for trade unionism in the United States.

It would be unjust not to record, however, that the great majority of union leaders are committed—to a greater extent than their members —to a much wider conception of the natural interests and proper obligations of trade unionism than would have sufficed in the days of Gompers. The labor movement does, of course, have its institutional instincts and priorities in matters of legislative policy; but it is by no means distinguished in that respect, and its record is better than most. There are, indeed, a number of issues—particularly civil rights and international trade—on which both federation and individual union leaders have risked or incurred the displeasure of their constituents by the stands they have taken on grounds of general principle or the public interest. Given the primacy in union affairs of direct service to the membership, and the indifference of many of the latter to the larger issues, such men deserve better of their critics.

Gus Tyler
TOWARD PARTY REALIGNMENT

The role of organized labor in American politics must flow from three considerations:

1. The nature of our American economic system;
2. The nature of the American working class;
3. The nature of American political parties.

Traditionally, the American radical has used all three (or any one) of these pivotal considerations to conclude that the nation requires a "class party" directed at Socialism:

1. The "capitalist" system is faulty, self-contradictory, and ultimately self-destructive: ergo, the inevitable imperative for a socialist transformation.

2. The working class, to realize this objective, must have a self-conscious power: ergo, a labor party.

3. A political party, to realize a basic reform of our society, must be a disciplined unit and not a loose fusion of social forces: ergo, a new party that will challenge the Republicans and Democrats in our national politics.

If these three traditional conclusions are checked out against either the realities of our culture or against pure logic, they now appear to be invalid.

1. Capitalist society may be beset with evils, may generate anti-capitalist forces, and may compulsively undermine the props of its existence, yet it does not follow that a socialist society, in the classic sense, is either preferable or inevitable. The welfare state, with all of its implications for a mixed economy, may offer a dynamic that allows for action along new frontiers without accepting socialism.

2. The working class should develop a cohesive political power but it does not follow that a "class party" of labor is either the most

From *New Politics*, Vol. 1, No. 2, Winter 1962. Reprinted by permission of the publisher.

desirable or even the possible instrument for doing so in the United States. An independent political *force*, rather than a *party*, has thus far proven to be more feasible and effective.

3. A political party, with a coherent program and an ideologically coherent leadership, is undoubtedly desirable but it does not follow that the way to attain this is by the organization of a national third party. The trend appears to be toward a realignment of political forces in America through the impact of pressure groups on our two major existing parties.

The peculiar behavior of labor in American politics flows at present from the fact that we live in a capitalist society that is not "capitalist," that we have a working class that does not think of itself as a "class," and that we have political parties that are not "parties" in the classic European sense. What makes this behavior "peculiar" is the fact that it is non-imitative, autochthonous, and deeply rooted in our culture. To American labor, the behavior appears natural; but it appears unnatural to those who would instruct labor from the texts of pre-World War II Europe, who believe that great masses learn from the poignant phrase and not from the searing experience, and who believe that the roots of human behavior spring from the insightless ratiocinations of those intellectuals who know what the masses *should* do.

Let's look at our economy, our working class and our political parties. Our economy is not running on Marxist schedule. The middle class is not disappearing. As an economic entity it is holding its own and as a socio-psychologic self-image it is growing almost disgustingly. The polarization of working class and capitalist class can only be proven by a semantic twist that defines poverty as "relative poverty" and defines wealth, not as ownership, but as "control." But defined common-sensically, the mounting poverty that was to drive the great mass to revolt against the handful who own the nation is not mounting at all. In short, the economic evolution that was to provide the socio-political dynamic for social revolution seems to be operating in reverse.

This has been the objective of the welfare state—and thus far, it has worked within limits. It has failed in those areas where political power has been lacking to apply the welfare idea more fully. The combined economic and political impact has been the development of a system that is neither capitalist, nor socialist, but a vacillating in-between that escapes classic radical categories because it was not envisioned in classic radical thought.

In fact, the inapplicability of the classic categories is presently almost universal. When Castro insisted that his was the first socialist state in the Western Hemisphere (is it socialist?) he was challenged by

Trujillo who claimed the credit for the Dominican Republic (anathema to both socialists and communists). The Soviet Union and Soviet China both claim to be socialist (to the annoyance and discredit of socialists) and find themselves joined by the United Arab Republic. If these societies, all closed and orderly, defy classic definition, how much more elusive is the character of the open and disorderly societies, such as the United States, Great Britain, Sweden and Mexico.

In the closed societies, the labor movements cannot make any operational adjustments to their circumstances: they are told that they are enjoying "socialism" and that if they do not like it neither can they lump it. They are the prisoners of clichés and commissars. In the open societies, especially where the welfare state is a functioning factor, the political movements of labor tend to adjust to reality, by modifying their definitions of socialism, by seeking alliances with other classes, by seeking to establish a national (not necessarily chauvinist) party in place of a class party. This even applies to the great socialist parties of England and Germany!

In America, where the labor movement was never deeply involved with socialist tradition, despite the tremendous contributions of individual socialist leaders, of socialist critique, and of socialist legislation, the labor movement as a political force moved easily into developing a program for the real society in which it lives and which it seeks to change.

The reluctance of American labor to accept a socialist orientation has been attributed, by some, to a certain *backwardness* on the part of the American worker. The assumption was that as American labor would become more educated and sophisticated it would move toward class party and socialism. In other words, as American labor grew up it would look more European.

Actually, the reverse seems to be the case. European socialists appear more American, deemphasizing the class nature of their social-democratic parties and moving toward mixed rather than purely nationalized economies.

Attempts to measure the "backwardness" or "sophistication" of American labor with, let us say, British labor, is rather a futile and meaningless exercise, like adding apple pies and Yorkshire puddings. The difference is more a matter of cultural taste than level of development. The American workers, for instance, were the first in the world to have their Workies' Parties, way back in the 1830's. Repeatedly, the American laborites reverted to class parties: Greenback, Labor, Populist, Socialist, Farmer-Labor, Communist. Ultimately, American workers—who had never accepted these ideas by majority support—abandoned the concept of a national third party, not because of stupidity or sin but because such parties did not jibe with their concepts of their society or themselves— and because they did not work!

The distinctive quality of American Labor is its mobility—a trait common to our total culture: an upward economic mobility, a horizontal geographic mobility, and a diagonal ethnic mobility that is reflected in greater earnings and in movement into new neighborhoods. This mobility smudges, blurs and sometimes even obliterates class lines.

To expect the average American worker, viewed not at a moment but over three or more generations, to be class conscious is to expect him to substitute an epigram for experience. And without class-consciousness, there can be no lasting class parties.

All this does not mean that there are no group or class conflicts in the United States. There are. But where American labor has moved into politics, as an expression of its class aspirations, it has done so for specific programs rather than for class power. And, to accomplish this, labor has found it more productive to work within and through the established political mores.

Under our mores, a political party is something vastly different from a European political party. A European political party starts as an ideology; it spells out a program that flows from its philosophy; it sets up a membership organization to back this program; this membership is *the party* legally, naming its candidate usually by convention action. An American political party does *not* start as an ideology; it writes a program that reflects the fused aspirations of all the elements primarily wooed by the party; the political clubs are *not legally the party;* candidates are named in *primaries* in which people participate who have never been in or near a club or who do not even consider themselves members of the party.

The European party is generally the expression of a fairly definable social grouping: economic, ethnic or religious. The American party is generally the expression of a fusion and mixture of social groupings. The European political party is a national entity; there is no legal national political party in America since all parties operate under state law and enjoy title according to state regulations. A European political party can, by convention, generally deny renomination to a non-conformist member of parliament; in the United States, a non-conformist can return to Congress for decades so long as the people who vote in the primary in *his district* stand behind him.

Whether the American system is better or worse than the European is of less relevance than the cold fact that the U.S. method is here, is deeply rooted, is the consequence of our social circumstances: geographic diversity, economic mobility, ethnic fractionalization.

The mechanical device that distinguishes the American system from the European is our primary. In the South, the struggle between liberals and reactionaries is fought out not through the organization of any liberal party but through the Democratic *primary*. In Wisconsin, LaFollette battled the Old Guard GOP through the *primary*. The primary is a mechanism that gives added flexibility to our highly flexible major parties. Farmer, labor, capital, Catholic, Baptist, Negro, prohibitionist—these and many others have used the primary as a way of turning a national party, a program, or a local candidate in their direction.

For all of these reasons, American labor is unlikely to move in the direction of a national third party of labor. (The fact that the blue collar worker, the backbone of the trade union, becomes increasingly a smaller part of the total population is a most realistic deterrent to launching any party with a trade union label on it—even if all the other deep-seated socio-historic reasons were absent.)

A *realignment* of the major parties is far more desirable—and even possible. Its desirability arises from the fact that an integrated governmental program requires a guiding intelligence and such an "intelligence" is most fittingly a national party with a purpose and with internal cohesiveness. The possibility arises from the fact that our national party system has been moving in the direction of purpose and cohesion.

The big trend toward party realignment begins with the New Deal. With FDR as standard bearer of social legislation, the Democratic Party—by and large—began to develop a New-Dealish complexion. The Republican Party—as opponent of FDR and New Deal—fixed upon itself the image of conservatism. This evolution of Democrats as New Deal and Republicans as the Old Order has continued for nearly a generation.

This process has not run off to its ultimate and natural conclusion primarily because of the North-South division in the Democratic Party. The schism in the Congressional delegation of the Democrats has created a Three Party system on Capitol Hill. There are the liberal Democrats, a reasonably cohesive formation, a large bloc but not a numerical majority; there are the Republicans who represent the hard steady core of conservatism (with about two dozen of them occasionally swinging to a liberal position); and, finally, there are the Southern Democrats, some of whom are liberal on economic matters and virtually all of whom are conservative on civil rights.

The great legislative obstacle of the labor and liberal forces in the United States is the simple fact that it is much easier for the Southern Democrats and Republicans to unite on an over-all program than it is for the Liberal Democrats to unite with their Southern party colleagues.

The conservative coalition in Congress is a "party" without a label. Since 1938, it has been the majority party in Congress. The struggle between the "coalition" and the "liberals" is the contest between the realigning elements in our national government.

To reduce the "coalition" to minority status is the first and most immediate mission of the liberal-labor forces in America. This can be done through two major pushes:

1. To get a system of fair districting in the House of Representatives, so that each representative comes from a district that is compact, contiguous and equal in population with other districts. As matters now stand, Congress is "gerrymandered" to favor Republicans over Democrats in the North and rural over urban in the South. The end result is an advantage of several dozen seats enjoyed by the "coalition" even before the election begins.

2. To continue and improve the efforts of labor and liberals to do the double job of ousting conservative Northern Republicans and entering primaries where a liberal Democrat or a liberal Republican can oust a conservative of either party.

The second project is well under way and accounts for the sizeable liberal delegations now in Congress that, at this moment, come close to a majority though still falling somewhat short. The first project will require extended education and action and constitutional reform within the states alongside of appropriate legislation in D.C.

In the push for a liberal majority, the strategy must shift from North to South. In the North, this is a matter generally settled in interparty struggle on Election Day. In the South, this is a matter generally settled in intraparty struggle on primary day. This last campaign is the more difficult of the two for labor and liberalism, but it can never be surrendered. The forces of progress must sooner or later emerge in the Southland, manned by native elements, reacting to on-the-spot issues and pressures. As such forces do emerge—and they are most apt to do so as part of the industrialization of the South and in line with trade union growth—a genuine realignment of liberalism "on the Hill" will be inevitable.

The realignment of forces should logically include liberal Republicans. This readiness of "liberal" Republicans to join with a Democratic Party that is solidly liberal in the North and sporadically liberal in the South is dependent on the direction of the GOP. So long as some urban and industrial Republicans feel that they can rescue their party for operation in the Twentieth Century, they are not apt to leave their party in chunks and they certainly must, for reasons of inner party strategy, deny any intent to break. But if the right wing of the GOP becomes the militant spokesman of the "new right" in America, a national party of liberalism will be able to form a liberal coalition "on the Hill" to include elements of the GOP—ultimately perhaps to include them in a national "liberal" party.

To be an effective part of such an evolution toward meaningful realignment, the labor movement must pursue a double strategy:

1. It must, as a political expression, win the confidence and loyalty of its rank and file. And to do this, labor must inescapably emphasize the economic aspects of politics, because it is the bread-and-butter appeal that ties dues payer to leadership in unions.

2. It must, to maintain firm coalition with other segments of American society in a political realignment, shape a program of progress that is "good" for all America and for all its democratic ideals.

The above strategy will not appeal to the impatient. Nor will it appeal to the gimmick-minded who seek solutions in mechanical decisions and devices. The above perspective assumes a mature labor movement, able to keep a long range social objective in mind while sweating its way from election to election to reach its goal.

Kirk Petshek

THE STAKE OF LABOR
IN THE URBAN COMMUNITY

During earlier eras, up to the time of the New Deal, the power structure of urban communities was clearly dominated by the entrepreneur of small and middle-sized firms. He affected the important decisions in small and middle-sized cities through a local elite. By World War II, the industrial unions, collective bargaining partners of corporate personnel managers, had sufficient strength to share in the role of decision-making in the metropolis. But their ability and will to do so has been affected by other changes in the urban community.

The local power elite has changed, to begin with. Locally owned businesses have largely been replaced by branch plants of national corporations, run by bureaucrats who see their career hopes pointing towards the magic of their company's headquarters. Absentee ownership has given way to absentee management by nonowners.

This paper is published here for the first time.
Mr. Petshek is Professor of Urban Affairs, University of Wisconsin.

The professionalization of the corporate bureaucracy, however, has mitigated this picture. Business-school trained local managers are aware of their public visibility and, thus, are likely to be sensitive to public relations implications. In order to avoid giving an "absentee" image, they try to become part of the community power structure and to participate in local decision-making—with the scions of local ruling families of long standing. In middle-sized cities, managers concentrate their attention first on fund-raising and charities—activities which have the most visible impact on corporate headquarters. Local firms, feeling a more direct responsibility for community problems, all too often imitate the corporate professionals by concentrating their efforts on publicly attractive programs. This leaves the difficult social problems of middle-sized urban communities without much leadership. Unions have developed a cadre of professionals—most of them at the national level but, increasingly, also at the metropolitan level in larger local union headquarters—who could fill this leadership vacuum, but they usually lack the concern, the interest, and the initiative to do so. The local inertia and the status-quo conservatism of many of these middle-sized communities, where labor faces an uphill fight for recognition, complicates the task even further.

In large and growing metropolitan areas, the picture is different. Here it is likely to fall to the corporate elite to take on true leadership functions in guiding urban development. This is most apt to happen where local government recognizes the need to move in new directions towards further community growth and knows how to co-opt local business leadership. Financial institutions may decide to guide the redevelopment of metropolitan downtown areas with their own capital (Baltimore, Rochester, Cleveland). Or various corporate executives and local leaders decide jointly with the public leadership of the city to bring about the changes necessary for creating a new image of the city and metropolis (Philadelphia, New Haven, Boston).

As with business executives, the union leaders' center of allegiance lies outside the local community—with the international union. But the interests of local union leaders are more permanently tied to the community than are those of mobile corporate executives. Recognizing that interest, labor representives have become members of local boards, committees, and agencies. They have equal status with business members, though their numbers are often smaller, as the company clearly considers this activity part of its corporate function. But labor's desire to penetrate the existing power structure has all too often meant an attempt at imitation—to be like "one of them." When business representatives participate actively in fund-raising activities and serve on private agency boards, they do so with an eye toward membership on boards making long-range development decisions which deal with problems affecting the entire metropolitan area. Labor, though vitally affected by such decisions, rarely takes independent positions on general community problems. Union leaders don't recognize that their members' livelihoods are affected by the development of the community. Instead, union representatives show their chief concern with short-term events. Hence, what has happened in many communities is that labor's status on boards and committees has been "frittered away" in terms of real influence because community leaders feel that the narrow parochial interests of labor leaders may blind them to the long-term interests of the community. The similarly parochial concerns of the other board members are generally better camouflaged!

Often union officers are asked to be members of voluntary agency boards like community services, Red Cross, hospitals, etc. But, here again, their role is only that of labor representative, making sure that union members' interests are safeguarded, rather than representing the citizenry at large—the consumers, the old or sick, the commuters, etc. But workers, after all, are consumers and commuters for more hours in the day than they are producers. Worker and community interests could be achieved more effectively if this fact were recognized by labor leaders. Notwithstanding increasing labor representation on all manner of community boards, community goals have not been noticeably influenced by labor.

For labor leaders, community-agency appointments have obvious status implications. Frequently, the top leader in the local labor hierarchy may keep most of these posts. He is often unable to do justice to the demands made by these different boards. He attends but, because he hasn't done his homework, his contribution and, thus, his influence are minimal.

It is also not lost on those making community appointments that they are able to choose those businessmen whom they know from other associations to be effective board members. On the other hand, they may be prohibited from appointing labor members with special qualifications for particular assignments, lest they incur labor's wrath: only the labor hierarchy can make the appointments (intra-union politics!), and if that affects the effectiveness of the appointees, so be it!

Where labor does not constitute a sizable part of the community it is difficult for labor leaders to get deeply involved in local politics. As every hour of their day is filled with union activities (not just from nine to five), they must be able to defend politics as essential to the members' welfare. Nor can an elected union officer take a "leave of absence" to take a political position and expect to find his office waiting for him at the end of the period!

There is still another difficulty for labor: the role it assigns to professionals. Labor unions are run by elected officials who are shrewd bargainers, are toughened in union politics, and have a sixth sense for their members' needs. Education, research for bargaining background, legal advice, legislative lobbying, and related functions are handed over to hired professionals—but only rarely do these experts have a direct influence on union decisions.

On the other hand, well-trained corporate managers do not limit their own professionals in the same way. Growing municipalities also hire professionals to assure that public decisions are carefully prepared. Civic groups and business associations hire professional managers. These different groups of professionals understand each other. All of these professionals are consulted by community board members. Many issues are, in effect, settled by the professional before their principals meet. Compromises on community problems emerge only from the full knowledge of all implications—and board members are frequently instructed by their professionals on the issues involved. Elected labor leaders, not having the time for thorough probing on their own or a willingness to use their professionals after the manner of the business community, may find themselves outguessed and out of their depth in dealing with community problems.

Labor's stake in a healthy metropolitan economy, an attractive community, satisfactory public services, and civic involvement is truly great. But its influence on the community, and in it, is small. Union leaders should begin to comprehend that their own and their members' interests are best served by improving the community as a whole. They should grasp the fact that the well-being of urban centers is of increasing importance to all its citizens. Most of the interest groups affected by the direction of urban development devote considerable effort to increasing the influence they exert and surround themselves for this purpose by well-trained professionals and technicians. Union leaders should realize that labor's affluence permits unions to do likewise. If they acted on this knowledge, unions would see their influence grow and their effect on community decisions increase. It would not take long for them to perceive how many of labor's vital interests are actually affected by community decisions.

In recent years, a third category, widely ignored but even more deeply affected by community decisions, has entered the picture: the disadvantaged, the poor, the deprived. Labor participates, but the underprivileged are not even aware of the decisions which are made. While only a minority of the deprived belong to organized labor, labor's representatives could have taken up the cudgel for them long ago. Organized labor could have been their spokesman, and, thus, increased the respect for labor's position in the councils of the community. If unions had done this, they would now, quite properly, reap the benefits from the changed atmosphere.

The disadvantaged are less likely than labor to be satisfied with "a place at the table" without much of a voice. They are not interested in status, they don't intend to imitate, they do not aspire to become part of the middle-class elite. They want to be listened to in their own right and not be brushed aside. Paradoxically, though they are latecomers to the table, the manner of their entry gives them their own kind of "status." Whether this change will make it easier or harder for labor to gain a louder voice in influencing community decisions, only time will tell.

Neil Chamberlain

HOW EFFECTIVE IS
LABOR'S POLITICAL ACTION?

. . . In recent years the question has been repeatedly asked, What influence do the unions really have over the voting of their members? If their bargaining power with the parties rests primarily on the influence which they have with their memberships, can they in fact "deliver the vote"?

Particularly after the 1950 election in Ohio, when Sen. Robert Taft, coauthor of the Taft-Hartley Act, won by an immense majority despite the active opposition of the unions in this highly unionized state, has it frequently been argued that there is no such thing as a "labor vote," that union members will not be bound by any ties with political parties which are effected by their officials, and hence that the political parties may very well ignore the unions without suffering any significant penalty. Others, a little more cautious, agree that the ability of union leaders to influence their members' voting has perhaps been overrated in the past but nevertheless does have its effect. What can be said about this issue?

The matter can be approached through a series of propositions.

1. Union members have more or less common economic aspira-

tions but a multiplicity of other values. Among the 17.5 million members in the labor movement in the United States can be found all forms of religion, a variety of views with respect to this country's proper role in world affairs, differing sectional interests, conflicting ideas of the proper spheres of government, and so on. But their economic aims are largely the same.

2. In times when their economic aims are being met reasonably well, they can afford to allow their other prejudices and interests to have political expression. They may well ignore the candidate whom their union has endorsed because he happens to be a Catholic and they are Protestant, or because he favors the United Nations and they are isolationist, or because he is for integration and they are for segregation, or because their brother-in-law is working for the other party's candidate and they'll do him a favor, or just because they don't like his looks. Thus the votes of union members are dispersed rather than concentrated.

3. At times when their economic interests appear to be threatened, however, particularly in time of spreading unemployment, then economic interests dominate other interests, and they coalesce politically. This can happen too if there is a prevalent enough belief among workers that they are sharing considerably less than proportionately in the benefits of a period of sustained prosperity. At such times there is a tendency for union votes to be concentrated on their common economic interest, rather than dispersed on their other multiple values.

4. Some party will usually appeal for the labor vote by promising to support its interests. In times of relative adversity, it is this party that will be the recipient of the bloc of worker (not just union) votes. In times of prosperity it is likely to gain a considerable portion of worker votes, but by no means can it count on a worker vote solid enough to ensure election. In recent times this role of labor's supporter has been played by the Democratic party.

5. Under such circumstances the influence of union leaders lies (a) in focusing the members' interest and intent, (b) in arousing their enthusiasm, and (c) in making sure that they vote. The union leaders do not control their members' votes, and except in times of stress they are only one of a number of influences determining how member votes are cast—not an insignificant influence, but nevertheless only one influence to be laid alongside many others. But in times of economic adversity, as so interpreted by workers generally, union leaders can effectively marshal the vote. They do not deliver it in the sense of controlling it, but they do deliver it in the sense that they see that it is counted. They can rely on the common economic interest and perception to ensure that the vote is cast the "right" way.

These propositions are stated categorically for purposes of clarity. Actually, even in economic matters workers do not think and feel politically as one. To the extent that unemployment and poverty are concentrated in certain classes, industries, or geographical sectors, this lessens the *general* impact of economic adversity and may disperse labor's vote. There is, however, greater unity of outlook in this area than in most others, so that the statements made can be looked upon as having a high degree of probability.

This approach is somewhat similar to the motivational approach underlying economic-indifference analysis, namely, that which is least satisfied is most stressed. The economic interest dominates a worker's political thinking when he becomes relatively more unhappy about it than about other interests. It is then that his union, his economic agent, mobilizes his sentiment and makes him politically more effective than he would be without it. In more prosperous times, he can afford the luxury of voting for a candidate who is personally more attractive than another or who appeals to him on some noneconomic issue.

One corollary of the above line of reasoning is that the surest antidote to a cohesive labor vote is a prosperous economy.

POLITICAL INFLUENCE

But there is more to the story than this. We earlier noted that the political process is composed of a network of bargains. The capacity of labor unions to deliver the vote, even in the limited sense suggested above, is not a measure of their political influence. While politicians and parties may be mindful of their commitments to union sympathizers and supporters and even seek to support their special interests, the bargaining process, as we know, continues within a city council or a state legislature or the Federal Congress. A majority must be put together in order to secure the actions which an interest group seeks, whether it be labor or business.

It is the uncertainty of how this legislative and administrative process will turn out which renders suspect any sweeping judgments as to the degree of political power residing in particular segments of the community. The 1958 congressional elections are instructive in this respect. Less than a month before they occurred, the chairman of the board of General Electric asserted that the AFL-CIO constituted the "most aggressive and successful force in politics." He spoke of their influence in the preceding session of Congress. "No bill was passed that they opposed," he said. "But now they seek—and most observers seem to believe they will gain in the coming election—the added eleven Senators and forty-one Representatives that will give the union officials an absolute majority and the power to pass or repeal legislation at will."[1]

The voting trend in 1958 was as this business spokesman had anticipated, and the new Congress reassembled with a larger proportion of labor-backed Democratic congressmen and senators. We may assume that the sharp rise in unemployment that year coalesced the labor vote along the lines we have just analyzed. Immediately following the election, an outstanding analyst of the contemporary labor scene commented as follows, in a private gathering:

". . . [What] is labor going to do in terms of government policy as a result of the substantial number of people who owe their election to labor's organizational support? My own guess is that the incoming Congress will not give labor a great deal. As a matter of fact, that seemed to me rather apparent when the Federation got around to holding its first Executive Council meeting after the election. It seemed to me that labor didn't have any very clearly defined goals. At the first council meeting, of course, the immediate announcement was that labor would expect repeal of 14B of Taft-Hartley, would knock out right-to-work laws, and that labor would like to see something along the lines of the Kennedy-Ives bill, or perhaps a somewhat less potent version of that bill. Reuther pointed out that labor ought to have some kind of affirmative program, and so at this point they reached into the bottom drawer and came out with a rather tired old program: for expanded housing, expanded education, higher minimum wages. It was clear that there had been a dearth of original thinking of what labor would do with its victory in the event that it won. . . ."

This prediction was more than justified. Not only was labor without an affirmative program to press for; ironically, in the light of the previous business warning as to labor's forthcoming political omnipotence, it was unable not only to secure amendment to the Taft-Hartley Act but even to prevent passage of the Landrum-Griffin Act, causing union spokesmen to comment bitterly that they could not afford many more such election successes. A UAW resolution in the convention of 1959 stated: "The Democratic victories in November 1958 were turned into Republican victories in 1959 on one vital bill after another through the clever use of negative Presidential vetoes and sharp revival of the Dixie-GOP coalition." The same resolution went on to explain, in an effort to save something from the ruins of the previous year's hopes, that most Northern Democrats whom the unions had supported had remained loyal to their supporters and had voted against the Landrum-Griffin measure, and that only the solid Southern Democrat-Republican combi-

[1] Ralph J. Cordiner, as reported in the *New York Times*, October 19, 1958.

nation had managed to put across the hated bill. But this only underscores the tenuousness of imputing some monolithic political power to either labor or business simply by assigning this senator or that congressman to one camp or the other, on one basis or another, and then tallying the score. There remains the hard and uncertain task of putting together a legislative majority on any given issue, usually with administration support, and that is a process scarcely susceptible to statistical prediction.

Arthur Kornhauser
Albert J. Mayer
Harold L. Sheppard

UNION MEMBERS AND
THE FUTURE OF POLITICAL ACTION

Labor Views or "Middle Class" Views?

To speak of labor's becoming "middle class" usually implies that working people not only are reaching a higher *economic* level but that they are adopting the social philosophy and standards of the fairly well off white collar sections of the population. This may be happening; but we believe that any conclusion to this effect is premature. The future is still in the making. Whether the trend is for working people to assimilate a "middle class" conception of their position in society or an alternative that stresses distinctive and divergent goals remains a crucial question. Our study of auto workers contributes rather striking evidence that it is possible for wage earners to experience vast social and economic gains and yet remain steadfastly union oriented in their political views. This may well be the most significant of our findings.

According to our results, Detroit area auto workers are not going "middle class" in political outlook. They are predominantly oriented in agreement with the union; they approve of union political activities; they

Excerpted from Arthur Kornhauser, Albert J. Mayer, and Harold L. Sheppard, *When Labor Votes* (New Hyde Park, New York: University Books, Inc., 1956), pp. 281–295. Reprinted by permission of the publishers.

Messrs. Kornhauser, Mayer, and Sheppard are all associated with Wayne State University.

trust labor's voting recommendations and the great majority cast their
ballots accordingly; they are inclined to distrust the recommendations of
business groups and newspapers; they want organized labor to have a
larger voice in government and they want business to have less influence;
they are overwhelmingly Democratic and they look upon the Democratic
Party as the party that protects and advances the interests of working
people; they identify themselves as members of the "working class"
rather than the middle class (78 per cent to 22 per cent). . . .

Choices of Political Direction: Job-Centered versus Broad Social Goals

The second broad question of workers' political orientation is
whether their interests as union members will be restricted to their own
job-centered problems. Or will they wish to use their unions' augmented
power and know-how to help achieve a variety of goals that spread out
from the job into their entire lives? We called attention to reasons for
believing that an exclusively "bread and butter," business unionism
limited to direct job interests does not meet the conditions and needs of
labor in the present period, regardless of whether or not it did in the past.
This is not to say that direct job interests are secondary. But it does assert
that workers have important non-job-related wants which they may also
expect their union to help solve. To the extent that they do look to their
union for such help it means a widening of union political perspectives.

Job-related interests themselves have far-reaching ramifications.
As unionists grow in their understanding of the forces affecting their
incomes, security, status, and rights as workers, and the forces threatening the strength and security of their unions, they are almost inevitably
impelled to see the need for exerting influence on governmental policies
as well as carrying on direct dealings with employers. Even with respect
to traditional union objectives, that is, we can expect members increasingly to look to *political* means, along with direct economic pressures, for
attaining their ends. . . .

Clearly economic advances are not all that matters to workers
and their unions. If this were the complete story, "why do not," to quote
J. B. S. Hardman, "the opponents dispose of the disturbing movement by
offering better bread and richer butter and more of both to the workers?
Of course, by 'bread alone,' even if buttered, unionism could not survive,
still less achieve its phenomenal growth and enhanced status in American
society."[1]

In other words, besides the material gains, *status* and other

[1] *The House of Labor*, edited by Hardman and Neufeld, Prentice-Hall, New
York: 1951, p. 58.

intangibles are involved. This becomes especially important as the working population is made up less and less of men and women with an under-dog mentality. The egalitarian ideology of American society has much to do with this force in workers' lives and the functioning of their union, whether it be in the shop, the local community, or the country. The desire to be treated as an equal, or to be treated fairly, to receive some kind of recognition, the belief that these are *deserved* forms of treatment and consideration (an expectation not present in the under-dog), all these are increasingly a characteristic of larger segments of our society. . . .

Too often this whole question is treated as if the objectives of self-interest and of reforms in the interest of all working people were alternatives. Obviously unions can and do work for both. But an unending dilemma of relative emphasis does exist. There are innumerable combinations and intermediate positions between the one extreme of exclusive concern with the union's own job-centered advantages and the opposite extreme of going all-out for grand programs of social change. Unions are forced constantly to decide and re-decide how much to emphasize each and how to fit the parts together.

To the extent that the preceding analysis holds water, it suggests that further trends will be toward wider union political perspectives. But certainly there is no settled answer. The vitally important thing is for people, in and out of unions, to keep asking the question and weighing all relevant evidence that bears on it. And the most important evidence consists of their own preferences in the light of their own situations. People's values and desires over the changing years *could* incline union political action more toward expanded, reform-oriented goals, with the general public interest in view, or toward more restricted objectives that have special importance for unions or for particular industries. Only time will tell which is to prevail.

Our study of auto workers contributes principally in a negative way on this entire issue. That is, the responses show a lack of enthusiastic involvement or deep emotional commitment, an absence of the "higher," more idealistic forms of political motivation. In the opposite direction, as has been pointed out, many auto workers express feelings of political futility and impotence, personal discouragement, social alienation, and authoritarian attitudes. We have no reason to suppose that these negative attitudes are any more common among Detroit auto workers than in other comparable groups. Indeed, one may suspect that the picture is usually more unfavorable elsewhere since UAW educational and political activities are among the best. But the fact remains that the union's political program, however liberally conceived by the top leaders, has not engendered much zeal among the members. This is not said in criticism.

Few people in our society, whatever their station in life, glow with political fervor. . . .

Business versus Labor Influence on Political Beliefs

In considering alternative paths that labor political action may travel, we have . . . referred to the decisive importance of the underlying structure of expectations, values, and beliefs that are held. The directions in which people seek political solutions for unsatisfied wants are defined by the accepted thought patterns of the times and by the social interpretations circulated and popularly approved within their groups. But the formation of opinions is complicated by the fact that divergent and contradictory views compete with one another. Individuals are exposed to an unending series of influences that tend to mold their opinions and their underlying aims and values in subtle, unnoticed fashion. It would be hard to maintain that these influences are balanced, that all sides are fairly presented in a manner that leaves people free to make up their minds. Many a person who protests most loudly that "nobody's going to tell me how to vote" is, in fact, induced to vote exactly as some newspaper or commentator wishes, without ever realizing what has happened.

What workers want and believe and act on inevitably reflects, in part, what they read in the daily papers and hear over the air, what they learned in school and what their children learn, what their neighbors, preacher, and corner grocer have to say. Since newspapers, magazines, radio, and television are controlled with few exceptions by persons having the viewpoint of business and the well-to-do, it is natural that they exert their influence predominantly toward preventing changes and ideas which run counter to business values and desires. They attempt to create and strengthen a faith among working people that the best solution to their problems lies in individual effort and loyal support of business leadership.

The crucial question is what counter-measures organized labor can and will take to offset the predominantly business-oriented presentation of the news, ideas, and interpretations. Will influence exerted by business in shaping public opinion through control of mass media and through pressures on schools, writers, clergymen, and other opinion leaders be felt as a serious threat to labor unions and their political programs? Will this aroused concern, if it grows, lead labor organizations to more vigorous attempts to combat one-sided influences by providing their own members, and the public generally, with other information and alternative views more favorable to union efforts and to social change in the interest of working people as the union sees it? What these questions mean to suggest is the probability that sophisticated labor and business leadership will increasingly perceive their long-run power relationship as determined in great measure by public opinion (including workers' opinions) and its political expression; that consequently they will carry on the struggle to achieve their respective goals largely through contending efforts to win moral approval and support in the public mind.

The serious problem for organized labor is whether continued reliance on the collective bargaining process, without much greater attention to public opinion and political influence than has been common, might mean that bargaining itself will become less usable for their purposes, tending more and more to be conducted within an atmosphere and a legal framework thoroughly in accord with management views and devoted to preserving management powers in an unmodified form. Collective bargaining, backed by the strike, is only as dependable as the state of opinion, law, and politics permits it to be. The position unions come to occupy over the next few decades will in all probability be determined more by events on the broad ideological and communications front, in politics broadly conceived, than by developments in the direct dealing between management and labor. The crucial question will persist: Who controls the social controls?

It is these considerations that are neglected in the persuasive case that has been argued by some liberal economists for "limited function" unions "integrated" into the pluralistic society. According to this conception unions should operate solely as bargaining agencies operating in the area of employment relations. No attention is paid to the unbalanced state of communications controls and social influence in the society, and the implications for unions. But if the dissemination of ideas, the inculcation of basic value premises, the control of rewards and penalties for thinking "right" or "wrong" are predominately under business influence, how do opposed views get an adequate hearing unless labor unions refuse to be "limited" or "integrated" into the going system with the going rules and power relations unchanged—or changed in ways unfavorable to labor? A "free pluralistic society" may become a pious phrase if there are no effective offsetting interest groups to challenge domination by corporations and their allies in shaping opinion on the social-political front. This counter-influence function could conceivably be taken over by new organizations but it is difficult now to picture an effective political organization representing broad labor interests that does not rest largely on labor union support.

All this points to the probability that the main body of American organized labor will feel compelled to engage in extensive programs of political education and political influencing. A major part of the effort will necessarily have to do with union members themselves, both because it is essential for unions to hold their loyalty and enthusiasm in the face of pervasive counter-pulls and likewise because of the enormous indirect effect that members' relations to the union are bound to exert on the general public. These indirect effects are of two kinds: (1) the personal influence of unionists on the attitudes of their family members, relatives and neighbors; (2) the picture that the union's way of dealing with its own members conveys as a demonstration of union-policy-in-action in regard to democratic process and individual rights, interest in goals beyond the pay envelope, and concern with the *public* welfare.

The successful accomplishment of these objectives is a most formidable assignment. Unions have the problem of so conducting their political education that it arouses positive, active enthusiasm among potential supporters while at the same time doing what it can to avoid alienation of middle class voters and unionists who are not "on side." Union political education confronts not only the obstacles of widespread indifference and the resistance created by opposed opinion-influencing agencies, but also the deeply ingrained belief that unions belong in the factory and should stay out of politics, and the even firmer adherence to belief in individual independence in politics, typified by the familiar "nobody can tell me how to vote." A profound change is occurring, too, in that the old stirring symbols of concrete evils to be destroyed by militant labor action have lost their force. The fight against starvation, long hours, intolerable working conditions; the battle for a "living wage" and "the right to organize"—for most workers these no longer represent vital issues. New moral justifications are needed, emotionally potent convictions, which by the nature of the changing times, will be more abstract and require more sophisticated understanding of society's—and working people's—problems.

These considerations, we believe, will more and more call for a freely inquiring, non-manipulative type of union political education, on pragmatic grounds even where the leadership may not be so inclined by reason of its own social values. Education of this kind must be mainly *self-education*. If workers are to become effectively and satisfyingly involved, they first have to understand what goes on, where their own interests as unionists and as members of the larger society lie. Working people will move toward solutions to their problems to the extent that they and their chosen leaders learn to inform themselves and to participate democratically in deciding the direction they, and our society, must take. . . .

Index of Authors